FRA

UNTOLD STORIES

Printed in the United States of America

First printing — June 2001

Cover photo of the Mission de Ras Shamra, 1979. Claude Schaeffer stands in the center. To his right is Odile Schaeffer and to his left is Marguerite Yon. Yves Calvet is second from the right. Courtesy of Yves Calvet and the Mission de Ras Shamra.

Digital image of the MRZḤ tablet from a photograph by Bruce and Kenneth Zuckerman, West Semitic Research, courtesy Martin Schøyen.

Library of Congress Cataloging-in-Publication Data

Smith, Mark S., 1955–
    Untold stories: the Bible and Ugaritic studies in the twentieth century / Mark S. Smith.
        p. cm.
    Includes bibliographical references and indexes.
    ISBN 1-56563-575-2 (cloth)
    1. Ugaritic philology—History. 2. Ugaritic literature—Relation to the Old Testament. 3. Old Testament scholars—History—20th century. 4. Ugaritic Literature—History and criticism. 5. Bible. O.T.—Criticism, interpretation, etc. I. Title.

PJ4150 .S65 2001
492'.67'09—dc21

                                                                2001016680

UNTOLD STORIES

The Bible and Ugaritic Studies
in the Twentieth Century

MARK S. SMITH

HENDRICKSON
PUBLISHERS

For my Ugaritic teachers,
Marvin H. Pope and Jonas C. Greenfield

For a word I have, I will tell you,
A message, I will recount to you:

The word of tree and the whisper of stone,
The converse of Heaven to Hell,
Of Deeps to Stars.

I understand the lightning
Which the Heavens do not know,
The word people do not know,
And Earth's clans do not understand.

Come and I will reveal it
In the midst of my mountain, Divine Ṣapan,
On the holy mount of my heritage,
On the beautiful hill of my might.

(*KTU* 1.3 III 20–31)

Table of Contents

Abbreviations, Terms, and Sigla

I. ABBREVIATIONS: Books, Journals, and Series

AAL	*Afroasiatic Linguistics*
AB	Anchor Bible
ABD	*The Anchor Bible Dictionary.* Edited by D. N. Freedman (6 vols.; New York: Doubleday, 1992)
AfO	*Archiv für Orientforschung*
AION	*Annali del'Istituto Universitario Orientale di Napoli*
AJA	*American Journal of Archaeology*
AJBA	*The Australian Journal of Biblical Archaeology*
AJP	*American Journal of Philology*
AJSL	*American Journal of Semitic Languages and Literature*
ALASP	Abhandlungen zur Literatur Alt-Syrien-Palästinas
AnBib	Analecta Biblica
AnOr	Analecta Orientalia
ANET	*Ancient Near Eastern Texts.* Edited by James Pritchard (3d ed. with supplement; Princeton: Princeton University, 1969)
AO	*Aula Orientalis*
AOAT	Alter Orient und Altes Testament
AOS	American Oriental Society
APS	Archives of the American Philosophical Society
ArOr	*Archiv Orientální*
AS	Assyriological Studies
BA	*Biblical Archaeologist*

BAR	*Biblical Archaeology Review*
BASOR	*Bulletin of the American Schools of Oriental Research*
BBB	Bonner Biblische Beiträge
BDB	*Hebrew and English Lexicon of the Old Testament.* Edited by F. Brown, S. R. Driver, and C. A. Briggs (Oxford: Clarendon, 1907)
BETL	Bibliotheca Ephemeridum Theologicarum Lovaniensium
BHS	Biblia Hebraica Stuttgartensia
Bib	*Biblica*
BibOr	*Biblica et Orientalia*
BiOr	*Bibliotheca Orientalis*
BJRL	*Bulletin of the John Rylands University Library of Manchester*
BN	*Biblische Notizen*
BSOAS	*Bulletin of the School of Oriental and African Studies*
BZ	*Biblische Zeitschrift*
BzA	*Beiträge zur Assyriologie*
BZAW	Beiheft zur *ZAW*
CAD	*Chicago Assyrian Dictionary*
CAT	*The Cuneiform Alphabetic Texts from Ugarit, Ras Ibn Hani, and Other Places.* Edited by M. Dietrich, O. Loretz, and J. Sanmartín (KTU: 2d, enlarged ed.) (ALASPM 8; Münster: Ugarit-Verlag, 1995). Cited by text number
CBQ	*Catholic Biblical Quarterly*
CBQMS	*CBQ* Monograph Series
CNRS	Centre Nationale de la Recherche Scientifique
ConBOT	Coniectanea biblica, Old Testament
CRAIBL	*Académie des Inscriptions et Belles-Lettres, Comptes rendus des scéances de l'année*
CTA	*Corpus des tablettes en cunéiformes alphabétiques découvertes à Ras Shamra-Ugarit de 1929 à 1939.* Edited by A. Herdner (Mission de Ras Shamra X; Paris: Imprimerie Nationale/Paul Geuthner, 1963)
DB	*Dictionnaire de la Bible.* Edited by F. Vigouroux. 5 vols. 1895–1912
DBAT	*Dielheimer Blätter zum Alten Testament und seiner Rezeption in der alten Kirche*
DBSup	*Dictionnaire de la Bible: Supplément.* Edited by L. Pirot and A. Robert. Paris, 1928–
DJD	Discoveries in the Judaean Desert
EA	El-Amarna letters
EI	*Eretz Israel*

Emar	*Recherches au pays d'Aštata. Emar VI; Tome 3. Texts sumériens et accadiens. Texte.* Edited by D. Arnaud (Paris: Editions Recherche sur les Civilisations, 1986). Cited by text number
EncJud	*Encyclopaedia Judaica* (1971)
FAT	Forschungen zum Alten Testament
FF	File Folder (system of the Cyrus Adler letters in the Dropsie College archives, Center for Judaic Studies of the University of Pennsylvania, Philadelphia)
FRLANT	Forschungen zum Religion und Literatur des Alten und Neuen Testaments
FuF	Forschungen und Fortschritte
GAG	*Grundriss der akkadischen Grammatik.* Edited by W. von Soden (AnOr 33; Rome: Pontifical Biblical Institute, 1952)
GKC	*Genesius' Hebrew Grammar.* Edited by E. Kautzsch (trans. A. E. Cowley; 2d ed.; Oxford: Clarendon, 1910)
HALAT	*Hebräisches und aramäisches Lexikon zum Alten Testament.* Edited by L. Koehler and W. Baumgartner (Leiden: Brill, 1958)
HAR	*Hebrew Annual Review*
HdO	Handbuch der Orientalistik
HS	*Hebrew Studies*
HSM	Harvard Semitic Monographs
HSS	Harvard Semitic Series
HTR	*Harvard Theological Review*
HUCA	*Hebrew Union College Annual*
IEJ	*Israel Exploration Journal*
IOS	*Israel Oriental Studies*
JANES	*Journal of the Ancient Near Eastern Society of Columbia University*
JAOS	*Journal of the American Oriental Society*
JBQ	*Jewish Bible Quarterly*
JBL	*Journal of Biblical Literature*
JCS	*Journal of Cuneiform Studies*
JEA	*Journal of Egyptian Archaeology*
JEOL	*Jaarbericht van het Vooraziatisch-Egyptisch Genootschap Ex Oriente Lux*
JNES	*Journal of Near Eastern Studies*
JNWSL	*Journal of Northwest Semitic Languages*
JPOS	*Journal of the Palestine Oriental Society*
JPS	Jewish Publication Society
JQR	*Jewish Quarterly Review*
JRAS	*Journal of the Royal Asiatic Society*

JSem	*Tydskrif vir Semitistiek/Journal for Semitics*
JSOTSup	Journal for the Study of the Old Testament Supplement Series
JSS	*Journal of Semitic Studies*
JTS	*Journal of Theological Studies*
KAI	*Kanaanäische und aramäische Inschriften.* Edited by H. Donner and W. Röllig (Wiesbaden: O. Harrassowitz, 1964-68). Cited by text number
KTU	*Die keilalphabetischen Texte aus Ugarit.* Edited by M. Dietrich, O. Loretz, and J. Sanmartín (AOAT 24/1; Kevelaer: Verlag Butzon & Bercker; Neukirchen-Vluyn: Neukirchener Verlag, 1976). Cited by text number
LAPO	Littératures anciennes du Proche-Orient
Leš	*Lešonénu*
MARI	*Mari Annales de Recherches Interdisciplinaires*
MIOF	*Mitteilungen des Instituts für Orientforschung*
MRS	Mission de Ras Shamra
MUSJ	*Mélanges de l'Université Saint-Joseph*
NK	Nikkal (*KTU* 1.23)
NJBC	*The New Jerome Biblical Commentary.* Edited by R. E. Brown, J. A. Fitzmyer, and R. E. Murphy (Englewood Cliffs, N.J.: Prentice Hall, 1990)
NJPS	*TANAKH, The Holy Scriptures: The New JPS Translation According to the Traditional Hebrew Text* (Philadelphia/New York/Jerusalem: Jewish Publication Society, 1988)
NRSV	New Revised Standard Version
NTT	*Norsk teologisk tidsskrift*
NUS	*Newsletter for Ugaritic Studies*
OBO	Orbis biblicus et orientalis
OLA	Orientalia lovaniensia analecta
OLP	Orientalia lovaniensia periodica
OLZ	*Orientalistische Literaturzeitung*
Or	*Orientalia*
OTA	*Old Testament Abstracts*
OTL	Old Testament Library
OTPs	*The Old Testament Pseudepigrapha.* Edited by James H. Charlesworth (2 vols.; Garden City, N.Y.: Doubleday, 1983–1985)
OTS	*Oudtestamentische Studiën*
PBI	Pontifical Biblical Institute
PE	Eusebius, *Praeparatio evangelica*, cited according to H. W. Attridge and R. A. Oden Jr., eds., *Philo of Byblos, The Phoenician*

	History: Introduction, Critical Text, Translation, Notes (CBQMS 9; Washington, D.C.: Catholic Biblical Association of America, 1981)
PEQ	*Palestine Exploration Quarterly*
PRU	*Le Palais Royal d'Ugarit* publié sous la direction de C. F. A. Schaeffer
QD	Quaestiones disputatae
RA	*Revue d'assyriologe et d'archéologie orientale*
RB	*Revue Biblique*
RES	*Revue d'Études Sémitiques (et Babyloniaca)*
RevQ	*Revue de Qumran*
RGG³	*Religion in Geschichte und Gegenwart* (3d ed.; Tübingen: Mohr Siebeck, 1986)
RGG⁴	*Religion in Geschichte und Gegenwart: Band 1. A-B* (4th ed.; Tübingen: Mohr Siebeck, 1998)
RNAB	Revised New American Bible
RR	*Review of Religion*
RSO	Ras Shamra–Ougarit
RSV	Revised Standard Version
SBL	Society of Biblical Literature
SBLCP	Society of Biblical Literature Centennial Publications
SBLDS	Society of Biblical Literature Dissertation Series
SBS	Stuttgarter Bibelstudien
Sef	*Sefarad*
Sem	*Semitica*
SEL	*Studi Epigrafici e Linguistici*
SJOT	*Scandinavian Journal of the Old Testament*
SSN	Studia Semitica Neerlandica
TA	*Tel Aviv*
TDOT	*Theological Dictionary of the Old Testament.* Edited by G. J. Botterweck and H. Ringgren (trans. J. T. Willis and D. E. Green; rev. ed.; Grand Rapids, Mich.: Eerdmans, 1977–)
TWAT	*Theologisches Wörterbuch zum Alten Testament.* Edited by G. J. Botterweck and H. Ringgren (Stuttgart: Kohlhammer, 1970–)
UBL	Ugaritisch-Biblische Literatur
UF	*Ugarit-Forschungen*
Ugaritica I	C. F. A. Schaeffer, *Ugaritica I* (MRS III; Paris: Librairie Orientaliste Paul Geuthner, 1939).
Ugaritica II	C. F. A. Schaeffer, *Ugaritica II* (MRS XIII; Paris: Librairie Orientaliste Paul Geuthner, 1949).

Ugaritica V	J. Nougayrol, E. Laroche, C. Virolleaud, and C. F. A. Schaeffer, *Ugaritica V* (MRS XVI; Paris: Imprimerie Nationale/Librairie Orientaliste Paul Geuthner, 1968)
Ugaritica VII	C. F. A. Schaeffer et al., *Ugaritica VII* (MRS XVII; Paris: Imprimerie Nationale/Librairie Orientaliste Paul Geuthner, 1978)
UT	C. H. Gordon, *Ugaritic Textbook* (AnOr 38; Rome: Pontifical Biblical Institute, 1965)
VT	*Vetus Testamentum*
VTSup	Vetus Testamentum Supplements
WMANT	Wissenschaftliche Monographien zum Alten und Neuen Testament
WO	*Die Welt des Orients*
WTJ	*Westminster Theological Journal*
WZUG	*Wissenschaftliche Zeitschrift der Ernst-Moritz-Arnd-Universität Greifswald*
ZA	*Zeitschrift für Assyriologie*
ZAH	*Zeitschrift für Althebraistik*
ZAW	*Zeitschrift für die alttestamentliche Wissenschaft*
ZDMG	*Zeitschrift der deutschen morgenländischen Gesellschaft*
ZDPV	*Zeitschrift des deutschen Palästina-Vereins*
ZTK	*Zeitschrift für Theologie und Kirche*

II. TERMS

1. Languages and Dialects

BH	Biblical Hebrew
ESA	Epigraphic South Arabian
Heb.	Modern Hebrew
Jap.	Japanese
MA	Middle Assyrian
MB	Middle Babylonian
NA	Neo-Assyrian
NB	Neo-Babylonian
OB	Old Babylonian
PS	Proto-Semitic

2. Grammatical Terms

acc.	accusative case
C	causative stem (BH Hiphil)

cst.	construct state
D	double stem (BH Piel)
DN	divine name
Dt	double stem with -*t* reflexive or reciprocal (BH Hitpael)
fem.	feminine gender
G	ground or simple stem (BH Qal)
Gt	ground stem with -*t* reflexive or reciprocal
impf.	imperfect or prefix tense
impv.	imperative
inf.	infinitive
masc.	masculine gender
N	*N*-prefix stem (BH Niphal)
p.	person
pl.	plural number
pass.	passive voice
perf.	perfect or suffix tense
pl.	plural
PN(s)	proper names(s)
prep.	preposition
ptcp.	participle
sg.	singular
St	causative stem with -*t* reflexive or reciprocal

3. Other Terms

DSS	Dead Sea Scrolls
EA	El-Amarna
LXX	Septuagint
MT	Masoretic Text
n(n).	footnote(s)
RIH	Ras ibn-Hani (text number)
RS	Ras Shamra (text number)
v(v).	verse(s)

III. SIGLA

ʾ	ʾ*aleph* (e.g., in Hebrew and Aramaic)
ḏ	Ugaritic sign 16
ʿ	ʿ*ayin*
*	hypothetical form or root

Introduction and Acknowledgments

Every student of the Old Testament would do well to work on Ugaritic.
—William Foxwell Albright

Albright's estimate of the importance of Ugaritic for the future development of biblical studies has proved correct.
—J. J. M. Roberts

⌧ AIMS AND RESOURCES

In 1927, a year before the first discovery of remains from the ancient culture of Ugarit, W. F. Albright looked back on the scholarly career of Paul Haupt, his mentor at Johns Hopkins University.[1] In the wake of Haupt's death, Albright could survey the history of Assyriology and Semitics and situate his teacher in a long line of accomplished scholars. He could acknowledge the disciplines' achievements and failures, the projects realized, and the research that failed. Albright recognized the importance of looking back, commenting that "every true scholar" should be aware of the history of her or his "science."[2] At that point, Albright could hardly know what the next few years would bring, but the discoveries that soon emerged from the ancient city of Ugarit quickly changed the field of biblical studies. Like the study of Assyriology before it, the field of Ugaritic studies forever altered the modern understanding of the Bible.[3] This book surveys the history of that field over the course of the twentieth century, and it focuses particular attention on its momentous contributions to the study of ancient Israel and the Hebrew Bible (Old Testament).

Before outlining the contents of this work, let me explain my reason for writing it now. A presentation of Ugaritic's historical importance for biblical studies entails more than reviewing the former field's developments,[4] its intellectual topics and trends in different periods, or the texts and tools developed for research in Ugaritic and biblical studies. These matters are included in this work, and indeed the following chapters are organized around them. Yet a proper treatment also benefits from the recollections of its most senior figures. The recent deaths of my two teachers of Ugaritic, Marvin H. Pope and Jonas C. Greenfield, have brought home to me the fact that an important generation of scholars working in Ugaritic and biblical studies now stands in its twilight years. (The most recently deceased of this generation are Albright's successor at Hopkins, Delbert Hillers, who died on 25 September 1999, William Moran, who passed away on 20 December 2000, and Cyrus Gordon, who passed away on 30 March 2001.) The names of this great generation, such as Professors James Barr, Henri Cazelles, Brevard S. Childs, Frank Moore Cross, Joseph Fitzmyer, David Noel Freedman, John Gibson, Cyrus H. Gordon, William W. Hallo, Wolfram Herrmann, Jacob Hoftijzer, Otto Kaiser, Klaus Koch, Thomas Lambdin, George Mendenhall, Franz Rosenthal, Stanislav Segert, John Strugnell, and Edward Ullendorff, grace the pages of this study because of the record of their achievements or the recollections that they very kindly sent to me (or both). I express my deep gratitude to Professors Childs, Cross, Fitzmyer, Hallo, Lambdin, Rosenthal, and Strugnell, former teachers of mine, for their correspondence and conversation. I owe a further debt to Professor Rosenthal, who communicated with me throughout my research. Our correspondence and even more our visit together on the afternoon of 30 November 1999 evoked not only his many memories about the field but also my recollections of our time together at Yale in the 1980s. I am further grateful to Professor Cross for his many acts of kindness, including several letters answering my inquiries for this project. I also acknowledge my appreciation to Cyrus Gordon, who took great interest in this work and who shared his experiences with me, both in letters and in personal conversations. Sadly he died as this book went to print. Readers interested in Gordon's career should consult his autobiography, *A Scholar's Odyssey* (Atlanta: Scholars Press, 2000). Finally, I am deeply grateful to David Noel Freedman, who edited an earlier version of this manuscript. This volume benefited from both his editorial hand and his knowledge of the field.

This study pays tribute not only to the figures of this previous generation, but also to their successors. They too have been generous in providing me with information, and I gratefully acknowledge their many letters and e-mails: Robert Althann, Hans Barstad, Adele Berlin, Pierre Bordreuil, David Clines, Chaim Cohen, Izaak Cornelius, Geoffrey Cowling, Jesus-Luis Cunchillos-Ilarri, Adrian H. W. Curtis, Graham I. Davies, John Day, Steven E. Fassberg, Terry Fenton,

Agustinus Gianto, C. H. J. de Geus, Bella Greenfield, E. L. Greenstein, Judith Hadley, Gordon J. Hamilton, John F. Healey, Jan Heller, Larry Herr, John J. Huehnergard, Finn Ove Hvidberg-Hansen, Avi Hurvitz, Rebecca G. S. Idestrom, Shlomo Izre'el, Bernd Janowski, William Johnstone, Jan Joosten, Peter J. Kearney, Marjo C. A. Korpel, Ingo Kottsieper, Charles Krahmalkov, Antti Laato, André Lemaire, Niels Peter Lemche, Oswald Loretz, Avraham Malamat, John Marks, Paolo Merlo, Walter Michel, Johannes C. de Moor, Tryggve N. D. Mettinger, Takamitsu Muraoka, David Owen, Dennis Pardee, Shalom M. Paul, Anson Rainey, Gary A. Rendsburg, Mervyn Richardson, Jack Sasson, Victor Sasson, Philip Schmitz, Anton Schoors, S. David Sperling, Jean-Michel de Tarragon, Jeffrey Tigay, Neal Walls, Wilfred van Soldt, Wilfred G. E. Watson, Gernot Wilhelm, Nick Wyatt, Petr Zemánek, and Ziony Zevit. Other scholars of this generation provided information during the 1998 national meeting of the Society of Biblical Literature: Wally Aufrecht, Bernard Batto, Herbert Basser, Joseph Blenkinsopp, Oded Borowski, Duane Christiansen, Richard J. Clifford, Michael Dick, John Elwolde, Erhard Gerstenberger, Barry Gittlen, Bob Haak, Joel Hunt, Bernard Lang, P. Kyle McCarter, Carol Meyers, Martti Nissinen, Kevin O'Connell, Simon B. Parker, Rolf Rendtorff, Thomas Römer, Bill Schniedewind, John Spencer, J. Glen Taylor, Marion Taylor, Sidnie White Crawford, Richard Whitaker, Ed Wright, and Nick Wyatt.

I very much enjoyed information given to me about the Dropsie College and the University of Pennsylvania by Drs. Sol Cohen and David Goldenberg, both long associated with the former institution. David Goldenberg also kindly read and commented on a draft of sections pertaining to Dropsie. Rabbi Alan Iser helped me track down information about Cyrus Adler's role in Jewish life in the United States and abroad. Victor (Avigdor) Hurowitz, Dennis Pardee, and Gary Rendsburg commented on an earlier draft of this manuscript. Gordon Hamilton offered critical comments on the sections in Chapters Two and Four pertaining to the alphabet. Jeffrey Ackler, an undergraduate at Saint Joseph's University, where I taught and worked on some of the issues involving Israelite religion (especially in Chapter Four), rendered invaluable assistance by reading over an earlier draft of the manuscript. I could not have completed this work without the tireless efforts on the part of the Interlibrary Loan office of Drexel Library at Saint Joseph's, and I thank the staff there: Mary Martinson, Patrick Connelly, Rebecca Reilly, and Naomi Cohen. Finally, I am grateful to my colleagues at New York University for their kind hospitality in my initial year on the faculty, which made the completion of this work easier.

Three institutions granted me access to their archives. First, Yale Divinity School provided access to Marvin Pope's letters and papers and granted me permission to cite them. I wish to express my appreciation to Dr. Roy Heller for organizing Pope's correspondence and bringing it to my attention. Thanks to

Dr. Heller, I spent many enjoyable hours on 12 January 1999 poring over this resource on Pope's life. I also had the opportunity to go over two boxes of Pope's unpublished papers during the 1998–1999 academic year. Second, Dr. David Goldenberg and Aviva Astrinsky of the Center for Judaic Studies of the University of Pennsylvania (formerly the Dropsie College for Hebrew and Cognate Learning) offered help with files on several key figures associated with Dropsie and granted permission to cite the Dropsie material. Third, William Foxwell Albright's correspondence, housed in the collection of the American Philosophical Society, yielded a gold mine of material for this study. I have consulted letters from 1928 to 1947. My thanks go to Robert Cox and Scott DeHaven of the society for their assistance with the Albright collection. Use of this material falls within the bounds of the fair use regulations (within the Copyright Act) concerning archival material.

Finally, some published resources aided this work. An unparalleled resource for bibliography in the area of Ugaritic and biblical studies is the four-volume work, *Ugarit-Bibliographie 1928–1966,* produced by M. Dietrich, O. Loretz, P. R. Berger, and J. Sanmartín (AOAT 20/1–4; Kevelaer: Butzon & Bercker; Neukirchen-Vluyn: Neukirchener Verlag, 1973); these were followed by two more volumes produced by the same publishers: M. Dietrich, O. Loretz, and W. Delsman, *Ugaritic Bibliography 1967–1971* (AOAT 20/5; 1986); and M. Dietrich and O. Loretz, *Analytic Ugaritic Bibliography 1972–1988* (AOAT 20/6; 1996). Information about dissertations completed in the United States partially derives from searches done at University Microfilms International on 3 October 1985 and 5 November 1998. Basic information on biblical scholars (especially in Germany) appears in *RGG*[3] and *RGG*[4]. Much helpful information on German and Scandinavian biblical scholars appears in D. A. Knight, *Rediscovering the Traditions of Israel: The Development of the Traditio-Historical Research of the Old Testament, with Special Consideration of Scandinavian Contributions* (rev. ed.; SBLDS 9; Missoula, Mont.: Scholars Press, 1975). Cullen Murphy's book, *The Word According to Eve: Women and the Bible in Ancient Times and Our Own* (Boston/New York: Houghton Mifflin, 1998), profiles the background of a number of female biblical scholars. The work of S. D. Sperling, *Students of the Covenant: A History of Jewish Biblical Scholarship in North America* (Atlanta: Scholars Press, 1992) provides a substantial amount of information concerning the work of many Jewish scholars. *Encyclopaedia Judaica* also surveys many biblical scholars and other figures, Jewish and non-Jewish alike. Basic information on members of the Catholic Biblical Association is provided by *Catholic Biblical Quarterly* 49, Supplement (1987) and 59, Supplement (1997), and by G. P. Fogarty's book, *American Catholic Biblical Scholarship: A History from the Early Republic to Vatican II* (San Francisco: Harper & Row, 1989). Numerous figures pertinent to this book appear also in the very helpful volume of P. J. King, *American Archaeology in the Mideast: A History of the American Schools of Oriental Research* (Philadelphia: American Schools of Oriental Research, 1983). For the situation at the Dropsie College and the University of Pennsylvania, Cyrus Gordon's survey of *The Pennsylvania Tradition of Semitics* (SBLCP; Atlanta: Scholars Press, 1986) was very useful.

For the figure of W. F. Albright and many of his students, two works were particularly helpful: L. G. Running and D. N. Freedman, *William Foxwell Albright: A Twentieth-Century Genius* (New York: Morgan Press, 1975); and B. Long, *Planting and Reaping Albright: Politics, Ideology, and Interpreting the Bible* (University Park, Pa.: Pennsylvania State University, 1997). Long stresses the ideological aspects of the "Albright school" in the United States. (And many of the points regarding class in archaeology[5] could equally well describe the study of ancient Near Eastern texts, including the Bible.) No similar emphasis is to be found in this present study, but the story recounted here does illustrate some aspects of the sociology of knowledge and academic advancement in this field. Finally, I will mention Bruce Kuklick's *Puritans in Babylon: the Ancient Near East and American Intellectual Life, 1880–1930* (Princeton: Princeton University Press, 1996), which tells the story of the early study of the ancient Near East by American scholars up to and including W. F. Albright and his generation. Kuklick's book will soon be joined by a history of American scholarship on the Near East for the period 1650–1950, which Professor Benjamin R. Foster of Yale University is now preparing.[6] The present book largely complements the works of Kuklick and Foster, for they analyze the intellectual milieu of American scholars who studied the ancient Near East in earlier periods. All of these resources—personal, archival, and bibliographic—provide an opportunity to capture thoughts from many generations of scholars who have contributed to the discipline over the twentieth century. Photographs were most kindly supplied by the American Schools of Oriental Research, Yves Calvet, Frank Moore Cross, Cyrus Gordon, the Jewish Theological Seminary, Ingrid Pope, and Franz Rosenthal. Finally, I am happy to express my gratitude to Hendrickson Publishers for publishing this work, and to my editor, Dr. John Kutsko, for invaluable editorial and production help. Without all this aid, this work would not have been possible; of courses, all errors and deficiencies remain my own responsibility.

⊠ GENESIS AND ORGANIZATION OF THIS WORK

This retrospective survey of the field of Ugaritic-biblical studies is a revision of a presentation made before the International Organization for the Study of the Old Testament in Oslo on 5 August 1998 and before the General Meeting of the Catholic Biblical Association of America in Scranton, Pennsylvania, on 10 August 1998. I thank the organizers of the Oslo conference, especially Hans Barstad, for the opportunity to present this talk. Indeed, I found the invitation to speak in Oslo on a subject so intimately associated with the names of the great Sigmund Mowinckel and Arvid Kapelrud very moving. I was also grateful for the opportunity to give this talk before the Catholic Biblical Association. The first time this scholarly organization heard such a presentation was in 1944, when the towering figure William Foxwell Albright addressed the association. Albright's presentation was published the following year in the association's house organ, *Catholic Biblical Quarterly*.[7] As his and other such works[8] indicate, this book broadly belongs to a long established genre of Ugaritic-biblical surveys.

The present work departs from the genre, however, in two respects: it selectively surveys Ugaritic and biblical studies in historical order from 1928 to 1999, and it focuses specifically on the Ugaritic texts (as opposed to the Akkadian texts and texts in other languages discovered at ancient Ugarit). In contrast, one may note the monumental 1999 *Handbook of Ugaritic Studies*,[9] exemplary for its treatment of most subjects in Ugaritic studies, not to mention the Akkadian and Hurrian texts at Ugarit as well as, to some degree, the site's history and archaeology. The *Handbook*, however, addresses little of the history of the field, except for the early years and most recent research, and even in discussing these periods, the work barely enters into the academic and intellectual context of the figures and their research. The present work, then, is intended to fill this gap, to tell the untold stories of Ugaritic studies. My wife, Liz Bloch-Smith, astutely suggested to me that this book be entitled *Untold Stories* because it relates both the larger, untold story of how Ugaritic studies contributed so massively to the study of the Bible in the twentieth century and many unknown stories involving the lives and scholarship of the field's major figures.

The volume proceeds in historical order, specifically covering four areas for each period. First, it provides a list of the basic texts and tools for the period in question. The list includes the most important works, but it is hardly comprehensive. Second, the major works and advances in language, literature, and religion are discussed. At some points this discussion overlaps with the listings. While I believe that repetition runs the risk of boring veterans of the field, I think that the reiteration of major works will help those encountering the discipline for the first time. This survey does not provide a comprehensive list of specific gains in Ugaritic and biblical studies for each period. Such a project would require far greater detail. Instead, this description of developments is representative of work taking place in each period. Third, I present the major figures in the study of Ugaritic and the academic programs with which they were associated. I have indulged in including some anecdotes available in letters and archival material.

Such material should interest readers even where the personal stories do not bear directly on academic developments. More importantly, such material furnishes a wider context for appreciating the academic developments outlined. (Or, in the words of one colleague who prefers to remain anonymous, "gossip is the first principle of hermeneutics.") I mean no disrespect in relating these untold stories. On the contrary, my admiration has only increased, as I have come to appreciate more deeply the contours of the lives of the scholars involved in the story of Ugaritic and biblical studies. Fourth and finally, I examine an issue representative of the intellectual climate of each period. For the prewar era, Chapter One presents the discussion of monotheism between W. F. Albright and Theophile Meek. For the postwar era, Chapter Two explores myth-and-ritual approaches to Ugaritic and biblical sources, especially Sigmund Mowinckel's theory of the New Year's Feast. Chapter Three revisits the impact of Mitchell Dahood's work in the 1970s. Chapter Four examines the use of Ugaritic in recent theories about Judean monotheism. The treatments of specific issues in the four chapters are designed in part to give some sense of the intellectual atmosphere of Ugaritic and biblical studies in different periods.

The chapters divide the history of the field into four periods: between the two world wars, 1928–1945; from the end of World War II to 1970; from 1970 to 1985; and from 1985 to the present. This division of periods requires some explanation:

1. As for the first period, the Second World War created a major shift in scholarship, as many leading figures emigrated from Germany. Within the field, the end of the war marked the completion of the initial stage of work, involving the discovery, decipherment, and publication of the major texts.

2. For the end of the postwar period, I have taken 1970 as a major break-point because of the publication of the important new texts in *Ugaritica V* (1968). While some might divide 1945–1970 into two periods, I see no compelling reason for doing so: no new major texts intervened, nor did a significant shift of perspective take place in this rather long period. Furthermore, the major figures who came of age before the war continued their research throughout most or all of this period (e.g., W. F. Albright, U. Cassuto, G. R. Driver, T. H. Gaster, H. L. Ginsberg, C. H. Gordon, F. Løkkegaard, C. F. A. Schaeffer, E. Ullendorff, and C. Virolleaud). The same point applies as well to those scholars whose studies began shortly after the war.

3. As for delineating 1970 as the beginning of a period, the publication of new texts in *Ugaritica V* generated new discussion and several journals commenced at this time.

4. For several reasons I have chosen 1985 as the end of one period (1970–1985) and the beginning of another (1985–present). By the mid-1980s the

field seemed to have slowed somewhat.[10] At the same time, a major shift emerged after 1985 resulting from the efforts of the French team. The archaeology of the sites as well as the sort of epigraphic work being produced showed major changes beginning around 1985. Finally, from around the mid-1980s onward, the field displayed a growing awareness of the field's methodological complexities, especially with respect to the relationship between Ugaritic and biblical studies.

⊠ DISCLAIMERS AND DISCLOSURES

This historical survey includes the voices of many scholars, some now almost forgotten, in order to evoke the atmosphere of the field in their times. In editing this book, D. N. Freedman quipped that the piece sometimes reads like a phone book, with too much detail and too many figures. I am afraid that his assessment is on the mark. However, it is not only the great ones of a generation *(gĕdōlê haddôr)* who move a field forward; this effort also requires the talents of a myriad of other figures. In recalling these scholars *(šuma zakāru)*, this work serves one of its primary goals.

Some further caveats about this work. Because of my background and access to archives in American institutions, it is evident that I do not know the European side of the story of Ugaritic-biblical studies as well as the American side. In spite of all the help provided by the many scholars mentioned above, mine may not be an entirely balanced view of the history of Ugaritic studies. Moreover, writers are necessarily implicated in their work, and I am no exception. I happily acknowledge my studies under S. Rosenblatt at Johns Hopkins in 1973–1975, with A. Fitzgerald, J. A. Fitzmyer, P. J. Kearney, and P. K. Skehan at the Catholic University of America in 1977–1978, with F. M. Cross, T. O. Lambdin, W. L. Moran, and M. D. Coogan at Harvard in 1979–1980, with M. H. Pope and F. Rosenthal as well as B. S. Childs, W. W. Hallo, and R. R. Wilson at Yale in 1980–1985, and with J. C. Greenfield in 1983–1984. Indeed, I offer my thanks to my many teachers at these institutions and to numerous friends and colleagues whom I met during visits to the University of Chicago (first during the summer of 1981 and many times afterward) and the W. F. Albright Institute, the Ecole Biblique and the Hebrew University (first in 1980, then in 1983–1984 and many occasions since). This narrative has also benefited from my relationships with both the Center for Judaic Studies (formerly Dropsie College) and the University of Pennsylvania. Much of this manuscript came not simply from book learning but from many experiences since I first entered the field of biblical studies at Catholic University in 1977 (thanks in large measure to the good graces of Aloysius Fitzgerald—on whom more in Chapter Two). It will be apparent the narrative stresses figures whom I have known best, and this experience perhaps skews matters somewhat; how much I will leave to readers to decide. Oversights or imbalances in discussions of various scholars or their work may appear here. For readers who find this narrative insufficiently critical, I plead guilty. While I have not ignored many negative aspects of research (much less the researchers in a few cases), I have dealt more with positive contributions. It will also be evident that I have stressed questions of grammar, literature, and religion over issues of archaeology and history.

I cannot escape the question of motive. For example, I am interested in the ideology underlying an intellectual project of this sort, specifically how this discourse serves to justify and rationalize the place of Ugaritic in the field of Bible and vice-versa (I critique this stance in Chapter Four). In so doing, I could note how the relationship of the two serves a larger ideology of reading (specifically "behind the text"—again, see the end of Chapter Four). Perhaps I might admit how this project secures and underscores my own place in the narrative of scholarship and as a result justifies my work and identity. I could then explore my background and the influence of various factors on the construction of meaning in this book's narrative. These would include, admittedly, the importance I attach to the Bible and its interpretation; my Catholicism, my particular interest in Judaism, and my sympathy for religion in general as well as the emphasis I give to religious texts among the ancient materials; my appreciation for various religious and nonreligious traditions alike; my interest in learning in general and the subdisciplines of a field; my respect for earned authority; my suspicion of theoretical discussions ungrounded in some sort of discourse involving "texts" or "evidence"; and what I hope is an appreciation for contributions made not only by important figures, but also by those now considered unimportant or, worse, simply forgotten. Then I could offer an extended analysis of the ideology lurking in such factors. I do not doubt that some or all of these are operative in this project, and I will leave it to readers to judge how much these factors have affected this book. Despite such motives, I hope that between the discussion of intellectual trends and topics and the bibliographical and anecdotal material, this narrative captures some of the life and brilliance as well as the difficulties and setbacks in Ugaritic and biblical scholarship over the last seventy-odd years.

I will end by returning to the two names invoked at the beginning of this introduction. This work is dedicated to my two teachers of Ugaritic, Marvin Hoyle Pope and Jonas Carl Greenfield, as a small token of my deep gratitude to them. Both were passionate and brilliant scholars, as well as good friends to each other for many decades since their first meeting at Yale University in the early 1940s. There they both began their careers as doctoral students with the great Albrecht Goetze and Julian Obermann, and the paths of their lives crossed repeatedly. Four decades later I took Ugaritic with Pope at Yale (1980–1983) and then with Greenfield at the Hebrew University (1983–1984). In her "Message" prefaced to the essays produced in 1952 to honor the memory of her husband, the great scholar Max Leopold Margolis (1866–1932), Evelyn Aronson Margolis wrote: "When a teacher dies and his students, in the first flush of grief, establish a memorial to his memory, it does credit to their sincere emotions."[11] It is my hope that this work honors Marvin Pope and Jonas Greenfield well. I basked in the wealth of their companionship and learning for years, first as their student and later as their friend. Since their deaths, I have often returned to their great insight and learning, and even more often and with greater gratitude, I recall their warmth and good humor.

Department of Hebrew and Judaic Studies
New York University

⚌ NOTES

1. Albright, "In Memoriam Paul Haupt," *BzA* 10/2 (1927): xiii–xxii.

2. Ibid., xiv.

3. Albright's statement in the epigraph above is quoted in C. H. Gordon, *The Pennsylvania Tradition of Semitics* (SBLCP; Atlanta: Scholars Press, 1986), 54. The quotation of Roberts comes from his essay "The Ancient Near Eastern Environment," in *The Hebrew Bible and Its Modern Interpreters* (ed. D. A. Knight and G. M. Tucker; Philadelphia: Fortress; Decatur, Ga.: Scholars Press, 1985), 77.

4. Roberts rightly characterizes Ugaritic studies (with respect to biblical studies) as "a quasi-independent specialization"; see Roberts, "Ancient Near Eastern Environment," 77.

5. R. H. McGuire and M. Walker, "Class Confrontations in Archaeology," *Historical Archaeology* 33 (1999): 159–83.

6. See B. R. Foster, "Edward E. Salisbury: America's First Arabist," *Al-'Usur al-Wusta: The Bulletin of Middle East Medievalists* 9/1 (April 1997): 15–17.

7. W. F. Albright, "The Old Testament and Canaanite Language and Literature," *CBQ* 7 (1945): 5–31. See also G. P. Fogarty, *American Catholic Biblical Scholarship: A History from the Early Republic to Vatican II* (San Francisco: Harper & Row, 1989), 241–42.

8. Other technical surveys of Ugaritic-biblical studies include: H. L. Ginsberg, "Ugaritic Studies and the Bible," *BA* 8 (1945): 41–58; E. Ullendorff, "Ugaritic Studies within Their Semitic and Eastern Mediterranean Setting," *BJRL* 46 (1963): 236–44; H. Donner, "Ugaritismen in der Psalmenforschung," *ZAW* 79 (1967): 322–50; H. Ringgren, "Ugarit und das Alte Testament: Einige methodologische Erwägungen," *UF* 11 (1979 = C. F. A. Schaeffer Festschrift): 719–21; P. C. Craigie, "Ugarit and the Bible: Progress and Regress in 50 Years of Literary Study," in *Ugarit in Retrospect: Fifty Years of Ugarit and Ugaritic* (ed. G. D. Young; Winona Lake, Ind.: Eisenbrauns, 1981), 99–111; J. J. M. Roberts, "Ancient Near Eastern Environment," 75–121, esp. 77–80; O. Loretz, *Ugarit und dei Bibel: Kanaanäische Götter und Religion im Alten Testament* (Darmstadt: Wissenschaftliche Buchgesellschaft, 1990); and W. G. E. Watson and N. Wyatt, eds., *Handbook of Ugaritic Studies* (HdO 1/39; Leiden: Brill, 1999).

Popular surveys include: M. Baldacci, *La scoperta di Ugarit: La città-stato ai primordi della Bibbia* (Spa: Piemme, 1996); P. C. Craigie, *Ugarit and the Old Testament* (Grand Rapids, Mich.: Eerdmans, 1983); A. H. W. Curtis, *Ugarit (Ras Shamra)* (Cities of the Biblical World; Cambridge: Lutterworth, 1985); E. Jacob, *Ras Shamra-Ugarit et l'Ancien Testament* (Neuchâtel/Paris: Delachaux et Niestlé, 1960); A. S. Kapelrud, *The Ras Shamra Discoveries and the Old Testament* (trans. G. W. Anderson; Norman, Okla.: University of Oklahoma Press, 1963); D. Kinet, *Ugarit—Geschichte und Kultur einer Stadt in der Umwelt des Alten Testamentes* (SBS 104; Stuttgart: Verlag Katholisches Bibelwerk, 1981); J. P. Lettinga, *Oegarit (rās esj-sjamrā), een nieuwe Phoenicische stad uit de Oudheid* (Cultuurhistorische Monografieën 11; La Haye: Servire, 1948); G. Saadé, *Ougarit: Métropole Canaanéenne* (Beirut: Imprimerie Catholique Beyrouth, 1979); and P. Xella, *La terra di Baal (Ugarit e la sua civiltà)* (Biblioteca di Archeologia; Rome: Armando Curcio Editore, 1984).

9. Watson and Wyatt, *Handbook of Ugaritic Studies.*

10. See the comments of Roberts, "Ancient Near Eastern Environment," 80.

11. *Max Leopold Margolis: Scholar and Teacher* (Philadelphia: Dropsie College for Hebrew and Cognate Learning, 1952), vii. I am grateful to David Goldenberg for drawing my attention to this work.

chapter one

Beginnings: 1928 to 1945

⊠ TEXTS AND TOOLS

Archaeology: C. F. A. Schaeffer, *CTA* xix–xxx, provides a convenient listing. See also the bibliography of J. C. Courtois, "Ras Shamra: I. Archéologie," *DBSup* 9 (1979): 1287–89, 1291–95.

Decipherment: On the work of H. Bauer, E. Dhorme, and C. Virolleaud, see below pp. 14–16.

Editio Princeps: C. Virolleaud's articles in *Syria*. See also the bibliography of Courtois, "Ras Shamra: I. Archéologie," *DBSup* 9 (1979): 1291–95.

Grammar: C. H. Gordon, *Ugaritic Grammar* (AnOr 20; Rome: Pontifical Biblical Institute, 1940).

Handbook: J. A. Montgomery and Z. S. Harris, *The Ras Shamra Mythological Texts* (Memoirs of the American Philosophical Society IV; Philadelphia: American Philosophical Society, 1935).

Translations: H. L. Ginsberg, *Kitbê ʾUgarit* (Jerusalem: Mosad Bialik, 1936). C. H. Gordon, *The Loves and Wars of Baal and Anat* (Princeton Oriental Texts 9; Princeton: Princeton University, 1943).

Synthetic Studies: W. F. Albright, *From the Stone Age to Christianity: Monotheism and the Historical Process* (Baltimore: Johns Hopkins University Press, 1940; 2d ed., 1957). R. Dussaud, *Les découvertes de Ras Shamra (Ugarit et l'Ancien Testament)* (2d ed.; Paris: Geuthner, 1941). J. W. Jack, *The Ras Shamra Tablets and Their Bearing upon the Old Testament* (Old Testament Studies 1; Edinburgh: T&T Clark, 1935). R. de Langhe, *Les textes de Ras Shamra–Ugarit et leur rapports avec le milieu biblique de l'Ancient Testament* (Gembloux: Duculot, 1945).

⊠ FIRST DISCOVERIES

The story of the discovery of the Ugaritic texts has been told many times. Here let me quote P. C. Craigie's account.

In the spring of 1928, a farmer was ploughing some land on the Mediterranean coast of Syria; his name was Mahmoud Mella az-Zir, and he lived close to a bay called Minet el-Beida. The tip of his plough ran into stone just beneath the surface of the soil; when he examined the obstruction, he found a large man-made flagstone. He cleared away the earth, raised the stone, and beneath it he saw a short subterranean passageway leading into an ancient tomb. Entering the tomb, he discovered a number of ancient objects of potential value; these he sold to a dealer in antiquities. Though he could not have known it at the time, the agricultural worker had opened up more than a tomb on that spring day. He had opened a door which was to lead to extraordinary discoveries concerning ancient history and civilization, and even to a new appraisal of the Old Testament.[1]

At this time Minet el-Bheida (the ancient Leukos Limen, "the white harbor") belonged to the Alouites (later Syria), then under the French mandate, specifically in the jurisdiction of the governor, M. Schoeffler. News of the discovery soon reached the director of the Antiquities Service of Syria and Lebanon, Charles Virolleaud (1879–1968), who sent out a reconnaissance team under L. Albanèse. After this initial investigation, a team was assembled under the leadership of C. F. A. Schaeffer (1889–1982), an Alsatian then employed in the archaeological museum in Strasbourg.

On April 2, 1929, Schaeffer's team commenced excavations. The crew discovered at Minet el-Bheida what he thought to be a cemetery adjoining a number of buildings, and then a series of rich deposits of objects (foreign and local pottery, two hawk figurines in Egyptian style, stone tablets uninscribed, pierced stelae, stone weights, bronze implements, and weapons). Later René Dussaud (then Keeper of the Department of Oriental Antiquities at the Louvre) visited the site, and on his advice the team moved on May 9 to the nearby tell of Ras Shamra ("Fennel Mound," named for the flowers that grew there). Five days later, late in the afternoon of May 14, the first clay tablet with writing came to light.[2] After this initial textual discovery, many more texts and objects were discovered. The first season was a great success, having yielded both artifacts and texts in a hitherto unknown cuneiform script.[3]

⊠ DECIPHERMENT

At this point the story of Ugarit turned to initial publication and decipherment,[4] with Virolleaud, himself a trained Assyriologist, taking the lead. Virolleaud quickly recognized that the texts were written in alphabetic cuneiform. Once this point was established, decipherment followed quickly. Virolleaud was joined shortly in the labor by two brilliant biblical scholars who had been cryptographers in the First World War. The first was Hans Bauer (1878–1937), professor of Semitic Languages at Halle from 1922 onward, already well-known for his studies of medieval Arabic philosophy (especially Al-Ghazali), his studies of the Semitic tenses, *Die Tempora im Semitischen* (1919), and his magisterial work, *Historische Grammatik der hebräischen Sprache des Alten Testaments* (1922), coauthored with Pontus Leander.[5] The second scholar was Père Edouard Dhorme (1881–1966), professor at the Ecole Biblique in Jerusalem (until 1931, when he returned to Paris).[6] At this time Dhorme was already famous for *Le livre de Job*, his 1926 commentary on the biblical book, as well as his work on the El-Amarna tablets. Less than a year's effort on the part of Virolleaud, Bauer, and Dhorme yielded the basic decipherment of Ugaritic, as the language was called after the ancient name of the site.[7]

Here we may cite an account of the events leading up to the decipherment, reported by a witness, William Foxwell Albright (1891–1971). Emerging as a dominant figure in biblical studies in the United States, Albright became the W. W. Spence Professor of Semitic Languages at The Johns Hopkins University in 1929:[8]

> Virolleaud recognized almost immediately that the script was alphabetic, not syllabic like Accadian, because of the number of separate letters (29 or 30). But he hesitated to proceed further with the available material, publishing it without extended comment in April, 1930. Before the end of the month Hans Bauer, professor of Semitic Languages at Halle, had succeeded in identifying over half of the letters correctly by clever use of decoding methods, with which he was familiar. In June he published a popular sketch of his results in the *Vossische Zeitung*, which reached my hands through the intermediation of Kurt Galling, then in Jerusalem. I took the article to Dhorme, who was working on the texts at that time, and he immediately recognized that Bauer was correct in a number of points which he had missed, but that he himself was right in other points. In September Dhorme published his improved results in the *Revue Biblique*, which was promptly sent to Bauer, causing him to revise his identifications and to make further improvements. Meanwhile the tablets found in the spring of 1930, which included long consecutive poems in the Canaanite alphabet, had reached Virolleaud, who was able to distance both Bauer and Dhorme, fixing nearly all remaining values.[9]

Albright's account omits his own small contribution to decipherment. Although he was fully engaged with excavations at Tell Beit Mirsim, Albright contributed to the correct identification of one letter, the dotted *z*.[10] Thus, by the second season of excavation at Ras Shamra, decipherment was essentially achieved.

Excavations were conducted in the second season again at Minet el-Bheida and then at Ras Shamra. With a library having been discovered in the second season, Ugaritic held out the promise of ever greater discovery. Albright identified the site with ancient Ugarit in 1931–1932,[11] and the proposal was independently confirmed in Schaeffer's publication of a tablet mentioning "Niqmaddu king of Ugarit."[12] Progress continued apace. By 1939, with the Second World War descending on Europe, the work had yielded more than 150 Ugaritic texts, along with numerous texts in several other languages. The Ugaritic texts discovered included the Baal Cycle (*KTU* 1.1–1.6), other pieces concerning Baal (1.8, 1.10, 1.12) and Anat (1.13), part of Keret (1.14), all of Aqhat (1.17–1.19), the Birth of the Beautiful Gods (1.23), and Nikkal wa-Ib (1.24). At Ras Shamra the archaeological team had uncovered two temples (which the excavators called the temples of Baal and Dagan), parts of a palace, and many private houses and streets. In addition, the work at Minet el-Bheida yielded remains of a seaport.

⊠ GRAMMAR AND POETRY

Immediately following the initial seasons of excavation, two tasks dominated the field. The first involved Ugaritic itself, the second its relationship to the Bible. This period saw the production of basic information and tools, in particular text editions and translations. Here we can look back with admiration on the labors of the pioneers, especially Schaeffer for his archaeological work[13] and Virolleaud,[14] as well as Bauer and Dhorme, for their epigraphical and philological discoveries. Schaeffer published a long series of archaeological reports in the journal *Syria,* which kept the field apprised of new discoveries. Similarly, the publications of Ugaritic texts by Virolleaud were admirable for the speed with which they appeared. Many of the best scholars tried their hand at the various texts, in particular the myths that Virolleaud published piecemeal. The main scholars who undertook textual studies in this early period were J. Aistleitner, W. F. Albright, G. A. Barton, U. Cassuto, R. de Langhe, R. Dussaud, J. Friedrich, T. H. Gaster, H. L. Ginsberg, F. F. Hvidberg, J. A. Montgomery, and J. Obermann.[15] Albright commented in 1943: "Again we see that the cooperation of successive students is necessary, and that no one man can hope to solve most of the difficulties with which Ugaritic mythological poems swarm."[16] Thanks to these scholars, it soon became obvious that the Ugaritic texts held a special key to understanding the linguistic and cultural conditions in Canaan in the very words of the indigenous population. Since the mythological texts appeared first, it was hardly surprising that Ugaritic attracted interest first and foremost from the biblical field.[17] Many scholars followed through the war with various grammatical and cultural studies (A. Alt, W. Baumgartner, A. Bea, H. Bauer, H. Birkeland, C. G. von Brandenstein, C. Brockelmann, J. Cantineau, O. Eissfeldt, J.-G. Février, J. Friedrich, C. H. Gordon, E. Hammershaimb, Z. Harris, A. Herdner, A. M. Honeyman, B. Hrozny, E. Jacobs, J. W. Jack, A. Jirku, P. Joüon, J. J. Kroeze, J. P. Lettinga, A. Lods, B. Maisler/Mazar, J. Pedersen, F. Rosenthal, A. D. Singer, and R. de Vaux). Cumulatively, the Ugaritic texts allowed scholars to penetrate "behind the Bible" and to understand its linguistic and cultural background.

The labor of these scholars produced detailed philological work yielding a rudimentary knowledge of the grammar. In this area Ugaritic provided an especially rich resource for comparison with biblical Hebrew. Ugaritic provided thirty symbols representing twenty-seven basic consonants with three variants for the letter *ʾaleph*. (The abecedaries published for the most part in the early 1950s list the *ʾa-ʾaleph* in first position, with the *ʾi-* and *ʾu-ʾalephs* appearing at the very end, except for the enigmatic *ś*, absent from literary texts and perhaps used only for loanwords.) This repertoire confirmed what Akkadian and Arabic together had already indicated about the merger of consonants lying behind Hebrew's smaller assemblage of twenty-three consonants. Ugaritic provided evidence that the older stages of West Semitic had employed this fuller repertoire, and it further clarified other details about the early alphabet. Initially, the usage of the three *ʾalephs* was a matter of controversy. Assuming that the *ʾalephs* varied largely according to the vowel that followed (except for the use of *ʾi* in syllable-closing contexts)[18] allowed for the successful reconstruction of the vowels inside Ugaritic words, at least to some extent. It was evident from a lack of *w-* and *y-* in some words where Hebrew showed *waw* and *yodh* that Ugaritic had fully contracted diphthongs, not only in construct forms, but also in absolute forms (as the discovery of the Samaria Ostraca would show for northern Hebrew, or more precisely, "Samarian" Hebrew).[19]

The understanding of Hebrew morphology benefited from Ugaritic in many ways as well. The case system of Ugaritic was evident to investigators early on.[20] The three *ʾalephs* at the ends of nouns showed that Ugaritic had a full system of case endings that later Hebrew lost around 1200 B.C.E. with the loss of other final short vowels.[21] The result in Hebrew was a modification and coalescence of endings, and for nouns, an end to case distinctions. Recognizing the loss of final short vowels in early Hebrew, scholars determined that the masculine plural dyptotic case system in Ugaritic (nominative *-ūma* and genitive/accusative *-īma*) had been reduced to the single plural ending *-îm* in Hebrew and that the masculine construct plural ending in Hebrew, namely *-ê*, derived from the dual construct ending *-ay* (reduced to *-ê* as in Ugaritic). Many of the nominal patterns shared by Ugaritic and Hebrew were identified early on, with their *ʾ-*, *m-*, and *t-* preformative elements, as well as sufformatives (morpheme added to the end of a word) such as *–n*. The basic nominal patterns in Ugaritic, where the internal structures could be discerned on the basis of the three *ʾalephs*, largely conformed to patterns known in Hebrew. The identification of anomalous long forms of third person pronouns in biblical Hebrew and apparently in some Qumran Hebrew found confirmation in similar forms in Ugaritic.

In the area of the verb, H. L. Ginsberg discovered the applicability of Barth's rule regarding theme vowels in the Ugaritic G-stem (Qal in Hebrew) "imperfect" or prefix indicative verbal forms; soon the rule became known as "the Barth-Ginsberg law" (dissimilation of prefix vowel from theme vowel in prefix forms).[22]

J. Friedrich contributed a description of the different modal endings of the verb.[23] The loss of final short vowels affected distinctions between certain verbal forms. Ugaritic apparently distinguished the old *yaqtul*-preterite form from the present-future prefix form, *yaqtulu (the use of both forms in Ugaritic poetic narrative apparently goes back to their original distinction, but this distinction was later lost).[24] However, when *yaqtulu lost its final short -*u*, this form was indistinguishable in Hebrew from the old *yaqtul preterite, subsequently preserved in Hebrew in *wayyiqtol forms (the so-called "*waw*-consecutive" or "converted imperfect") and as a variant form to narrate past events in Hebrew poetry.[25] In Ugaritic and biblical poetry, the two prefix indicative forms are interchangeable, apparently a relic of an older distinction in the verbal system.

Ugaritic was recognized as having a full range of verbal stems, including the old "Qal passive" (*G*-stem passive), which, apart from the participle, Hebrew preserved only vestigially.[26] Thanks to forms recognized in Ugaritic, Qal-passive forms vocalized in the MT as either Pual perfects or Hophal imperfects (with corresponding active forms in the Qal) were more easily recognized as Qal passive. Disputing the traditional view of the *D*-stem (BH Piel) as the "intensive" stem,[27] Albrecht Goetze produced a 1942 study that had wide application to the derived stems in Ugaritic and Hebrew. Although Goetze's view that *D*-stem forms of *G*-stem active verbs are resultative did not win acceptance (many regard such forms as pluralitive),[28] he made three crucial points (as summarized by S. A. Kaufman):

> Goetze did establish three fundamental and correct approaches to the study of Semitic lexical morphology: (1) that the semantic lexical modification imparted by stem variation differs for active and stative verbs; (2) that the D-stem is never "intensive"; and (3) that the D-stem is "factitive" (not causative) for stative verbs.[29]

Goetze's article on the *D*-stem was so insightful and influential that it has remained the basis of discussion up to the present.[30]

Ugaritic offered a valuable new resource for etymologies of Hebrew words and articles. Vocabulary specifically enlightened by recourse to Ugaritic include: *št^c (= Ugaritic ṯt^c), "fear" (Isa 41:10, 23);[31] *šulḥan (= Ugaritic ṯlḥn), "table"; and *derek*, "way," but also "dominion" (= Ugaritic drkt). Many Hebrew particles were elucidated by means of Ugaritic. For example, Albright and others recognized that "the -*h* locale" (or "directive" or "terminative" -*h*), long known in biblical Hebrew, was a particle in its own right in Ugaritic, since that language does not mark case endings on singular nouns consonantally.[32] Accordingly, it was evident that "the -*h* locale" was not an accusative case ending as some had supposed. Similarly, the Ugaritic asseverative *kaph* and emphatic (or asseverative) *lamed*,[33] as well as the enclitic *mem* first identified by H. L. Ginsberg,[34] have been generally accepted for Hebrew as well. Other particles seen in Ugaritic, such as vocative *lamed*,[35] have been more controversial when identified in Hebrew. Many of the diachronic developments and particles illustrate many changes during the long evolution of grammar. Therefore, many of the features in Ugaritic should remain relatively rare for Hebrew. Despite the chronological gap between the texts written in Ugaritic and Hebrew, the grammars of these two languages had so much in common that many in the field began to characterize Ugaritic as Canaanite, and a debate over this linguistic classification ensued, with pieces authored on the subject in this period by, for example, Albright and Goetze.[36]

The new Ugaritic texts also enriched other areas of biblical studies. For example, Ugaritic poetry showed the sorts of syntax and parallelism of lines well-known in Hebrew poetry. Psalms 92:10 and 145:13 were cited early on as examples of biblical poetry demonstrating great congruence with Ugaritic poetry (in particular *KTU* 1.2 IV 8–10).[37] Both Ugaritic and Hebrew poetry exhibited distinct examples of closely matching parallel terms (a-b-c // a'-b'-c' or a-b-c // a'-b'), but also what E. L. Greenstein in the 1970s aptly termed "staircase" parallelism (a-b-c // a-b-d // a'-b'-d').[38] Many of the same standard pairs of words in parallelism ("word pairs") appeared in both languages. The feature of the "double-duty" pronominal suffix (used in the first line and implied in the second line) generally found acceptance among commentators.

⋈ COMPARISONS OF LITERATURE AND RELIGION

Literary analysis of Ugaritic and Hebrew showed a common repertoire of themes and type-scenes. Ugaritic also provided a whole new corpus of texts pertinent to the literature and religion of the Canaanites, thus elucidating the Bible.[39] For example, Ps 29 seemed now to swarm with so many features known from Ugaritic that, following Ginsberg,[40] scholars began to debate whether this psalm was originally Israelite or not. The figure of the biblical Daniel in Ezek 14:14, 20 seemed to be attested now as Dan'ilu in the story of Aqhat.[41] The very names of Baal's mountain and his cosmic enemies now appeared in the Bible as well: like Baal, Yahweh had an abode called ṣapôn (Ps 48:3), and like Baal, Yahweh battled cosmic adversaries with the same names, such as Leviathan.[42] Now the polemics of Israel's prophets against its Canaanite neighbors seemed to have a clearer context, with the very names of Baal and Asherah familiar from the Bible now appearing in Ugaritic texts.[43]

However, there were occasional missteps. Early treatments of some mythological texts sometimes posited personal names as a last resort in interpreting difficult Ugaritic words. For example, Dussaud and Virolleaud proposed to see the biblical names of Terah and Negeb behind similar Ugaritic words. Context suggested otherwise, but it would take some time to root these ideas out of the scholarly literature.[44] A longer-lasting mistake involved Ginsberg's ingenious suggestion that the biblical prohibition against boiling (or seething) a kid in its mother's milk (Exod 23:19, 34:26; Deut 14:21) represented a polemic against a Canaanite ritual practice evidenced in *KTU* 1.23.14.[45] This proposal long remained a standard example of Ugaritic-biblical connections,[46] until M. Haran[47] and then J. Milgrom[48] demonstrated otherwise. Later photographic studies of the original Ugaritic letters[49] in question confirmed the substantial impediments to understanding *KTU* 1.23.14 as evidence of such a Canaanite ritual. As these examples illustrate, Ugaritic texts early on offered many fine insights for the Bible, but occasionally there would be some misfires. Similarly, it was clear already at this early stage that the myths and legends engaged scholars' interest far more than did ritual and administrative texts. The new interest that Ugaritic generated for studying the Bible reaped immediate results in the academic community. Still, those involved in the interpretation of the texts, as Albright was in 1936, could "foresee ten years of concerted effort on the part of scholars before there is a real communis opinio with regard to details of grammar and vocabulary, to say nothing of interpretation."[50]

☒ ACADEMIC DEVELOPMENTS IN EUROPE AND PALESTINE

The successes of the discoveries helped to bring Ugaritic into the curriculum of academic programs. A handful of examples may convey some of the university activity in Ugaritic through the Second World War.

Paris: C. Virolleaud

At the Ecole Pratique des Hautes Etudes (fifth section), Charles Virolleaud was the only teacher offering Ugaritic in France in this period. His students included the leading French scholars of the next generation, including Andrée Herdner, André Caquot, Henri Cazelles, and R. Largement.[51]

Copenhagen: J. Pedersen, F. Løkkegaard, D. Nielsen, and F. F. Hvidberg

Faculty at Copenhagen took up Ugaritic before the war. Johannes Pedersen (1883–1977) and Frede Løkkegaard themselves wrote on Ugaritic.[52] Other figures at Copenhagen also produced both cultural and grammatical studies: Ditlef Nielsen's comparative study of astral deities in West Semitic and Epigraphic South Arabian texts, *Ras Šamra Mythologie und Biblische Theologie* (1936);[53] Flemming Friis Hvidberg's work, *Graad og Latter i det Gamle Testmente*, published originally as an annual University-Programme (1938) and translated into English after his death by Løkkegaard under the title *Weeping and Laughter in the Old Testament*;[54] and Erling Hammershaimb's doctoral dissertation on "Das Verbum im Dialekt von Ras Schamra" (1941).[55] Nielsen, for many years librarian at the Royal Library at Copenhagen, continued to publish studies in the history of Semitic religions.[56]

Halle and Berlin: H. Bauer and F. Rosenthal

Germany produced major figures by the eve of the war. At Halle, Hans Bauer provided instruction in Ugaritic. Born in Bavaria, Bauer (1878–1937) had been appointed as professor at Halle in 1922.[57] One of his students was the distinguished Otto Eissfeldt,[58] already professor there beginning the year before.[59] Franz Rosenthal (1914–) was the first faculty member to teach Ugaritic in Berlin, his hometown, in 1937 following his doctoral studies there in 1932–1935 under Hans Heinrich Schaeder as his "principal teacher and adviser," "wonderful and helpful in both capacities."[60] After a year in Florence following the completion of his dissertation, *Die Sprache der palmyrenischen Inschriften*, he returned to Berlin in 1937 to take up a post as Dozent für orientalische Sprachen an der Lehranstalt

Franz Rosenthal. Courtesy of Michael Marsland, Yale University Office of Public Affairs.

für die Wissenschaft des Judentums, and as such he first taught Ugaritic. However, Rosenthal lost his academic position in 1938,[61] and he fled Germany in December of that year. Thanks to Schaeder's contact with H. S. Nyberg, Rosenthal acquired a visa for Sweden. In 1938 he won the Lidzbarski Prize of the International Congress of Orientalists for his book, *Die aramaistische Forschung seit Theodor Noeldekes Veroeffentlichungen*. In the same year Rosenthal also authored one of the first studies of parallels within the Ugaritic literary corpus.[62]

The Hebrew University: U. Cassuto

Another refugee from the war established a program in Jerusalem. Umberto Moshe David Cassuto (1883–1951), Chief Rabbi of Florence and head of the Rabbinical School, left his post at the University of Florence for a professorship at the University of Rome. Dismissed from his position in October 1938 on

account of Jewish racial laws (along with about one hundred other Jewish professors), Cassuto departed for a new position at the Hebrew University in 1939.[63]
For decades prior to emigrating, Cassuto had produced significant work on Italian classics, the Judeo-Italian dialect, Hebrew inscriptions of southern Italy, and
related topics. (The most important artifact of this research was his 1918 study in
Italian Jewish history, *Gli ebrei a Firenze nell' età del rinascimento.*) At the Hebrew
University, Cassuto wrote and taught in the area of Ugaritic and biblical comparisons. His most famous students included Edward Ullendorff[64] and later Samuel
Loewenstamm, Abraham Malamat, and A. D. Singer.[65] Cassuto was well known
for many studies of Ugaritic passages, especially in the myths and legends.[66] Besides his text studies and literary observations, one major contribution was
Cassuto's attempt in 1943 to demonstrate an early literary epic tradition in Israel
that was distinctly indebted to the "Canaanite" culture, as represented by the
Ugaritic texts.[67] This prompted a major discussion regarding the shared literary
traditions between the two cultures (as Canaan and Israel were viewed in this period and afterward—and in some quarters, to this day). Perhaps it was Cassuto's
first raising the issues that later led scholars to develop the topic of "Hebrew
epic."[68] At Tel Aviv in this period we may note the figure of Samuel Yeivin. Known
mostly for his work in archaeology and the Bar Kochba revolt, he occasionally
wrote on Ugaritic.[69]

✄ ACADEMIC DEVELOPMENTS IN THE UNITED STATES

The University of Pennsylvania and Dropsie College:
J. A. Montgomery, G. Barton, and E. A. Speiser

Schools in the United States also incorporated Ugaritic into their curricula.
Apparently, the first dissertation involving Ugaritic was the 1934 Chicago work of
Walter George Williams, "The Ras Shamra Inscriptions and Israel's Cultural Her-
itage."[70] However, Chicago did not develop a program in this field in the prewar
period. The program that first integrated Ugaritic into its curriculum was the
University of Pennsylvania.[71] A longtime member of the Penn faculty, James A.
Montgomery (1866–1949), was joined in 1923 by George Barton (1859–1942), a
Canadian Quaker, who had been teaching at Bryn Mawr College. (Montgomery
and Barton taught also at the Philadelphia Divinity School.) Both scholars published early studies on Ugaritic. In 1935, Montgomery and his student, Zellig
Harris, cowrote a handbook, *The Ras Shamra Mythological Texts.* In the fall of
1935, Montgomery offered a course entitled "The Hebraic Ras Shamra Texts." By
1937–1938, Harris teamed up with Montgomery to teach Ugaritic.

Ugaritic also found a home across town at the Dropsie College for Hebrew and Cognate Learning. Beginning in the 1930s, the outstanding faculty at Dropsie embraced the riches of the Ugaritic texts. Ephraim Avigdor Speiser (1902–1965)[72] first taught Ugaritic there.[73] Born in Skalat, Galicia (then part of Austrian Poland, now in Ukraine), Speiser graduated from the Gymnasium of Lemberg, Austria, in 1918. He took a master's degree from the University of Pennsylvania in 1923, with a thesis on "The Hebrew Origin of the First Part of the Book of Wisdom," and a doctorate from Dropsie College in 1925, with a dissertation on "The Pronunciation of Hebrew according to the Transliterations in the Hexapla," supervised by Max Margolis. In this period he also worked with Edward Chiera (1885–1933), an Assyriologist at the University of Pennsylvania.[74] Underwritten by Dropsie College, the two-time Guggenheim winner surveyed northern Iraq in 1926–1927, excavated at Tell Billa from 1930 to 1932 (with the work greatly improving his knowledge of Arabic),[75] and once again at Tell Billa and at Tepe Gawra from 1936 to 1937. In 1928, Speiser succeeded Chiera on the faculty of the University of Pennsylvania and served there into the war and then again from 1947 until his death in 1965.

The standard necrologies of Speiser[76] overlook his early career at Dropsie. In the early 1930s Speiser became a lecturer and in 1934 a professor at Dropsie. The *Dropsie College Register* for 1935–1936 lists the "Ras Shamra Texts" under its courses of study, and it requires the Montgomery and Harris textbook for the course, which was restricted to "specially qualified students."[77] Speiser worked from 1936 to 1937 as director of excavations at Tepe Gawra (a site he had discovered in 1926–1927); afterward he would not offer the subject again at Dropsie. By 1939 Speiser abandoned the revision and expansion of his doctoral dissertation on the Hexapla, realizing that in the area of West Semitic studies, Ugaritic now had assumed a place of major importance. In a letter dated 13 February 1939, he informed his patron at Dropsie College, its president Cyrus Adler, of his decision not to proceed with the revision of his dissertation, which Adler had long encouraged. In part, Speiser's argument involved the appearance of the new materials from Ugarit:

> Ras Shamra has furnished and keeps on furnishing extensive material that is basic for the earliest history of Hebrew phonology. This material cannot be ignored. At the same time, our knowledge of the Ras Shamra documents is as yet inchoate and the annual campaigns add regularly fresh and important evidence. It will probably require many years before the new source has been exhausted, and additional years before the total yield can be evaluated.[78]

Speiser apparently planned to continue with Ugaritic in his teaching at Dropsie, but he did not. Other matters intervened.

Speiser taught at Dropsie until 1941, shortly after the death of the school's first president, Cyrus Adler. Although Speiser emerged as one of the finalists in the running as his successor, the position went instead to Abraham A. Neuman. Disappointed with the school's choice, Speiser abandoned his teaching mid-semester at Dropsie, which he announced in a letter to Newman dated 16 February 1941.[79] (In 1940–1941 and 1942–1943, Joseph Reider taught the Ugaritic course.) Like many other scholars, Speiser then joined the war effort, leaving Penn to work for the Office of Strategic Services (precursor to the Central Intelligence Agency). He did return to Philadelphia to serve as professor of Assyriology at the University of Pennsylvania from 1947 to 1965, and he wrote occasional pieces on Ugaritic subjects (described in the following chapter in the section on the University of Pennsylvania), but not as an affiliate of Dropsie.[80] Still, the college awarded an honorary doctorate to him in 1965, the year he died of cancer.

The Johns Hopkins University: W. F. Albright and F. R. Blake

Thanks to William Foxwell Albright (1891–1971), Johns Hopkins became a well-known program for Ugaritic and the Bible up through the war. In 1929 he returned there from the American School in Jerusalem, and in 1930 he succeeded his great teacher, Paul Haupt (1858–1926), as W. W. Spence Professor of Semitic Languages.[81] Haupt regarded Albright as "the most brilliant man he has seen for forty years."[82] In 1934 Albright was offered the Laffan Chair of Assyriology and Babylonian literature at Yale University, only to decline and recommend instead Albrecht Goetze for the position.[83] Albright remained at Hopkins until he retired in 1958.

William F. Albright. Courtesy of the American Schools of Oriental Research.

Also deeply influential on the Hopkins students was Frank Ringold Blake, himself a teacher of Albright and later his colleague.[84] Following his 1902 dissertation at Hopkins,[85] Blake had become a part-time instructor there. When Albright returned to Hopkins in 1929, the staff of the department also included Rabbis William Rosenau (retired in 1935, died in 1943) and Samuel Rosenblatt, a student of Albright's in Jerusalem.[86] Son of the famous cantor Yossele Rosenblatt and a scholar of Arabic and Hebrew, Rosenblatt wrote many books, perhaps the best-known being his translation of

Saadia Gaon's *The Book of Beliefs and Opinions*.[87] While Rosenblatt held a full-time position in the rabbinate, Blake maintained a full-time job as the principal of City College High School in Baltimore. Today Blake is largely forgotten, but his place in the Hopkins program was an important one, providing doctoral training especially in Hebrew grammar.[88] One of his famous students, Frank Moore Cross, remembers Blake as "the best language teacher I ever had."[89] Moreover, his studies of vowels and the verb in biblical Hebrew were models of grammatical methodology, and his work has been the basis of studies by his student Thomas Lambdin and Lambdin's own Harvard students. Together, Albright, Blake, and their colleagues during this period produced a number of very strong doctoral students who would eventually assume major university posts of their own, including Abraham Biran, John Bright, George Mendenhall, Abe Sachs,[90] and G. Ernest Wright.

As for the Ugaritic texts, work at Hopkins before the close of the war is represented primarily by Albright's many studies.[91] Along with Ginsberg and others, he offered editions of the texts as soon as Virolleaud made them available. Albright gave an informal seminar on Ugaritic in 1936–1937, and followed with a formal one in 1941.[92] With so many fine doctoral students to follow after the war, it is easy to forget that Albright had already reached the apex of his career as the dominant American figure in the biblical field. In 1943 Albright wrote that he was feeling his age and suffering from diminished vision and a crippled left hand.[93] In 1944 he also suffered attacks of sacroiliac pain and later sciatica as well as kidney trouble, fever, and infection of the tonsils, and in 1945 his back trouble required an operation.[94] In the meantime, Albright's own work on Ugaritic would continue, namely, as one of a dozen subfields to which he contributed. By the end of the war, he had charted a course of integrating knowledge of the Ugaritic texts into the wider context of ancient Near Eastern and biblical studies. Exemplifying this project were his two best-known works on history and religion, *From the Stone Age to Christianity* (1940) and *Archaeology and the Religion of Israel* (1942). The next chapter discusses the program at Hopkins in the postwar period.

The Jewish Theological Seminary: H. L. Ginsberg

At the Jewish Theological Seminary of America (JTS),[95] meanwhile, the dominant figure was Harold Louis Ginsberg (1903–1990).[96] Born in Montreal, Ginsberg studied Semitics at the University of London. Afterward he lived in Jerusalem in the 1930s and served as a visiting instructor at the Hebrew University.[97] Among his students of Ugaritic there was the undergraduate Edward Ullendorff.[98] Although he lacked a university post (he apparently supported himself at least in part by teaching in the Mizrachi Boys High School),[99] it was during this period in Jerusalem that Ginsberg made some of the most fundamental observations on Ugaritic grammar and posited the linguistic proximity between Ugaritic and Phoenician.[100] He also produced the most important translation of the Ugaritic mythological texts of this period, *Kitbê ʾUgarit* (1936),[101] publishing it when he was only thirty-three![102] This translation noted numerous parallels between Ugaritic and Hebrew words and poetic lines. Many of the important observations went beyond matters of grammar, lexicography, and poetic style. As noted above, Ginsberg recognized the cumulative weight of so many connections between the Ugaritic texts and Ps 29 that he deduced that the psalm was an ancient Phoenician hymn devoted to the storm-god, Baal, secondarily revised as a hymn to Yahweh.

Louis Ginsberg. Courtesy of The Joseph and Miriam Ratner Center for the Study of Conservative Judaism, The Jewish Theological Seminary of America.

He also came into contact with important Semiticists in Jerusalem, including Albright, then director of the American School. In a 1936 letter to Cyrus Adler, Albright described Ginsberg as "the best Jewish comparative Semitic grammarian living, in spite of his youth (in his early thirties)," and Albright goes on to offer high praise for his work on the Ras Shamra texts.[103] Ginsberg set the highest grammatical and philological standards for the field. By the end of the war—though only in his early forties—Ginsberg was the internationally acknowledged master of Ugaritic. In 1945 Albright singled out Ginsberg as *primus inter pares*.[104] In 1936, Ginsberg had begun a teaching career at JTS that lasted until his death in 1990. At JTS, his students included many figures who came to hold positions in biblical studies at major universities, notably Moshe Held (Dropsie and Columbia), Jacob Milgrom (Berkeley), Baruch A. Levine (New York University), Seymour (Shalom) M. Paul (Tel Aviv University and then the Hebrew University), Jeffrey Tigay (University of Pennsylvania), Yohanan Muffs (JTS), and Tikva Frymer-Kensky (Reconstructionist Rabbinical College and the University of Chicago).[105]

In this period, down the street from JTS, Columbia University employed the talents of another contributor to Ugaritic and biblical studies, namely, Isaac Mendelsohn, professor from 1932 to 1965. Primarily an Assyriologist, Mendelsohn contributed some of the first treatments of Ugarit's legal and social institutions through the 1940s,[106] culminating in his 1949 book, *Slavery in the Ancient Near East: A Comparative Study of Slavery in Babylonia, Assyria, Syria, and Palestine from the Middle of the Third Millennium to the End of the First Millennium*. He also taught Ugaritic, and his students included Jeffrey Tigay and Stephen Geller before they pursued doctoral studies at Yale and Harvard, respectively.[107]

Yale University: A. Goetze and J. Obermann

Franz Rosenthal was not alone in departing from Germany because of the war. A non-Jew who opposed the Nazis, Albrecht Goetze left his homeland for the United States, taking up the Laffan Chair of Assyriology and Babylonian Literature at Yale University. He soon became one of the major figures in the ancient Near Eastern field in the United States. Goetze was a giant in Assyriology and Hittitology, and he attracted students from both America and abroad. Besides teaching Ugaritic, he is perhaps best known for his article on the linguistic classification of Ugaritic as a Canaanite language,[108] but he also offered other studies, including one on Nikkal wa-Ib (*KTU* 1.24) and another on a passage from the Baal Cycle with the catchy title "Peace on Earth."[109] Clearly Goetze's great strengths lay in Akkadian and Hittite, and some of his contemporaries recognized that his knowledge of Akkadian overly influenced his analysis of Ugaritic grammar. Indeed, his 1938 debut at the American Oriental Society meeting treating the Ugaritic verb tenses sullied his reputation in the area of West Semitics.[110]

Goetze's colleague at Yale, the Arabist Julian Obermann, devoted more of his energies to Ugaritic.[111] He authored many works on subjects ranging from grammar to mythology.[112] However, the work was not without its problems. For example, in January 1937 Albright described his and Ginsberg's reactions to a paper given by Obermann, probably the one given at the meeting of the Society of Biblical Literature held in the fall of 1936:

> It will take me a long time to get over the superlatively dreadful paper by Obermann. While my opinion of his work in his pre-Arabic field was previously very low, it has descended into the depths of Arallu. When he finished both Ginsberg and I were completely paralyzed; we had not dreamed that such a paper was possible.[113]

However, Obermann's work on Ugaritic improved over the next decade. His 1946 article on sentence negations in Ugaritic and his 1947 article on Baal's conflict with Yamm in *KTU* 1.2 IV won him some respect from the field.[114] *Ugaritic Mythology* (1948), an early effort at a literary study of motifs in the texts,[115] earned a polite review by Ginsberg. While he offered some praise for the book's higher criticism, Ginsberg noted the intractability of some problems and judged that "complete success was not to be expected." Obermann's treatment of grammar and poetry fared about the same. In defending two of his own views against Obermann, Ginsberg declared with his typical wit, "I cannot find it in my heart to deny salvation to anyone who questions [them]."[116] Obermann's most useful contribution, Ginsberg recognized, was his efforts to study the larger motifs and type-scenes in the texts. Obermann was clearly ahead of Albright and Ginsberg in studying the literary character of the Ugaritic mythological texts. In the 1940s, apart from Obermann and Cassuto, hardly anyone was working on literary issues. Obermann's case represents an interesting example of how reputation in the field was assessed. Scholars working on literary problems who showed philological weaknesses found their work being considered inferior to that of researchers who confined their efforts to successful philological study.

Goetze and Obermann offered the first instruction in Ugaritic at Yale in 1939 to a single student, Marvin H. Pope. Later wartime students included Bernhard Anderson and John Trever.[117] The two teachers disagreed greatly over Ugaritic grammar, Goetze being influenced by Akkadian grammar and Obermann by Arabic grammar. Goetze and Obermann each claimed Ugaritic as his own domain at this time. Pope recalled that Goetze and Obermann clashed so much in the beginning of the course that he met separately with them.[118]

⊠ GORDON'S ENTRY INTO UGARITIC: *From Speiser to Albright*

Two of the most famous scholars of biblical studies coming from Penn and Dropsie were E. A. Speiser and his student, Cyrus Herzl Gordon (born on June 29, 1908).[119] Gordon pursued a B.A., M.A., and Ph.D. at Penn, while he took courses under Max Leopold Margolis at Dropsie College.[120] Gordon received his doctorate in 1930, a few weeks before he turned twenty-two. Speiser was Gordon's Akkadian teacher at Penn, a relationship fraught with complications. On the face of it, the story of this relationship might seem peripheral to the history of Ugaritic and biblical studies. However, had it not been for Speiser's early antipathy toward Gordon, the latter might have concentrated on Assyriology— he might never have moved to Ugaritic studies and written his 1940 *Ugaritic Grammar*.[121] Accordingly, I relate the story of their relationship here. Moreover, the Dropsie records and the Albright papers have yielded new information, adding to the picture of the situation presented in Gordon's own published accounts.

After Gordon studied under Speiser at Penn,[122] he joined his former teacher in the field in Iraq. At Tell Billa in 1931, Speiser and Gordon read cuneiform copies of Nuzi texts at night by the light of kerosene lamps.[123] In his 1986 book, *The Pennsylvania Tradition of Semitics*, Gordon recounts those days:

Though I respected Speiser's gifts as a savant and teacher, he took a dislike to me and, while denying any prejudice or animosity, proved to be the most damaging professional enemy of my entire career. I left an instructorship at Penn to go into the field where I began to work with Speiser in 1931–1932 at Billa and Gawra. In the evenings we read Chiera's published corpus of Nuzi tablets. Those sessions got me started in Nuzi studies. As far as I can tell, it was my following in his footsteps in Nuzi scholarship—including the biblical parallels—that kindled his ire against me. I always felt pleased when a student emulates me and walks in my footsteps, but Speiser was resentful and jealous. He wanted me to work on Aramaic incantations *instead.* I indeed kept working on those incantations, but not *instead* of Assyriology.

I continued to look up to Speiser throughout most of 1931–1932, until I made the mistake of asking his advice on a project that I wanted to undertake: a beginner's manual of Akkadian based exclusively on Hammurapi's laws. He forbade me to undertake it because "only a senior scholar should write an elementary textbook in any field." I still think his advice was wrong, but since I had sought his advice, I was loath to flout it. That was the last time I sought a superior's advice on any project I wished to undertake.[124]

Gordon proceeds to label Speiser "a bully" with "more than a touch of a Napoleonic complex,"[125] adding that "he was skilled at kissing up and kicking down." Gordon does balance his picture, noting Speiser's capabilities as "a savant and teacher," "a remarkable linguist at all levels," "an accomplished scholar," and "an outstanding teacher." As accounts by others indicate, Speiser's demeanor was authoritarian and critical, and he sometimes showed an intolerance for "losing" (as the incident over the appointment of Neuman as Adler's successor, recounted above, illustrates).

Complementing Gordon's view of Speiser, published more than two decades after the latter's death, is Speiser's view of Gordon, which was confined to personal communications. In a letter to Cyrus Adler dated 4 November 1931, Speiser wrote from Tell Billa:

I am very fortunate to have this year a splendidly balanced and capable staff. Gordon is very willing and takes occasional rebuffs in a nice spirit. He is really growing up, though he will probably never lose the unfortunate knack of saying trite and commonplace things at the worst time imaginable.[126]

The season at Tell Billa clearly had a deleterious effect on their relationship. Speiser's view of a senior scholar taking on a project such as a grammar stood in the norms of scholarly tradition. A younger scholar was expected to begin with more focused studies and move progressively toward larger projects. Gordon would have nothing of this; he already had his eye on bigger projects (a constant feature of his career). After this dispute over the proposed grammar, Gordon pursued publication of a catalogue of cylinder and stamp seals, as well as studies of Nuzi texts and Aramaic incantations.[127]

Speiser's criticism of Gordon did not end with the excavations, but dogged him through the 1930s. In a letter to Albright in March of 1936, Speiser faults the "kind of rut in which Gordon seems to revel in wallowing,"[128] referring to Gordon's series of studies on women in Nuzi texts, with "meaningless transliterations . . . full of ridiculous errors." The norm for working on texts was a high level of careful and precise craftsmanship, a touch that Speiser saw lacking in Gordon. Then Speiser continues with a general assessment:

> I feel that he is off on the wrong foot, following the line of least resistance instead of doing solid and honest work, modestly and with humility. He is much too young to attempt to cash in on a reputation that does not exist. I feel it is a pity, because he can do good work when not overimpressed with himself.

Here Speiser reiterates the old scholarly model of beginning with smaller and more careful projects that yield surer results. At the same time we should bear in mind his critical cast—the same letter contains sharp criticism of Ginsberg's work. Despite such criticism, Gordon would not submit to the brilliant but difficult Speiser. The relationship between the two men was decidedly negative, yet this does not tell the whole story. Even if Speiser criticized his student privately, this did not prevent him from commending Gordon to others. In a letter of recommendation written on Gordon's behalf to Sir Leonard Woolley (at the time seeking an epigrapher for his excavations at Ur), the director of the University Museum at Penn remarked that "Dr. Speiser tells me that Dr. Gordon is perfectly competent."[129]

The conflict between Speiser and Gordon was well-known in the field. Albright provides a third view. Asked by Theophile Meek (1881–1966) in the summer of 1936 to recommend candidates for a post in Akkadian, Arabic, and Hebrew at the University of Toronto, Albright provided the following summation:

> Cyrus Gordon you know; you also know that he has been in Speiser's bad graces recently. Being a friend of both, I am rather neutral. Gordon used to be a bit cocky. . . . He has improved greatly since I first knew him in 1930, and is much more adaptable and much better liked by his contemporaries. . . . Speiser's strictures on his scholarly work are only fair to a certain very limited extent; he did publish a few papers which were a mistake from the standpoint of his career—but who of us has not done that—and even Speiser is not guiltless in this respect. However, Gordon is a very competent Semitist, and knows all the important Semitic languages. His Hebrew is excellent, including the spoken language of the day; he was trained grammatically by Margolis and Speiser. His Arabic is good, and he speaks both Syrian and Iraqi dialects very well, besides having a respectable knowledge of the classical tongue. He is entirely at home in Aramaic and Syriac, and is an excellent teacher.[130]

In a subsequent letter to Meek, Albright lauded Gordon's research on the Nuzi material and its parallels with the patriarchal stories in Genesis.[131] In a card written shortly thereafter to Albright,[132] Ginsberg, too, praised Gordon's work, specifically on Ugaritic:

> Gordon has done valiantly in the interpretation of the Marriage of Gods [1.24]. I have no time for RS work since coming to this country [in 1936], but on reading the text in question over a few times shortly after the arrival of the relevant number of *Syria* I reached the same conclusions regarding the verb *trḥ* and the nouns *mtrḥt* and *mlg* as Gordon. I was able to do so thanks to the talks I used to have with him and the manuscripts of his that I used to read concerning Nuzi.

Albright would be more direct in a letter later that year to Nathaniel Schmidt of Cornell University: "Speiser's opposition to him, which is quite without foundation, as I can assure you with absolute confidence, has done him a great deal of harm."[133] Clearly Albright and Ginsberg, the two leading American scholars of Ugaritic in the 1930s, showed a more balanced view of Gordon than did Speiser. Yet clearly Speiser's view of Gordon was not entirely negative. In fact, two letters written by Gordon's teacher, J. A. Montgomery, in 1932 tell how "Dr. Speiser reports in very warm terms" concerning Gordon's work, which "confirms our notion that you would make good."[134] Similarly, in the summer of 1939 Speiser wrote to Albright: "I am sincerely happy that Gordon will be in Princeton next year and I hope from the bottom of my heart that this appointment will lead to something permanent."[135] Albright would report to Gordon in 1941 that "Speiser said that you gave a good paper at Chicago."[136] Two personal letters in Gordon's possession written by Montgomery likewise confirm Speiser's modified view of his former student.

In retrospect, a number of factors influenced Gordon's early rejection by Speiser (and later by Albright as we will see in the following section). Grand projects executed quickly by a scholarly neophyte sullied Gordon's reputation in the eyes of his mentors. Where most scholars might spend a decade or longer on a single subject, he moved by comparison with great dispatch, sometimes with results that dismayed his teachers. Clearly the standard hierarchical model of mentor-student relations suited Gordon only up to a certain point. As a result, Speiser did not aid him in his academic advancement, and even Albright's letters (cited above) perhaps compounded the difficulty of Gordon's situation. In a conversation with me, Gordon observed that a letter of recommendation hardly need recount the past troubles of a student, yet Albright regularly did just that. Perhaps, however, Albright's letters of recommendation mention Gordon's troubles with Speiser in order to counteract Speiser's negative comments, since it would be expected that Speiser's advice would be sought in any Gordon job candidacy. Or perhaps Albright's allusions to Gordon's difficulties with Speiser allowed him to reveal his own mixed feelings about Gordon. Finally, Gordon's background as a nonobservant Jew made him suspect in Jewish circles but perhaps "too" Jewish in non-Jewish circles. (In a letter of recommendation to Sir Leonard Woolley, the director of the University Museum at Penn remarked that "while he [Gordon] is of Hebraic origin, it is not too obvious.")[137] Owing to his problems with Speiser and his Jewish background, Gordon thought that Albright would not push hard for his candidacy in most universities.

There would be no reason to rehearse this story of animosity except that it profoundly affected Ugaritic studies. Speiser's rejection of Gordon's plans for an Akkadian grammar led the younger man to other projects. When Albright mentioned the importance of Ugaritic to Gordon (as the following section will recount), the comment fell on receptive ears. Gordon pursued Ugaritic with great passion and speed, and he soon produced the *Ugaritic Grammar,* an early classic in

Cyrus H. Gordon.
Courtesy of Cyrus H. Gordon.

the field. Because of the immense importance of this book and the distance it created between Albright and Gordon, the next section takes up the story of its publication.

⋈ ALBRIGHT, GINSBERG, AND GORDON

The end of this initial period coincided with the Second World War. Although the war took a toll on trans-Atlantic communication, research continued. As Albright put it, "Though we have been cut off in America from French publications in the field of Ugaritic studies since 1940, it is still possible to make many contributions in detail to the understanding of the previously published texts."[138] Perhaps the most important publication in the field during the war was Gordon's 1940 work, *Ugaritic Grammar.*[139] In 1931, while excavating at Beit Zur, Albright had pointed out to Gordon the importance of Ugaritic for biblical studies.[140] Gordon recalls what he told him: "Every student of the Old Testament would do well to work on Ugaritic."[141] Gordon followed Albright's cue. He began working on Ugaritic grammar in 1933 (unbeknownst to Albright),[142] under the influence of H. L. Ginsberg's many fine grammatical observations in his published work. Gordon remembers meeting Ginsberg in the early 1930s in Jerusalem at the American School of Oriental Research (later the Albright Institute).[143] As Gordon recalled,[144] "Albright brought us together."

Gordon also had additional sources of inspiration for his work on Ugaritic grammar, including his Dropsie training. He wrote that "I formulated my *UG* [*Ugaritic Grammar*] on the principles of Semitic linguistics exclusively on what Max Margolis drummed into me."[145] Furthermore, Gordon mentions in the foreword to the *Ugaritic Grammar* that he often consulted the best translations, in particular those of Ginsberg, and he would have been familiar with the sketch of Ugaritic language and literature in the 1935 book, *The Ras Shamra Mythological Texts*, by his old Penn teacher James Montgomery along with Z. S. Harris. Gordon particularly acknowledged his debt to Ginsberg's translations.

After his split with Speiser, Gordon was a postdoctoral fellow at Johns Hopkins, thanks to Albright's support. The year before the war broke out, Gordon proposed to Father Alfred Pohl that the Pontifical Biblical Institute Press publish his grammar of Ugaritic. When Albright learned of the *Ugaritic Grammar*, he opposed its publication. In Gordon's words,

> He was furious and informed me in no uncertain way that my plan was not only presumptuous but impossible: no one could do it in the foreseeable future. I realized then and there that Baltimore was no longer big enough for the two of us and I moved to Smith College in the fall of 1938.[146]

According to his account, Gordon wrote the grammar in the summer of 1939 in Uppsala and completed it during the 1939–1940 academic year at Smith College.[147] Although the war started on September 3, 1939, this event did not interfere with the project. Gordon used the Vatican's diplomatic pouch service, which Fr. Pohl placed at his disposal, and the book was published in 1940.

When the *Ugaritic Grammar* appeared, it was generally very well received.[148] In a review, Albright publicly retracted his opposition, welcoming the publication of the work. Still, his published remarks are qualified: such "a detailed grammatical treatment of the new Canaanite dialect seemed premature to many, including the reviewer. The author refused to be daunted by dissuasion."[149] The accepted path for young scholars was to work up from small problems to major ones, but Gordon had set his sights on major projects beyond the capabilities of most persons, younger or more established. Albright further characterized the work as "collaborative" with Ginsberg, and ends oddly: "we congratulate him [Gordon] and ourselves on the appearance of the book!"[150] Later, in 1945, Albright referred to the work as "the excellent *Ugaritic Grammar* of a young scholar who began Ugaritic with me and continued working under Ginsberg's influence."[151] And in 1950 Albright would describe the work as "invaluable."[152] Despite such public acclamation, privately Albright withheld full approval, attributing the best of the grammar to Ginsberg's influence.[153] Despite Albright's misgivings, the appearance of this book marked a new level of synthesis in the area of grammar, a trend that extended to other areas as well. One of these involved the discussion of monotheism in ancient Israel.

⊠ ALBRIGHT, MEEK, AND MONOTHEISM

The prewar period witnessed major efforts to understand the Bible and ancient Israel in the light of the Ugaritic texts. Some of the discussion involved a myriad of linguistic and religious details, but it also concerned the larger question of the nature of ancient Israelite religion, notably of Israelite monotheism. Here I single out two figures for their contrasting views on the subject, Theophile J. Meek and W. F. Albright. In his 1936 book, *Hebrew Origins*,[154] Meek criticized Albright's view of Mosaic monotheism, pointing to the lack of early evidence for monotheism predating the later attestation of monotheistic declarations in the sixth-century prophets. In 1938 Meek put his reservations about the definition of monotheism to Albright in a personal letter:

> Since returning home I looked up the dictionary definitions of henotheism, monolatry, and monotheism, and I feel more convinced than ever that you are using monotheism in a sense not supported by the dictionaries. By monotheism in my book [*Hebrew Origins*] I mean exclusive belief in and worship of one god and the denial of even the existence of other gods, which when believed in are merely figments of the imagination, with no reality at all. Our difference seems to be largely one of definition, but it is unfortunate when people define words in different ways.[155]

Indeed, Meek had a good point. In 1940 Albright presented the word's meaning along lines that suited his view of matters:

> If . . . the term "monotheist" means one who teaches the existence of only one God, the creator of everything, the source of justice, who is equally powerful in Egypt, in the desert, and in Palestine, who has no sexuality and no mythology, who is human in form but cannot be seen by human eye and cannot be represented in any form— then the founder of Yahwism was certainly a monotheist.[156]

Apart from the initial point, Albright's definition of monotheism had little to do with the normal meaning of the word. Most problematic for Albright's position, the early parts of the Bible simply do not teach the existence of only one God, as mentioned above. As this quote would suggest, Albright's representation of monotheism drew upon different parts of the Bible and combined into a single original picture.

For Albright, the Ugaritic texts and other Late Bronze Age corpora provided both antecedents of and contrasts with Mosaic monotheism. As Albright understood it, Late Bronze Age evidence demonstrated preconditions for monotheism. These included multiple divine abodes, power in a multitude of locales, and the god's role as a creator god. All had parallels in fully polytheistic religions. However, the Ugaritic texts also showed manifest differences between the polytheism of the other nations and Israel's monotheism. Albright's definition (quoted above) focuses on what seemed to be patently different, for example, the mythology of the Ugaritic deities and their sexual relations. The model implicit here, namely the contrast between "Canaanite polytheism" and "Israelite monotheism," dominated the discussion of Israelite religion through this period and well into the next (1945–1970). Indeed, this model became the conceptual cornerstone of Albright's later treatment of this subject, his 1968 book, fittingly entitled *Yahweh and the Gods of Canaan: A Historical Analysis of Two Contrasting Faiths*.[157] This oppositional paradigm would come under fire during the 1960s and later.[158]

For the roots of Albright's viewpoint, we have to look deeper. He undoubtedly believed in the historical reality of Sinai monotheism. In 1943 he wrote to his former student, G. Ernest Wright, that his book, *From the Stone Age to Christianity,* conceded too much to his critics.[159] For example, he felt that he could base Mosaic monotheism on the first of the Ten Commandments, that the Israelites "shall have no other gods besides me *(ʿal pānay)*" (Exod 20:3; Deut 5:7). Albright thought that he could defend this translation based on the Punic use of *ʿlt pn-,* "besides," in the Marseilles tariff (*KAI* 69:3),[160] and that such a meaning served to establish monotheism. On the first claim, Albright had a good point; the use is attested in Punic. But whether this interpretation of the First Commandment demonstrated monotheism was in fact problematic. Most scholars take the commandment not as a denial of other deities, but as a prohibition against devotion to them. Indeed, such a commandment suggests to many a problem of the other gods competing with Yahweh. The question is why Albright allowed himself these historical leaps. Indeed, it was only in the religious area that he did so.[161] Perhaps his tremendous personal faith in the biblical texts is the source of his position. He believed that the biblical narrative was essentially historical, even when the biblical sources involved were later.[162] Moreover, it was later biblical texts that provided him with his historical paradigm of opposition between Canaanites and Israelites, between the polytheism of the former and the monotheism of the latter. Albright the believer convinced Albright the historian despite the lack of historical evidence.

For a number of reasons, the debate between Albright and Meek solved nothing. The failure to resolve the issue would hinder the ability of scholars to discuss the historical issues. However, there was a deeper problem. Scholars on both sides of the divide failed to address the more constructive points made by their opponents. Albright, for example, did not address the fundamental question concerning later monotheistic formulations. If Israel were basically monotheistic from an early time, as he claimed, then why did its rhetoric of monotheism appear in clearer, less ambiguous forms only in the seventh and sixth centuries B.C.E.? And Meek, for all his correctly placed concerns over definition, did not solve the problem raised by the distinctive form of Israelite polytheism, which was certainly a far more reduced form of polytheism compared to the pantheons found in the Ugaritic record.[163] Finally, neither camp attempted to situate the issues in terms of Judah's larger social structure and historical context in the seventh and sixth centuries. Meek's basic point remains valid, yet the relatively late emergence of the monotheistic rhetoric defies understanding until it is set against the background of discourse about divinity during the late Judean monarchy. Unfortunately, questions of monotheism's sociopolitical context would not take center stage for decades,[164] that is, until the final phase of Ugaritic studies discussed in Chapter Four.

⊠ WORLD WAR II AND ITS EFFECTS ON SCHOLARSHIP

As the *Ugaritic Grammar* shows, the end of this period witnessed greater efforts toward synthesis. In 1937, the final year of his life, Hans Bauer produced *Der Ursprung des Alphabets,* the first book on the alphabet that integrated the Ugaritic texts into the wider discussion described by its title.[165] Syntheses were not limited to the grammatical field. A case in point is Cassuto's brief for an early literary epic tradition in Israel, which argued for a distinct debt to the "Canaanite" culture independently represented by the Ugaritic texts. In addition to works cited above, the first syntheses in the area of Ugaritic and biblical studies came from European scholars: J. W. Jack's 1935 book, *The Ras Shamra Tablets and Their Bearing upon the Old Testament;*[166] R. Dussaud's 1941 volume, *Les découvertes de Ras Shamra (Ugarit et l'Ancien Testament);*[167] and the massive two-volume 1945 study by the Belgian scholar R. de Langhe,[168] entitled *Les textes de Ras Shamra-Ugarit et leur rapports avec le milieu biblique de l'Ancient Testament.*[169] Finally, Albright and others also realized that Christianity, Judaism, and Islam show deep continuity with earlier West Semitic religions (including those that the Bible depicts).[170] These studies, as well as many others, gathered evidence and presented larger issues derived from the numerous points of comparison between Ugaritic and the Bible. The work of synthesis, especially by the biblicists, would herald the basic future course of Ugaritic studies. Hugely learned and talented biblical scholars with training in extrabiblical languages and history turned to the challenge of Ugaritic with great energy and began to produce results that would alter the modern understanding of the Bible.

The war arrested this trend, however, which, again, caused a migration of many scholars and restricted academic correspondence and exchange. For example, the texts published during the war remained unknown to many scholars until its end. The number of students dwindled as military service and other more pressing needs took their toll on the field. In America alone, for example, Albright taught Arabic and geography for the army at Hopkins (he also unsuccessfully applied for a commission for the Military Government School in Charlottesville, Virginia); Gordon served in army intelligence, first in Washington and then in the Persian Gulf; and Speiser and Rosenthal worked for the Office of Strategic Services in Washington (Rosenthal was first an army private). In England J. W. Jack was killed by a truck during a blackout in 1944.[171] Many figures of the next scholarly generation also joined the war effort. For example, Marvin Pope's doctoral studies were interrupted by his military service at a weather station in northern Australia. The war also interrupted George Mendenhall's academic program under Albright, as he undertook service in the army in the Pacific theater. John Patton was an army chaplain, and John Bright, Alexander D. Goode, Paul Reich, and John Zimmerman served as navy chaplains. Rabbi Goode drowned in the North Atlantic in January 1943 when his transport ship was torpedoed.[172] In Germany[173] many figures suffered through the war, standing staunchly against the Nazis; these included A. Alt, O. Eissfeldt, J. Friedrich, and K. Galling.[174] Others such as A. Jirku, J. Hempel,[175] G. Kittel, and E. Sellin served or sympathized with the terrible regime.[176] In Israel, A. D. Singer died in the war that led to the founding of the state. Fortunately, the majority of scholars survived the war, and the age of great syntheses in Ugaritic and biblical studies would unfold in its wake.

✄ NOTES

1. Craigie, *Ugarit and the Old Testament* (Grand Rapids, Mich.: Eerdmans, 1983), 7. The following account represents a drastic synopsis of pp. 7–25, supplemented by C. F. A. Schaeffer's own shorter 1930 account translated into English in his article, "The Discovery of Ugarit," in *Hands on the Past* (ed. C. W. Ceram; New York: Knopf, 1966), 301–6 (I thank my father, Donald Eugene Smith, for bringing this article to my attention). See also Schaeffer's later account in his *The Cuneiform Texts of Ras Shamra-Ugarit* (London: The British Academy, 1939). For more details of the story, readers should consult these accounts. See also A. H. W. Curtis, *Ugarit (Ras Shamra)* (Cities of the Biblical World; Cambridge: Lutterworth, 1985), 18–33; and idem, "Ras Shamra, Minet el-Beida, and Ras Ibn Hani: The Material Sources," in *Handbook of Ugaritic Studies* (ed. W. G. E. Watson and N. Wyatt; HdO 1/39; Leiden: Brill, 1999), 5–9; O. Loretz, *Ugarit und der Bibel: Kanaanäische Götter und Religion im Alten Testament* (Darmstadt: Wissenschaftliche Buchgesellschaft, 1990), 1–2.

2. For the story, see Schaeffer, "La première tablette," *Syria* 33 (1956): 161–68.

3. See Schaeffer, "Les fouilles de Minet-el-Bheida et de Ras Shamra," *Syria* 10 (1929): 285–97. Schaeffer continued to publish results from the ongoing excavations in issues of *Syria*.

4. The best account, with very good details, is that of K. J. Cathcart, "The Ugaritic Language," in *Handbook of Ugaritic Studies*, 76–80. A more detailed account by P. L. Day is in progress.

5. *EncJud* 4:330.

6. Information courtesy of Professor J. M. de Tarragon, e-mail 8 March 1999. In a letter dated 23 September 1932, Dhorme wrote to Albright from his new home in Paris (APS archives Albright Corresp.-Misc. 1925–1933). Albright mentioned the appointment in a letter to John Garstang dated 26 January 1946 (APS Albright correspondence 1946).

7. See Virolleaud, "Les inscriptions cunéiformes de Ras Shamra," *Syria* 10 (1929): 304–10; H. Bauer, "Ein kanaanäisches Alphabet in Keilschrift," *ZDMG* 84 (1930): 251–54; idem, "Zum Alphabet von Ras Schamra," *OLZ* 33 (1930): 1062–63; idem, "Die Entzifferung des Keilschriftalphabets von Ras Schamra," *FuF* 6 (1930): 306–7; idem, *Die Entzifferung des Keilschrifttafeln von Ras Schamra* (Halle/Saale: Max Niemeyer, 1930); Dhorme, "Trouvailles sensationelles en Syrie," *RB* 39 (1930): 152–53; idem, "Un nouvel alphabet sémitique," *RB* 39 (1930): 571–77. See also R. Dussaud, "Déchiffrement par M. Hans Bauer des textes de Ras Shamra," *Syria* 11 (1930): 200–202.

8. See the section on Albright at Hopkins below in this chapter as well as the discussion of the Hopkins program in the next chapter.

9. Albright, "The Old Testament and Canaanite Language and Literature," *CBQ* 7 (1945): 9. The reference is to *Vossische Zeitung Unterhaltungsblatt* 128 (June 4, 1930): 17. For the *Revue Biblique* reference, see the preceding note. See the detailed reconstruction of J. M. de Tarragon, "Philologie sémitique," in *L'Ancien Testament: Cent ans d'exégèse de l'Ecole Biblique* (ed. Jean-Luc Vesco; Cahiers de la Revue Biblique 28; Paris: Gabalda, 1990), 41–42. See also C. H. Gordon, *Forgotten Scripts: Their Ongoing Discovery and Decipherment* (rev. and enlarged edition; New York: Basic Books, 1982), 103–10. In his personal copy of Bauer's *Das Alphabet von Ras Schamra* (now in the library of Southern Baptist Theological Seminary), on page 4, Albright penciled in a more precise breakdown: he credited the decipherment of nineteen signs to Bauer, five to Dhorme, and six to Virolleaud (with clarifications by himself, Friedrich, and Ginsberg).

10. Albright, "The North-Canaanite Epic of 'Al'êyan Ba'al and Môt," *JPOS* 12 (1932): 186–87. See Hillers, "William F. Albright as a Philologian," 52, and Cross, "The Contributions of W. F. Albright to Semitic Epigraphy and Palaeography," 25, in *The Scholarship of William Foxwell Albright: An Appraisal* (ed. G. W. Van Beek; HSS 33; Atlanta: Scholars Press, 1989).

11. Albright, "The Syro-Mesopotamian God Šulman-Ešmun and Related Figures," *AfO* 7 (1931–1932): 165 n. 9.

12. See Curtis, "Ras Shamra," 9.

13. See P. Amiet, "Claude Schaeffer (1889–1982)," *RA* 77 (1983): 1–2; J. M. Robinson, "An Appreciation of Claude Frederic-Armand Schaeffer-Forrer (1898–1982)," *BAR* 9/5 (1983): 56–61.

14. In a letter dated 31 October 1933, Albright recommends to T. H. Robinson: "For the North-Canaanites follow Virolleaud; Dussaud is stimulating, but unsafe" (APS archives Albright Corresp.-Misc. 1925–1933).

15. For the authors involved in interpreting the mythological texts, see the bibliographies preceding the beginning of each text treated in *CTA*.

16. Albright, "The Furniture of El in Canaanite Mythology," *BASOR* 91 (1943): 39.

17. Assyriologists have made many significant contributions to the study of Ugaritic. Examples of Assyriologists who followed Virolleaud in the field would include G. Dossin, A. Goetze, F. Thureau-Dangin, and E. Weidner; later I. Mendelsohn, E. A. Speiser, and W. von Soden (to an incidental degree); and more recently W. Dietrich, D. O. Edzard, W. W. Hallo, A. R. Millard, W. L. Moran, D. Owen, D. J. Wiseman, as well as J. Huehnergard, S. Izre'el, and W. van Soldt. Many of these figures and their work play a role in subsequent chapters. For a partial listing of the early figures' contributions to Ugaritic, see *CTA*, 293–339.

18. As solved by Friedrich, "Zu den drei Aleph-Zeichen des Ras-Schamra-Alphabets," *ZA* 41 (1933): 305–13. See the description of the consensus emerging by 1935 in Montgomery and Harris, *Ras Shamra Mythological Texts*, 16.

19. Albright, "The Old Testament and Canaanite Language and Literature," 28 n. 80.

20. Albright receives credit for this discovery from Cross, "The Contributions of W. F. Albright to Semitic Epigraphy and Palaeography," 25.

21. Albright, "The Old Testament and Canaanite Language and Literature," 18. Later the issue of case endings on construct forms in Ugaritic would arise. Two later studies demonstrated their existence: G. A. Tuttle, "Case Vowels on Masculine Singular Nouns in Construct in Ugaritic," in *Biblical and Near Eastern Studies: Essays in Honor of William Sanford LaSor* (ed. G. A. Tuttle; Grand Rapids, Mich.: Eerdmans, 1978), 253–68; and J. Huehnergard, "Akkadian Evidence for Case Endings for Case-Vowels on Ugaritic Bound Forms," *JCS* 33 (1981): 199–205; cf. Z. Zevit, "The Question of Case Endings on Ugaritic Nouns in Status Constructus," *JSS* 28 (1983): 225–32.

22. See J. Barth, "Zur vergleichenden semitischen Grammatik. II. Zu den Vocalen der Imperfect-Präfize," *ZDMG* 48 (1894): 4–6; H. L. Ginsberg, "Two Religious Borrowings in Ugaritic Literature," *Or* 8 (1939): 319–22. See *UT* 9.9.

23. Cross credits Friedrich for this discovery ("The Contributions of W. F. Albright to Semitic Epigraphy and Palaeography," 25).

24. See *UT* 9.10.

25. Especially in earlier Hebrew poetry. Whether or not this development relates to the reduction of diphthongs and triphthongs in third weak nouns and verbs cannot be determined at this point, although this is a logical supposition.

26. Albright, "The Old Testament and Canaanite Language and Literature," 22.

27. Goetze, "The So-Called Intensive of the Semitic Languages," *JAOS* 62 (1942): 1–8.

28. Represented by the doubling of the middle radical; so see J. Joosten, "The Functions of the Semitic D stem: Biblical Hebrew Materials for a Comparative Hebrew Approach," *Or* 67 (1998): 202–30. A. Malamat ("Mari and the Bible: Some Patterns of Tribal Organization and Institutions," *JAOS* 82 [1962]: 148 esp. n. 27) notes *nhl in *G*-stem refers to singular (Num 34:17, 18, possibly Josh 19:49), but *nhl in *D*-stem is plural (Num 34:29, Josh 13:32, 51); he cites P. Joüon, *Grammaire de l'hébreu biblique* (Rome: Institut Biblique Pontifical, 1923; reprinted with corrections, 1965), 117; *GKC*, 148.

29. Kaufman, review of P. A. Siebesma, *The Function of the Niph'al in Biblical Hebrew in Relationship to Other Passive-Reflexive Verbal Stems and to the Pu'al and Hoph'al in Particular*, *CBQ* 56 (1994): 571–73.

30. Goetze was followed in the main by E. Jenni, *Das hebräische Pi'el* (Zurich: EVZ-Verlag, 1968); and S. A. Ryder, *The D-Stem in Western Semitic* (Janua Linguarum, Series Practica 131; The Hague/Paris: Mouton, 1974). For a recent discussion, see J. Joosten, "Functions of the Semitic D stem," 202–30. Joosten modifies and applies to Hebrew the work of N. J. C. Kouwenberg, *Gemination in the Akkadian Verb* (SSN 32; Assen/Maastricht: Van Gorcum, 1997). The *D*-stem verbs, described by D. Hillers ("On Delocutive Verbs in Biblical Hebrew," *JBL* 86 [1967]: 320–24), may be viewed as "verbally" factitive of *G*-stem statives. On the issue of *D*-stem morphology, see J. Huehnergard, "Historical Phonology and the Hebrew Piel," in *Linguistics and Biblical Hebrew* (ed. W. R. Bodine; Winona Lake, Ind.: Eisenbrauns, 1992), 209–29.

31. Ginsberg, "The Rebellion and Death of Ba'lu," *Or* 5 (1936): 170 n. 1; idem, "Ugaritic Studies and the Bible," 58.

32. Albright, "The Old Testament and Canaanite Language and Literature," 22.

33. Ibid., 24.

34. Ginsberg, "A Phoenician Hymn in the Psalter," in *Atti del XIX Congresso Internazionale degli Orientalisti. Roma, 23–29 Settembre 1935–XIII* (Rome: Tipografia del Senato, 1938), 476. As acknowledged by Albright, "The Old Testament and Canaanite

Language and Literature," 23. Ibn Janah already recognized the "superfluous" character of some cases of final *mem;* for discussion and references, see E. Tov, *Textual Criticism of the Hebrew Bible* (Minneapolis: Fortress; Assen/Maastricht: Van Gorcum, 1992), 364 n. 20. See the defense of the enclitic *mem* in Ps 29:6 by S. E. Loewenstamm, " *'Wyrkydm kmw 'gl,'" Leš* 47 (1983): 70–73 [Heb.].

35. See P. D. Miller, "Vocative Lamed in the Psalter: A Reconsideration," *UF* 11 (1979): 617–37; and a response by M. H. Pope, "Vestiges of Vocative Lamedh in the Bible," *UF* 20 (1988): 201–7 = *Probative Pontificating in Ugaritic and Biblical Literature: Collected Essays* (ed. M. S. Smith; UBL 10; Münster: Ugarit-Verlag, 1994), 317–24.

36. W. F. Albright, "The Northwest-Semitic Tongues before 1000 B.C.," in *Atti del XIX Congresso Internazionale degli Orientalistici. Roma, 23–29 Settembre 1935–XIII* (Rome: Tipografia del Senato, 1938), 445–50; A. Goetze, "Is Ugaritic a Canaanite Dialect?" *Language* 17 (1941): 127–38. See shortly after the war, J. Friedrich, "Kanaanäiche und Westsemitische," *Scientia* 84 (1949): 220–23.

37. See Albright, "New Light on Early Canaanite Language and Literature," *BASOR* 46 (1932): 15–20; Ginsberg, "The Victory of the Land-God over the Sea-God," *JPOS* 15 (1935): 327; and "Ugaritic Studies and the Bible," 54–55.

38. Albright, "The Egypto-Canaanite Deity Haurôn," *BASOR* 84 (1941): 10; Ginsberg, "Ugaritic Studies and the Bible," 54. See Greenstein, "One More Step on the Staircase," *UF* 9 (1977): 77–86. See also his article, "Two Variations of Grammatical Parallelism in Canaanite Poetry and Their Psycholinguistic Background," *JANES* 6 (1974): 87–105.

39. Albright, "The North-Canaanite Epic of 'Al'êyan Ba'al and Môt," *JPOS* 12 (1932): 188–95, 208.

40. Ginsberg, *Kitbê 'Ugarit*, 129–30; also "Phoenician Hymn in the Psalter," 472–76. Ginsberg's view found a following by, for example, Albright, "The Old Testament and Canaanite Language and Literature," 29; T. H. Gaster, "Psalm 29," *JQR* 37 (1946–1947): 55–56; F. M. Cross, "Notes on a Canaanite Psalm in the Old Testament," *BASOR* 117 (1950): 19–21; A. Fitzgerald, "A Note on Psalm 29," *BASOR* 215 (1974): 61–63. See further J. Day, "Echoes of Baal's Seven Thunders and Lightnings in Psalm XXIX and Habakkuk III 9 and the Identity of the Seraphim in Isaiah VI," *VT* 29 (1979): 143–51. On Ps 29, see the survey of views in Y. Avishur, *Studies in Hebrew and Ugaritic Psalms* (Jerusalem: Magnes, 1994), 67–71; see also Chapter Three below.

41. G. Barton, "Danel, A Pre-Israelite Hero of Galilee," *JBL* 60 (1941): 213–25; Ginsberg, "Ugaritic Studies and the Bible," *BA* 8 (1945): 50. For a recent challenge to this identification, see H. H. P. Dressler, "The Identification of the Ugaritic Dnil with the Daniel of Ezekiel," *VT* 19 (1979): 152–61; cf. J. Day, "The Daniel of Ugarit and Ezekiel and the Hero of the Book of Daniel," *VT* 30 (1980): 174–84, and B. Margalit (Margulis), "Interpreting the Story of Aqht: A Reply to H. H. P. Dressler," *VT* 30 (1980): 361–65; and Dressler's response in his "Reading and Interpreting the Aqhat Text," *VT* 34 (1984): 78–82. See further L. L. Grabbe, " 'Canaanite': Some Methodological Observations in Relation to Biblical Study," in *Ugarit and the Bible: Proceedings of the International Symposium on Ugarit and the Bible. Manchester, September 1992* (ed. G. J. Brooke, A. H. W. Curtis, and J. F. Healey; UBL 11; Münster: Ugarit-Verlag, 1994), 119–20. As Grabbe's discussion indicates, the Ugaritic figure may correspond to the Daniel of Ezek 14, but certainly not the Daniel of the book of Daniel, whom the book locates in "historical time" in the sixth century, although this book may use the name to evoke the older tradition.

42. Albright, "The Old Testament and Canaanite Language and Literature," 29–30; Ginsberg, "Phoenician Hymn in the Psalter," 472; and "Ugaritic Studies and the Bible," 52.

43. See, for example, in this early period O. Eissfeldt, "Neue Götter im alten Testament," in *Atti del XIX Congresso Internazionale degli Orientalisti. Roma, 23–29 Settembre 1935–XIII* (Rome: Tipografia del Senato, 1938), 478–79. Curiously, Eissfeldt makes no mention of the Ugaritic texts in this communication.

44. For references and discussion, see Kapelrud, *The Ras Shamra Discoveries and the Old Testament*, 18–19. Note also the identification of Ashdod in *KTU* 1.23 by Montgomery and Harris, *The Ras Shamra Mythological Texts*, 39.

45. Ginsberg, *Kitbê 'Ugarit*, 77; "Notes on the Birth of the Gracious and Beautiful Gods," *JRAS* (1935): 45–72, esp. 65.

46. For example, Cassuto, *The Goddess Anath*, 40; Ullendorff, "Ugaritic Studies," 240; B. S. Childs, *The Book of Exodus* (OTL; Philadelphia: Westminster, 1974), 485–86; J. C. de Moor, *New Year with Canaanites and Israelites* (2 vols.; Kampen: Kok, 1972), 2:18 n. 76. To Childs's credit, he notes the difficulties with the Ugaritic passage in question.

47. Haran, "Seething a Kid in Its Mother's Milk," *JJS* 30 (1979): 23–35; "Das Böchlein in der Milch seiner Mutter und das säugende Muttertier," *Theologische Zeitschrift* 41 (1985): 135–59.

48. Milgrom, " 'You Shall Not Boil a Kid in Its Mother's Milk': An Archaeological Myth Destroyed," *Bible Review* 1/3 (1985): 48–55.

49. R. Ratner and B. Zuckerman, " 'A Kid in Milk'?: New Photographs of *KTU* 1.23, Line 14," *HUCA* 57 (1986): 15–60. For further references, see Loretz, *Ugarit und der Bibel*, 124–25.

50. Letter to R. Dussaud, dated 7 August 1936 (APS archives Albright Personal Corresp. 1936–1938).

51. So according to H. Cazelles, in an undated letter to me (received 12 January 1999). So, too, Cazelles mentions Herdner and Largement as students with him in 1941–1944.

52. Information courtesy of N. P. Lemche (e-mails on 3, 5, and 7 October 1998), as well as a letter from F. O. Hvidberg-Hansen dated 14 January 1999. Pedersen wrote on "Die Krt Legende," in *Berytus* 6 (1941): 63–105. For a discussion of Pedersen's thought, see E. S. Frerichs, "The Social Setting of the Peoples of the Ancient Near East: An Assessment of Johannes Pedersen (1883–1977)," in *Ancient Egyptian and Mediterranean Studies in Memory of William Ward* (ed. L. H. Lesko; Providence, R.I.: Department of Egyptology, Brown University, 1998), 111–15. Løkkegaard's best-known work on Ugaritic was published up through the 1950s. For discussion, see E. Keck, S. Søndergaard, and E. Wulff, eds., *Living Waters: Scandinavian Oriental Studies Presented to Dr. Frede Løkkegaard on His Seventy-Fifth Birthday, January 27th 1990* (Copenhagen: Museum Tusculanum Press, 1990); reference courtesy of Professor Hvidberg-Hansen. Eduard Nielsen came to the faculty at Copenhagen after the war, serving from 1953 to 1991.

53. Nielsen, *Ras Šamra Mythologie und Biblische Theologie* (Abhandlungen für die Kunde des Morgenlandes XXI/4; Leipzig: 1936; repr. Nendeln, Liechtenstein: Kaus Reprint, 1966).

54. Hvidberg, *Weeping and Laughter in the Old Testament* (trans. F. Løkkegaard; Leiden: Brill; Copenhagen: Nyt Nordisk Forlag/Arnold Busck, 1962).

55. Published as Hammershaimb, *Das Verbum im Dialekt von Ras Schamra* (Copenhagen: Munksgaard, 1941).

56. Information courtesy of Professor Hvidberg-Hansen. For example, Nielsen, "Die altsemitische Muttergöttin," *ZDMG* 92 (1938): 504–51.

57. *EncJud* 4:330.

58. Information courtesy of a letter from Klaus Koch dated 31 October 1998.

59. *EncJud* 6:557. Eissfeldt had been a *Privatdocent* in Berlin.

60. Following the International Meeting of Orientalists in Brussels in 1938, Rosenthal wrote to American scholars seeking their help and provided the names of his teachers in his curriculum vitae (preserved in Albright's Corresp. 1938–1940 in APS archives). For Semitics Rosenthal studied under Professors Mittwoch, Schaeder, Meissner, Ebeling, and Kraus; for Iranian philology Schaeder; and for classical philology Professors Jaeger, Norden, Deubner, and Deichgräber. Rosenthal believed that Ugaritic had not been formally taught in other German universities prior to that year (oral communication to

me on 17 September 1998), but I am unable to verify this point. The further information about Rosenthal's life comes from a letter to me dated 23 January 1999.

61. So James Montgomery informed Albright in a letter dated 9 September 1938 (APS archives [Albright] Corresp. 1938–1940).

62. Rosenthal, "Die Parallelstellen in den Texten von Ugarit," *Or* 8 (1939): 213–17; and "Some Minor Problems in the Qur'ân," in *The Joshua Starr Memorial Volume: Studies in History and Philology* (Jewish Social Studies, Publications No. 5; New York: Conference on Jewish Relations, 1953), 67–84. For a number of Rosenthal's reviews in Ugaritic studies in 1939–1952, see the listing in Herdner, *Corpus des tablettes*, 323. A brief profile of Rosenthal appears in *EncJud* 14:292–93.

63. See *EncJud* 5:234–35; and C. Adler, *I Have Considered the Days* (Philadelphia: Jewish Publication Society of America, 1941), 343. The Hebrew University was founded in 1925.

64. Information courtesy of Edward Ullendorff in a letter to me dated 31 December 1998.

65. Information courtesy of Avraham Malamat in a letter to me dated 3 April 1999.

66. For Cassuto's work in this area, see his *The Goddess Anat: Canaanite Epics of the Patriarchal Age* (trans. I. Abraham; Jerusalem: Magnes, 1971); and his two volumes of *Biblical and Oriental Studies* (trans. I. Abraham; Jerusalem: Magnes, 1975).

67. Cassuto, "The Israel Epic," *Knesset* 8 (1943): 121–42; published in English in *Biblical and Oriental Studies*, 2:69–109.

68. C. H. Gordon, "Indo-European and Hebrew Epic," *EI* 5 (1958 = B. Mazar volume): *10–*15. See F. M. Cross's best-known work, *Canaanite Myth and Hebrew Epic;* and his more recent work, *From Epic to Canon* (Baltimore/London: Johns Hopkins University Press, 1998), 28. To be sure, Cross understands the works traditionally known in biblical scholarship as the J and E sources to be repositories of Israelite epic tradition. So, too, the work of Cross's student, S. Niditch, *Oral World and Written Word: Ancient Israelite Literature* (Library of Ancient Israel; Louisville, Ky.: Westminster John Knox, 1996), 120–25.

69. For example, Yeivin, "An Ugaritic Inscription from Palestine," *Qedem* 2 (1945): 32–41 (Heb.). For a brief biography, see *EncJud* 16:733.

70. See his article, "The Ras Shamra Inscriptions and Their Significance for the History of Religion," *AJSL* 51 (1934–1935): 128–39.

71. This information about the University of Pennsylvania derives from C. H. Gordon, *The Pennsylvania Tradition of Semitics* (SBL Centennial Publications; Atlanta: Scholars Press, 1986), 6, 41, 43, and 44. Gordon cites J. A. Montgomery's article on Semitics at Penn entitled "Oriental Studies in the University," *The General Magazine and Historical Chronicle* 36 (1933–1934): 205–16.

72. See the accounts of Speiser's career by two of his devoted students, J. J. Finkelstein, "E. A. Speiser: An Appreciation," in *Oriental and Biblical Studies: Collected Writings of E. A. Speiser* (ed. J. J. Finkelstein and M. Greenberg; Philadelphia: University of Pennsylvania, 1967), 605–16; and M. Greenberg, "In Memory of E. A. Speiser," *JAOS* 88 (1968) = *Essays in Memory of E. A. Speiser* (ed. W. W. Hallo; AOS 65; New Haven: American Oriental Society, 1968), 1–2; *EncJud* 15:258–59. See also S. D. Sperling, *Students of the Covenant: A History of Jewish Biblical Scholarship in North America* (Atlanta: Scholars Press, 1992), 71–73. Missing from these descriptions of Speiser are his involvement at Dropsie and the qualities of his personal demeanor; see below. Some of the following information pertaining to Dropsie College derives from its *Registers*.

73. This information, absent from Finkelstein or Greenberg's account (see the preceding note), derives from the record of the *Dropsie College Registers* for these years.

74. On this figure, see Gordon, *The Pennsylvania Tradition of Semitics*, 24; P. J. King, *American Archaeology in the Mideast: A History of the American Schools of Oriental Research* (Philadelphia: American Schools of Oriental Research, 1983), 68–69; and

B. Kuklick, *Puritans in Babylon: the Ancient Near East and American Intellectual Life, 1880–1930* (Princeton: Princeton University Press, 1996), 169–70.

75. Letter of E. A. Speiser to Cyrus Adler, dated 25 April 1927, in the Dropsie College Adler papers, Box 100, FF 15.

76. Finkelstein, "E. A. Speiser: An Appreciation," 605–16; Greenberg, "In Memory of E. A. Speiser," 1–2.

77. Letter to Cyrus Adler, dated 6 October 1935, in the Dropsie College Adler papers, Box 100, FF 17.

78. In the Dropsie College Adler papers, Box 100, FF 17.

79. In the Dropsie College Adler papers, Box 100, FF 17, addressed as "Bram" and signed off as "Fred Speiser." Neuman responded cordially in a letter of 19 February 1941 addressed to "Fred" and signed "Abraham A. Neuman."

80. For example, Speiser honored the memory of his Dropsie professor with his essay entitled "The Contribution of Max Leopold Margolis to Semitic Linguistics," in *Max Leopold Margolis*, 27–33.

81. A student of the great Friedrich Delitzsch at Leipzig, Haupt came to Hopkins shortly after its inception in 1876. For an appreciation of Delitzsch, see I. M. Price, "Friedrich Delitzsch," *Beiträge zür Assyriologie* 10/2 (1927): i–xii. On Haupt, see Albright, "In Memoriam Paul Haupt," *Beiträge zür Assyriologie* 10/2 (1927): xiii–xxii; *EncJud* 7:1475–76. For a fine evocation of Haupt as well as the period, see Kuklick, *Puritans in Babylon*, esp. 17–34 (esp. 18 and 24) and 125–26.

82. So according to a letter of Albright's co-student, Paul Bloomhardt, to Albright, dated 3 February 1920, APS archives (Albright Corresp.-Misc. 1925–1933).

83. See L. G. Running and D. N. Freedman, *William Foxwell Albright: A Twentieth-Century Genius* (New York: Morgan Press, 1975), 185; W. W. Hallo, "Albright and the Gods of Mesopotamia," *BA* 56/1 (1993): 20. Concerning the early history of the chair, see Kuklick, *Puritans in Babylon*, 107–8.

84. On Blake as one of Albright's teachers, see Running and Freedman, *William Foxwell Albright*, 32. On Blake further, see pp. 72, 139, 172, 196, 211–12, 256–57, 269, and 296.

85. Blake, "The So-Called Intransitive Verbal Forms in the Semitic Languages."

86. Mentioned by Albright to Sam Geiser, an old friend and professor of Biology at Southern Methodist University, in a letter dated 31 October 1929 (APS archives, Albright Corresp. Misc. 1929–1932).

87. *Saadia Gaon. The Book of Beliefs and Opinions* (trans. S. Rosenblatt; Yale Judaica Series 1; New Haven: Yale, 1948). He also published works on *The Interpretation of the Bible in the Mishnah* (Baltimore: Johns Hopkins, 1935); and *Interpretation of the Bible in the Tosefta* (JQR monograph series 4; Philadelphia: Dropsie University, 1974). Like Blake, Rosenblatt enjoyed longevity at Hopkins from 1930 through the 1970s. I myself recall fondly my lunchtime courses on Josephus with him; my co-student was his grandson, Jonathan Rosenblatt. See *EncJud* 14:278–79.

88. See Running and Freedman, *William Foxwell Albright*, 212.

89. Letter to me dated 7 December 1998. Cross recalls that Blake "constantly gave examples of grammatical phenomena from Tagalog. I think I was half through the first term before I discovered that Tagalog was not a Semitic language, and tradition has it that several finished their degrees still under the impression that Ugaritic and Tagalog were sister languages." Blake had learned Tagalog after Paul Haupt told him that there would be a great need for the language after the United States took over the Philippines.

90. According to D. N. Freedman (personal communication, 8 August 1999), Albright regarded Sachs as his best student ever.

91. On Albright's contributions to the field of Ugaritic, see F. M. Cross, "The Contributions of W. F. Albright to Semitic Epigraphy and Palaeography," in *The Scholarship of*

William Foxwell Albright: An Appraisal (ed. G. W. Van Beek; HSS 33; Atlanta: Scholars Press, 1989), 24–26; and in the same volume D. R. Hillers, "William F. Albright as a Philologian," 51–53. For Albright and further assessments of his work, see (by year) J. A Miles, Jr., "Understanding Albright: A Revolutionary Etude," *HTR* 69 (1976): 151–75; D. N. Freedman, "W. F. Albright as an Historian," in *The Scholarship of William Foxwell Albright: An Appraisal*, 33–43; P. Machinist, "William Foxwell Albright: The Man and His work," in *The Study of the Ancient Near East in the Twenty-First Century* (ed. J. S. Cooper and G. M. Schwartz; Winona Lake, Ind.: Eisenbrauns, 1996), 385–403 (with further bibliography); Kuklick, *Puritans in Babylon*, 185–93; B. Long, *Planting and Reaping Albright: Politics, Ideology, and Interpreting the Bible* (University Park, Pa.: Pennsylvania State University, 1997), 156–57. See also the essays in *BA* 56/1 (1993) devoted to Albright and his work. For a critique of Albright's use of "logic," see A. Gibson, *Biblical Semantic Logic: A Preliminary Analysis* (New York: St. Martin's Press, 1981), 225–31. For Albright's later story, see the next chapter.

92. So Albright in a letter to Cyrus Gordon dated 7 December 1941 in APS archives Albright Corresp. 1941, 42.

93. So Albright in a letter to A. Honeyman dated 13 June 1943 in APS archives Albright Corresp. 1943.

94. So Albright in letters in February 1945 and October 1945 in APS archives Albright Corresp. 1945.

95. For the early history of JTS, see *EncJud* 10:95–97. For personal accounts, see Adler, *I Have Considered the Days*, 66, 78, and 242–44; L. Finkelstein, "Preface," in *Cyrus Adler: Selected Letters* (ed. I. Robinson; 2 vols.; Philadelphia: Jewish Publication Society of America; New York: Jewish Theological Seminary of America, 1985), 1:xvii–xxiv; and N. W. Cohen, "Introduction," in *Cyrus Adler: Selected Letters*, 1:xxv–xliii. The founding and renovation of the seminary issued largely from the efforts and vision of two Philadelphians, Sabato Morais and Cyrus Adler. Morais and Adler his student were close associates at Mikveh Israel Synagogue in Philadelphia. As the next chapter notes, Adler was also a seminal figure in the founding of the Dropsie College in Philadelphia. Since Morais, his teacher, was the founder of JTS, Adler felt deep personal ties to it and undertook its renovation. In a letter to Jacob Schiff written to allay fears that Dropsie would compete with JTS, Adler writes: "I am more interested in the Seminary than I am in the Dropsie Foundation. My interest has been in it since the beginning from the days of its early foundation by Dr. Morais" (letter to Jacob H. Schiff on 15 November 1906 published in *Cyrus Adler: Selected Letters*, 1:129). Adler's letters and autobiography (which quote the letters directly at many points) shine with his affection and concern for the seminary. They also reflect his many years of close contact with Solomon Schechter, from their first meeting in England through the negotiations bringing Schechter to the seminary to be a professor there and then its president until his death in 1915. Afterwards Adler served as Acting President and then President until his own death in 1940. It is also not well known that Leon Metoff was the ghostwriter for Adler's *I Have Considered the Days*; C. H. Gordon informed me of this when I visited his home on 18 November 1999.

96. Much of the following information comes courtesy of Professor Cohen, in an e-mail of 6 December 1998, supplemented by Sperling (*Students of the Covenant*, 75–77) and other sources cited below.

97. For Ginsberg's associations with the Hebrew University at this time, see A. Hurvitz, *ET LA'ASOT* 3 (Summer 1991): 16 [Heb.]; and "H. L. Ginsberg as a Linguist (Kehoqer Hallashon)," *Shnaton* 11:19 [Heb.].

98. Information courtesy of Edward Ullendorff in a letter to me dated 31 December 1998.

99. As Cyrus Adler mentioned in his letter to Albright dated 6 February 1936, APS archives Albright Personal Corresp. 1936–1938.

100. See the formulation in Ginsberg, "The Northwest Semitic Languages," in *Patriarchs* (vol. 2 of *The World History of the Jewish People*; ed. B. Mazar; Tel Aviv: Jewish History Publications, 1967; Rutgers, 1970), 102–24.

101. Ginsberg's translations appeared not only in *Kitbê 'Ugarit*, but also in several issues of the journal *Tarbiz*.

102. A point nicely appreciated by M. Haran, *ET LA'ASOT* 3 (Summer 1991): 18 [Heb.].

103. Letter dated 8 February 1936, APS archives Albright Personal Corresp. 1936–1938.

104. Albright, "The Old Testament and Canaanite Language and Literature," 13. Cross offers a similar estimate; see his comments in his article, "The Contributions of W. F. Albright to Semitic Epigraphy and Palaeography," 26. Pope likewise stressed to his students Ginsberg's greatness in Ugaritic studies. For scholarly appreciations of Ginsberg's work, see the essays devoted to him in *ET LA'ASOT* 3 (Summer 1991): 9–34, especially those of A. Hurvitz and S. Paul.

105. These figures are all profiled in Sperling's *Students of the Covenant*. Most pursued doctorates elsewhere.

106. Mendelsohn's name first appears in the *Ugarit-Bibliographie* in 1939–1940 for his review of P. D. M. Burrows, *The Basis of Israelite Marriage*, *RR* 4 (1939–1940): 108–9. In Ugaritic studies, Mendelsohn is perhaps best known for articles such as "The Canaanite Term for 'Free Proletarian,'" *BASOR* 83 (1941): 36–39; "State Slavery in Ancient Palestine," *BASOR* 85 (1942): 14–17; "The Family in the Ancient Near East," *BA* 11 (1948): 24–40; "Samuel's Denunciation of Kingship in the Light of the Akkadian Documents from Ugarit," *BASOR* 143 (1956): 17–22; "A Ugaritic Parallel to the Adoption of Ephraim and Manasseh," *IEJ* 9 (1959): 180–82. For further information on Mendelsohn, see Sperling, *Students of the Covenant*, 139–40 n. 58.

107. For Geller, see Sperling, *Students of the Covenant*, 128. My information about Tigay derives from his e-mail dated 25 October 1998.

108. Goetze, "Is Ugaritic a Canaanite Dialect?" *Language* 17 (1941): 127–38.

109. See Herdner, *Corpus des tablettes*, 309.

110. This was published as his piece on "The Tenses of Ugaritic," *JAOS* 58 (1938): 266–309. Z. Harris remarked in a letter to Albright dated 11 June 1937 after Goetze presented this paper to the American Oriental Society in Cleveland that year (APS archive Albright Personal Corresp. 1936–1938): ". . . many linguistic arguments can be adduced against his attempt to divorce Ras Shamra genetically from Canaanite (I think I had a mixed metaphor there)." Albright also voiced concerns to Goetze in a letter dated 7 July 1937 (APS archive Albright Personal Corresp. 1936–1938); he did accept Goetze's idea of a present tense verb **yaqattal* for Ugaritic (so in a letter to Goetze dated 4 October 1940, APS archives [Albright] Corresp. 1938–1940), but was put out that Goetze had not read up on the subject (including Albright's writings). In a letter to Albright dated 26 July 1938, Ginsberg wrote: "I'm sorry to say my verdict on Goetze's study on the Ugaritic tenses is: *zift*" (APS archive [Albright] Corresp. 1938–1940). On the proposal to see a Ugaritic verbal form morphologically analogous to Akkadian *iqattal*, see the discussion and refutation of T. L. Fenton, "The Absence of a Verbal Formation *yaqattal* from Ugaritic and Northwest Semitic," *JSS* 15 (1970): 31–41; see also Moran, "Early Canaanite *yaqtula*," *Or* 29 (1960): 1–19.

111. For examples of Obermann's work in this period besides the following discussion mentions, see his *Votive Inscriptions from Ras Shamra* (New Haven: American Oriental Society, 1941). Obermann's work in Arabic includes his edition of Ibn Shahin's *Book of Comfort*.

112. See Herdner, *Corpus des tablettes*, 321.

113. Letter written to Theophile Meek on 5 January 1937 (APS archives Albright Personal Corresp. 1936–1938). Given the timing of this letter, I believe that the paper in question would have been Obermann's "The Historic Significance of Ugaritic Script," given at the Society of Biblical Literature in the Fall of 1936, mentioned in "The Society of Biblical Literature and Exegesis: Proceedings," *JBL* 56 (1937): iv.

114. Obermann, "Sentence Negations in Ugaritic," *JBL* 65 (1946): 233–48; "How Baal Destroyed a Rival," *JAOS* 67 (1947): 195–208. See Ginsberg, review of Obermann, *Ugaritic Mythology, JCS* 2 (1948): 139–140.

115. Obermann, *Ugaritic Mythology: A Study of Its Leading Motifs* (New Haven: Yale University, 1948).

116. Ginsberg, review of Obermann, *Ugaritic Mythology,* 141.

117. Anderson, personal communication on 27 May 1999.

118. Pope, personal communication. For further discussion of these figures, see the following chapter.

119. Sperling, *Students of the Covenant,* 73–74.

120. Gordon's Penn dissertation is entitled "Rabbinic Exegesis in the Vulgate of Proverbs" (1930); an extract of the work appeared in *JBL* 49 (1930): 384–416. On Dropsie, see the relevant section in the following chapter. In "Interview with Cyrus H. Gordon, Center for Judaic Studies at the University of Pennsylvania, February 3, 1998" (a videotape taped and housed at Dropsie), Gordon tells of immigrant parents, and how his Lithuanian father became a doctor. Gordon first attended Gratz College, then Dropsie and Penn.

121. When I proposed this reading of his early history over the telephone in spring, 1999, Gordon pronounced it plausible. The following section discusses the production of the grammar.

122. "Interview with Cyrus H. Gordon, Center for Judaic Studies at the University of Pennsylvania, February 3, 1998."

123. Ibid.

124. Gordon, *Pennsylvania Tradition of Semitics,* 70–71 (his italics). One should read Gordon's sharper comments against the background of his later efforts to secure a university post. In this he struggled for some time. Following his years at Hopkins and Smith College, he cast about for a position and struggled to make ends meet. In September 1941 he expressed his willingness to consider other means of support, including popular writing if necessary (so in a letter to Albright dated 22 September 1941 [APS archives Albright Corresp. 1941]).

125. Gordon, *Pennsylvania Tradition of Semitics,* 72.

126. Dropsie College Adler files, Box 100, FF 16.

127. There was a dispute over the rights to publish the seals from Ur, which resulted in a flurry of correspondence among Speiser, Albright, Gordon, and Sidney Smith in the first half of 1935 (APS archives, Albright Corresp. 1920–1935).

128. Letter dated 15 March 1936, APS archives Albright Personal Corresp. 1936–1938.

129. Horace H. F. Jayne, letter dated 8 July 1931 (University Museum of the University of Pennsylvania archive, cited with permission). My thanks go to Professor Richard Zettler for bringing this letter to my attention.

130. Letter dated 23 June 1936, APS archives Albright Personal Corresp. 1936–1938. The same letter highly praises Ginsberg as well.

131. Letter of 5 January 1937 (APS archives Albright Personal Corresp. 1936–1938).

132. Written on 5 March 1937 (APS archives Albright Personal Corresp. 1936–1938).

133. Letter to Schmidt on 21 June 1937 (APS archives Albright Personal Corresp. 1936–1938).

134. Letter dated 14 March 1932 from Montgomery to Gordon's mother; and letter of 9 June 1932 from Montgomery to Gordon. Both are in Gordon's personal possession.

135. Letter dated 7 June 1939 (APS archives Albright Corresp. 1938–1940).

136. Letter dated 30 April 1941 (APS archives Albright Corresp. 1941).

137. Horace H. F. Jayne, letter dated 8 July 1931 (University Museum of the University of Pennsylvania archive, cited with permission). My thanks go to Professor Richard Zettler for bringing this letter to my attention.

138. Albright, "The Furniture of El in Canaanite Mythology," *BASOR* 91 (1943): 39.

139. Gordon, *Ugaritic Grammar* (AnOr 20; Rome: Pontifical Biblical Institute, 1940). For Gordon's account of this story, see also his article, "Sixty Years in Ugaritology," in *Le pays d'Ougarit au tour de 1200 av. J. C. Historie et archéologie. Actes du Colloque International, Paris, 28 juin–1ᵉʳ juillet 1993* (ed. M. Yon, M. Sznycer, and P. Bordreuil; RSO 11; Paris: Editions Recherche sur les Civilisations, 1995), 41–42. Gordon also recalls his "close and cordial friendship" with Virolleaud.

140. Gordon gave the date of the quote in his oral history, "Interview with Cyrus H. Gordon, Center for Judaic Studies at the University of Pennsylvania, February 3, 1998." In this interview Gordon mentions that he first met Albright in Max Margolis's office at Dropsie.

141. Quoted in Gordon, *Pennsylvania Tradition of Semitics*, 54.

142. So by Gordon's accounts. Among Albright's 1938 papers is Gordon's two-page "Plans for Work" which does not mention the *Ugaritic Grammar* (APS archives Albright Corresp. 1938–1940). So too in 1938 when Albright wrote a letter on Gordon's behalf to the American-Scandinavian Foundation for Gordon's year in Uppsala (APS archives Albright Personal Corresp. 1936–1938). Also earlier in a letter recommending Gordon to Dr. Goodchild dated 23 February 1933, Albright mentions the Aramaic incantation texts and "a grammatical analysis of the Kirkuk tablets" as the younger man's main projects (APS archives Albright Corresp.-Misc. 1925–1933). He wrote further: "I do not know of a single Orientalist in America (under thirty) who shows anything approaching Dr. Gordon's promise. He is also endowed by nature with a handsome physique and an attractive personality. He sometimes irritates younger men by an unconscious attitude of superiority, but I have never noted any tendency of the sort in his contacts with older men." In another letter of recommendation dated 11 January 1935, written to Henry Allen Moe of the Guggenheim Foundation, Albright again shows no awareness of the grammar project. The letter is unfailingly positive in this case: "Dr. Gordon is a most able young man, well trained under Speiser and others at the University of Pennsylvania, and an indefatigable worker. . . . He is undoubtedly the most promising young scholar who has passed through the American Schools of Oriental Research in the last ten years. . . . His character is excellent" (APS archives Albright Corresp. 1920–1935).

143. So "Interview with Cyrus H. Gordon, Center for Judaic Studies at the University of Pennsylvania, February 3, 1998." So also Cyrus Gordon personal communication, via Constance Gordon, e-mail communication to me, 18 October 1998.

144. So Gordon in our conversation together on 18 November 1999.

145. So Gordon's letter to me of 9 October 1998. For further background to this story and for Gordon's development up and through this period, see the discussion of Dropsie College in this and the following chapter.

146. Gordon, *Pennsylvania Tradition of Semitics*, 55. Gordon reiterated this story in a letter to me dated 9 October 1998. Albright thought that Gordon would be working on Akkadian material at Smith College (letter to Speiser dated 2 July 1938, and Gordon's letter to Albright from Smith College dated 30 September 1938, APS archives Albright Corresp. 1938–1940).

147. So Cyrus Gordon personal communication via Constance Gordon, e-mail communication to me, 18 October 1998. See also *Ugaritic Grammar*, vii.

148. For example, see F. Rosenthal, review of Gordon, *Ugaritic Grammar*, *Or* 11 (1942): 171–79.

149. Albright, review of Gordon, *Ugaritic Grammar, JBL* 60 (1941): 434.

150. Ibid., 448. This episode also appears in M. Lubetski and C. Gottlieb, " 'Forever Gordon': Portrait of a Master Scholar with a Global Perspective," *BA* 59 (1996): 7.

151. Albright, "The Old Testament and Canaanite Language and Literature," 13.

152. Albright, review of Gordon, *Ugaritic Handbook, JBL* 69 (1950): 385.

153. So Gordon's letter of 9 October 1998 and Freedman's letter of 24 October 1998. In Gordon's words, "Albright maliciously spread the rumor that I stole everything from Ginsberg." Cf. *Ugaritic Grammar*, 7. I have not discovered such a sentiment in Albright's correspondence. It is reported that Ginsberg directly tutored (dictated to) Gordon in writing the *Ugaritic Grammar*. Moreover, Ginsberg and Gordon enjoyed friendly relations after the publication of *Ugaritic Grammar*. Several of Ginsberg's later notes to Albright speak well of Gordon (APS archive [Albright] Corresp. 1938–1940), and Ginsberg read Gordon's chapter on Ugaritic for the latter's book *The Living Past* before publication (so Gordon's postcard to Albright postmarked 19 April 1941 in APS archive Albright Corresp. 1941). The two also worked together in the summer of 1946 on Martha's Vineyard (as Ginsberg reported to Albright in a letter dated 3 July 1946, APS archive Albright Corresp. July 1946). See also Ginsberg's praise of Gordon's work in "Interpreting Ugaritic Texts," *JAOS* 70 (1950): 156–60.

154. Meek, *Hebrew Origins* (New York: Harper & Row, 1936), 204–28.

155. Letter dated 22 January 1938, American Philosophical Society Albright Personal Corresp. 1936–1938. For their exchange in print, see also their contributions to *Monotheism and Moses* (ed. R. J. Christen and H. E. Hazelton; Lexington, Mass.: Heath, 1969). Albright added a little-known rejoinder in this volume (pp. 78–79) mixing later claims against all deities with earlier claims against specific cults (1 Kgs 18:27, 2 Kgs 1:6).

156. Albright, *From the Stone Age to Christianity: Monotheism and the Historical Process* (2d ed.; Baltimore: Johns Hopkins University Press, 1946), 207.

157. Albright, *Yahweh and the Gods of Canaan: A Historical Analysis of Two Contrasting Faiths* (New York: Doubleday, 1968; repr. Winona Lake, Ind.: Eisenbrauns, 1994).

158. See the end of Chapter Two below.

159. Letter dated 31 January 1943 (APS Albright Personal Corresp. 1943).

160. So J. Hoftijzer and K. Jongeling, eds., *Dictionary of the North-West Semitic Inscriptions. Part Two: M-T* (HdO 21/2; Leiden: Brill, 1995), 919–20.

161. See B. Long, "Mythic Trope in the Autobiography of William Foxwell Albright," *BA* 56/1 (1993): 36–45; and idem, *Planting and Reaping Albright: Politics, Ideology, and Interpreting the Bible* (University Park, Pa.: Pennsylvania State University, 1997), 156–57.

162. Albright, *From the Stone Age to Christianity*, 197.

163. I have addressed some possibilities for this issue in *The Early History of God: Yahweh and the Other Deities in Ancient Israel* (San Francisco: Harper & Row, 1990), 154–56.

164. The task of working out Albright's agenda contrasting Mosaic monotheism and Canaanite polytheism in political terms fell to his student G. Mendenhall in his book, *The Tenth Generation: The Origins of the Biblical Tradition* (Baltimore/London: Johns Hopkins University Press, 1973); and in his article, "The Worship of Baal and Asherah: A Study in the Social Bonding Functions of Religious Systems," in *Biblical and Related Studies Presented to Samuel Iwry* (ed. A. Kort and S. Morschauser; Winona Lake, Ind.: Eisenbrauns, 1985), 147–58. In an e-mail to me dated 30 April 1999, Mendenhall writes of Baal as the symbolization of political force and Asherah as the representation of "GNP" (Gross National Product). Or, as he writes in *The Tenth Generation* (p. 223), "The fertility cult is the deification of the process of production and, appropriately, is usually represented as a Great Mother and a god of the storm who brings the fertilizing rainfall."

165. Bauer, *Der Ursprung des Alphabets* (Der Alte Orient 36.1/2; Leipzig: Hinrichs, 1937).

166. Jack, *The Ras Shamra Tablets and Their Bearing upon the Old Testament* (Old Testament Studies 1; Edinburgh: T&T Clark, 1935).

167. Dussaud, *Les découvertes de Ras Shamra (Ugarit et l'Ancien Testament)* (2d ed.; Paris: Geuthner, 1941).

168. From the 1940s into the 1960s, de Langhe taught at Leuven/Louvain. His students there included Antoon Schoors. De Langhe also held a visiting appointment at Nijmegan in the 1950s (information courtesy of Schoors and de Geus).

169. De Langhe, *Les textes de Ras Shamra-Ugarit et leur rapports avec le milieu biblique de l'Ancient Testament* (Gembloux: Duculot, 1945).

170. Albright, "Islam and the Religions of the Ancient Orient," *JAOS* 60 (1940): 283–301. For a comparable range, see F. Rosenthal, "Some Minor Problems in the Qur'ân," in *The Joshua Starr Memorial Volume: Studies in History and Philology* (Jewish Social Studies, Publications No. 5; New York: Conference on Jewish Relations, 1953), 67–84. For a later comparison with Islam, see C. H. Gordon, "The Three Graces," *NUS* 31 (April 1984): 11. For later reflexes in Jewish and Christian literature, see A. Goetze, "Peace on Earth," *BASOR* 93 (1944): 17–20; M. S. Smith, *The Ugaritic Baal Cycle. Volume 1: Introduction with Text, Translation, and Commentary to the First Two Tablets (KTU 1.1–1.2)* (VTSup 55; Leiden: Brill, 1994), xxvii, *inter alia*.

171. Reported by J. H. Patton to Albright in a letter dated 22 March 1944 (APS archives Albright Personal Corresp. Jan.-Aug. 1944).

172. Letter written to "Father and Family," dated 30 March 1943 (APS archives Albright Personal Corresp. 1943). Goode had completed his doctorate in 1940.

173. The following assessments depend partially on information reported to Albright in the letters cited below; one of his sources was H. H. Rowley, for example in a letter dated 8 January 1946 (APS archives Albright Personal Corresp. April 1946), but in 1946 Albright also alludes to hearing about the situation from people in Germany, the Netherlands, and Switzerland. Albright also exchanged letters with Goetze and Mowinckel over the culpability of German scholars. For further information, see the book of M. Weinreich, *Hitler's Professors: The Part of Scholarship in Germany's Crimes against the Jewish People* (New York: Yiddish Scientific Institute—YIVO, 1946); Weinreich exchanged letters with Albright in the first half of 1946.

174. Letter of 10 March 1946 to his son Paul (APS archives Albright Personal Corresp. March 1946).

175. Albright reports that Hempel and Jirku were fired from their positions (letter of 2 March 1946 to Orlinsky, APS archives Albright Personal Corresp. March 1946; letter of 8 April 1946 to Samuel Terrien, APS archives Albright Personal Corresp. March 1946). Jirku was replaced "by his great enemy Noth" (letter to Nelson Glueck, dated 9 February 1946, APS archives Albright Personal Corresp. 1946).

176. Weinreich (*Hitler's Professors*, 41–43, 215–16) discusses the pro-Nazi activities of Kittel, son of the famous Rudolph Kittel (1853–1929); on the latter, see *EncJud* 10:1079–80). Albright learned that Kittel was jailed in France (letter to Nelson Glueck, dated 9 February 1946, APS archives Albright Personal Corresp. 1946), and that Sellin was shot by the Russians (letter of 2 March 1946 to Orlinsky, APS archives Albright Personal Corresp. 1946). Weinreich also cites the broader phenomenon of pro-Reich sympathies among biblical scholars (for an example, see *Hitler's Professors*, 68–69 n. 144).

Synthesis and Comparisons: 1945 to 1970

The postwar era was the period of greatest achievement in many key respects for both Ugaritic and biblical studies. This was the time of many scholarly giants: C. Virolleaud, J. Nougayrol, and R. Dussaud in France; R. de Langhe in Belgium; G. R. Driver and E. Ullendorff in the United Kingdom; W. Baumgartner and L. Koehler in Switzerland; A. Alt and O. Eissfeldt in Germany; J. Pedersen in Denmark; H. S. Nyberg[1] in Sweden; S. Mowinckel[2] in Norway; J. Aistleitner in Hungary; U. Cassuto first in Italy, then Israel; A. van Selms in South Africa; and W. F. Albright, T. H. Gaster, H. L. Ginsberg, A. Goetze, C. H. Gordon, and J. Obermann in the United States.[3] The next generation emerging in the wake of the great prewar generation included A. Kapelrud, H. Ringgren, and G. W. Ahlström in Scandinavia; A. Herdner, A. Caquot, and H. Cazelles in France; J. A. Emerton, J. C. L. Gibson, and J. Gray in the United Kingdom; W. Herrmann, J. Jeremias, O. Kaiser, K. Koch, and O. Loretz in Germany; P. Fronzaroli in Italy; S. Segert in Czechoslovakia; and F. M. Cross, D. N. Freedman, M. Held, J. C. Greenfield, and M. H. Pope in the United States.

Up through the war some of the best Ugaritic scholars in the United States were immigrants, mostly from Europe, as they were in many other academic fields. For example, with Gaster from England and Ginsberg from Canada (via Israel), the circle of Columbia University and Jewish Theological Seminary drew on the learned heritages of the British Commonwealth and Jewish tradition.[4] As we noted in the preceding chapter, Goetze and Obermann (and later Rosenthal) came from Germany to Yale University. One might say that they created a German center of Ugaritic studies at Yale. Emphasizing the German origins of Ugaritic at Yale may sound like an exaggeration, but in the postwar era a number of European students, including A. Kapelrud, H. Gese, J. Jeremias, and E. Gerstenberger, came to study at Yale, especially with Goetze. (In the 1960s S. Segert would come to the United States from Prague.) The great immigration of Semitic scholars to the United States clearly had a major effect. Albright anticipated this change in a letter written to Goetze in 1934: "We need your assistance to help us raise our standards, which, though probably better than ever before, are not yet equal to those which prevailed until recently in Germany."[5] In 1937 Albright felt that the United States had a strong core of scholars in West Semitics, thanks to the presence of Goetze, Obermann ("not so good"), Ginsberg ("first-class"), Montgomery, Harris, Gordon, and himself. He concluded: "America is rapidly becoming the center of research in Canaanite philology, especially since H. Bauer died."[6] (And in the following year Rosenthal also came to the United States.) In view of the war, Albright's assessment of the situation was understandable. Indeed, all the figures named by Albright held posts at universities from Baltimore to New Haven, and they enjoyed a regular exchange of communications. Albright's assessment was not entirely correct, however, given the presence of Baumgartner, Dhorme, Driver, Friedrich, Eissfeldt, and others on the Continent, as well as Cassuto and de Vaux in Jerusalem. Moreover, Europe and Israel would produce major centers of study in the postwar era. In the United States, Israel, and Europe, this period marked a high point in all areas of synthesis. Armed with the pioneering efforts of the prewar period, postwar research took great strides forward, not only in many details of archaeology and texts, but also in the synthetic broad strokes that portrayed the relations between Ugarit and the Bible in matters of language, literature, and religion. Let us first chronicle some of the texts and tools dating to the postwar period.

⊠ TEXTS AND TOOLS

Archaeology: C. F. A. Schaeffer (in issues of the journal *Syria*). See the bibliography of J. C. Courtois, "Ras Shamra: I. Archéologie," *DBSup* 9 (1979): 1287–89, 1291–95.

Text Editions: *CTA* (including bibliography). *Ugaritica I–II. PRU II–VI.* Courtois, "Ras Shamra: I. Archéologie," *DBSup* 9 (1979): 1287–89, 1291–95.

Grammars and Lexica: J. Aistleitner, *Untersuchungen zur Grammatik des Ugaritischen* (Berlin: Akademie-Verlag, 1954). *Wörterbuch der ugaritischer Sprache* (ed. O. Eissfeldt; Berlin: Akademie-Verlag, 1958; 2d ed., 1965; 3d ed., 1967). C. H. Gordon, *Ugaritic Handbook* (Rome: Pontifical Biblical Institute, 1947); *Ugaritic Manual* (Rome: Pontifical Biblical Institute, 1955); *Ugaritic Textbook* (Rome: Pontifical Biblical Institute, 1965).

Concordance: G. D. Young, *Concordance of Ugaritic* (AnOr 36; Rome: Pontifical Biblical Institute, 1956).

Proper Names: F. Gröndahl, *Die Personennamen der Texte aus Ugarit* (Studia Pohl 1; Rome: Päpstliches Bibelinstitut, 1967).

Translations: J. Aistleitner, *Die mythologischen und kultischen Texte aus Ras Shamra* (Budapest: Akadémiai Kiadó, 1959; 2d ed., 1964). U. Cassuto's articles later published in his two-volume *Biblical and Oriental Studies* (trans. I. Abrahams; Jerusalem: Magnes, 1975); and his book, *The Goddess Anat* (trans. I. Abrahams; Jerusalem: Magnes, 1971). G. R. Driver, *Canaanite Myths and Legends* (Old Testament Studies 3; Edinburgh: T&T Clark, 1956). T. H. Gaster, *Thespis: Ritual, Myth, and Drama in the Ancient Near East* (New York: H. Schuman, 1950). H. L. Ginsberg, *ANET* 129–55. C. H. Gordon, *Ugaritic Literature: A Comprehensive Translation of the Prose and Poetic Texts* (Rome: Pontifical Biblical Institute, 1949). A. Jirku, *Kanaanäische Mythen und Epen aus Ras Schamra-Ugarit* (Gütersloh: Gerd Mohn, 1962). Z. and S. Rin, *The Acts of the Gods* (Jerusalem: Iblan, 1968 [Heb.]).

Studies and Commentaries: H. L. Ginsberg, *The Legend of King Keret* (New Haven: American Schools of Oriental Research, 1946). J. Gray, *The Keret Text in the Literature of Ras Shamra: A Social Myth of Ancient Canaan* (Leiden: Brill, 1955).

Synthetic Studies on Grammar: J. Barr, *Comparative Philology and the Text of the Old Testament* (Oxford: Oxford University Press, 1968).

Synthetic Studies on Religion: G. Ahlström, *Aspects of Syncretism in Israelite Religion* (Horae Soederblomianae 5; Lund: Gleerup, 1963). B. Albrektson, *History and the Gods: An Essay on the Idea of Historical Events as Divine Manifestations in the Ancient Near East and in Israel* (ConBOT 1; Lund: CWK Gleerup, 1967). W. F. Albright, *Yahweh and the Gods of Canaan: A Historical Analysis of Two Contrasting Faiths* (London, 1968; repr. Winona Lake, Ind.: Eisenbrauns, 1994). O. Eissfeldt, *El im ugaritischen Pantheon* (Berlin: Akademie Verlag, 1951). J. Emerton, "The Origin of the Son of Man Imagery," *JTS* 9 (1958): 22–42. G. Fohrer, *History of Israelite Religion* (German original 1969; trans. D. E. Green; Nashville, Tenn.: Abingdon, 1972). J. Gray, *The Canaanites* (Ancient Peoples and Places 38; New York: Frederick A. Praeger, 1964); and *The Legacy of Canaan* (VTSup 5; Leiden: Brill, 1957; 2d ed., 1965). O. Kaiser, *Die mythische Bedeutung des Meeres in Ägypten, Ugarit, und Israel* (BZAW 78; Berlin: Töpelmann, 1958; 2d ed., 1967). A. Kapelrud, *Baal in the Ras Shamra Texts* (Copenhagen: Gad, 1952); *The Violent Goddess: Anat in the Ras Shamra Texts* (Oslo: Universitetsforlaget, 1969). S. Mowinckel, *The Psalms in Israel's Worship* (2 vols.; repr. of 1962 English original; trans. D. R. Ap-Thomas; Biblical Seminar 14; Sheffield: JSOT, 1992). U. Oldenburg, *The Conflict between El and Ba'al in Canaanite Religion* (Supplement to Numen 3; Leiden: Brill, 1969). M. H. Pope, *El in the Ugaritic Texts* (VTSup 2; Leiden: Brill, 1955). M. H. Pope and W. Röllig, "Syrien: Die Mythologie der Ugariter und Phönizier," in *Wörterbuch der Mythologie I:1* (ed. H. W. Haussig; Stuttgart: Ernst Klett, 1965), 235–312. W. Schmidt, *Königtum Gottes in Ugarit und Israel* (BZAW 80; Berlin: de Gruyter, 1961). N. Tromp, *Primitive Conceptions of Death and the Nether World in the Old Testament* (BibOr 21; Rome: Pontifical Biblical Institute, 1969).

⌘ TEXT EDITIONS, LANGUAGE, AND GRAMMAR

The field recovered from the war with some figures picking up where they had left off in 1939. Schaeffer served as head of the French archaeological team through 1971, and he continued to publish archaeological reports in the journal *Syria*. He never completed a final report, and no synthetic archaeological work on Ugarit would appear until the 1980s. As a result, it was often difficult to discern from report to report the stratigraphy and its relation to the finds.

In the area of text editions, the beginning of this period marked the end of the publication of *editio princeps* by Charles Virolleaud, while the end (almost) of this period witnessed the important 1963 publication of the standard text edition by his student, A. Herdner, entitled *Corpus des tablettes alphabétiques (CTA).*[7] Virolleaud's wartime publications of new texts began to receive attention. These included two of the three tablets of Keret (*KTU* 1.15 and 1.16), the Rephaim texts (1.20–1.22), and some other mythological pieces (1.7, 1.9, 1.11). Herdner's edition later marked a new high point. The field may be grateful for both Virolleaud's expeditious publication of the tablets and for Herdner's comprehensive edition. By the same token, the readings of many letters in the texts would remain unresolved throughout this period. In part this situation is to be attributed to the nature of the discovery at Ras Shamra: no multiple copies of texts were found, so differing readings would continue. Today's standard practice of working with both the original tablets and highly detailed photographs had not yet developed. Moreover, in the case of postwar editions of tablets, the epigraphers did not work with the originals in Syria (Virolleaud's reliance on photographs and casts after World War II seriously detracted from his editions of the postwar period).

Despite the great help that it provided, Herdner's edition produced yet another numbering of the Ugaritic texts. Up to the time of *CTA,* the field had used the numbering system first developed by Virolleaud or the original "RS" numbers (the numbers given to the tablets in the field). In addition, Gordon devised a system for his *Ugaritic Textbook,* and Otto Eissfeldt added his own numbering.[8] From 1970 to 1985, the field reached a consensus on the numbering system advanced by *Die keilalphabetischen Texte aus Ugarit (KTU),*[9] but in the interim the confusion in nomenclature ill served the field. If Ugaritic scholars found correlating the different numbering systems confusing at times, this situation made entry into the field forbidding to those in related areas of research.

In the postwar era, the nature of the Ugaritic written characters became a matter of some controversy.[10] From the outset it seemed clear that Mesopotamian culture influenced the cuneiform shapes of the thirty Ugaritic alphabetic graphemes. However, the limited number of signs indicated a development not from syllabic cuneiform writing, but from the local West Semitic alphabetic writing. Five issues about the alphabetic classification surfaced in the postwar era. First, some argued that the forms of the signs drew on Mesopotamian models,[11] while others suggested a relationship to the pictographic West Semitic letters known from Middle or Late Bronze Age inscriptions attested at Serabit el-Khadem and elsewhere, or even to hieroglyphs without any intermediary step.[12] For example, A. T. Olmstead and H. Bauer had noted many similarities between the Phoenician and Ugaritic alphabets.[13] F. Rosenthal argued that the Ugaritic alphabet imitated West Semitic letter forms, noting the correspondence of circular shapes in letters of Late Bronze noncuneiform scripts with the wedge shape *Winkelhaken* used in the same letters in the alphabetic cuneiform forms (for example, in the five letters *tet, ʿayin, ghayin, qoph, th*).[14] Forms with only linear wedges, whether vertical or horizontal, also arguably follow the form of their local noncuneiform counterparts, although in Rosenthal's view some forms present difficulties. (His approach has found a more recent advocate in E. Puech,[15] who has nicely lined up the letter forms of the West Semitic cuneiform and noncuneiform alphabets from the Late Bronze Age.)[16] Still others felt that the shapes resulted from aesthetic combinations of the three basic wedges, the single horizontal and vertical as well as the *Winkelhaken* (possibly for mnemonic purposes).[17] A view combining the two approaches has been voiced recently as well:

> This alphabet seems to have been invented in the fourteenth century B.C. under Proto-Canaanite influence, but cuneiform shapes were adapted to it to suit the requirements of the Ugaritic scribes. The similarity of the shape of some of the letters to their Proto-Canaanite prototypes can hardly be a coincidence, while other letters seem to have been invented independently.[18]

Second, why did the Ugaritic alphabet have three *ʾalephs*? Clearly this feature marked a departure from other West Semitic alphabets. H. Bauer's proposal that the *ʾalephs* served for writing foreign words[19] has failed to convince.[20] Rosenthal suggested another view: "The Accadian signs expressing a mere vowel might indeed have attracted the attention of the inventor, because in spelling often enough they took the place of *aleph*."[21] At present the question remains open.[22]

Third, whether the letters constituted an alphabet or a reduced syllabary (where each symbol stood for a consonant plus any vowel) became an issue in this period. Clearly, scholars trained primarily in West Semitic languages followed the former view (such as W. F. Albright and later his students, F. M. Cross and T. O. Lambdin),[23] while the latter found support from some Assyriologists (such as I. J. Gelb and W. W. Hallo, his student from the University of Chicago).[24] In part Gelb's view represented a refutation of the majority view held since A. Gardiner[25] that the linear alphabet attested at Serabit el-Khadem derived from a prior Egyptian model using the acrophonic principle (that is, the phonetic value of a sign is based on the initial sound of the object represented).

Fourth, this issue raised a further question as to whether or not the letter names were old and original. If so, this would tally with arguments for the acrophonic alphabetic principle proposed originally for West Semitic scripts. If the latter, then perhaps Ugaritic could be regarded as a reduced syllabary. The publication of a scribal text (*KTU* 5.14 = RS 19.159) with the Ugaritic signs in one column matched by syllabic signs in another column fueled this debate. Two of Albright's students, F. M. Cross and T. O. Lambdin,[26] would argue in 1960 that the signs in the right-hand column represent the first syllable of the letter names of the signs in the left-hand column. Evidence presented in an article by the Assyriologist E. A. Speiser bolstered this argument.[27] However, other scholars, such as W. W. Hallo,[28] dismissed this view especially after scholars such as E. Ullendorff[29] cast serious doubt on other putative evidence for the antiquity of the letter names (in particular in Ethiopic). Yet, after initially following Ullendorff on this point, J. Ryckmans would later turn up new evidence that he felt refuted the position.[30]

Fifth and finally, many scholars would raise the issue of the relationship between alphabetic writing and the rise of literacy, since the Ugaritic alphabet had relatively few signs compared to scripts in either Egypt or Mesopotamia.[31]

Defining the nature of the alphabet became further complicated in the postwar period, after texts in a short cuneiform alphabet were discovered at various sites (1933–1988). Four of these texts came to light near ancient Ugarit itself, including one text on an inscribed jar handle from Minet el-Bheida, *KTU* 1.77 (discovered in 1934), and three tablets from Ras Shamra, *KTU* 4.31 (discovered in 1933), *KTU* 4.710 (discovered in 1959), and RS 88.2215 (discovered in 1988).[32] *KTU* 7.60, an inscription on the head of a clay nail from Ugarit, is sometimes included in this group. A handful of other texts written in alphabetic cuneiform would be found at sites throughout the Levant, including (from north to south): Qadesh on the Orontes (Tell en-Nebi Mend),[33] discovered in 1975 (*KTU* 6.71); Kumidi (Kamid el-Loz),[34] discovered in 1967 (*KTU* 6.2, 6.67); Sarepta, found in 1972 (*KTU* 6.70); Tabor, excavated in 1944 (*KTU* 6.1); Taanach, discovered in 1963 (*KTU* 4.767); Beth Shemesh, found in 1933 (*KTU* 5.24 = 8.1);[35] and also at Hala Sultan Tekke in Cyprus (*KTU* 6.68).[36] In most, if not all, of these cases, the shorter alphabet prevailed.[37] To many scholars, it seemed as if these cases of the shorter alphabet provided a missing link between the longer Ugaritic alphabet and the shorter alphabets of the Iron Age Levant.[38] In sum, scholars raised many questions about the Ugaritic signs, but they reached little consensus on these issues. Still, the Ugaritic alphabet remained immensely important for biblical studies, since it provided the fuller repertoire of consonants that lay behind the reduced Phoenician, Aramaic, and Hebrew alphabets. However, even this limited consensus would come under fire in the mid-1980s, as we will see in Chapter Four.

The understanding of Ugaritic texts and language developed in the postwar period, as the successive editions of Cyrus Gordon's 1955 *Ugaritic Manual* reflect. The *Ugaritic Manual* was to include a concordance produced by G. D. Young, Gordon's student at Dropsie (discussed below),[39] but the concordance appeared separately in 1956.[40] Gordon's own labors culminated in the appearance of the three fascicles of his 1965 *Ugaritic Textbook*. J. C. Greenfield caustically declared the *Ugaritic Textbook* to be out of date when it was published,[41] but for lack of any other such tool, the volumes served scores of students right into the 1990s. In this period Gordon was one of the best propagators of the field, thanks to these volumes and his other works, including his translations.

After the war, Ugaritic assumed increasing significance for studying biblical Hebrew. As Ugaritic and Hebrew continued to illuminate one another, a subfield that one might call "Hebrew historical grammar" came into being within the older discipline of comparative Semitics.[42] Scholars such as Albright, Ginsberg, Gordon, Greenfield, Held, and Pope refined the historical study of West Semitic languages. Ugaritic provided many Hebrew "proto-forms," explaining anomalous-looking older Hebrew grammatical forms and vocabulary, and it provided an overall set of paradigms that helped elucidate the early development of classical Hebrew. The inventory of consonants in biblical Hebrew, its basic vowel structure, its nominal types and endings, and the entire verbal system continued to be clarified by Ugaritic.

⊠ ACADEMIC DEVELOPMENTS IN EUROPE AND ISRAEL

Lexicography and G. R. Driver at Oxford

One of the major challenges facing the study of Ugaritic involved its lexicon. Scholars turned to biblical Hebrew and the other Semitic languages in order to discern the meanings of words. Arabic especially helped to clarify the consonantal inventory of Ugaritic and its verbal system, and the wealth of the Arabic lexicon provided many possible etymologies for Ugaritic. In the British isles, this work is perhaps most associated with Sir Godfrey Rolles Driver, the son of the great Hebraist S. R. Driver, Regius Professor of Hebrew at Oxford and a canon in the Church of England. G. R. Driver was a young prodigy.[43] At age sixteen he helped his father with the 1910 production of *Gesenius' Hebrew Grammar* (commonly called Gesenius-Kautzsch-Cowley and abbreviated *GKC*). In his appointment as professor of Semitic Philology at Oxford (1938–1962) as well as Fellow of Magdalen College, Driver exercised a further act of filial piety in offering additions ("many hundreds in number") to the 1953 reprint edition of the 1907 *A Hebrew and English Lexicon of the Old Testament Based on the Lexicon of William Gesenius* (commonly called by the names of its editors, Brown-Driver-Briggs, and abbreviated *BDB*), which were based on his father's later work.[44] Throughout his career, G. R. Driver was a prolific author and well-known for his research and writing on Ugaritic, especially his much-used *Canaanite Myths and Legends* (1956).[45]

Driver taught many fellow Englishmen who would become well-known scholars of Bible and West Semitic languages in their own right. Two, John A. Emerton and D. Winton Thomas,[46] served as Regius Professor of Hebrew at Cambridge. Another was the illustrious Semiticist Edward Ullendorff, who had begun his Ugaritic studies in Jerusalem with Ginsberg and Cassuto and taught later at a number of schools, including Manchester. Driver acknowledged Ullendorff's contributions to his seminar in *Canaanite Myths and Legends* under the abbreviation "Ull."[47] Like Ullendorff, another Driver student, the biblicist and Ugaritologist T. L. Fenton, later taught at Manchester University. Driver also taught other significant figures in Ugaritic studies, including the eminent Scottish scholar J. C. L. Gibson, later a professor at Edinburgh; the English Assyriologist Alan Millard, longtime professor at Liverpool and a regular contributor to Ugaritic studies; and Chaim Rabin, professor of Hebrew at the Hebrew University and occasional author of studies involving Ugaritic vocabulary.[48] In addition, many biblical scholars studied with Driver, including John Rogerson at Sheffield, Anthony Gelston at Durham, John Strugnell at Duke University and Harvard University (as well as a major figure in the study of the Dead Sea Scrolls and longtime director of the international team responsible for their publication, in the series Discoveries in the Judaean Desert, published by the Clarendon Press), and T. W. Thacker, a comparative Semiticist and teacher of M. E. J. Richardson at Durham.

Strugnell would make the Dead Sea Scrolls his lifelong passion, but he fondly remembers his Ugaritic class with Driver:

> It is pleasant to summon up remembrance of things past, and collect my scattered memories of the days in 1955 when I and four or five others sat around Driver's seminar table in his rooms in Magdalen [College]. Remember how in those days Gordon *[Ugaritic Textbook]* had not been published, and Driver's own "Canaanite myths" was another year in the future . . . his interest was in the lexical side, and did not require much vocalisation. His interest, I repeat, was lexical, with few interests in the poetic, mythical or (in general) cultural elements in the texts; this was also in general the influence behind his studies in the Psalms and the Prophets. Perhaps things changed with the appearance of "Canaanite Myths and Legends," but I remember how the principal book beside him as he lectured was Hava's Arabic Lexicon; the students imitating the English Schoolboy books like "With Clive in India" or "With Livingstone in Darkest Africa" referred to his forthcoming book as "With Lane through Darkest Ugarit."[49]

As Strugnell's comments suggest, the appearance of Driver's *Canaanite Myths and Legends* in 1956 marked a watershed event in Ugaritic studies. Driver set the text of most of the main Ugaritic myths line by line next to his English translation, with further notes at the bottom of the page. *Canaanite Myths and Legends* also offered helpful introductions to the mythological texts, as well as a glossary at the back of the volume.

Increasingly from the 1950s onward, scholars called for controls on the use of Arabic in Ugaritic lexicography.[50] A fundamental critique that touched in particular on Driver's work appeared toward the end of the postwar period, namely, James Barr's seminal 1968 study, *Comparative Philology and the Text of the Old Testament*.[51] Grandson of James Barr, a member of Parliament from 1924 to 1931 and from 1935 to 1945, and son of Allan Barr, a professor in the Free Church College at Edinburgh, Barr was born in Glasgow on 20 March 1924. At Edinburgh, he pursued classics (1941–1942) before serving as a pilot in the Fleet Air Arm of the Royal Navy (1942–1945). Afterward he returned to the university to complete his study of classics (1945–1948), and then he turned to theology and the Bible (1948–1951).[52] During this period, Norman Porteous, professor of Semitic Languages (who turned one hundred years old in 1998), and Oliver Rankin, professor of Old Testament Language, Literature, and Theology, taught biblical studies at Edinburgh. Ugaritic was not part of the curriculum, but Barr managed to teach himself the language. After Rankin died a few years later, Barr succeeded him as professor of Old Testament Literature and Theology at Edinburgh (1955–1961) after a stint as professor of New Testament Literature and Exegesis at Presbyterian College in Montreal (1953–1955). After 1961, the prolific Barr taught at Princeton Theological Seminary (1961–1965), Manchester (1965–1976), and Oxford (1976–1978 Oriel Professor; Regius Chair of Hebrew 1978–1989). In 1989 he took up his current position as professor of Hebrew Bible at Vanderbilt University in Nashville, Tennessee.

Barr was a capable lexicographer, and he came to challenge the freewheeling use of Arabic in Ugaritic studies, writing: "[B]ut it is here, among the Drivers and Dahoods of scholarship working on the detailed biblical text, that I find not just an empiricism or positivism but an almost entirely *uncritical* and *unanalytical* empiricism and positivism."[53] As this quote suggests, he was highly critical of the methods that both Driver and Dahood (a controversial figure treated in the next chapter) used to interpret the Hebrew Bible. To be fair, Barr elsewhere would defend Driver against a caricatured grouping with Dahood,[54] and Barr also writes positively of a number of Driver's philological suggestions (e.g., his comparisons of Ethiopic *leḥiq* and BH *lḥqh* in 1 Sam 19:20; Ugaritic *bṣql* and BH *bṣqln* in 2 Kgs 4:42; and Driver's skepticism about the enclitic *mem* in Hebrew).[55]

Also criticizing the uncritical use of Arabic was Marvin Pope's 1966 review of John Gray's *The Legacy of Canaan*.[56] Gray's free equation of sibilants in Arabic and Ugaritic garnered the label of "phonological heresy" from Pope. Indeed, Arabic seemed to offer so many lexicographical possibilities that even a learned Semiticist could err. To illustrate, I cite an anecdote from Otto Kaiser, who studied Ugaritic with Otto Rössler at Tübingen in 1954–1955:

> It happened during my work on the mythological concern of the sea[57] that I found an etymological explanation of an Ugaritic word by an Arabic word by C. H.

Gordon. I had an indistinct feeling of irritation and went by bicycle to Prof. Rössler (at that time in Germany scholars usually did not own a car) to ask him for his opinion. He immediately laughed and said: "Well, this is a loanword from Byzantine Greek which means 'Imperial Mail' "![58]

Nevertheless, a more critical use of Arabic in Ugaritic as well as Hebrew lexicography was increasing throughout this period. Questions about proper lexicographical procedure, and in particular mistaken consonantal correspondences between Arabic and Ugaritic, helped to produce greater clarity about Ugaritic grammar in the postwar era.

Halle (O. Eissfeldt), Leipzig (A. Alt, J. Friedrich, and S. Herrmann), Tübingen (O. Rossler and W. Röllig), and Heidelberg (C. Westermann and R. Rendtorff)

In the postwar period, Ugaritic had an enormous impact in both England and in the divided Germany. In East Germany, Ugaritic was taught primarily at two universities. At Halle, Hans Bauer had taught Otto Eissfeldt. Even though Eissfeldt served as rector of the university after the war, he continued to be incredibly prolific. His scholarship touched on nearly every aspect of Ugaritic and biblical studies. His 1951 study *El im ugaritischen Pantheon*[59] is one of a series of works aimed at understanding divinity in Israel with the help of Ugaritic and other West Semitic texts: "Ba'alsamem und Jahwe" (1939); "Jahwe Zebaoth" (1950); "El and Yahweh" (1956);[60] and "Adonis und Adonij" (1970).[61] Eissfeldt also studied the Ugaritic texts in their own right,[62] and taught Ugaritic to a number of students, including K. H. Bernhardt, R. Hillmann, and H. Goeseke.[63] Bernhardt's contributions included a 1956 article on Keret and a 1975 survey of the Ugaritic texts.[64] Goeseke wrote an article on the language of the Ugaritic texts based on his 1954 Halle dissertation.[65] Hillmann wrote his 1965 dissertation on "Kosmische Verbindungslinien zwischen dem kanaanäischen Wettergott und Jahwe." In the mid-1950s Eissfeldt developed a working relationship with Joseph Aistleitner of Budapest (d. September 9, 1960), whose grammatical work appeared in 1954,[66] and whose 1963 *Wörterbuch* appeared posthumously, thanks to Eissfeldt's editorial efforts.[67] Eissfeldt issued a second edition of the wordbook in 1965 and a third edition in 1968. Despite some questionable etymologies, the work has remained a standard tool in the field for four decades. Between the two of them, Eissfeldt and Aistleitner covered the fields of the grammar, literature, and religion of Ugarit. A number of scholars followed Eissfeldt in working on Ugaritic at Halle, including H. J. Zobel and A. Mustafa,[68] whose 1974 dissertation was entitled "Untersuchungen zu den Satztypen in den epischen Texten von Ugarit."

At Leipzig, the old tradition of Semitics that Friedrich Delitzsch (1850–1922)[69] passed on to his students Paul Haupt (1858–1926)[70] and Benno Landsberger

(1890–1968)[71] continued, now in the field of Ugaritic with Johannes Friedrich. Friedrich was an accomplished linguist of ancient Near Eastern languages, known especially for the basic tools that he produced for the study of Hittite. He also wrote occasionally on matters pertaining to Ugaritic,[72] including work on the Ugaritic alphabet that Albright respectfully characterized as a "brilliant and incisive linguistic paper."[73]

In Leipzig after the war, Friedrich had a famous colleague, the great Albrecht Alt (1883–1956).[74] Although Alt is primarily remembered as an immensely important biblical scholar, his work in the 1940s treated Ugaritic occupations and place names.[75] During the 1950s he addressed some Egyptian-Ugaritic interconnections,[76] and he offered some of the first sustained treatments of Ugaritic economy.[77] His use of feudal terminology for ancient Ugaritic society began a trend that John Gray sustained in the early 1950s and Anson Rainey in the early 1960s.[78]

In part because of his opposition to the Nazis, Friedrich became the rector of Leipzig University after the war.[79] In 1950, unhappy over Communist control, Friedrich moved to the new Freie Universität in West Berlin (he retired in 1964). Under Friedrich's supervision in Berlin, F. Gröndahl produced a dissertation published as *Die Personennamen der Texte aus Ugarit*.[80]

In time W. Herrmann who, at Alt's suggestion, had studied Ugaritic under Friedrich in 1948–1949,[81] would himself become professor at Leipzig, where he regularly offered a course entitled "Canaanite Gods in the Old Testament."[82] During the 1960s Herrmann was perhaps the most prolific German author, devoting his attention primarily to Ugaritic. He produced a score of studies on divinity[83] and on Ugaritic texts.[84] Indeed, that productivity continues, most recently in his 1999 book on West Semitic deities and the Bible.[85]

In West Germany, several universities provided instruction in Ugaritic. At Tübingen, Semiticist Otto Rössler taught Ugaritic and occasionally wrote on Ugaritic grammar.[86] One of his better-known students was Otto Kaiser, whose dissertation on the mythological sea helped to draw attention to the ways Ugaritic provided background to Israelite cosmology.[87] Afterward, Kaiser wrote occasionally on Ugaritic subjects[88] and taught Ugaritic for many years at Marburg. In the 1960s at Tübingen, W. Röllig taught Ugaritic, sometimes with H. P. Rüger.[89] One of their better-known students was B. Janowski, now professor at Tübingen (after positions in Hamburg and Heidelberg).

At Heidelberg, the major force in ancient Near Eastern studies in the pos.-war period was Adam Falkenstein. Students engaged with Ugaritic there in the early 1950s included Gerhard von Rad, Klaus Koch, Otto Plöger, and R. Rendtorff.[90] Von Rad became professor at Heidelberg, while Koch eventually taught at Hamburg. While von Rad's interests hewed closely to the biblical canon, the prolific and insightful Koch wrote extensively on Bible, Egypt, and the rest of the ancient Near East, including Ugaritic. Later at Heidelberg (1963–1990), Rendtorff taught Ugaritic after a stint in Göttingen (1956–1963). (There in 1956–1957, Rendtorff had learned and then cotaught Ugaritic with R. Borger and C. Colpe, and from 1958 to 1963 Rendtorff himself provided instruction in Ugaritic to some well-known students of the Bible, including R. Smend and R. Schmitt.) At Heidelberg, Rendtorff aimed to establish a translation project in Ugaritic and initiated a study of Nikkal wa-Ib (*KTU* 1.24). Although he nearly completed a book-length manuscript on this text, he actually published only an article out of it.[91] Rendtorff was not the only figure at Heidelberg interested in Ugaritic in the postwar era. The great biblicist Claus Westermann employed Ugaritic in his work, for example, in his 1976 study of the patriarchal narratives.[92]

In retrospect, the flight of scholars from Germany slowed the growth of Ugaritic studies there during the postwar era. Despite this situation, the study of Ugaritic continued to exert a significant impact on biblical studies in Germany through the 1970s and beyond.

Ugarit and the Bible in Switzerland: W. Baumgartner and L. Koehler

After the war, Basel was an exciting center for students of Bible and theology. Baumgartner was a major figure there, as were Karl Barth, Oscar Cullman, and Walter Eichrodt. W. F. Albright regarded Baumgartner highly, and in a letter of 28 March 1931 answering Professor George Dahl of Yale University's request for suggestions for a position at Yale, Albright proposed Baumgartner's name: "Baumgartner has published some exceedingly able, really brilliant monographs on biblical and Semitic philological subjects. If Baumgartner came to America, we should lose all anxiety with regard to the maintenance of high philological standards in American Biblical Scholarship."[93] In a letter written in 1933 to Baumgartner, Albright urges him to take up the study of Ugaritic: "With your exceptional linguistic training, in both lexicography and morphology, covering the three most useful languages, Accadian, Hebrew, and Aramaic, you are evidently the man for it. Besides, you are the man to study comparative mythological implications of these documents."[94] Nowadays Baumgartner is still known for the 1953 "Koehler-Baumgartner" dictionary of biblical Hebrew (abbreviated as *HALAT*).[95] (His coeditor, L. Koehler, held a post in Zurich.) The dictionary was the first to use etymological evidence from Ugaritic to elucidate Hebrew. Baumgartner also was a prolific generalist on biblical and Ugaritic topics.[96]

In the postwar period, many German and Swiss students flocked to Baumgartner, such as E. Jenni, Baumgartner's successor at Basel; E. Nielsen, later professor at Copenhagen;[97] P. Raymond; R. Smend, later at Göttingen; and

J. Alberto Soggin, later at Rome. A number of Americans studied Ugaritic, Hebrew, and Old Testament in Basel at this period, including Brevard Childs (later at Yale) and John Marks (later at Princeton). Marks recalls Baumgartner as "a brilliant linguist, interested primarily in the *Realien* of history. He was also a modest and friendly person."[98]

Ugaritic at Leiden: P. A. H. de Boer, J. P. Lettinga, and J. Hoftijzer

In the Netherlands the tradition of Ugaritic goes back to P. A. H. de Boer at the Rijks Universiteit te Leiden. Shortly after World War II, he organized a study group for Ugaritic at Leiden.[99] W. W. Hallo of Yale University[100] recalled joining this group in 1950–1951. According to his recollection, the others in the class were T. Jansma, professor of Aramaic at Leiden from 1950; J. Hoftijzer, later a major scholar of West Semitics; the great Assyriologist R. Borger; the accomplished Hebraist J. P. Lettinga; and the Arabist A. J. Drewes. According to Hallo, the study of Ugaritic was new, and the students and professors were on about the same footing. J. P. Lettinga is perhaps best known for his grammar of biblical Hebrew *(Grammatica van het Bijbels Hebreeuws)*, but he also produced in 1948 a small introductory work for the general public, called *Oegarit (ras esj-sjamra), een nieuwe Phoenicische stad uit de Oudheid*, as well as articles on Ugaritic.[101] In 1952, Lettinga took a post as lecturer at one of the theological seminaries in Kampen (the Theologische Hogeschool van de Gereformeerde Kerken). In the early 1950s, Jansma began giving lectures on Ugaritic at Leiden. Beginning in 1962, in his capacity as *wetenschappelijk hoofdambtenaar* (roughly Associate Professor), Hoftijzer joined Jansma at Leiden in providing training in West Semitic languages, including Ugaritic. Hoftijzer's students of Ugaritic have included many eminent Dutch figures: M. J. Mulder, B. Hartmann, A. J. Drewes, K. R. Veenhof, M. Stol, J. Fokkelman, J. C. de Moor, W. van Soldt, and J. W. Wesselius.

Prague: S. Segert, J. Heller, and P. Zemánek

Eastern Europe produced no major programs of Ugaritic studies, but its scholars deserve mention. Charles University in Prague[102] produced few figures in the field, but they made significant contributions. The university's best-known product was Stanislav Segert (1921–), who took a doctorate in 1947 under Rudolph Růžička. In 1951–1958 Segert taught Ugaritic at the same institution to students including Stanislav Hermensky, Jan Heller, Jaroslav Oliverius (later professor of Arabic), and Vladimír Sadek (later professor of Jewish Studies). In November 1963, Segert worked as an archaeologist for the twenty-sixth season of excavation at Ras Shamra. After teaching at the University of Chicago in 1966 and at Hopkins in 1968–1969, he assumed a professorship at UCLA, where he served until his retirement in 1991. All the while, Ugaritic continued in Prague, thanks to Jan Heller.[103] Heller has had one major student of Ugaritic in Petr Zemánek, who has authored *Ugaritischer Wortformenindex*.[104] Zemánek also took one semester with Segert during Segert's visit to Prague in 1980. That Segert's class attracted the attention of twenty students attests to the interest that this subject commands in Czechia.

Jerusalem and the Literary Studies of U. Cassuto and S. E. Loewenstamm

The history of Ugaritic studies in Israel is an interesting one. As we noted in Chapter One, the tradition of Ugaritic studies began with H. L. Ginsberg and Umberto Cassuto at the Hebrew University in Jerusalem. Cassuto's student, Samuel Ephraim (Fritz) Loewenstamm (1907–1987), who had been trained in law at the Friedrich-Wilhelm Universität in Berlin, his hometown, succeeded him.[105] After his dismissal from his position as *Gerichtsreferendar* in the Prussian judiciary, he undertook formal Jewish studies at the Lehranstalt für die Wissenschaft des Judentums in 1936. In 1939 Loewenstamm emigrated to Israel, but it was only in 1951 that he took his master's degree from the Hebrew University, and his doctorate followed in 1962. In the meantime his reputation grew for his work on the *Encyclopaedia Biblica* and his role as editor in chief of the *Thesaurus of the Language of the Bible*. In 1962 he began as a lecturer at the Hebrew University and progressed through the ranks to full professor in 1971. He retired in 1975, at the age of sixty-eight. Like Cassuto his mentor, he paid close attention to literary features and conventions in the Ugaritic texts.[106] Occasionally, other scholars in Jerusalem, such as E. Y. Kutscher,[107] Yigael Yadin,[108] Moshe Goshen-Gottstein,[109] and Abraham Malamat,[110] also made contributions to Ugaritic studies. Ugaritic was taught by a variety of people at the Hebrew University: in addition to Loewenstamm, these included Z. Ben-Hayyim, E. Y. Kutscher, and M. Goshen-Gottstein. Loewenstamm's major student in Ugaritic was Yitzhak Avishur, mentioned in the next chapter in the section on Haifa.

⋈ ACADEMIC DEVELOPMENTS IN THE UNITED STATES

Grammar and Mythology at Yale:
A. Goetze and J. Oberman, M. H. Pope, and J. C. Greenfield

As noted in the preceding chapter, the Second World War brought both Albrecht Goetze and Julian Obermann to Yale from Germany. The works of the two men on Ugaritic have been largely surpassed, and nowadays in biblical studies their names are hardly remembered. However, their contributions extended beyond their own publications to producing important students of Ugaritic and the Bible, most notably Marvin Hoyle Pope and Jonas Carl Greenfield. Their backgrounds could hardly have been more different: Pope, born in Durham, North Carolina, a Methodist and a product of Duke University (1934–1939); and Greenfield, an Orthodox Jew bred in Brooklyn and a graduate of City College of New York (B.A. in English in 1949).

Pope's parents worked in a cotton mill. Writing of the year the Ugaritic texts were discovered, Pope talks about his early interest in religion:

> The year 1928 of the Common Era was notable in my own life because at the age of 12 I began my work experiences, first as a water-boy for bricklayers building tobacco warehouses and then as clerk and soda "jerk" in a Drug Store. The presidential election of 1928 was the beginning of my interest in religion, economics, and politics. I didn't even know there was a small RC [Roman Catholic] church in town when I heard that the Pope would move to the US if a Catholic became president. My boss was an ardent Democrat and he used the front windows of the store for political pronouncements. He had a set of Tom Paine's writings, Voltaire's Philosophical Dictionary, a Bible, and the Pharmacopeia. Between customers and chores, I read these books and found religious issues fascinating.[111]

Pope began his academic life at Duke University in 1934 and graduated with an A.B. in 1938 and an A. M. in 1939. He studied Hebrew with William Stinespring in 1936–1937. Yet Duke had long been part of Pope's life, as he would recall: "As a lad I roamed what was to become Duke Forest and watched the University being built."[112] Later Pope wrote: "Time and chance happen to all and Duke gave me an opportunity to pursue my interest. . . . My mother's early death at 57 was eased by her hearing of my graduation from her death bed in Duke Hospital."[113] He taught a semester of New Testament Greek at Duke in 1939 and then left for doctoral studies at Yale.

Marvin Pope. Courtesy of Ingrid Pope.

Pope might have pursued doctoral studies with Albright at Hopkins. After all, Pope first studied Hebrew with William Stinespring, Albright's brother-in-law. (Stinespring was also a friend of Albright's student, John Bright.) However, Stinespring's own teacher was C. C. Torrey at Yale and in 1939 Pope followed that path. Upon his arrival, Pope discovered the challenges of the Yale program. As noted in Chapter One, Goetze and

Obermann together taught him Ugaritic at Yale in 1939. As a result of the dis-
agreements between Goetze and Obermann, Pope's way through Yale was not
without its adventures.

After his studies at Yale with intervening war service (his doctoral studies
were interrupted by military service at a weather station in northern Australia),
Pope returned as an instructor in English Bible at Duke in 1947–1949. In 1949 he
completed his dissertation entitled "A Study of the Ugaritic Particles W, P, and M,
with an Excursus on B, L, and K." Albright later congratulated Pope on receiving
his doctorate and surviving the conflicts between Goetze and Obermann.[114] The
thesis was safe enough, showing how many of these particles' functions in
Ugaritic texts illuminated their use in biblical texts. With the completion of his
dissertation, Pope left Duke for a post at Yale:

> [I] supposed I might continue there [at Duke] for the rest of my life. But when I
> submitted my dissertation at Yale (on Ugaritic Particles) I was totally surprised by a
> job offer as Assistant Professor of Hebrew [at Yale] . . . The point of this missive is
> that I owe a great debt of gratitude to Duke which I could never repay in money but
> (while I still have breath in my mouth and thinks I have sense in my head) I could
> in part offer some specialized perspectives on erudition and religion touching the
> ancient background of the Bible.[115]

Pope returned to Yale as assistant professor in 1949, and later became Louis
J. Rabinowitz Professor of Semitic Languages.[116] From Goetze he had mastered
the linguistic details, and from Obermann he developed an interest in mythology.
Pope went beyond what his professors taught him, breaking new ground on a
number of topics, including deities and the devotion to the dead. His 1955 book,
El in the Ugaritic Texts,[117] combines a high level of philological work with a great
depth of religious knowledge in studying the traditions about El. Moreover, he
started his research program to devote a major study to each deity,[118] and in his
contribution to the 1965 *Wörterbuch der Mythologie*, he undertook just this
task.[119] With these studies a fresh voice emerged in the area of mythology, fully
supported by the fundamentals of philology. In the world of biblical studies, Pope
later became known for his learned Anchor Bible commentaries on the books of
Job and Song of Songs,[120] which brought Ugaritic to bear on many difficult textual and thematic difficulties. Reading the manuscript of the Job commentary
before publication (itself a sign of his interest in Pope), Albright called it "certainly one of the best of the Anchor series."[121] (An indication of the two men's relationship appears in Albright's signing these letters at this time with "William,"
an advance over "W. F. Albright," which shows up in the correspondence in the
1950s.) Pope's imagination sometimes ran ahead of the data available, yet his fer-
tile mind enriched the field.

In the meantime, Greenfield's 1956 Yale dissertation, "The Lexical Status of
Mishnaic Hebrew," offered master studies of etymological information.[122] This

dissertation traced complex relationships between many Ugaritic words and their cognates in biblical and Mishnaic Hebrew. In contrast to Pope, Greenfield led a peripatetic academic life. After two years teaching at Brandeis from 1954 to 1956, he served at UCLA from 1956 to 1965, and then he was professor at the University of California, Berkeley, from 1965 to 1971. Greenfield found his final academic home at the Hebrew University in 1971. He taught the full range of West Semitic languages and texts, including Ugaritic, until his death in April 1995. His most important work was his many important contributions to Aramaic language and lexicography, but he also returned regularly to questions of Ugaritic. Greenfield had a genius for the details. His control over many fields aided in his many sharp insights. Greenfield's mind moved so quickly that the articles flowed fast; by the same token, he regretted that he never stopped to produce a book of his own. Fortunately, this situation has been remedied. Greenfield's collected essays have appeared, thanks to Shalom Paul and Michael Stone (two of his former colleagues at the Hebrew University) and to Magnes Press. (The next chapter relates Pope's and Greenfield's tenures at Yale and the Hebrew University, respectively.) It is fitting to remember Pope and Greenfield together, for they not only were graduate students together at Yale but also were friends for over forty-five years.

Jonas Greenfield. Courtesy of Bella Greenfield and Joel Fishman.

Biblical Comparisons: W. F. Albright and F. R. Blake at Johns Hopkins

The postwar period was a golden age for the "Oriental Seminary" at Hopkins. With Albright at the helm of the program and F. R. Blake teaching West Semitic grammar, Hopkins thrived.[123] Unlike the wide-ranging comparative linguistic focus that Driver brought to Ugaritic from Arabic and Hebrew, the program at Johns Hopkins concentrated more on the Bible. Prior to the war's end, limited doctoral work on Ugaritic had taken place there, but the situation with dissertations changed dramatically in the postwar era. Ugaritic quickly came to play a larger role not only in Hebrew language but also in many other areas, including poetry, history, religion, tradition criticism, form criticism, and even occasionally textual criticism.[124] At Hopkins, grammar and poetic analysis remained central interests of Albright, and they became the driving force of doctoral research. For these subjects, Ugaritic played a crucial role. Already the grammar of Ugaritic as well as the structures of cola, word pairs, poetic syntax, and stylistic devices so clear in its poetry had already aided Cassuto, Ginsberg, Gordon, and later Gevirtz, Loewenstamm, and Tsevat in the study of Hebrew poetry.[125] The combination of historical grammar and poetic analysis was perhaps never so powerful as in the double dissertations of Frank Moore Cross and David Noel Freedman,[126] lifelong partners in scholarship.[127] Albright and even his teacher Paul Haupt had laid out some elements in the agenda of their doctoral project,[128] but Cross and Freedman advanced the discussion, building on earlier research by others in the field (such as Ginsberg) and adding their own formidable text-critical skills, inculcated not only by Albright but also by Monsignor Patrick Skehan, who was visiting profesor from the Catholic University of America in nearby Washington.

A third postwar dissertation directed by Albright was Moshe Held's 1957 study of Ugaritic lexicography.[129] Born in Poland in 1924 and an immigrant to Israel in 1935, Held was raised in Tel Aviv (he attended secondary school with Abraham Malamat).[130] After his studies with Cassuto at the Hebrew University (including a master's degree) and with Ginsberg at the Jewish Theological Seminary, Held began doctoral work with Albright and wrote his Hopkins dissertation while studying with Landsberger in Chicago. Held's work was a model of precision, demonstrating a very high linguistic and literary standard for comparison of words in different languages.[131] When he compared words, he not only identified cognates but also compared their contexts (especially poetic parallelism and genre) as well as their syntax and usage. In S. D. Sperling's fine summary:

> Held's work reveals the man's exceptional talent in lexicography, in which he synthesized method derived from his teachers, both immediate and removed, and made it his own. From Albright and Landsberger he learned to stress usage over etymology in comparative lexicography. Second, he followed Cassuto's insistence that comparisons take account of diction so as to distinguish among everyday language, technical language such as one finds in economic or ritual texts, and the language of poetry. Third, Held, with many scholars, relied heavily on parallelism in delineating the semantic range of lexemes. These three principles were steps towards plotting the "interdialectical distribution."[132]

If we compare the lexicographical studies of Driver with those of Held, what stands out in the latter's work is its combination of genre considerations with the wealth of Akkadian material, as well as a deeper awareness of medieval Jewish grammarians. One cannot help admiring Held's singular distinction of studying with Cassuto, Ginsberg, Albright, and Landsberger, whose methods he implemented with vigor and insight.

As these stories suggest, students came to Hopkins on the strength of Albright's reputation as a scholar of Bible, ancient languages and literatures, and archaeology. These figures included not only Cross, Freedman, and Held, but many others who would become important scholars of the Hebrew Bible and Dead Sea Scrolls, Semitics, and archaeology, such as Francis I. Andersen, Abraham Bergman (later Biran), Robert Boling, John Bright, Raymond Brown, Edward Campbell, Mitchell J. Dahood, Joseph A. Fitzmyer, George S. Glanzman, Victor Gold, Robert Hansen, John Huesman, Delbert Hillers, Samuel Iwry, Thomas O. Lambdin, Paul and Nancy (Renn) Lapp, George Mendenhall, William L. Moran, Frederick Moriarty, Jacob Myers, Roger T. O'Callaghan, Abe Sachs, Cullen Story, and G. Ernest Wright. Cyrus Gordon and Harry Orlinsky were post-doctoral students at Hopkins.[133] Other less well known figures there also pursued doctoral research on Ugaritic-biblical parallels: J. H. Patton, "Canaanite Parallels in the Book of Psalms" (1944); F. L. Feinberg, "Canaanite Influence on the Book of Job" (1945); H. Hummel, "Enclitic 'Mem' in Early Northwest Semitic, with Special Reference to Hebrew" (1955); P. Proulx, "Ugaritic Verse Structure and the Poetic Syntax of Proverbs" (1956); and F. J. Neuberg, "Ugaritic and the Book of Isaiah" (1959). The agenda of these works (and also R. G. Boling's 1959 dissertation entitled " 'Synonymous' Parallelism in the Book of Psalms") would anticipate the general approach that Albright's (in)famous student Mitchell J. Dahood would inculcate in his own students at the Pontifical Biblical Institute following the completion of his own 1951 Hopkins dissertation, "Canaanite-Phoenician Influence on Qoheleth." To judge from the sheer volume of correspondence regarding scholarships and other needs, Albright took considerable interest in his students and their careers. (As a single example, Albright underwrote the publication of Patton's dissertation, a work he regarded as "a model of its kind.")[134] His influence on students extended beyond Hopkins. For example, in 1941, James Pritchard, then a doctoral candidate at the University of Pennsylvania, wrote to ask him about a dissertation topic on figurines; Pritchard felt the project was looking like a dead end. Albright wrote back suggesting the topic of figurines of goddesses, an idea that eventually became the basis for Pritchard's famous work on the subject.[135] Albright also corresponded with Bernhard Anderson in 1943 concerning his Yale dissertation on the root *$špṭ$, "judge, rule."[136] The following year, Albright answered H. N. Richardson's request for advice about a dissertation topic.[137]

Another notable point concerning the historical importance of Albright and the Hopkins program was their openness to scholars of different religious backgrounds (this despite the university's attempts to impose restrictions on the number of Jewish students enrolled).[138] As a result of the openness at Hopkins, Albright trained talented figures from varied religious backgrounds. Few other programs of the postwar era would have had Moshe Held and Joseph Fitzmyer together in a Ugaritic class.[139] Albright's friendly relations with Jewish scholars had also long marked his career. In 1929 the Hopkins staff included two rabbis,

William Rosenau and Samuel Rosenblatt, and in 1936 Albright received two honorary doctorates from the Jewish Theological Seminary and the Jewish Institute of Religion, both in New York City. In a letter to the latter institution conveying his gratitude for the degree, Albright declared: "To associate with my Jewish colleagues and to collaborate with them in the advancement of our common interests have always been one of the joys of my scholarly career."[140] Later in the same year Albright deplored American anti-Semitism even as he saw it gathering force in Germany.[141] Albright refers occasionally in his correspondence to his "Jewish cousins" in Chicago.[142] Besides his students and two Hopkins postdocs, Cyrus Gordon and Harry Orlinsky, Albright enjoyed good relations with H. L. Ginsberg and Nelson Glueck.[143] In 1958–1959, the first year of his retirement, Albright spent a year at the Jewish Theological Seminary, with Shalom Paul as his research assistant.[144] In 1967 Albright received an honorary doctorate from Dropsie College. As the story of Dropsie College in the next section demonstrates, Jewish scholarship was already well established, but the contacts of Jewish scholars with Albright helped to spread their work to wider circles in the United States.

Despite the anti-Catholic prejudices in his background,[145] Albright became open to Catholicism and Catholics during his time in Jerusalem in the 1920s, even as he continued to be a practicing Methodist.[146] In October 1922, his wife, Ruth, converted to Catholicism and became a third-order lay Dominican,[147] thanks to her contact with the fathers at the Ecole Biblique, especially Père Vincent.[148] Through his wife's conversion, Albright had gained a greater appreciation of Catholicism. Later in life he briefly contemplated converting as well,[149] in part because of his unhappiness with the liberal trend of the Methodist Church, a feeling attested in his correspondence as early as 1941.[150]

Albright made a major impact on Catholic biblical scholarship in the United States. He trained many Catholics in Old Testament and the ancient Near East. Indeed, it may be noted that American Catholics entered the field of Ugaritic only beginning with the war period, before which they usually enrolled at the Catholic University of America in Washington or Catholic schools in Europe such as the Pontifical Biblical Institute. In his correspondence, Albright first mentions Catholic students, two of them, in the fall of 1937,[151] but according to Ruth Norton Albright,[152] it was the war that helped divert Catholics from Europe to Hopkins. Many of these (as Ruth Albright also observed) were Jesuits: Dahood, Fitzmyer, Glanzman, Huesman, McCool, Moran, Moriarty, and O'Callaghan.[153] Of these figures, O'Callaghan is today most obscure because he died young in a car accident in Iraq in 1954.[154] His body lies today in the cemetery of the former Baghdad College, a high school run by New England Jesuits until they were expelled from Iraq by the Ba'ath Party.[155] O'Callaghan did write an important study on the history of upper Mesopotamia, *Aram Naharaim*.[156] After his doctoral program at Hopkins, he taught biblical archaeology and history at the Pontifical Biblical Institute from 1946 to 1952, when he returned to the United States.[157] Albright's first Catholic student, O'Callaghan was in Albright's words "a very nice fellow and a brilliant linguist,"[158] "nothing short of brilliant."[159] David Noel Freedman describes him as "a favorite of Albright."[160] Fortunately, O'Callaghan's contribution included some Ugaritic notes, yet his influence continued beyond his short life: he had a number of students at the Pontifical Biblical Institute including Dermont Ryan, later professor of Semitics in Dublin.

Besides his Catholic students, Albright also enjoyed a good working relationship with Catholic biblical scholars. His 22 August 1944 lecture at the national meeting of the Catholic Biblical Association, held at St. Mary's College in South Bend, Indiana,[161] was published the following year in the *Catholic Biblical Quarterly,* the first article by a non-Catholic in the journal.[162] Albright became an honorary life member of the association. From 16 to 25 August 1946, he participated in the program of the "Biblical Summer School" sponsored by the Catholic Biblical Association at Niagara University. He shared the platform with the diocesan priest Monsignor Patrick W. Skehan, the two Jesuits J. J. Collins and M. J. Gruenthaner, and a Dominican, J. M. Vosté. Albright also worked with a number of established Catholic scholars, including Fr. Romain Butin and Fr. Albert Jamme, and he corresponded with many others, including E. A. Cerny and John Courtney Murray. Beginning in 1947, Skehan served as visiting professor at Hopkins while Albright was conducting excavations.[163]

Albright's acceptance of Catholic students and scholars contributed to Catholic scholarship in both Old and New Testaments. Doctoral students of Albright included the two greatest Roman Catholic scholars in New Testament in the United States after the Second World War, the greatly lamented Raymond Brown (1928–1998), S.S., and Joseph A. Fitzmyer (1920–), S.J. In the 1950s, Hopkins was an attractive program because, in Fitzmyer's words,

> We came to JHU [Johns Hopkins University] not only because of Albright's reputation as a biblical interpreter but also because JHU was the rare American University where future NT professors could be trained in the Semitic background of the NT and an ability to read the Dead Sea Scrolls, which were then just beginning to be published.[164]

Thanks in part to the Hopkins program with Albright at the helm, Catholic biblical scholarship became more ecumenical and matured significantly.[165] All in all, he nurtured an academic environment that helped shape the ecumenical environment of the biblical field as a whole. At the end of a thirteen-year retirement filled with publications and public lectures, Albright died on 19 September 1971.[166]

After his departure from Hopkins, the school enjoyed the services of Wilfred G. Lambert, Thomas O. Lambdin, and Delbert Hillers. Blake's student and successor, Lambdin left Hopkins in 1960 and Lambert departed in 1964. Hillers, at the time a recent Hopkins graduate, assumed Albright's chair as W. W. Spence Professor. He also took over Albright's editorial responsibility for *Biblical Archaeologist*, a venue for many Ugaritic articles throughout the postwar period. With the departures of Lambdin and Lambert from Hopkins, other scholars served as visiting professors of West Semitic languages; these included two great Jesuit scholars, Joseph Fitzmyer and George Glanzman, as well as Herbert Huffmon and Stanislav Segert.[167] Throughout this period, Hillers maintained the house that Albright built. He modestly quipped: "Ugaritic is a bit of a mystery, and I have done nothing to relieve that situation." In reality, he published many fine articles on the subject. Using his knowledge of Ugaritic and other Semitic languages, he became known for his Anchor Bible commentary on Lamentations, his Hermeneia commentary on Micah, his leadership as a cofounder of the Comprehensive Aramaic Lexicon project, and his copublications with E. Cussini of about two hundred new Palmyrene texts in a volume entitled *Palmyrene Aramaic Texts* (Baltimore/London: Johns Hopkins University Press, 1996). Despite the shifting fortunes of the Hopkins program in the 1960s and 1970s, it continued to produce impressive figures working on Ugaritic and related areas, including D. L. Magnetti, Simon B. Parker, James Rimbach, David L. Thompson, J. Ivan Trujillo, Bernard Batto, and later Michael Dick and Michael L. Barré. For Ugaritic studies we may point in particular to Parker's fine 1967 dissertation entitled "Studies in the Grammar of Ugaritic Prose Texts," and Trujillo's 1973 thesis, "The Ugaritic Ritual for a Sacrifical Meal Honoring the Good Gods (Text *CTA:* 23)." Sadly, after a long and productive career, Delbert Hillers died on 25 September 1999.

Looking back over the academic tradition of Hopkins, it gradually expanded from a center of German Semitic scholarship and then Palestinian archaeology to a program of scholarship revolving around the integration of available textual and archaeological materials from across the ancient Near East. Albright began his career there in the renowned Leipzig tradition of his teacher and predecessor, Paul Haupt, and during his teaching career he kept in touch with scholars not only in America and Palestine, but also in Europe (such as A. Alt, W. Baumgartner, J. Cantineau, F. M. Th. Böhl, H. Danby, W. Eichrodt, I. Engnell, A. Gardiner, J. Garstang, A. M. Honeyman, J. Pedersen, F. Petrie, T. H. Robinson, H. H. Rowley, C. F. A. Schaeffer, C. Virolleaud, C. Watzinger, E. Weidner, and H. Zimmern). And his respect for these scholars, especially Alt and Baumgartner (as noted above), was considerable. Regarding the former, Albright wrote to Theodore Robinson in 1929,

> I wonder whether you have seen Alt's brilliant monograph on *Der Gott der Väter*, just out. It is the best thing in the field of Old Testament religion since Mowinckel. You can make no mistake in reading every paper of Alt's on which you can lay your

hand. He is head and shoulders above all other Old Testament historians, including his old master, Kittel—for whom, incidentally, I have all respect.[168]

By the 1950s, Albright would also express considerable respect for his contemporaries in Europe, such as O. Eissfeldt. If many today think of Albright as a quintessentially American figure, with his appetite for solving problems, he was also a scholar in the German tradition, with its stress on encyclopedic knowledge of the fields. From his earliest days, Albright was an international figure, even as he "invented" an American school consisting of the "very good men" (as he sometimes referred to them) whom he had trained at Hopkins.

Philology and Comparative Literature at Dropsie College: T. H. Gaster, C. H. Gordon, and M. Held

The first major figure at Dropsie working squarely in Ugaritic was Theodor Herzl Gaster (1906–1992),[169] the son of Moses Gaster (1856–1939), the famous chief rabbi of the Sephardic Jewish community in London (the family name had been Castro according to the son's recollection). Great scholar and Zionist, the senior Gaster named his son after his friend, Theodor Herzl. When the junior Gaster was a boy, his father became blind, and the son used to read books to him; this experience furthered his interest in language and mythology.[170] His childhood friends included the Jewish luminaries Abba Eban and Isaiah Berlin.

Gaster took several degrees at the University of London (B.A., 1928, in Classics; M.A., 1936, in Near Eastern Archaeology; and an honorary D. Lit., 1971) and did museum work at the Wellcome Museum in London (1928–1932, 1936–1939). His M.A. thesis shows his early devotion to the Ugaritic texts: "The Ras Shamra Texts and the Origins of Drama." Even before the completion of the M.A., he wrote more than ten articles on Ugaritic that showed the skill and knowledge of a mature scholar.[171] Many of these reveal his early emphasis on the mythological texts as ritual drama. Besides his position in the Wellcome Museum, Gaster served as lecturer on Biblical and Near Eastern Archaeology at New College and Institute of Archaeology, University of London, from 1937 to 1939.

After losing his museum post as curator in the Department of Egyptian and Semitic Antiquities at the Wellcome,[172] Gaster arrived in the United States in the fall of 1939.[173] He next pursued a doctorate at Columbia, and in 1943 he completed a dissertation, "A Canaanite Ritual Drama: The Spring Festival at Ugarit."[174] While pursuing many other part-time jobs, Gaster taught at Dropsie College in Philadelphia (1944–1981). Gaster offered two courses during the 1944–1945 academic year, one on the "Religions of the Ancient Near East," and a second on "Religious Literature of the Ancient Near East." In 1945–1946 he taught "Introduction to Comparative Religion" and "The Sacred Scriptures of the World." In 1951–1952 the *Dropsie College Register* introduces two new titles,

"The Mythology of the Ancient Near East" and "Religion and Magic," and in 1961–1962 he added "Types of Ritual" and "The Idea of God in Ancient Religions." These course titles reflected Gaster's interest in comparing the religions of the ancient Near East, but his approach was not narrowly focused around the Ugaritic texts (except for his 1960–1961 course, "Religion of the Canaanites"). In 1954, Gaster became professor of comparative religion at Dropsie. He later assumed a full-time post at Barnard (1966–1985), and throughout the postwar period he taught part-time at Columbia (1942–1985). Even after taking his post at Barnard, Gaster continued to serve at Dropsie as a visiting professor through 1981. During this period he served as reader for a number of linguistic and poetry dissertations, even as recently as the 1970 Dropsie thesis of R. Bornemann. In 1978, Dropsie awarded Gaster an honorary doctorate for his achievements and his decades of service to the institution.

Even before his years at Dropsie, Gaster studied the ritual influence on, and background of, many of the Ugaritic literary texts. Armed with a keen philological sense and knowledge of the Bible, he tried to reconstruct a broad cultural setting for Ugaritic and biblical texts. At Dropsie, he published many works, including *Passover: Its History and Tradition* (1949),[175] which shows his wide-ranging interest in using folk customs and ritual practices to illuminate the background of the Jewish festival. This interest in ritual and folklore is already apparent in his M.A. thesis, and one may detect the influence of Sir James George Frazer's *The Golden Bough* even earlier. Indeed, Gaster's interest in literature and folklore parallel Frazer's literary and "anthropological" concerns closely despite their different focal points: Gaster's knowledge of the Bible and the ancient Near Eastern literatures served as his focus, in contrast to Frazer's intellectual "point of gravity" in the classics. The latter's influence on Gaster will be discussed later in this chapter.

A native Philadelphian and student at Dropsie in the 1920s, Cyrus Gordon returned to the school as professor of Assyriology and Egyptology from 1946 to 1956 after serving in military intelligence during World War II.[176] In 1946–1947 he offered three courses on "Great Literatures of the Ancient Middle East," one of which was "Ugaritic Mythological Poems." (Gaster continued to offer Ugaritic as well.) In the following years, this course was offered intermittently (1948–1949; 1950–1951, with *Ugaritic Handbook* and *Ugaritic Literature* as textbooks; and 1953–1954). During Gordon's Dropsie years, he also produced the *Ugaritic Manual* (1955). His course offerings included Sumerian and Akkadian, Egyptian and Coptic, "Hamito-Semitic," and history of the Middle East. Not knowing Egyptian very well when he became professor of Egyptology at Dropsie, he taught himself.[177] And his interests in this area were reflected in his supervision of the doctoral dissertation on Coptic by D. W. Young, later his protégé at Brandeis (see below). The *Dropsie College Register* for 1956–1957 lists both a course on Ugaritic and another on the Akkadian tablets from Ras Shamra, a topic of his doctoral students' research after he moved to Brandeis in 1956 to establish a program that flourished under his leadership (described in the following section).

With Gordon's departure from Dropsie, Moshe Held taught at Dropsie from 1957 to 1966. Held took over Gordon's Assyriology and Ugaritic courses, while Gaster continued his own teaching at Dropsie. Most years, Held offered one Ugaritic course. In 1957–1958 and 1960–1961, however, the *Dropsie College Register* lists both an introduction to Ugaritic and readings courses (consisting of Keret and the Baal Cycle). And in 1963–1964, Held taught courses on introductory Ugaritic, Akkadian texts from Ras Shamra (as well as Alalakh and Nuzi), and Northwest Semitic inscriptions, including Ugaritic. Following his dissertation (completed for Hopkins in 1957), Held continued his philological studies using his "interdialectical" method. In addition, he pioneered at Dropsie a comparative agenda in the area of poetic syntax, as exemplified by his essays "The *YQTL-QTL (QTL-YQTL)* Sequence of Identical Verbs in Biblical Hebrew and in Ugaritic" and "The Action-Result (Factitive-Passive) Sequence of Identical Verbs in Biblical Hebrew and Ugaritic."[178] As these two titles indicate, Held had particular insight into the use of verb forms in parallelism. Ugaritic perhaps never received more coverage in an American institution of higher learning than it did from 1957 until 1966, when both Gaster and Held served as full-time professors at Dropsie (before Held moved to Columbia).[179] (Together the two scholars would reprise these roles in the program at Columbia-Jewish Theological Seminary, as I will discuss further in the following chapters.)

Dissertations from the period 1945–1970 that Gordon, Gaster, and Held directed at Dropsie reflect the deeply grounded philological orientation of the institution. They include G. D. Young, "The Structure of the Poetry of Ugarit" (1948); W. LaSor, "Semitic Phonemes: with Special Reference to Ugaritic and in the Light of the Egyptian Evidence" (1949); L. N. Manross, "The Combinatory Method in Ugaritic Exegesis" (1950); F. E. Young, "The Epic of Baal and Anath: With Special Reference to Old Testament Literary Parallels" (1954); J. Kaster, "The Archaeological Background of the Ugaritic Texts" (1954); N. Sarna, "Studies in the Language of Job" (1955); D. W. Young, "The Coptic Tenses in the Writings of Shenoute" (1955); G. Schramm, "Judeo-Baghdadi: A Descriptive Analysis of the Colloquial Arabic of the Jews of Baghdad" (1956); R. F. Youngblood, "The Amarna Correspondence of Rib-Haddi, Prince of Byblos (EA 68–96)" (1961); W. Gerhardt, "The Weather God in Ancient Near Eastern Literature, with Special Reference to the Hebrew Bible" (1963); J. D. Falk, "The Plants of Mari and Ugarit: With Special Reference to the Hebrew Bible" (1966); L. L. Walker, "Studies in Ugaritic Grammar" (1966); F. R. McCurley, Jr., "A Semantic Study of Anatomical

Terms in Akkadian, Ugaritic, and Biblical Literature" (1968); K. L. Barker, "A Comparative Lexical and Grammatical Study of the Amarna Canaanisms and Canaanite Vocabulary" (1969); R. Bornemann, "Verbal Parallelism in Ugaritic and Biblical Poetry" (1970); and N. Waldman, "Akkadian Loanwords and Parallels in Mishnaic Hebrew" (1972). As this list indicates, Dropsie was a Jewish institution that opened its doors to Jews and non-Jews interested in the philological and religious study of the Bible and the ancient Near East. Moreover, Dropsie matched the faculty talent at other leading institutions.

In the 1970s, however, as more universities welcomed Jewish students into their doctoral programs and created graduate programs in Jewish studies, the raison d'être for Dropsie faded. Owing to a fire and financial difficulties, the institution moved on 1 January 1984 to the empty school building of Adath Israel synagogue on Highland Avenue in Merion (a western suburb of Philadelphia) and finally closed its doors in 1985. However, thanks to Walter Annenberg, the honorary chairman of its board of trustees, and under the leadership of David M. Goldenberg, Dropsie's last president and a 1978 doctorate, Dropsie returned to life in 1986 as the Annenberg Research Institute, which provided a home to postdoctoral research and seminars. In the fall of 1993, the institution merged with the University of Pennsylvania and became the Center for Judaic Studies. Today at its location behind Independence Hall on Walnut Street, it flourishes as a unique center for bringing together scholars, Jewish and non-Jewish alike, for yearlong conversations on Jewish studies. For the biblical field, the center devoted the 1997–1998 academic year to a program titled "Text, Artifact, and Image: Revealing Ancient Israelite Religion." The history of Dropsie is a glorious one.

Administrative Texts and "Hellenosemitica" at Brandeis University: C. H. Gordon and D. Young

One scholar in the early postwar era fostering an interest in Ugaritic ritual and administrative texts was Cyrus Gordon, who taught at Brandeis University from 1956 to 1973 (before filling his last post at New York University from 1973 to 1989).[180] Jonas Greenfield had already introduced Ugaritic into the curriculum at Brandeis during the period 1954–1956,[181] but it was Gordon who developed Ugaritic studies. His learned and talented students would color in many of the areas Gordon outlined in his writings. Baruch A. Levine (1930–) made ritual texts in Ugaritic and the Bible a lifelong interest,[182] beginning with his 1962 dissertation "Survivals of Ancient Canaanite in the Mishnah." David T. Tsumura (1944–), later devoted his dissertation to the one Ugaritic text clearly containing both myth and ritual, *KTU* 1.23.[183] Two other students, Anson Rainey (1930–)[184] and later Robert Stieglitz (1943–),[185] wrote on administrative and economic texts. Here Rainey continued some of the earlier "feudal" terminology in his discussion of Ugaritic society.[186] Other, less well known Brandeis doctorates also pursued Ugaritic topics during the 1960s and early 1970s: R. Y. Uyechi, "A Study of Ugaritic Alphabetic Personal Names" (1961); A. H. Lewis, "Ugaritic Place-Names" (1966); W. C. Kaiser, "The Ugaritic Pantheon" (1973); and J. T. Lee, "The Ugaritic Numeral and Its Use as a Literary Device" (1973).

Some of Gordon's students used the Akkadian texts from Ras Shamra to produce new insights into the formulas of administrative texts, while others pursued comparative subjects: G. G. Swaim, "A Grammar of the Akkadian Tablets Found at Ugarit" (1962); D. Kinlaw, "A Study of the Personal Names in the Akkadian Texts from Ugarit" (1967); M. C. Fisher, "The Lexical Relationship between Ugaritic and Ethiopic" (1969); and S. Ahl, "Epistolary Texts from Ugarit: Structural and Lexical Correspondences in Epistles in Akkadian and Ugaritic" (1973). Apart from Gordon and his students, the field showed limited interest in administrative texts,[187] in part owing to the biblical orientation of the scholars in it. Finally, Gordon fostered an interest in connections between Ugarit and surrounding cultures: H. Hoffner focused on Hittite with occasional attention to Ugaritic; W. A. Ward worked on Ugaritic and Egyptian; and F. Bush tackled Hurrian.

In the area of Ugarit's relations with its neighbors, the issue took a new turn in the 1960s, thanks to Anson Rainey's provocative observation that a person called a "Canaanite" appeared alongside other persons with other ethnic designations (e.g., "Egyptian" and "Ashdodite") in a Ugaritic text (*KTU* 4.96.7).[188] Rainey also observed a further reference to the "people of the land of Canaan" in an Akkadian text from Ugarit.[189] From these texts he deduced that the people of Ugarit did not consider themselves Canaanites. This historical issue impinged on the earlier discussion about whether or not Ugaritic was a Canaanite language.[190] Albright's reaction was not atypical. Citing Rainey's articles, he comments:

> This approach is decidedly misleading, since "language" and "nationality" are both fluctuating terms. For example, it would obviously be absurd to say that the Austrians and Swiss do not speak German because their countries are not part of Germany. . . . The fact is that "Canaan" was never, so far as we know, a national unit. The geographical extension of this term undoubtedly fluctuated, and we cannot attribute the same borders to it when we find it mentioned in different periods and literatures.[191]

Whether one should call Ugaritic Canaanite or not became both a linguistic and a historical issue. This question would remain problematic for decades.

To return to Brandeis, Gordon's contributions hardly ended with Ugarit and the surrounding cultures. He also inaugurated a wider comparative agenda between the Aegean world and the Levant, in an enterprise that his student M. Astour would dub "Hellenosemitica."[192] For example, C. McDowell wrote a dissertation on "Parallels between Ancient Greek and Hebrew Poets" (1965). The literary evidence for Levantine and Greek connections was sometimes clear, sometimes merely tantalizing. If in retrospect Gordon and Astour seemed to pursue specters with little methodological control, many scholars embraced their work.[193] (It would be especially attractive to Semitic scholars who trained in classical languages before their doctoral studies.) Nowadays, Gordon's research seems almost prophetic. The study of the eastern Mediterranean has emerged as a subject of special attention, thanks mostly to the sophisticated combination of archaeological and textual evidence from both the classical world and the Levant. Representing these advances on the Near Eastern side are J. Muhly, O. Negbi, and E. Puech,[194] and on the classical side H. G. Niemeyer, W. Burkert, and S. Morris.[195]

Unfortunately, Gordon and Astour did not have the benefit of doctoral-level training in classical literature. And, of course, they did not have access to later archaeological discoveries, such as the shipwrecks discovered off southern Turkey at Cape Gelidonya (ca. 1200 B.C.E.) and Ulu Burun (ca. 1300 B.C.E.).[196] They therefore deserve credit for investigating an area that enjoyed less respectability at that time. Soon, however, scholars would consider more likely cultural connections between the eastern Mediterranean and the ancient Near East, especially as they investigated questions, such as the date of the borrowing of the Phoenician alphabet by the Greeks[197] and the presence of Greek pottery during the Iron I period in the Levant.[198]

For decades Gordon's students would continue this line of research, as represented by the work of G. A. Rendsburg and his own student, S. Noegel.[199] Gordon also had a fundamental influence on Martin Bernal's famous and controversial work, *Black Athena,* published in two volumes in 1987 and 1991.[200] Aimed as a broadside against the field of classical studies, this work attempted to identify West Semitic influence as one of the bedrocks of Greek culture.

In retrospect, it was perhaps natural given Gordon's interest in "Hellenosemitica" that in the late 1950s and early 1960s, he would use his knowledge of classical and Semitic languages to pursue the larger challenge involving the decipherment of Minoan Linear A.[201] He also investigated the arrival of Indo-Europeans in northern Mesopotamia as well as Europe, as a means of accounting for parallels between the West Semitic and Aegean worlds.[202] Later in the 1960s Gordon would explore American connections with the West Semitic world,[203] and in the mid-1970s he would investigate the texts from Ebla.[204] All the while, he continued to offer advanced instruction in Ugaritic until his retirement from Brandeis in 1973.

He then moved to New York University, where he taught until 1989. To anticipate later developments, one should note that he continued his many interests, especially in the Ebla texts, but in the late 1980s he also began to venture further afield. In 1987 he started to explore the possible relationship between the Ugaritic alphabet and twenty-two Chinese letters that are not part of the repertoire of Chinese signs but appear to be cuneiform, deducing that they are not Mesopotamian but Ugaritic.[205] In the early 1990s, he studied the West Semitic words in the Bengali vocabulary known as Desi words.[206] As a result of these investigations, he concluded in 1998: "Intercontinental trade going back at least to Neolithic times supplied the impetus and since traders have to keep records, the idea of writing spread globally. . . . In the twenty-first century that is soon to dawn, Ugaritic studies should have more meaning than ever before."[207]

Gordon has been an adventurer throughout his academic life, and it is no accident that *A Scholar's Odyssey* is the title for his autobiography.[208] An Odysseus figure himself, Gordon traveled the Near East and Aegean and beyond not only by land and sea, but also by new texts and scripts. Explorations following the trail of newly discovered texts moved him from Akkadian and Aramaic to Ugaritic, from Ugaritic to Linear A, to the Phoenicians in South America, to the texts from Ebla, and then to China and India. Deciphering new texts opened ever-expanding horizons. Accordingly, his book *Forgotten Scripts*[209] reads in part like a record of Gordon's scholarly pursuits. The jury is still out on Gordon's views of Linear A, the texts from Ebla, or points beyond the Near Eastern and Aegean worlds, but the scope of his work elicits admiration.

Like the Hopkins program under Albright in the 1950s and later Harvard under Cross from the 1960s to the 1980s, Brandeis under Gordon in the 1960s enjoyed many excellent graduate students, including (in addition to those mentioned above) Loren Fisher, Martha Morrison, David Neiman, David Owen, Svi Rin, Jack Sasson, and Edwin Yamauchi.[210] Aiding the doctoral program there were colleagues, especially Dwight Young, who could provide the basic language instruction in Ugaritic.[211] One story about Young's teaching method, from Professor Joel H. Hunt, a student at Brandeis and presently a professor at Fuller Theological Seminary, deserves mention:

> Dwight believed in learning languages inductively. So the first day of Ugaritic, my first day in graduate school, Dwight handed out xerox copies of the cuneiform of the snake text UT 607 [*KTU* 1.100]. I had never seen this script, so I assumed that he would distribute some additional materials for the class. Much to my discomfort, and quickly believing that I had made a mistake in moving to Boston, Dwight returned to the desk at the front of the room and said, "Mr. Hunt, will you begin reading?" I looked at the paper before me, upon which was written an incomprehensible series of symbols and, trying to buy time, muttered, "Um." At this, Dwight complimented me and wrote the word *um*, "mother," the first word of UT 607, on the blackboard. He then turned to the other new student and said, "Now Mr. Stapleton, would you continue?"[212]

Many of the students of Gordon and Young hold major university positions in the United States. Loren Fisher, for example, built a program for Ugaritic studies at Claremont through the 1970s. Aided by his student Stan Rummel, Fisher was the guiding force behind the three volumes of *Ras Shamra Parallels*.[213] Highly influential in the 1970s and 1980s, these volumes documented in exhaustive detail the many parallels between Ugaritic and biblical texts that Gordon had long championed.

Philology and Translation at the University of Pennsylvania: E. A. Speiser, F. Rosenthal, and S. Rin

As the previous chapter recounted, Speiser returned to Philadelphia after his war service to serve as professor of Assyriology at the University of Pennsylvania from 1947 until his death in 1965. He is now perhaps best known for his commentary on Genesis, the first volume in the Anchor Bible series, which appeared the year before his death. Less well known were his occasional contributions to Ugaritic.[214] In one that reflects his fine training at Dropsie and Penn, Speiser demonstrated the varying correspondences between the forms of locative-terminative ending, the prefix consonant of the *C*-stem (e.g., Hiphil in Hebrew), and the prefix consonant of the independent third person pronouns. In Akkadian these forms are all *š*, and in many West Semitic languages this element is *h*; Ugaritic departed from this pattern in attesting a *h*-locative and *h*-prefix to the independent pronoun, but even as it exhibited a *š*-prefix *C*-stem.[215]

The prewar animosity between Gordon and Speiser continued to affect the course of Ugaritic studies in the postwar era. While Gordon was teaching at Dropsie, Speiser apparently blocked his candidacy in 1948 for a position in West Semitics at Penn by including Arabic in the job profile.[216] Speiser recruited a world-class scholar, Franz Rosenthal, instead. (After leaving Germany, Rosenthal first went to the Hebrew Union College in Cincinnati and was by this time an acknowledged expert in West Semitic languages, especially Aramaic, as well as Arabic.) Before leaving for Yale in 1956, Rosenthal taught Ugaritic[217] once, in 1950–1951, to three students: J. J. Finkelstein, Edmund I. Gordon, and Moshe Greenberg. Despite the talent of this small group, Ugaritic did not become a major area of research at Penn.

Penn remained a major program in Assyriology and Bible. Speiser in particular was one of the acknowledged postwar giants in the United States, and he produced many important doctoral students who would assume significant university posts. He was immensely productive and learned, and largely because of him, the Penn program was one of the most important in the postwar era in the United States. Despite what has been reported by Gordon (as detailed in Chapter One), the Penn program, and Speiser in particular, created an inspirational graduate experience for many doctoral students.[218] For example, Moshe Greenberg would write of "the collegial ethos" of the program, "an ethos that inspired everyone who was lucky enough to participate" in Speiser's weekly seminar on the "Interconnections of Oriental Civilizations."[219] Finally, the relationship between Gordon and Speiser affected the later development of the academic programs in Ugaritic and biblical studies: Gordon and Speiser would both depart from Dropsie. As a result, Dropsie lost the talents of two major scholars: Gordon moved to Brandeis, with Ugaritic as one of its major foci; Speiser, a graduate of Dropsie and Penn, left the first alma mater in a disagreement, and built his house at the second until his death in 1965. Two years later, Speiser's devoted students J. J. Finkelstein and M. Greenberg would publish his collected essays.[220]

In 1956, when Rosenthal left Penn, he was not replaced in West Semitics. A product of Brandeis, Svi Rin, though not hired for Ugaritic, did offer it in the early 1960s, and his students included Sol Cohen and Jonathan Paradise. In Ugaritic studies Rin was best known for his 1968 book, *'Alilot Ha'Elim (Acts of the Gods)*, a translation of the Ugaritic poetic texts (coauthored with his wife, Shifra, a Hebrew cataloger and book selector at the University of Pennsylvania libraries), as well as *Third Column of Acts of the Gods* (1979; rev. 1992), and a number of articles.[221] A superb Hebrew stylist, he originally came to Penn to teach Modern Hebrew, and he translated several works from Hebrew to English and from English to Hebrew, the latter including *The Wizard of Oz*.[222]

Other Programs

The various academic programs in Europe, Israel, and the United States exemplify the research conducted in the areas of grammar and philology, poetry and social structure. Other programs, not surveyed above, did not invest as heavily in Ugaritic, but they produced some dissertations in the field. I mentioned H. N. Richardson's 1951 Boston University dissertation above, and another BU dissertation was G. S. Thoburn's "Old Testament Sacrifice in the Light of Ugaritic Literature" (Th.D. diss., 1954). Elmer A. Leslie and Robert H. Pfeiffer were readers for both dissertations.[223] Victoria College (Toronto) sponsored W. Roth's "The Numerical Sayings in the Old Testament and in the Ancient Near East" (1959).[224] At the University of Michigan, George Mendenhall directed K. L. Vine's 1965 dissertation, "The Establishment of Baal at Ugarit." H. B. Huffmon's 1963 Michigan dissertation, entitled "Amorite Personal Names in the Mari Texts: A Structural and Lexical Study," drew extensively on Ugaritic evidence.[225] The University of Chicago produced two substantial dissertations in 1960 with the help of I. J. Gelb, R. A. Bowman, and others: S. Gevirtz's "Curse Motifs in the Old Testament and in the Ancient Near East";[226] and H. S. Haddad's "Baal-Hadad: A Study of the Syrian Storm-God." Another followed in 1964: W. E. Barr, "A Comparison and Contrast of the Canaanite World View and the Old Testament World View."

In 1966, U. Oldenburg wrote a Chicago dissertation entitled "The Conflict between El and Ba'al in Canaanite Religion."[227] M. Tsevat revised his 1953 Hebrew Union College dissertation, supervised by Sheldon Blank, and published it as *A Study of the Language of the Biblical Psalms*.[228] L. I. Stadelmann, a Swiss-born Jesuit, wrote "The Hebrew Conception of the World: A Philological and Literary Study" (1967, Hebrew Union College).[229] At Concordia Seminary in St. Louis, N. Habel completed a 1962 study on "A Conflict of Religious Cultures: A Study in the Relevance of the Ugaritic Materials for the Early Faith of Israel."[230] As these dissertations indicate, work continued intensively on grammar, poetry, and religion. On the literature of Ugarit, the dissertations of Tsevat and Gevirtz stand out. These combined lexicographical, grammatical, and poetic research similar to the previous studies of Ginsberg and Cassuto and like the contemporary dissertation research of M. Held. In addition to these doctoral programs and the scholars guiding them, other figures made contributions to the field during this period: J. Cantineau, M. S. Drower, K. Galling, R. Largement, E. Laroche, E. Lipiński, B. Mariani, R. du Mesnil du Buisson, N. M. Nicolsky, S. Spiegel, H. Stocks, and U. V. Struve.[231]

The research done on religion comes through imperfectly in the descriptions of these programs. The direction of the field cannot be appreciated without a closer look at research on both sides of the Atlantic. An illustrative case involves the so-called myth-and-ritual approach to Ugaritic and Israelite texts.

⋈ MYTH-AND-RITUAL STUDIES ON BOTH SIDES OF THE ATLANTIC

In the postwar era, the study of Ugaritic myth reached a new level of synthesis. As I noted above, book-length investigations of deities first appeared in the 1950s. On both sides of the Atlantic, the examination of Israelite religion showed advanced integration of biblical and Ugaritic textual material. Here I am thinking especially of W. F. Albright, F. M. Cross, and M. H. Pope in the United States, and A. Caquot, O. Eissfeldt, G. Fohrer, H. Gese, J. Jeremias, W. Herrmann, O. Kaiser, A. Kapelrud, K. Koch, E. Lipiński, H. Ringgren, and W. H. Schmidt in Europe.[232] Less important in Germany and the United States but extremely influential in Scandinavia and the United Kingdom was a ritually oriented approach to Ugaritic and biblical texts. This approach interpreted the two corpora as the products of cult. That is, the texts were used for cultic recitation, and they seemed to manifest a pattern of "myth and ritual," common to many cultures across the ancient world.[233]

Before the war, this approach was associated with Sidney H. Hooke,[234] and it spread rapidly in the United Kingdom and Scandinavia,[235] where it centered around Uppsala and the scholars Ivan Engnell (1906–1964) and Geo Widengren, as well as Engnell's successor, Helmer Ringgren (and his own student, Gösta Ahlström, later professor at the University of Chicago).[236] Other scholars showed a related interest with that of the so-called myth-and-ritual school,[237] notably Sigmund Mowinckel (1884–1965) and Arvid Kapelrud in Oslo; John Gray (1913–)[238] in Aberdeen; and Theodor Gaster (1906–1992), first at Dropsie College[239] and later at Barnard and Columbia. A constellation of topics sharing a ritual (and largely royal) background became the focus of the myth-and-ritual approach. Sacred or divine kingship and the New Year Feast throughout the ancient Near East (including Israel) had already drawn attention during the Second World War,[240] and soon other topics followed, such as "dying and rising gods."[241] With certain caveats, myth-and-ritual research, at least in England, had roots in comparative folklore studies, pursued before the turn of the century by Sir James George Frazer, W. Mannhardt, and others.[242] Indeed, much of the myth-and-ritual agenda appears in Frazer's classic, *The Golden Bough.*[243] Scholars other than those already mentioned applied this approach, and even if they critiqued those more closely associated with this method, one may speak of a "family resemblance" among them.

One should note that the biblical and ancient Near Eastern fields in Germany and the United States were hardly predisposed to myth-and-ritual research. Germany in this period enjoyed a well-established scholarly tradition of research grounded in form- and tradition-criticism as well as history of religion and language. The orientation toward myth also ran against the grain of the philological and historical orientation that dominated biblical scholarship in the United States.[244] Some of the objections involved the use of evidence,[245] but another issue concerned Israel's putatively historical and linear religious outlook in contrast to the mythical, cyclical religious orientation of its neighbors. Indeed, some Germans and Americans shared an emphasis on history as opposed to myth. The focus on covenant and law in biblical narrative, as stressed by Alt, Noth, von Rad, and others in Germany and by Albright, Wright, Mendenhall, and others in America, stood squarely against a myth-and-ritual agenda. It probably explains part of Albright's deep admiration for Alt and the convergence of theological views between Wright and von Rad. Indeed, the biblical theology movement, in both Germany and the United States up through the 1960s, laid considerable emphasis on a theology of the "mighty acts of God." Wright, partly influenced by Emil Brunner,[246] exemplified this agenda in his influential books, *God Who Acts* (1952) and *The Old Testament against Its Environment* (1950), as did von Rad in his monumental *Old Testament Theology* (1957)[247]

Scholarship must still explore the deep problem of labeling any ancient text either myth or history, as these terms are anachronistic for the ancient Near East.

The modern category of myth derives from an ancient critique of religion alien to the authors of the ancient texts (including the Bible), and the modern category of history differs from what the ancients understood as historical writing.[248] However, this point is getting ahead of our story. This cautionary tale begins with Sigmund Mowinckel.

⊠ SIGMUND MOWINCKEL AND THE FALL ENTHRONEMENT FESTIVAL

The work of Mowinckel offers a case study into the use of Ugaritic texts in biblical studies during the postwar period. In his *Psalmenstudien II* (1922),[249] Mowinckel had laid out a detailed theory of a fall enthronement festival,[250] reconstructing a feast, based on Pss 47 and 93–100, with a number of other psalms reflecting related themes (Pss 24, 65, 67, 68, 81, 84, 95, 118, and 132). The festival involved a number of themes: creation and its renewal; Yahweh's enthronement over creation and judgment of the nations; the revelation at Sinai and the establishment of the covenant; the giving of divine teaching; the procession of the ark; and the purification and rededication of the Temple. Mowinckel described the ritual procession with the ark as a reflection of a drama reenacting Yahweh's defeat over the cosmic enemies resulting in the renewal of creation. He situated this drama in the New Year festival known from Mesopotamian literature. Indeed, the Mesopotamian fall *Akitu* festival provided Mowinckel with an allegedly analogous ritual drama. In any case, Mowinckel returned to his reconstruction of the enthronement festival in his 1951 work, *Offersang og Sangoffer* (literally, "Offering-song and Song-offering"), which was translated into English in 1962 as *The Psalms in Israel's Worship*.[251] Mowinckel had no access to the Ugaritic texts in his 1922 *Psalmenstudien II*, but his 1951 *Offersang og Sangoffer* used the Baal Cycle to defend the reconstructed festival. Following Hvidberg and Gaster (discussed further below), Mowinckel saw this Canaanite fall festival as the background to the Israelite enthronement festival.[252]

Mowinckel's reconstruction and the subsequent criticism that it met have been fully critiqued.[253] For example, it was not clear whether some texts and themes fit a fall festival (such as the debate over Pss 50 and 81).[254] It was also evident that the reconstruction lacked some basic information. The notion of an annual ritual enthronement of Yahweh depended on a problematic interpretation of the expression *mālak yhwh* ("Yahweh has become king") as an acclamation of Yahweh's kingship during an annual ritual.[255] The accompanying ritual drama, with the procession of the ark serving to express the enthronement of Yahweh, also lacked convincing evidence. Van der Toorn has criticized the textual basis for any ritual combat in the *Akitu* festival[256] and has questioned the evidence for the recitation of *Enuma Elish* at that time. Moreover, the New Year's festival is never mentioned by name in ancient Israel. As a result, many scholars doubt the existence of an Israelite New Year's festival.[257]

⊠ BASIC EVIDENCE FOR A NEW YEAR'S ENTHRONEMENT FESTIVAL

Despite his criticisms, van der Toorn has defended the plausibility of such an autumn festival in ancient Israel, with modifications, and he has shown that none of the objections is insurmountable. Indeed, if we may prune back certain claims (such as the eschatological ideology of the feast in the preexilic period) and adduce further evidence, the core of Mowinckel's rich reconstruction retains merit. While his theory exceeds the evidence, some basic points may be made at the outset in its defense. I would amplify van der Toorn's presentation of evidence for a major feast in ancient Israel centered on Sukkot. In early texts, Sukkot is the early fall feast of the summer fruit harvest associated with the wine, accompanied by dancing and joy (Judg 9:27; 21:19, 20–21; Isa 16:10; 2 Macc 10:6; *m. Taʿan.* 4.8).[258] Judges 21:19–20 refers to the annual feast of Yahweh, and the context indicates that it coincides with wine making (i.e., after the harvest of the summer fruit, including grapes). Eli's suspicion that Hannah is drunk with wine makes sense in the context of the grape harvest at the time of Sukkot (1 Sam 1:14–15).[259] The northern and southern dynasties seem to regard the autumn as central to the royal cult. For example, the Jerusalem Temple was inaugurated in the fall (1 Kgs 8), an event accompanied by the procession of the ark. This event is recognized as "the feast" (*heḥāg,* 1 Kgs 8:2, 65; 12:32; cf. Hos 9:5 [?]), even as it goes unnamed (later rabbinic tradition taking "the feast" as one of the names of Sukkot). Jeroboam I is said to have instituted a parallel fall pilgrimage festival (1 Kgs 12:32–33).[260]

In later texts a festival occurs at the "end of the year" (Exod 23:16) or "turn of the year" (Exod 34:22). In the late biblical apocalyptic of Zech 14:16, all the nations will make a pilgrimage to Jerusalem. Whoever refuses to do so will not receive the rain (except the Egyptians, who will receive a different punishment because they have the Nile River and do not depend on rain). As this passage indicates, Sukkot marked the harvest of fruit and was the crucial time for the rain, the expected blessing of the season (Pseudo-Philo, *Liber antiquitatum biblicarum* 13.7[261]; *m. Taʿan.* 1.1–7). The rain in due season was anticipated with anxiety (Job 29:23), and at the time of Sukkot Israelites were to pray for rain (Zech 10:1) If rain did not appear, it was interpreted as a divine curse that would prompt public lamentation (Joel 2; *m. Taʿan.* 1–3).[262] To bestow rain is to bestow life on a land solely dependent on rain for water. Drought jeopardizes everything: crops, animals, humans, and the offerings to the deity who provides rain in the first place.

The Mishnah attests a water libation ritual performed at Sukkot (*m. Sheq.* 6.3; *Sukk.* 4.1, 9; *Zeb.* 6.2; *Mid.* 1.4; 2.6).[263] Its roots appear to be biblical (1 Sam 7:6; 1 Kgs 18:30–35).[264] Some of the Mishnaic passages (e.g., *m. Mid.* 2.6) discussing the water libation mention Rabbi Eliezer b. Jacob's citation of Ezek 47:1–2, itself a reference to the old idea of the cosmic life-giving waters that flow from beneath the Jerusalem Temple. The Talmud (*b. Ta'an.* 25b) remarks in a similar vein: "When the libation of water takes place during the feast, one flood *[thwm]* says to the other: 'Let your waters spring, I hear the voice of the two friends.' "[265] This passage may indicate that the water-libation ritual functioned as a gesture to accompany the prayers to induce rain.[266]

The symbols in the Jerusalem Temple emphasize the theme of divine enthronement. Mowinckel noted the cherubim throne in the inner sanctum.[267] And an insightful study by E. M. Bloch-Smith argues that a symbolic repertoire signifies the coming of the deity in the rains after the victorious battle with the cosmic sea (evoked by the superhuman-sized bronze sea), the homage paid to the deity in the form of sacrifices (the wheeled carts), the enthronement of the the divine warrior (the throne) and the deity's blessing upon the people (reflected in the names of the pillars, Yakin and Bo'az).[268] Bloch-Smith suggests that this ritual "narrative" is encoded in the symbolic repertoire of the Jerusalem Temple, and Ps 29 matching it thematically, element for element. The procession of the people (cf. Ps 68:25–28) and the ark (e.g., Ps 47:6 and the material cited in Pss 24 and 132; cf. 2 Sam 6; 1 Kgs 8) fit well in this larger context.[269] Admittedly, some evidence is problematic. For example, despite the widespread view that Ps 132 is preexilic, a postexilic date for the psalm has been argued.[270] The dating hardly precludes postexilic reuse of preexilic material. Van der Toorn likewise suggests a late monarchic influence on the ark procession in the Samuel and Kings passages.[271] Finally, it is striking that this festival continues "fourteen days in all" (1 Kgs 8:65), since the span of holy days from Rosh Hashanah through Yom Kippur to the beginning of Sukkot in the later Jewish calendar spanned about two weeks. Jewish tradition compartmentalized the symbolic and ritual repertoire of the autumn feast: in general terms, the renewal of creation was associated with Rosh Hashanah; divine judgment (Ps 94; cf. Ps 99), holiness, and purification (see Ps 93:5;[272] cf. 1 Kgs 8:64, Ezek 45:20;[273] Ps 65:4) with Yom Kippur; and procession and rain with Sukkot.[274] This is not to preclude the additional development of features of these three holidays.

Based on this evidence, the festival may have celebrated rain and the renewal of nature. Mowinckel stressed cosmic renewal in the festival, but van der

Toorn questions this point. Rain certainly expresses the renewal of nature, but whether rain signifies the earthly manifestation of the deity's renewal of the cosmos is unclear. The promotion of divine kingship at the season of the Israelite storm-god's greatest beneficence makes sense. Under the Davidic dynasty, divine kingship, indirectly promoting human kingship, perhaps emerged as a central theme of the festival. By the postexilic period, the theme of divine kingship would be linked to or perhaps displaced by the theme of Israel's sojourn in the wilderness after the Sinai revelation. Van der Toorn nicely summarizes: "It would be fairer to say that the rites as we know them met the need for a public confirmation of the social and ideological values of participants."[275] Stated differently, the rites evolved, celebrating an integrated vision of reality, stressing at different times a constellation of natural and historical aspects and varying social and political themes.

The question of the feast's name is not to the point. It is clear that in Mesopotamia the name of the fall *Akitu* festival derived from local conditions associated with the *akitu*-house.[276] Similarly, the names of Sukkot and perhaps the related feast of Rosh Hashanah were inner-Israelite developments that evolved from an older fall New Year's festival. The name "New Year Feast," however, misleadingly reduces the full complex of festival celebration, but the rejection of this detail of Mowinckel's theory hardly precludes the validity of his insights pertaining to the fall festival as a whole. Indeed, he downplayed the issue of the name.[277] He commented: "We cannot possibly draw a hard-and-fast line between the 'enthronement festival' and the great festal complex of which it is only a separate aspect."[278]

A further problem involves the gaps in evidence. The biblical material may reflect considerable range in time and place, as F. M. Cross[279] stresses in his discussion of Mowinckel and one that I will discuss shortly. V. Hurowitz pointed out that the fall festival in Mesopotamia differs widely among the many calendars (see those studied by M. E. Cohen).[280] Local variety is therefore to be expected at sites such as Jerusalem, Shechem (Judg 9:27), Shiloh (Judg 21:19–21), and Bethel (1 Sam 1:19; Amos 4:4).[281] Differences are not necessarily an indication of a weak theory; instead, they may reflect the social conditions and evolving historical practice.

Given Mowinckel's comprehensive and persuasive theory, it is not surprising that it has enjoyed considerable longevity. Mowinckel's approach appears in later research on Ugaritic and the Psalms, for example, in studies of the Psalms by John H. Eaton and John Gray,[282] in Johannes de Moor's monumental 1971 study of weather and ritual patterns in the Baal Cycle,[283] to some extent in a 1984 book by Oswald Loretz,[284] and in the unpublished work of Aloysius Fitzgerald and his students. Yet already in the postwar era, like-minded scholars would explore the possibilities that the Ugaritic texts offered. Two of the better-known figures drawing heavily from Ugaritic were John Gray and Theodor Gaster.

⊠ MYTH AND RITUAL IN THE WORK OF J. GRAY AND T. H. GASTER

In the United Kingdom, the myth-and-ritual approach played a role in the Ugaritic studies of John Gray (1913–).[285] Gray had taken his M.A., B.D., and Ph.D. at Edinburgh, and in the late 1930s he excavated at Tell ed-Duweir with J. L. Starcky. In 1936, Gray was the Blackie Travelling Fellow of Edinburgh University when he began his study of the Ugaritic texts in the library of the Ecole Biblique in Jerusalem.[286] From 1939 to 1941 Gray served as chaplain to the Palestine Police in the northern area of Palestine, where he learned Arabic.[287] After serving for a half dozen years as a minister in the Church of Scotland, he came to Manchester in 1947 first as an assistant lecturer and later a lecturer in Semitic Languages and Literatures (with H. H. Rowley). In 1952 Gray became lecturer in Hebrew and Biblical Criticism at the University of Aberdeen and a decade later became professor of Hebrew and Semitic Languages. There he established the first program of Ugaritic and biblical studies in Scotland, and many of his students became prominent in their own right: W. Johnstone (later Gray's successor at Aberdeen),[288] G. Cowling, P. C. Craigie, K. T. Aitken, W. G. E. Watson,[289] D. J. Weston, and J. Elwolde.

Gray worked on the Ugaritic economy,[290] but his primary focus lay in Ugaritic literature and religion.[291] In this area his main scholarly influence was Mowinckel, in particular his *Psalmenstudien*.[292] Like Mowinckel, Gray entertained ritual contexts even for texts that lacked ritual indicators. According to Gray, the texts of the Baal Cycle

> relate to the rituals throughout the agricultural year, being originally designed, we believe, to make the significance of such rites explicit and to double their efficacy. These were in fact the effectual word as counterpart and complement to the effectual rite, both having the purpose of influencing the deity by auto-suggestion.[293]

Yet Gray admits: "We unfortunately do not know the rites associated with this myth."[294] Another case in point was Gray's study of Krt (also Keret or Kirta; *KTU* 1.14–1.16).[295] He interpreted the text as "a glorified version of the marriage blessing," with some possible "association with the cult," perhaps even on "the New Year Feast."[296] Moreover, "The consummation of the marriage, and especially the royal marriage, in turn, would serve the purpose of a rite of sympathetic marriage on the eve of the new agricultural year."[297] In his many books and articles, he continued to emphasize the fall New Year Feast as the ritual context for texts, including in his most recent work, *The Biblical Doctrine of the Reign of God*.[298]

This approach to the Ugaritic texts (especially the Baal Cycle) and the Bible (especially the Psalms) was influential throughout the 1950s and 1960s in the United States. Theodor Herzl Gaster's synthesis *Thespis* exemplifies this direction.[299] At Barnard and Columbia, Gaster added a further dimension to the Ginsberg-Mendelsohn (later Held) team at Columbia-JTS[300] insofar as he worked on a broader literary and comparative agenda. *Thespis* traced basic patterns or types of myth and folklore across the ancient Near East and the classical world— indeed, around the globe. Gaster was profoundly influenced by Sir James George Frazer's *The Golden Bough*,[301] so much so that in 1959 he produced an abridged version, *The New Golden Bough*.[302] To cite only one example of their similar thinking, both Frazer and Gaster posited a seasonal background to the mythology of the "dying and rising gods." For both scholars, rituals celebrated the death and revival of these deities according to the seasons.[303] Armed with a far greater knowledge of the ancient Near East and the Bible, Gaster extended Frazer's approach to Ugaritic mythology by comparing it to the folklore of many different cultures, both ancient and modern. He viewed ritual as the context for the production and recitation of a culture's myths, and his parade example from Ugaritic was the Baal Cycle. Here he followed a long line of scholars, including Virolleaud, Dussaud, Hvidberg, and Gray.[304] Gaster formulates this as follows:

> . . . seasonal rituals are accompanied by *myths* which are designed to present the purely functional acts in terms of ideal and durative situations. The interpenetration of the myth and ritual creates *drama*. . . . The texts revolve around different elements of the primitive Seasonal pattern, some of them concentrating on the ritual combat, others on the eclipse and renewal of kingship, and others again on the disappearance and restoration of the genius of topocosmic vitality . . . myth is not . . . a mere outgrowth of ritual, an artistic or literary interpretation imposed later upon sacral acts; nor is it merely . . . the spoken correlative of "things done." Rather, it is the expression of a parallel aspect inherent in them from the beginning; and its function within the scheme of the Seasonal Pattern is to translate the punctual into terms of the durative, the real into those of the ideal.[305]

Gaster's application of ritual theory to the Baal Cycle involves ritual drama. Baal's fight against Yamm mirrors the cosmogonic battle with the "dragon" (or "monster").[306] The house of Baal is the enduring counterpart of the annual installation of the king. The Baal-Mot conflict introduces the motif of the dying and reviving god. The end of the cycle describes ritual wailing for Baal ("a projection of the seasonal ululations"), usurpation by Athtar ("a projection of the interrex"), the restoration of Baal through Shapshu ("a projection of the solar aspects of the seasonal festival"), and the final defeat of Mot ("a projection of the Ritual Combat"). Gaster concludes: *"On both internal and external grounds, therefore, there is every reason for seeing in the Canaanite Poem of Baal a seasonal myth based on the Traditional drama of the autumn festival."*[307] Another feature of Gaster's interpretation, widespread in the postwar era, was an assumption that the same ritual backgrounds applied to texts from different periods and places. He groups features common to myths from various areas: "What is at issue is, in fact, the history of the literary genre as a whole, not of the particular compositions."[308] The explanatory power of Gaster's interpretation was immense. His work achieved a massive synthesis tying cosmic and royal dimensions into the religious nature of the Baal Cycle and the seasonal realities facing Ugaritic society, along with the ritual medium that expressed them.[309]

⋈ THE CONTRIBUTION OF J. C. DE MOOR

Up to the 1960s, myth-and-ritual research focused its attention on the myths from Ugarit. J. C. de Moor contributed to the debate by adding one crucial royal ritual to the corpus of texts considered relevant to a fall festival of the sort that Mowinckel and others envisioned. De Moor argued further for such a festival based on two exemplars of the same text, *KTU* 1.41.1–49 = 1.87.[310] De Moor is right to draw attention to this text because it ritually celebrates the fall vintage and provides evidence for the chronological arrangement that also structures the Israelite fall festivals. That the vintage is ritually marked is evident from the opening lines of the text:[311]

byrḫ rʾiš yn	In the month of First Wine,
bym ḥdṯ	On the day of the (new) moon (= the first day),
šmtr ʾuṯkl	a cutting of a cluster (of grapes)
lʾil šlmm	for El: a *šlmm*-offering.

The text does not explicitly call this day a New Year festival, but merely the first day of this autumnal month. The text places relatively little importance on this celebration but seems to focus more on the rituals for the fourteenth day of the month. Lines 3–48a describe this ritual complex for the fourteenth day in much greater detail than is the case in the mere two lines devoted to the first day of the month. The ritual begins with the royal washing on the thirteenth day (line 3). The fourteenth day is the focus of offerings and other royal actions, both in the morning and at midday (lines 4–38a). The ritual then shifts to offerings made on "the fifth day" (lines 38b–45a), "the sixth day" (lines 45b–46), and "the seventh day" (lines 47–48a). These are the last three days of the seven-day celebration of the festival initiated on the fourteenth day. It would appear then that the first day of the month served as a prelude to the more extensive seven-day festival in the middle of the month.[312] In short, de Moor deserves credit for drawing attention to the importance of this text for the reconstruction of the West Semitic fall festival.

The comparison with biblical texts seems evident. Numbers 29 and other biblical texts indicate that the Israelite calendar has three fall feasts.[313] Numbers 29 preserves a proximate temporal structure for the fall ritual cycle (with the Day of Atonement added): the first day in verses 1–6; the tenth day (identified in Lev 16 as the Day of Atonement) in verses 12–16; and the fifteenth day followed by days two through eight of this holiday in verses 12–38. This fifteenth day initiates an eight-day festival comparable to the seven-day celebration beginning on the fourteenth day in *KTU* 1.41//1.87. Like the Ugaritic evidence, the biblical texts emphasize this third holiday. When we compare *KTU* 1.41//1.87 to biblical texts, two major differences emerge. The first is the emphasis on the first day of the month as the first day of the year. Clearly the Ugaritic and biblical evidence indicate that royal ritual could take place on this date. The increased importance that the "New Year" day assumes in biblical tradition represents a secondary Israelite development perhaps under the influence of the Babylonian calendar, as the later month names suggests. Many of the priestly references treat this day primarily as a celebration of the new moon of the seventh month (so Lev 23:24; Num 29:1–6), while other biblical versions of the festival calendar omit the day altogether (so Exod 23 and 34; cf. the different chronological arrangement of Neh 8). In short, there is little evidence for an indigenous Israelite New Year festival apart from Sukkot.

The second difference involves the emergence of Yom Kippur (Day of Atonement) in the Israelite calendar. The importance of this day, while grounded in indigenous tradition of communal repentance and lamentation,[314] may have grown under Mesopotamian influence. [315] Other external influences and internal developments undoubtedly had an impact over the long history of the fall festival complex.

Despite the plausibility of this overall reconstruction of the West Semitic fall calendar, two major problems remain for positing an enthronement festival complex for Ugarit as many writers reconstructed it. The first involves the apparently minor importance of the fall festival at Ugarit, even if it is possible to understand how de Moor and others can construe elements associated with the fall (such as references to the rains, a fall harvest, and the consumption of wine) as evidence for such a festival. Yet it is striking how the Ugaritic royal rituals speak so "quietly" of a fall festival.[316] It may be impossible to preclude such a festival, but evidence for it is weak. Perhaps we should understand the evidence to mean that a purely literary production on the theme of "divine enthronement" predominated at Ugarit. There may have been no massive royally sponsored enthronement ritual of the sort posited by Mowinckel and others. In this case, myth would function independently of ritual. The second problem involves the appropriateness of correlating the ritual information and the mythological texts, as de Moor and his myth-and-ritual predecessors did. This issue is the subject of the following retrospective sections.

⋈ MYTH AND RITUAL IN RETROSPECT

The work of J. C. de Moor marks the last flowering of the main myth-and-ritual studies at the end of the postwar period. At this point we may offer some further reflections on "myth and ritual" and the Ugaritic texts. Early on, Mowinckel and others argued that the Baal Cycle showed Baal to be a "dying and rising god" whose death part of the Canaanite festival ritually lamented. In his reconstruction of the Canaanite fall festival, Mowinckel and other scholars assumed a ritual celebration of Baal's death and resurrection on the basis of the literary presentation in the Baal Cycle. The view, even in modified forms, continues to exert great influence, as one may see from a passing remark by F. M. Cross in his 1998 book, *From Epic to Canon:* ". . . the Ba'l cycle served in some sense as an accompaniment to the New Year's Festival. . . ."[317]

Yet, was Baal of Ugarit a "dying and rising god"? Here discoveries made since Mowinckel's time contribute something new to this discussion. At the outset, I would argue that there is no firm category of the kind according to the terms set forth by Sir James George Frazer.[318] Dumuzi and Adonis hardly resemble Baal, or Osiris for that matter. Moreover, there are approximately seventy ritual texts from Ugarit, but not one of them clearly reflects the notion of Baal as a "dying and rising god." Instead, the only clear ritual evidence pertaining to Baal's death and return to life comes from a funerary text attesting the royal cult of deceased tribal and royal ancestors. This royal funerary text, *KTU* 1.161, does not support a ritual background behind the literary description of Baal's death and return to life, but it does point to the application of ritual material from the royal funerary tradition to the literary presentation of the figure of Baal.[319] This claim may be supported by the four major features that this funerary text shares with the Baal-Mot (Death) section of the Baal Cycle (*KTU* 1.5–1.6), especially 1.5 VI–1.6 I (here the studies of B. A. Levine and J. M. de Tarragon as well as T. J. Lewis and G. A. Anderson are instructive):[320]

First, in the Baal Cycle, El and Anat both mourn the fallen Baal. In order to lament him properly, El descends from his throne to his footstool and then from his footstool to the dust and finally utters words of lamentation (1.5 VI 11–25a). After similarly lamenting (1.5 VI 31, 1.6 2–10), Anat conducts the proper burial of Baal's corpse (1.6 I 10–18a). *KTU* 1.161 reflects a similar pattern of funerary practices. The family of the deceased king performs the funerary liturgy in order to lament him. Moreover, lines 14–15 call on the royal table and footstool to engage in lamentation by weeping, a means of signaling the sorrow expressed by the royal participants who customarily use these pieces of furniture. As Levine and de Tarragon note, the "appurtenances *swallow* their tears [*KTU* 1.161.15–16], just as Anath *drinks* her tears [*KTU* 1.6 I 9–10]."[321]

Second, in the ritual, either the deceased Niqmaddu[322] or, perhaps more likely, the living king Ammurapi[323] moves the deceased ancestors into the netherworld. In the myth Anat, Baal's sister, locates him in the underworld.[324] Levine and de Tarragon note the wording shared by the two texts and a third text as well, namely Jacob's words spoken in mourning the loss of his son Joseph (Gen 37:35):

Liturgy: ʾaṯr bʿlk ʾarṣ rd,
After your lord(s) *(bʿl)* to the underworld descend. (1.161.20–21)

Myth (1): ʾaṯr bʿl ʾard bʾarṣ,
After Baal *(bʿl)* I will descend into the underworld. (1.5 VI 24b–25)

Myth (2): ʾaṯr bʿl nrd bʾarṣ//ʿmh trd nrt ʾilm špš,
After Baal *(bʿl)* we will descend into the underworld.
To him descends[325] the Divine Light, Shapshu.[326] (1.6 I 7b–9a)

Family Legend: kî-ʾēred ʾel-běnî ʾābēl šěʾōlâ,
"For I will descend to my son in mourning to Sheol." (Gen 37:35)

In the myth Anat, the sister of the deceased, declares her intention to descend to the underworld. The liturgy apparently calls on the family member, the king, to make a similar ritual descent. Illustrating the close relationship between royal funerary ritual and the literary setting of the Baal Cycle is the use of *bʿl* for the deceased human king in the ritual and the divine king in the myth.[327]

Third, as Anat's words to Shapshu in 1.6 I 7b–9a indicate (quoted above), the sun-goddess accompanies the mourning family member in the ritual descent. Levine and Tarragon comment:[328] "In the myth, the descent into the netherworld is accomplished by a goddess. In the ritual, it is acted through recitation." As the quote above shows, 1.6 I 7 reads the plural *nrd*,[329] indicating that Anat intends Shapshu to join her, and the following line explicitly mentions the sun-goddess's attending role in the ritual descent. In the myth, Shapshu and Anat descend together and remove Baal's corpse from the underworld in order to render it a proper burial (1.6 I 10b–18a). In the ritual, too, Shapshu participates in the ritual directions to make the ritual descent into the underworld (*KTU* 1.161.18–19). The directions may even direct her to "burn bright" *(ʾišḫn)* in order to illuminate the underworld. Or, if this verb is to be taken in the sense of descent, then it would cohere with the sun-goddess's well-known night journey through the underworld (see 1.6 VI 45a–53). Accordingly, she plays the role of intermediary between the realms of life and death. The same wording introduces her two speeches in the myth and the ritual: *ʿln špš tṣḥ*, "On high Shapshu cries out" (*KTU* 1.6 VI 22b–23a; 1.161.19).

Fourth, a less noticed point is that both the funerary liturgy (*KTU* 1.161.27–30) and the mythological presentation (*KTU* 1.6 I 18b–29 [or 31?]) end the funerary rites with a series of offerings.

To judge from these four points of comparison,[330] the tradition of royal f neral ritual practice (though perhaps not this text specifically)[331] has influenced the presentation of Baal's death and return to life.[332] This influence operates at the level of specific wordings and motifs. Baal's death is modeled after human royal death as attested in *KTU* 1.161, much as other mythological presentations of deities imitate human experience. A later reflex of the idea of Baal's return to life may appear in the first-millennium royal funerary text of Panammu of Samal (*KAI* 214.21). Here a deceased king may eat and drink with the great West Semitic storm-god.[333]

Baal's fate in the Baal Cycle mimics that of Ugarit's dynasty, both the deceased king and his living successor. Kings died, but they were thought to have a continued existence in the afterlife.[334] Moreover, their successors continued the dynasty and its role in Ugarit. *KTU* 1.161 witnesses to these aspects of royal life. The text, at once mourning the deceased king and identifying his living successor, ultimately celebrates the link between the two; indeed, the text's list of ancestors highlights dynastic continuity, the common "baal-ship" of both deceased and living kings.[335] Baal's death reflects the demise of Ugaritic kings, but his return to life heralds the role of the living king in providing peace for the world. The storm-gods of Hatti disappear, sleep, and return at will, and ritual propitiation was the price of their return. In contrast, Baal does not choose to disappear.[336] His special form of disappearance, death, accords on the literary level with the weakness that Baal manifests throughout the cycle.[337] This divine death likewise mirrors the potential failure of agricultural fertility and other threats confronting human society as a whole and, in particular, the maintainer of societal order, the monarch. The Baal Cycle offers a literary rendering of the god that encodes the fertility and fragility of life on the natural, human, and cosmic levels. So, at this point the evidence provides a literary representation of Baal's death. Unfortunately, however, the texts do not preserve a description of his return to life (after a gap the text describes Baal alive again). There is thus no evidence for the ritual celebration of Baal's death and resurrection, a fact that seriously undermines the notion of a ritual component in the definition of "dying and rising gods" as Frazer, Mowinckel, Gray, Gaster, and others understood the concept.

Less known in the scholarly community is the more recent attempt by A. Fitzgerald to bolster Mowinckel's and Gray's work through a detailed analysis of the language for weather in the Psalms and prophetic corpus, which led him to conclude that weather patterns in many biblical texts suggest the centrality of autumn in the thinking of ancient Israel. In his review of Gray's *The Biblical Doctrine of God*, which drew heavily on Mowinckel's work, Fitzgerald gives hints of his approach:

> What I am ultimately suggesting is that, for the believer [of Mowinckel's theory], this monograph will be a welcome and attractively presented confirmation of his faith; that those who have not believed Mowinckel will not believe Mowinckel as presented by Gray; that more work is needed in the trenches before this kind of superstructure can be built. That has been the problem from the start. Mowinckel,

in presenting his hypothesis that explains so much, tended to write *about* texts too [as opposed to working through them detail by detail].

In particular, two problems with Mowinckel's preexilic New Year, the foundation of Gray's whole superstructure, have to be addressed more seriously. Some explanation has to be given for the gulf that exists between Sukkoth as revealed by the liturgical and historical texts in prose and the New Year uncovered by Mowinckel in basically poetic texts. Some way has to be found to tie Mowinckel's New Year more directly to Sukkoth or at least the autumn. For the second problem a partial solution is suggested here. Both Mowinckel and Gray understand Sukkoth as a New Year feast because it is located just before the coming of the first rains and the start of the agricultural cycle. It is remarkable how many of Mowinckel's texts are shot through with precisely this imagery though little attention is paid to it.[338]

Fitzgerald directed two dissertations that helped to establish a connection between the weather of the autumn and Sukkot and to investigate the accompanying language of divine kingship. One student, M. Futato, wrote on the meteorology in Pss 29, 65, and 104,[339] while another, K. Nash, examined the weather patterns mentioned in the book of Joel.[340]

Briefly, Fitzgerald and his students argued that only one time of year fits the weather patterns of specific psalms, namely, the fall when the desiccating east winds give way to the rain-bearing clouds driven by the westerly winds. For a brief period, the two sets of wind alternate, until the west winds finally predominate and the east winds desist; the result is the arrival of the fall rains. (Fitzgerald calls this "the fall interchange period.") Accordingly, biblical texts that emphasize rain and the storm theophany could be located in the context of the autumn festival, Sukkot. The time of year that would best fit the combination of no rain followed by rains and a feast is the fall period when the rains come from the west.

Candidates for Sukkot psalms include Pss 29, 65, 68, and 85, although they are not reflections of a single liturgical complex, as they vary widely in date and point of origin. H. L. Ginsberg early on observed the parallels that Ugaritic provided for Ps 29.[341] This text describes the procession of the storm-god terrestrially manifest in the rains moving from the Mediterranean Sea across the Lebanon and Anti-Lebanon mountain ranges and then into the Syrian desert. Psalm 29:9c mentions in the context of the eastward-moving storm theophany that the divine glory *(kābôd)* becomes visible in an unnamed temple.[342] A similar setting may be posited for Pss 65, 68, and 85. Psalm 65:5 refers to the rich fare of the Jerusalem Temple, and then vv. 6–14 ask Yahweh for rain that will bless the earth with growth. Psalm 68:8–10 makes specific reference to theophany and rain.[343] Psalm 85:13–14 refers to the divine bounty of the land and then the procession of Yahweh, connecting rain with a theophany.

Psalms 29, 65, 68, and 85 derive from different periods and locations. Psalms 29 and 68 seem to be earlier than the other psalms, the first being northern (or originally non-Israelite?) and the second drawing on southern traditions.

Psalm 65 may be later and belongs to the Jerusalem cult. Psalm 85 may derive from the northern kingdom (note the reference to Jacob in v. 2). It is also difficult to know whether these psalms derive from a specific cultic setting. For example, while Ps 63 may draw on the imagery of the fall rains and Sukkot, it is entirely metaphorical: in v. 2 the psalmist describes himself as parched like a waterless land and then in v. 6 as one sated on the rich fare of the Temple. It is also possible that Ps 65 draws on the imagery of the fall rains without being located in a specific Sukkot setting. Psalms 29, 68, and 85 are probably not metaphorical in the same manner, but they may refer to different points in the fall period. Psalm 29 charts a fall storm, possibly at Sukkot; and this feast is named as the time frame for the psalm in its superscription in the Septuagint. The setting of Ps 68 is very unclear, given the difficulty of the language in general. Psalm 85 is a thanksgiving for rain or a lament for the delayed rain, depending on how the verbal forms are to be understood. In sum, Pss 29, 65, 68, and 85 reflect disparate geographical and temporal backgrounds. Therefore, they hardly appear connected to one another or to other psalms in a Sukkot liturgy.

In contrast, Pss 93 and 95–100 may constitute some sort of Sukkot complex. All six of these psalms involve theophany and divine kingship. For example, Ps 96:11 refers to the roaring sea, thus evoking a storm that bears the theophany of Yahweh mentioned in the previous verse. The fields and trees of the forest therefore have good reason to "shout for joy at the presence of Yahweh, for He is coming" in the storm in v. 12. Psalm 97 presents an additional feature, a theophany (vv. 2–5) not from the west, but the east. The images of fire and cloud (ʿānān) do not suggest a rainstorm, but the windstorm coming from the eastern desert. Psalm 97 can be read with the other psalms in Pss 95–100, as the autumn witnesses the east and west winds alternating until the west wind brings the rains. This extended metaphor serves as the victorious sign of Yahweh's abundant care for Israel.

In view of the thematic congruence and juxtaposition of Pss 93 and 95–100, Fitzgerald's use of these psalms in support of Mowinckel's thesis has merit. It is unclear, however, whether these psalms were part of the Sukkot liturgy or secondarily inspired by it. The difficulties with the first alternative are that the texts lack liturgical characteristics (e.g., communal refrains), and, as Ginsberg noted, Ps 96:7–9 depends on Ps 29:2–3.[344] The better explanation, then, is that someone incorporated prior psalmic materials into a cycle of psalms created for Jerusalem devotion (see Pss 97:8 and 99:2), not necessarily for use in the cult.[345] Moreover, while Zion is mentioned (Pss 97:8, 99:2, 9), instead of the human king Moses, Aaron, and Samuel lead the community (Ps 99:6; cf. Massah and Meribah in Ps 95:8). This possibly suggests a postexilic adaptation. Mowinckel was aware of the issue of date, which the references to Moses and company raises, and he even acknowledges the issue of a literary versus a cultic setting.[346]

At this point it may be recalled that Mowinckel's reconstruction utilized Ugaritic evidence. Fitzgerald's hypotheses likewise suit an understanding of the Baal Cycle that is ultimately indebted to Mowinckel.[347] Despite the criticisms leveled against the interpretation of the Baal Cycle as a New Year's liturgical piece, it would appear that poem does draw on the language and imagery of the fall. Gaster, de Moor, and others have already argued this in general, but thanks to Fitzgerald's specific observation about the fall rains following a period of no rain, it is now possible to refine the older arguments. To be specific, each of the three sections of the Cycle culminates with the fall rains: Baal's victory over Yamm became manifest in the coming of the rains off the Mediterranean in 1.2 IV; the building of Baal's palace signals the coming of the rains with the opening of the window in 1.4 VII; and Baal's temporary victory over Death in 1.6 VI marks the shift of the direction of the prevailing winds to west from the east.[348] Mowinckel's work has been advanced by Fitzgerald's meteorological work on biblical texts, and to my mind a comparable meteorological approach illuminates the Baal Cycle.

Now, as is well known, scholars even predating Mowinckel and continuing through Gaster, de Moor, and right into the 1990s in the work of M. Yon have often read the cycle against the background of ritual.[349] When it comes to the Baal Cycle, I would turn the ritual paradigm on its head by arguing that the seasonal and ritual information was incorporated into the literary production of the myth, rather than the other way around.[350] Over the course of the unfolding of the West Semitic tradition, at times myth shaped ritual and at other points ritual influenced the formation of mythic narrative.[351] In short, Mowinckel's basic insights regarding Sukkot, the meteorological and agricultural cycles, and the political interpretation of divine and human reality built upon these cycles retain substantial merit despite major gaps. Mowinckel's theory continues to appeal to scholars other than "believers" (to recall Fitzgerald's term). For example, J. J. M. Roberts has stressed the political dimension of many of the psalms marshaled by Mowinckel, and their two treatments are compatible at many points.[352] In sum, it is clear that despite many subsequent discoveries and corresponding changes in perspective, the influence of Mowinckel endures (cf. *KTU* 1.6 III 20: *ḥy ʾalʾiyn bʿl*).

⊠ THE COMPARATIVE ENTERPRISE IN RETROSPECT

The myth-and-ritual approach generated much later scholarly discussion, but it is not uncommon today for this stage of research to be overlooked or even denigrated.[353] Indeed, to dismiss the work because of its speculative character would force the rejection of a good deal of other scholarship in the field (e.g., some of the work of C. H. Gordon or M. H. Pope). It might be preferable to await new evidence before ruling out such possibilities. In any case, despite some spec-ulation, Scandinavian scholarship rightly raised questions about a possible fall enthronement feast. Furthermore, scholars especially in Scandinavia deserve their due for helping demonstrate the divine *mythos* of Judean royal ideology,[354] commonly using the Ugaritic texts to do so. Despite the shift away from recon-structions heavily grounded in myth-and-ritual theory, the approach remains important for the discussions of kingship, especially in the Psalms.[355] In sum, this line of scholarship deserves credit for appreciating ritual and its influence in the shaping of both Ugaritic and biblical literature. Despite this important point, the excesses of this approach were becoming clearer in the 1960s even to some of its adherents.

In 1963 G. W. Ahlström produced a study that heralded a shift in perspective regarding Israelite religion.[356] Having shed most of the excesses of myth-and-ritual speculations evident in his 1959 dissertation, Ahlström used extrabiblical texts (including Ugaritic) and archaeological materials to question the model of Israel-ite-Canaanite opposition regnant in the postwar period. In particular, he rejected the widespread belief in the "superiority" of Israelite religion. A parade example of the view that Ahlström rejected comes from W. F. Albright, who noted

> the extremely low level of Canaanite religion, which inherited a relatively primitive mythology and had adopted some of the most demoralizing cultic practices then existing in the Near East. . . . The brutality of Canaanite mythology . . . passes belief.[357]

In retrospect, it is remarkable that Albright could make such a statement despite the lack of Ugaritic ritual or cultic texts to support his claims or the attestation of comparable motifs in other ancient Middle Eastern mythologies.[358] Yet Albright was hardly alone in such views. J. Gray could write of the Ugaritic texts, "there was no moral purpose in the fertility cult"[359] and Canaanite "religion was essen-tially magical and, as such a-moral."[360] U. Oldenburg, in his University of Chi-cago dissertation, also contrasted Canaanite and Israelite religion in highly personal terms:

> The more I studied pre-Israelite religion, the more I was amazed with its utter depravity and wickedness. Indeed, there was *nothing* in it to inspire the sublime faith of Yahweh. His coming is like the rising sun dispelling the darkness of Canaanite superstition.[361]

Clearly such statements reflected the belief structures of these scholars more than the beliefs of the authors of the Ugaritic texts.

Sometimes condemnation of the Canaanites took subtler form. For ex-ample, we may note the contrast drawn between the historical outlook of Israel and the nature and mythic religion of Canaan in the work of G. Ernest Wright and many others,[362] or G. E. Mendenhall's later distinction between the covenant religion of Israel and the power religion of Canaanite polytheism.[363] Albright's influence on his students is evident here, but the oppositional mindset operated in wider circles. Others, such as N. Habel, drew a contrast between the historical religion of Israel and Canaan's "nature religion."[364] To dramatize the contrastive approach, we may list the main categories:

Canaan	*Israel*
polytheistic	monotheistic
wicked/depraved	moral
natural (fertility)	historical
mythical	historical
magical	moral
power	covenantal

These oppositions all share modern values associated with modern Western religion, in particular the so-called "Judeo-Christian tradition" (itself a Christian ideological construct). Scholars have since criticized the weaknesses in the contrastive views,[365] including the tendency of many who championed such contrasts to overlook the mythic elements in Israelite literature,[366] including the nature imagery characterizing Yahweh in the earliest Israelite literature (Judg 5:4–5), the concern for fertility in the same literature (Gen 49:25–26; Deut 33:13–16; Judg 5:4–5),[367] and the presentation of divinity in royal terms (Exod 15:18). The very antiquity of these texts suggests that such features in Israel do not reflect secondary, negative Canaanite influences on the original Israelite covenantal identity.

Despite its problems, the contrastive theology has retained its hold, albeit in new forms. The contrast posed between Canaan and Israel continues under the related rubrics of power and liberation.[368] The ground for such a contrast has shifted to areas other than religion, for example in the literary contrast drawn in F. M. Cross's magisterial volume, *Canaanite Myth and Hebrew Epic*.[369] All of these contrasts were assumed at the outset, and the Ugaritic texts were made to fit neatly into these conceptual frameworks of opposition. Thanks to the work of G. Ahlström and others, however, this contrastive approach would shift in the 1970s toward a model of symbiosis and even identification. As a result, many of these "biblical values" no longer seemed parts of Israel's original constitution in contrast to Canaan but products of inner-societal developments during the Israelite monarchy and afterwards.

On balance, then, Ugaritic offered both major advances and problems for the biblical field. On the one hand, Ugaritic served as an indispensable part of the biblical field throughout the postwar period. A good example of this appears in the standard American tool in the field published in 1962, *The Interpreter's Dictionary of the Bible*. On the Continent, especially, form critics such as O. Eissfeldt,

C. Westermann, K. Koch, and R. Rendtorff included type-scenes in Ugaritic myths and legends. Moreover, the Scandinavian scholarship in Ugaritic and biblical studies in this period deserves great appreciation despite some well-placed criticisms. The fine 1976 study of royal ideology by T. N. D. Mettinger only reinforces this view.[370] Another positive advance in this period was an increased concern for ritual in literary texts and ritual texts. Finally, the level of synthesis in all of these areas was massive.

Finally, as the multitude of studies in language, poetry, and religion during this period suggests, some areas of Ugaritic studies surged ahead as long as the relevance for biblical studies was apparent. Indeed, this was an era that discovered parallels aplenty between Ugarit and the Bible, so much so that this "parallelomania," as Samuel Sandmel labeled it, came increasingly under fire by the end of this period.[371] Moreover, the work of Mowinckel, Gray, Gaster, Gordon, and Pope exemplified large-scale syntheses covering various topics and features, attested in a multitude of cultures. Compounding these difficulties at times was an absence of theoretical foundations, an issue evident in the discipline of ancient Near Eastern studies in the postwar era. To cite only one example, C. H. Gordon could claim that "we should not bring a prefabricated methodology or viewpoint to the problem, but rather let the methodology and conclusions come from the material itself."[372] While the statement shows a legitimate aversion to the importation of perspectives foreign to the world of the ancient texts (and perhaps a more covert aversion to politics or ideology), it also exposes a methodological illusion that texts somehow speak for themselves, and a corollary that interpreters can be objective or at least neutral. While other scholars hardly expressed themselves on the issues so openly, Gordon's statement reflected the attitude of many in the field. However, the late 1960s and the early 1970s would see societal changes that would put political and social issues in the forefront of biblical interpretation. Indeed, the next period would tend to the problems inherent in presupposing objective methods and perspective.

⊠ NOTES

1. For Nyberg's life and work, see S. Kahle, *H. S. Nyberg: En vetenskapmans biografi* (Stockholm: Norstedt, 1991). For bibliography, see also C. Toll, "Bibliographie H. S. Nyberg," in *Monumentum H. S. Nyberg* (Acta Iranica 4; 2 vols.; Tehran/Liège: Bibliothèque Pahlavi, 1975), 1:x–xxxi; the volume also contains two discussions of Nyberg: B. Utas, "H. S. Nyberg" (1:1–5); and F. Rundgren, "H. S. Nyberg" (1:7–14) (references courtesy of Hans Barstad).

2. Several aspects of Mowinckel's work are the subject of the articles published in *SJOT* 2 (1988). My thanks go to Hans Barstad for providing me with this volume. These essays do not touch on Mowinckel's treatment of the Ugaritic texts, but the piece by M. R. Hauge, "Sigmund Mowinckel and the Psalms—a Query into His Concern," 56–71, dis-

cusses several weaknesses in his theories about the New Year festival. For further on Mowinckel, see S. Hjelde, "Sigmund Mowinckels Lehrjahre in Deutschland," *ZAW* 109 (1997): 589–611; and the sections below on his work.

3. Albright, "The Old Testament and Canaanite Language and Literature," 14.

4. On Ginsberg and Gaster, see especially the profile on Columbia and Jewish Theological Seminary in the following chapter.

5. Letter dated 5 March 1934 (APS archives Albright Corresp. 1920–1935). This file box at APS includes an entire folder labeled "Dossier of Correspondence Relating to Yale Call Including Correspondence with Götze Dec 1933–1934 (May)." Speiser, too, considered applying for the post at Yale, as he wrote to Albright on 18 March 1934 (APS archives Albright Corresp. 1920–1935).

6. Letter written to E. M. Honeyman on 22 April 1937 (APS archives Albright box Personal Corresp. 1936–1938). The same letter sharply denigrates the work of Gaster, who had not yet come to the United States. On this point, see below.

7. The full reference is A. Herdner, *Corpus des tablettes en cunéiformes alphabétiques découvertes à Ras Shamra-Ugarit de 1929 à 1939* (Mission de Ras Shamra 10; Paris: Imprimerie Nationale/Paul Geuthner, 1963). One of Virolleaud's other students was Michael Astour, who worked with him before going to Brandeis to study with Gordon. Astour's *Hellenosemitica: An Ethnic and Cultural Study in West Semitic Impact on Mycenaean Greece* (Leiden: Brill, 1967) is dedicated to Virolleaud.

8. See Eissfeldt, *Neue keilalphabetische Texte aus Ras Schamra–Ugarit* (Berlin: Akademie-Verlag, 1965), 3.

9. M. Dietrich, O. Loretz, and J. Sanmartín, *Die keilalphabetischen Texte aus Ugarit: Einschliesslich der keilalphabetischen Texte ausserhalb Ugarits* (AOAT 24/1; Kevelaer: Butzon & Bercker; Neukirchen-Vluyn: Neukirchener Verlag, 1976). See the following chapter.

10. For the issues raised here about the alphabet, see W. W. Hallo, *Origins: The Ancient Near Eastern Background of Some Modern Western Institutions* (Leiden: Brill, 1997), 35–41.

11. Yet note the limits of Syro-Babylonian influence at Ugarit, discussed by M. Dietrich, "Aspects of Babylonian Impact on Ugaritic Literature and Religion," in *Ugarit, Religion and Culture: Proceedings of the International Colloquium on Ugarit, Religion and Culture. Edinburgh, July 1994. Essays Presented in Honour of Professor John C. L. Gibson* (ed. N. Wyatt, W. G. E. Watson, and J. B. Lloyd; UBL 12; Münster: Ugarit-Verlag, 1996), 33–47.

12. For this range of views, see G. R. Driver, *Semitic Writing from Pictograph to Alphabet* (rev. ed.; London: Oxford University Press, 1954), 148–49; B. Sass, *The Genesis of the Alphabet and Its Development in the Second Millennium B.C.* (Ägypten und Altes Testament 13; Wiesbaden: Harrassowitz, 1988), 163–64. C. T. Hodge attempted to derive the Ugaritic alphabet directly from Egyptian writing (which he prefers to call "hieratic" instead of "hieroglyphics"); Hodge, "The Hieratic Origin of the Ugaritic Alphabet," *Anthropological Linguistics* 11 (1969): 277–89.

13. Olmstead, "Excursus on the Cuneiform Alphabet of Ras Shamra and Its Relation to the Sinaitic Inscriptions," in *The Alphabet, Its Rise and Development from the Sinai Inscriptions* (ed. M. Sprengling; Oriental Institute Communications 12; Chicago: University of Chicago, 1931), 57–62; Bauer, *Der Ursprung des Alphabets* (Der Alte Orient 36. 1/2; Leipzig: Hinrichs, 1937), 39–40.

14. F. Rosenthal, review of C. Gordon, *Ugaritic Handbook, Or* 18 (1949): 254–56. Rosenthal has recently returned to this line of argument by noting the further correspondence between the form of the Ugaritic and South Arabian forms of the letter *ṯ*. See Rosenthal, review of Garbini and Durant, *Introduzione alla lingue semitiche, JAOS* 166 (1996): 280.

15. Puech, "Quelques remarques sur l'alphabet au deuxième millenaire," in *Atti del I Congresso Internazionale di Studi Fenici e Punici: Volume secundo* (Rome: Consiglio Nazionale delle Ricerche, 1983), 574–75. See also R. R. Steiglitz, "The Ugaritic Cuneiform and Canaanite Linear Alphabets," *JNES* 30 (1971): 135–39; and A. R. Millard, "The Ugaritic and Canaanite Alphabets: Some Notes," *UF* 11 (1979): 613–16.

16. See especially the lineup of forms on the chart in Puech, "Quelques remarques sur l'alphabet," 575–76.

17. So G. L. Windfuhr, "The Cuneiform Signs of Ugarit," *JNES* 29 (1970): 48–51.

18. Sass, *Genesis of the Alphabet,* 5, 163–64.

19. Bauer, *Ursprung des Alphabets,* 39.

20. So Driver, *Semitic Writing from Pictograph to Alphabet,* 151.

21. Rosenthal, review of Gordon, *Ugaritic Grammar, Or* 11 (1942): 172. This suggestion goes uncited in the Ugaritic grammars.

22. D. Sivan, *A Grammar of the Ugaritic Language* (HdO 28; Leiden: Brill, 1997), 9: "The reason for their invention is not known."

23. Albright, "The Early Alphabetic Inscriptions from Sinai and Their Decipherment," *BASOR* 110 (1948): 6–22; Cross, "The Evolution of the Proto-Canaanite Alphabet," *BASOR* 134 (1954): 15–24; and "The Origin and Early Evolution of the Early Alphabet," *EI* 8 (1969): 8*-24*; Cross and Lambdin, "A Ugaritic Abecedary and the Origins of the Proto-Canaanite Alphabet," *BASOR* 160 (1960): 21–26. So also Sass, *The Genesis of the Alphabet,* 163–64.

24. See Gelb, *A Study of Writing: The Foundations of Grammatology* (London: Routledge and Kegan Paul, 1952), 138–43; Hallo, "Isaiah 28:9–13 and the Ugaritic Abecedaries," *JBL* 77 (1958): 324–38. See also P. Swiggers, "Some Remarks on Gelb's Theory of Writing," *General Linguistics* 23 (1983): 198–201. Cf. the critiques of S. Segert, "Charakter des westsemitischen Alphabet: Eine Entgegnung an Ignace J. Gelb," *ArOr* 26 (1958): 243–47, 657–59; P. T. Daniels, "Fundamentals of Grammatology," *JAOS* 110 (1990): 727–31. Daniels distinguishes the Greek alphabet with its symbols for both consonants and vowels from the West Semitic scripts with their symbols only for consonants; he calls the latter *abjad*s after the Arabic word for the traditional order of its script. He regards Ugaritic as an "augmented abjad" because of the three ʾ*aleph*s or "syllablograms." Note also M. P. O'Connor: "The standard practice of referring to the West Semitic scripts as 'alphabets' could be defended on the grounds that no writing system notates everything relevant to language" ("Epigraphic Semitic Scripts," in *The World's Writing Systems* [ed. P. T. Daniels and W. Bright; New York/Oxford: Oxford University Press, 1996], 88). See also "Addendum: Alphabets ou syllabaires?" in P. Xella's article, "Tradition orale et rédaction écrite au Proche-Orient ancien: Le cas des textes mythologiques d'Ugarit," in *Phoinikeia grammata, lire et écrire en Méditerranée: Actes du colloque de Liège, 15–18 novembre 1989* (ed. C. Baurain, C. Bonnet, and V. Krings; Studia Phoenicia, Collection d'études classiques 6; Namur: Société des Etudes Classiques, 1991), 83–85.

25. Gardiner, "The Egyptian Origin of the Semitic Alphabet," *JEA* 3 (1916): 1–16. See also A. E. Cowley, "The Origin of the Semitic Alphabet," *JEA* 3 (1916): 17–21. The majority view includes the work of Albright, Cross, and Puech. For a standard treatment (with bibliography), see Puech, "Origine de l'alphabet," *RB* 93 (1986): 161–213 + plates I–III.

26. Cross and Lambdin, "A Ugaritic Abecedary," 21–26. This article responds directly to the case made by Gelb and Hallo.

27. Speiser, "The Syllabic Transcription of Ugartic [ḫ] and [ḥ]," *BASOR* 175 (1964): 42–47.

28. Hallo, "Isaiah 28:9–13 and the Ugaritic Abecedaries," 324–38. See Cross's response in his article, "The Origin and Early Evolution of the Alphabet," 24*.

29. Ullendorff's attack largely involves the putative letter names for Ethiopic. See Ullendorff, "Studies on the Ethiopic Syllabary," *Africa* 21 (1951): 211–13; reprinted in Ullendorff, *Studies in Semitic Languages and Civilizations* (Wiesbaden: Harrassowitz, 1977), 230–40.

30. Ryckmans, "A. G. Lundin's Interpretation of the Beth Shemesh Abecedary: A Presentation and Commentary," *Proceedings of the Seminar for Arabian Studies* 18 (1988): 123–29, esp. 127–28.

31. See W. F. Albright in *City Invincible* (ed. C. H. Kraeling and R. A. Adams; Chicago, 1960), 122–23; D. Diringer, *The Alphabet* (2d ed.; London/New York: Hutchinson, 1949), 37, 214; and more recently, C. Myers, *Discovering Eve: Ancient Israelite Women in Context* (New York: Oxford University Press, 1988), 152–53; G. Barkay, "The Iron II–III," in *The Archaeology of Ancient Israel* (ed. A. Ben-Tor; New Haven: Yale University Press/ Open University of Israel, 1992), 349; and W. E. Aufrecht, "Urbanization and Northwest Semitic Inscriptions of the Late Bronze and Iron Ages," in *Aspects of Urbanism in Antiquity: From Mesopotamia to Crete* (ed. W. E. Aufrecht, N. A. Mirau, and S. W. Gauley; Sheffield: Sheffield Academic Press, 1997), 116–29. Several articles appeared in response to A. Lemaire's claims for widespread schools in ancient Israel in his book, *Les écoles et la formation de la Bible dans l'Ancien Israël* (OBO 39; Freiburg, Switzerland: Universitätsverlag; Göttingen: Vandenhoeck & Ruprecht, 1981). For example, see M. Haran, "On the Diffusion of Literacy and Schools in Ancient Israel," in *Congress Volume: Jerusalem 1986* (ed. J. A. Emerton; VTSup 40; Leiden: Brill, 1988), 81–95; and in the same volume, E. Puech, "Les écoles dans l'Israël préexilique: Données épigraphiques," 189–203. These articles contain references to other responses to Lemaire's study. On the issue of literacy in Israel more recently, see S. Niditch, *Oral World and Written Word: Ancient Israelite Literature* (Library of Ancient Israel; Louisville, Ky.: Westminster John Knox, 1996), 39, 69–77; and M. D. Coogan, "Literacy and the Formation of Biblical Literature," in *Realia Dei: Essays in Archaeology and Biblical Interpretation in Honor of Edward F. Campbell, Jr. at His Retirement* (ed. P. H. Williams Jr. and T. Hiebert; Atlanta: Scholars Press, 1999), 47–61. For historical considerations militating against the importance of alphabetic writing for ancient literacy, see Niditch, *Oral World and Written Word,* 39–40; and P. Saenger, "The Separation of Words and the Physiology of Reading," in *Literacy and Orality* (ed. D. R. Olson and N. Torrance; Cambridge: Cambridge University Press, 1991), 208. Clearly, the alphabet is attested already in Iron I Israel prior to the Iron II rise of literacy (apart from traditional royal and priestly scribes); for the extension of literacy in Israel in the eighth century and afterwards, see M. S. Smith, *The Early History of God: Yahweh and the Other Deities in Ancient Israel* (San Francisco: Harper & Row, 1990), 148–49, 152; Coogan, "Literacy and the Formation of Biblical Literature," 47–61; and W. M. Schniedewind, "Orality and Literacy in Ancient Israel," *Religious Studies Review* 26/4 (2000): 327–32. For a critical, theoretical response to the importance given to the alphabet in the history of writing, see R. Harris, *The Origin of Writing* (La Salle, Ill.: Open Court, 1986).

32. For these texts, see P. Bordreuil, "Cunéiformes alphabétiques non-canoniques. 1) La tablette alphabétique sénestroverse RS 22.03," *Syria* 58 (1981): 301–10; and P. Bordreuil and D. Pardee, "Un abécédaire du type sud-sémitique découvert en 1988 dans les fouilles archéologiques françaises de Ras Shamra-Ougarit," *CRAIBL* (1995): 855–60. See also Puech, "Quelques remarques sur l'alphabet au deuxième millenaire," 570–75, with a fine comparative chart on p. 572; Sass, *Genesis of the Alphabet,* 164–66. Information about and readings for these first three texts appear in *CAT.*

33. See in addition to *CAT,* A. R. Millard, "A Text in a Shorter Cuneiform Alphabet from Tell Nebi Mend," *UF* 8 (1976): 459–60.

34. See in addition to *CAT,* G. Wilhelm, "Noch einmal zu der keilalphabetischen Kruginschrift aus Kumidi KL 67:428p," *WO* 28 (1997): 85–88.

35. In addition to *CAT,* see E. Puech, "La tablette cunéiforme de Beth Shemesh, premier témoin de la séquence des lettres du sud-sémitique," in *Phoinikeia grammata, lire et écrire en Méditerranée: Actes du colloque de Liège, 15–18 novembre 1989* (ed. C. Baurain, C. Bonnet, and V. Krings; Studia Phoenicia, Collection d'études classiques 6; Namur: Société des Etudes Classiques, 1991), 33–47. For further discussion, see Chapter Four.

36. See in addition to *CAT,* R. R. Stieglitz, "The Ugaritic Inscription from Hala Sultan Tekke," *Opuscula Atheniensia* 15 (1984): 193.

37. Dietrich and Loretz see the longer alphabet in the inscriptions from Hala Sultan Teke, Tell Nebi Mend, and Beth Shemesh; see Dietrich and Loretz, "The Cuneiform Alphabets of Ugarit," *UF* 21 (1989): 109, 111. On one page, the text from Kamid el-Loz is said to be in the long alphabet, and on another in the short alphabet. See further M. Dijkstra, "Another Text in the Shorter Cuneiform Alphabet (*KTU* 5.22)," *UF* 18 (1986): 121–23; B. Sass, "The Beth Shemesh Tablet and the Early History of the Proto-Canaanite, Cuneiform, and South Semitic Alphabets," *UF* 23 (1991): 315–25.

38. On the grammar of these inscriptions, see now J. Tropper, "Zur Sprache der Kurzalphabettexte aus Ugarit," in *"Und Mose schrieb dieses Lied auf": Studien zum Alten Testament und zum Alten Orient. Festschrift für Oswald Loretz zur Vollendung seines 70. Lebenjahres mit Beiträgen von Freunden, Schülern, und Kollegen* (ed. M. Dietrich and I. Kottsieper; AOAT 250; Münster: Ugarit-Verlag, 1998), 732–38.

39. So Gordon, *Ugaritic Textbook,* sect. 3.2.

40. Young, *Concordance of Ugaritic* (AnOr 36; Rome: Pontifical Biblical Institute, 1956).

41. Greenfield, review of Whitaker, *Concordance, JCS* 29 (1967): 126. Also note the many well-placed comments of Gordon's student, Anson Rainey, in his article, "Observations on Ugaritic Grammar," *UF* 3 (1971): 151–72.

42. This discipline is recently represented by E. Lipiński's book, *Semitic Languages: Outline of a Comparative Grammar* (OLA 80; Leuven: Uitgeverij Peeters en Department Oosterse Studies, 1997).

43. Information courtesy of John Strugnell, in a letter dated 16 December 1998.

44. *BDB* (1953), p. xii.

45. Driver, *Canaanite Myths and Legends* (Old Testament Series 3; Edinburgh: T&T Clark, 1956).

46. One of Thomas's students was D. J. A. Clines (later professor at Sheffield), who offers recollections of his student days with Thomas in Clines, *On the Way to the Postmodern: Old Testament Essays, 1967–1998* (2 vols.; JSOTSup 293; Sheffield: Sheffield Academic Press, 1998), 2:616–17.

47. Driver, *Canaanite Myths and Legends,* 133.

48. Professor Ullendorff's classmate in Ugaritic was Rabin (Ullendorff, letter dated 31 December 1998). Rabin authored a number of the well-known articles that use a good deal of Ugaritic including: "Hebrew *D* = 'Hand,'" *JSS* 6 (1955): 111–15; and "Hittite Words in Hebrew," *Or* 32 (1963): 113–39. Rabin was the supervisor of T. Muraoka, presently in Leiden, who will feature in the next chapter.

49. John Strugnell, in a letter dated 16 December 1998.

50. See L. Kopf, review of Al-Yasin, *The Lexical Relations between Ugaritic and Arabic, BiOr* 12 (1955): 134–36. Al-Yasin's 1950 Princeton thesis appeared in book form as *The Lexical Relation between Ugaritic and Arabic* (New York: Shelton College, 1952).

51. Barr, *Comparative Philology and the Text of the Old Testament* (Oxford: Oxford University Press, 1968), 100.

52. Information courtesy of J. Barr, in a letter dated 18 December 1998, and J. C. L. Gibson, in a letter dated 4 December 1998. Gibson knew Barr's family. A good deal of this information appears in S. E. Balentine and J. Barton, "The Reverend Professor James Barr, MA, BD, SS, D. Theol., FBA," in *Language, Theology, and the Bible: Essays in Honour of*

James Barr (ed. S. E. Balentine and J. Barton; Oxford: Clarendon, 1994), 1–4. The same volume contains a listing of Barr's bibliography on pp. 398–413.

53. Barr, *Comparative Philology and the Text of the Old Testament: With Corrections and Additions* (Winona Lake, Ind.: Eisenbrauns), 383. For further criticism of Driver's philological work, see pp. 185 n. 1, 193 n. 1, 284, 290–91.

54. Ibid., 112 (but cf. 385).

55. Ibid., 24, 26 with 294 n. 33; see also 188–89.

56. *JSS* 11 (1966): 228–41; reprinted in Pope, *Probative Pontificating in Ugaritic and Biblical Literature,* 109–26; discussed by Barr, *Comparative Philology and the Text of the Old Testament,* 85 n. 1. See also E. Ullendorff, "Ugaritic Studies within Their Semitic and Eastern Mediterranean Setting," *BJRL* 46 (1963): 249. See more recently the fine article by F. Renfroe, "Methodological Considerations Regarding the Use of Arabic in Ugaritic Philology," *UF* 18 (1986): 33–74 (with bibliography on this issue); and idem, *Arabic-Ugaritic Lexical Studies* (ALASP 5; Münster: Ugarit-Verlag, 1992).

57. Here Kaiser refers to his well-known dissertation published as *Die mythische Bedeutung des Meeres in Ägypten, Ugarit, und Israel* (BZAW 78; Berlin: Töpelmann, 1959).

58. Kaiser, letter dated 15 October 1998.

59. Eissfeldt, *El im ugaritischen Pantheon* (Berlin: Akademie Verlag, 1951).

60. Eissfeldt, "El and Yahweh," *JSS* 1 (1956): 25–37.

61. Albright writes on Eissfeldt's interpretive tendencies: "Eissfeldt is too inelastic, too apt to push an idea to the last possible conclusion, and lacking the wide background in ancient oriental lore which is necessary for the greatest success." Letter to Baumgartner, dated 16 June 1933, in APS archives (Albright box Corresp.-Misc. 1925–1933). Later Albright would come to express great respect for Eissfeldt.

62. Eissfeldt, "The Alphabetical Cuneiform Texts from Ras Shamra Published in Palais Royal d'Ugarit, Vol. II, 1957," *JSS* 5 (1960): 1–49.

63. Information on these figures comes courtesy of letters from Klaus Koch dated 31 October 1998 and from Wolfram Herrmann dated 2 May 1999.

64. Bernhardt, "Anmerkungen zur Interpretation des KRT-Textes von Ras Schamra-Ugarit," *WZUG* 5 (1955–1956): 101–21; and idem, "Ugaritische Texte," in *Religionsgeschichte Textbuch zum Alten Testament* (ed. W. Beyerlin; Göttingen: Vandenhoeck & Ruprecht, 1975), 224–38.

65. Goeseke, "Die Sprache der semitischen Texte Ugarits und ihre Stellung innerhalb des Semitischen," *Wissenschaftliche Zeitschrift der Martin-Luther-Universität Halle-Wittenberg, Gesellschafts- und sprachwissenschaftliche Reihe* 7.3 (1958): 623–52.

66. Aistleitner, *Untersuchungen zur Grammatik des Ugaritischen* (Berlin: Akademie-Verlag, 1954).

67. For this information, see Eissfeldt, introduction to J. Aistleitner, *Wörterbuch der ugaritischer Sprache* (ed. O. Eissfeldt; 2d ed.; Berlin: Akademie-Verlag, 1965), iii.

68. For this information, my thanks go to Wolfram Herrmann (letter of 2 May 1999).

69. *EncJud* 5 (1971): 1475–76.

70. See further in Chapter One. For Haupt at Hopkins, see B. Kuklick, *Puritans in Babylon: The Ancient Near East and American Intellectual Life, 1880–1930* (Princeton: Princeton University Press, 1996), 18, 24, 58–59, 104–7.

71. *EncJud* 10 (1971): 1411–12. Landsberger had fled Leipzig for Ankara at the beginning of the war before assuming his position at the University of Chicago.

72. For example, see Friedrich, "Zu den drei Aleph-Zeichen des Ras Shamra-Alphabets," *ZA* 41 (1933): 305–13; "Kanaanäisch und Westsemitisch," *Scientia* 84 (1949): 220–23.

73. Letter to Baumgartner, dated 16 June 1933, in APS archives (Albright Corresp.-Misc. 1925–1933). Albright would again offer very high praise of Friedrich's work in a letter dated 3 October 1936 to Roland Kent (APS archives Albright Corresp. 1936–1938).

74. See *EncJud* 2 (1971): 759–60. Alt's greatest disciple was Martin Noth (1902–1968), who wrote occasionally on Ugaritic: "Die Herrenschicht von Ugarit im 15/14. Jahrhundert v. Chr.," *ZDPV* 65 (1942): 144–64. Noth held professorships at Königsberg (1930–1945) and Bonn (1945–1965); see *EncJud* 12 (1971): 1232–33.

75. Alt, "Zu einigen Bezeichnungen von Berufen im Ugaritischen," *ZAW* 58 (1940–1941): 277–79; and "Nichtsemitische Ortsnamen im Gebiet von Ugarit," *ZDPV* 67 (1944–1945): 113–27.

76. Alt, "Ägyptisch-Ugaritisches," *AfO* 15 (1945–1951): 139–44; and "Hohe Beamte in Ugarit," in Alt, *Kleine Schriften zur Geschichte des Volkes Israel III* (ed. M. Noth; Munich: Beck, 1959), 186–97.

77. Alt, "Bemerkungen zu den Verwaltungs- und Rechtsurkunden von Ugarit und Alalach," *WO* 2/1 (1954): 7–18; *WO* 2/3 (1956): 234–43; *WO* 2/4 (1957): 338–42. See also Alt, *Kleine Schriften*, 186–213.

78. Gray, "Feudalism in Ugarit and Early Israel," *ZAW* 64 (1952): 49–55; Rainey, "The Social Stratification of Ugarit" (Ph.D. diss., Brandeis University, 1962); and "The Kingdom of Ugarit," *BA* 28 (1965): 102–25. This is not to suggest that these authors endorse the full baggage of such terminology. This discussion is laid out in J. D. Schloen, "The Patrimonial Household in the Kingdom of Ugarit: A Weberian Analysis of Ancient Near Eastern Society" (Ph.D. diss., Harvard University, 1995), 66–83.

79. For this information about Friedrich I am indebted to Gernot Wilhelm, e-mail dated 3 February 1999.

80. Gröndahl mentions Professors Friedrich and von Schuler as supervisors for her dissertation: *Die Personennamen der Texte aus Ugarit* (Studia Pohl 1; Rome: Pontifical Biblical Institute, 1967). Gröndahl has since left the field. For Professor von Schuler, see also the mention of Aartun in the following chapter.

81. Herrmann, in a letter to me dated 4 January 1999.

82. As reported in *NUS* 31 (April 1984): 12.

83. For example, Herrmann, "Götterspiese und Götterrank in Ugarit und Israel," *ZAW* 72 (1960): 205–16; "Die Göttersöhne," *Zeitschrift für Religions- und Geistesgeschichte* 12 (1960): 242–51; "Astart," *MIOF* 15 (1969): 6–55.

84. For example, Herrmann, *Yariḫ und Nikkal und der Preis der Kuṯarat-Göttinen: Ein kultisch-magischer Text aus Ras Shamra* (BZAW 106; Berlin: Töpelmann, 1968).

85. Herrmann, *Von Gott und den Göttern: Gesammelte Aufsätze zum Alten Testament* (BZAW 259; Berlin/New York: de Gruyter, 1999).

86. Well-known for an article, "*Ghain* im Ugaritischen," *ZA* 54 (1961): 158–72 (cf. Sivan, *A Grammar of the Ugaritic Language*, 23). See also Rössler, "Eine bisher unerkannte Tempusform im Althebräischen," *ZDMG* 111 (1961–1962): 445–51.

87. Published as *Die mythische Bedeutung des Meeres in Ägypten, Ugarit, und Israel* (BZAW 78; Berlin: Töpelmann, 1959). Cf. the review of J. C. Greenfield, *JBL* 80 (1961): 91–92.

88. Kaiser, "Zum Formular der in Ugarit gefundenen Briefe," *ZDPV* 86 (1970): 10–23.

89. Information courtesy of Professor Janowski, e-mail dated 2 January 1999.

90. Information courtesy of a letter of 31 October 1998 from Professor Koch.

91. R. Rendtorff and J. Stolz, "Die Bedeutung der Gestaltungstruktur für Verständnis ugaritischer Texte. Ein Versuch zu *CTA* 24 [= *KTU* 1.24] [NK] 5–15," *UF* 11 (1979 = C. F. A. Schaeffer Festschrift): 709–18. Information here courtesy of R. Rendtorff, personal communication, 21 November 1998. Thomas Römer (personal communication, 21 November 1998) reminded me that he took Rendtorff's course on Ugaritic and the Bible at Heidelberg in 1976–1977.

92. Westermann, *Die Verheissungen an die Väter: Studien zur Vätergeschichte* (FRLANT 116; Göttingen: Vandenhoeck & Ruprecht, 1976), published in English as *The Promises to the Fathers: Studies on the Patriarchal Narratives* (Philadelphia: Fortress, 1980).

93. Letter in APS archives (Albright box Corresp.-Misc. 1925–1933). In the same letter, Albright also praises Millar Burrows, who in time received the post.

94. Letter to Baumgartner, dated 16 June 1933, in APS archives (Albright box Corresp.-Misc. 1925–1933).

95. The full reference is Koehler and Baumgartner, *Lexicon in Veteris Testamenti Libros* (Leiden: Brill, 1953).

96. For a partial listing, see Herdner, *Corpus des tablettes*, 296, 332.

97. Nielsen was professor at Copenhagen in 1953–1991. Nielsen had studied also at Uppsala and was influenced by the circle of scholars there (see Knight, *Rediscovering the Traditions of Israel*, 352–66). Information courtesy of N. P. Lemche, e-mails on 3, 5, and 7 October 1998.

98. This information comes courtesy of B. S. Childs (letter to me dated 22 January 1999) and John Marks (letter dated 13 February 1999). Childs offered the same information during moving recollections of his time in Basel, Heidelberg, and Yale on the evening of 12 January 1999.

99. See references to Ugaritic, for example, in Jansma, "Some Notes on Hebrew Grammar and Etymology," *OTS* 9 (1951): 1–17. Reference and information, courtesy of Hoftijzer, in a letter to me dated 28 October 1998.

100. E-mail communication, 5 October 1998. According to his letter of 28 October 1998, Hoftijzer did not recall Lettinga as a member of this group. For Hallo's background, see Sperling, *Students of the Covenant*, 90–92.

101. Lettinga, *Oegarit (ras esj-sjamra), een nieuwe Phoenicische stad uit de Oudheid* (Cultuurhistorische Monografieën 11; La Haye: Servire, 1948). For further listings of Lettinga's contributions, see Herdner, *Corpus des tablettes*, 317–18.

102. Information courtesy of Professor Segert, in a letter to me dated 5 December 1998; Professor Heller, in an e-mail (via Robert Rehak) dated 22 December 1998; and Dr. Zemánek, e-mail 17 December 1998. Further information on Professor Segert appears in *CBQ* 49, Supplement (1987): 125.

103. See his study on Ugaritic mythology in *Prameny zivota* (ed. J. Vrbensky; Prague: Vysehrad, 1982).

104. Zemánek, *Ugaritischer Wortformenindex* (Lexicographie Orientalis 4; Hamburg: Buske, 1995).

105. For a biographical sketch of Loewenstamm, see Y. Avishur and J. Blau, "Samuel E. Loewenstamm. The Man and His Work," in Loewenstamm, *From Babylon to Canaan: Studies in the Bible and Its Oriental Background* (Jerusalem: Magnes, 1992), ix–xvii. My summary draws heavily on this essay.

106. In addition to the studies in Loewenstamm, *From Babylon to Canaan*, a fine representation of his studies appears in his book, *Comparative Studies in Biblical and Ancient Oriental Literatures* (AOAT 204; Kevelaer: Butzon & Bercker; Neukirchen-Vluyn: Neukirchener Verlag, 1980).

107. See "Ugaritic Marginalia" in Kutscher's book, *Hebrew and Aramaic Studies* (ed. Z. Ben-Hayyim, A. Dotan, and G. Sarfatti; Jerusalem: Magnes, 1977).

108. For example, Yadin, "An Ugaritic List of Spices and Ointments," *Tarbiz* 18 (1947): 125–28 [Heb.]; "The Composite Bow of the Canaanite Goddess Anath," *BASOR* 107 (1947): 11–15. See also his comments in "Symbols of Deities at Zinjirli, Carthage, and Hazor," in *Near Eastern Archaeology in the Twentieth Century: Essays in Honor of Nelson Glueck* (ed. J. A. Sanders; Garden City, N.Y.: Doubleday, 1970), 199–231. At a Thanksgiving dinner in 1983 at the Jerusalem home of Joy Ungerleider-Mayerson, Yadin, only months before his death, discussed with me (then a doctoral candidate) his views of Resheph in Egypt and Ugarit. His article on this topic appeared posthumously as "New Gleanings on Resheph from Ugarit," in *Biblical and Related Studies Presented to Samuel Iwry* (ed. A. Kort and S. Moschauser; Winona Lake, Ind.: Eisenbrauns, 1985), 259–74.

109. For example, Goshen-Gottstein, " 'Ephraim Is a Well-Trained Heifer' and Ugaritic *mdl*," *Bib* 41 (1960): 64–66.

110. Born in 1922 in Vienna, Malamat moved to Israel in 1935 and became a lecturer at the Hebrew University in 1954 after completing his M.A. (1952) and Ph.D. (1954) there. His many publications have occasionally touched on Ugaritic. Malamat's Schweich lectures contain many references to Ugaritic: *Mari and the Early Israelite Experience: The Schweich Lectures of the British Academy 1984* (Oxford: Oxford University Press, 1989); see Malamat, *Mari and the Bible* (Studies in the History and Culture of the Ancient Near East 12; Leiden: Brill, 1998). For a piece strongly drawing on Ugaritic, see his "The Divine Nature of the Mediterranean Sea in the Foundation Inscription of Yaḫdunlim," in *Mari in Retrospect: Fifty Years of Mari and Mari Studies* (ed. G. D. Young; Winona Lake, Ind.: Eisenbrauns, 1992), 211–15.

111. Pope's unpublished address for the Dahood Memorial Lecture at the 1995 Annual Meeting of the Society of Biblical Literature.

112. Pope's letter to Professor Russell Richey on 10 February 1995 (Yale Divinity School archive).

113. Pope's letter to President Keohane of Duke (undated, Yale Divinity School archive).

114. So Pope to me in conversation in the preparation of his volume, *Probative Pontificating in Ugaritic and Biblical Literature*, 1.

115. Pope's letter to President Keohane of Duke (undated, Yale Divinity School archive).

116. Rabinowitz also supported the important Yale Judaica Series. On Rabinowitz, see W. F. Albright, "Louis Rabinowitz in Memoriam," *BASOR* 146 (1957): 2–3.

117. Pope, *El in the Ugaritic Texts* (VTSup 2; Leiden: Brill, 1955). The book received widespread praise. Albright, for example, called it "very well done" (24 September 1955, letter in Yale Divinity School collection).

118. Pope, *El in the Ugaritic Texts*, vii.

119. M. H. Pope and W. Röllig, "Syrien: Die Mythologie der Ugariter und Phönizier," in *Wörterbuch der Mythologie I:1* (ed. H. W. Haussig; Stuttgart: Klett, 1965), 235–312. For a full listing of Pope's contributions, see *Probative Pontificating in Ugaritic and Biblical Literature*, 380.

120. Pope, *Job* (AB 15; New York: Doubleday, 1965; rev. ed., 1973); idem, *Song of Songs* (AB 7C; New York: Doubleday, 1977). Pope accepted the offer to produce the latter commentary in letters dated 22 January 1967 and 13 March 1967, both written to D. N. Freedman. Pope proposed a deadline of 31 December 1968 (letters in Yale Divinity School collection).

121. Albright to Pope on 4 June 1962 and 23 March 1965 (letters in Yale Divinity School collection).

122. For a listing of Greenfield's publications, see חֹיֹים לֹיונה, in *Solving Riddles and Untying Knots: Biblical, Epigraphic, and Semitic Studies Presented to Jonas C. Greenfield* (ed. Z. Zevit, S. Gitin, and M. Sokoloff; Winona Lake, Ind.: Eisenbrauns, 1995), xiii–xxvii. The preface to the volume contains a fine precis of Greenfield's academic career. Other essays on Greenfield's career were composed by J. H. Tigay, "Jonas Carl Greenfield (October 20, 1926–March 13, 1995)," *AfO* 42/43 (1995–1996): 329–31; and Z. Zevit, "Jonas Carl Greenfield," in *The Oxford Encyclopedia of Archaeology in the Near East* (ed. E. M. Meyers; 5 vols.; New York/Oxford: Oxford University Press, 1997): 2.440–41. For Greenfield's background, see Sperling, *Students of the Covenant*, 100–101. The Greenfield Prize was established in his memory by the American Oriental Society, thanks to a gift donated by his widow, Bella Greenfield. The first winner was Christa Mueller-Kessler in 1998, for her re-edition of a Mandaic magic bowl in the Yale Babylonian Collection ("The

Story of Bguzan-Lilit, Daughter of Zanay-Lilit," *JAOS* 116 [1996]: 185–95). See http://www.umich.edu/~aos/greenfie.htm.

123. So Blake's letter to Albright dated 24 January 1946 (APS Albright Papers Corresp. 1946).

124. For discussion of Ugaritic and text-criticism of the Hebrew Bible, see the famous proposal made for the emendation of 2 Sam 1:21 via *KTU* 1.19 I 44–45 by H. L. Ginsberg, "The Ugaritic Texts and Textual Criticism," *JBL* 62 (1943): 109–15. Later the proposal would be rejected by J. P. Fokkelman, "*Sdy trwmh* in 2 Sam. 1.21—a Nonexistent Crux," *ZAW* 91 (1979): 290–92. For further discussion, see S. Talmon, "Emendation of Biblical Texts on the Basis of Ugaritic Parallels," *Scripta Hierosolymitana* 31 (1986): 279–300; E. Tov, *Textual Criticism of the Hebrew Bible* (Minneapolis: Fortress; Assen/Maastricht: Van Gorcum, 1992), 363–69 (with bibliography); and more recently, reprising earlier discussions, T. L. Fenton, "Nexus and Significance: Is Greater Precision Possible?" in *Ugarit and the Bible: Proceedings of the International Symposium on Ugarit and the Bible. Manchester, September 1992* (ed. G. J. Brooke, A. H. W. Curtis, and J. F. Healey; UBL 11; Münster: Ugarit-Verlag, 1994), 85–91. An emendation proposed for Ps 42:2, ʾ*ayyāl* to **ʾayyelet* founded on a possible dittography and identified based on an incongruence of gender with *ta⁽ărōg*, is further plausible when compared to a similar image predicated of ʾ*aylt* in *KTU* 1.5 I 17. See M. Held, "The *YQTL-QTL (QTL-YQTL)* Sequence of Identical Verbs in Biblical Hebrew and in Ugaritic," in *Essays Presented to A. A. Neuman* (ed. M. Ben-Horin; Leiden: Brill, 1962), 285 n. 5.

125. The work of these figures is cited elsewhere in this volume, except for the fine study of Stanley Gevirtz (*Patterns in the Early Poetry of Israel* [2d ed.; Chicago: University of Chicago, 1973]), which grew in part out of his 1960 University of Chicago dissertation, "Curse Motifs in the Old Testament and in the Ancient Near East." Work on word pairs culminated in the work of Loewenstamm's student, Y. Avishur, *Stylistic Studies of Word-Pairs in Biblical and Ancient Semitic Literature* (AOAT 210; Neukirchen-Vluyn: Neukirchener Verlag, 1984). See below for further discussion.

126. Cross and Freedman, *Early Hebrew Orthography: A Study of the Epigraphic Evidence* (American Oriental Series 36; New Haven: American Oriental Society, 1952); and idem, *Studies in Ancient Yahwistic Poetry* (SBLDS 21; Missoula, Mont.: Scholars Press, 1975; 2d ed.; Biblical Resources Series; Grand Rapids, Mich./Cambridge, England: Eerdmans; Livonia, Mich.: Dove, 1997). For further bibliography by Cross and Freedman, see p. vii of the second edition of the latter work. See their quoted remarks together on their early experience of Ugaritic with Albright in L. G. Running and D. N. Freedman, *William Foxwell Albright: A Twentieth-Century Genius* (New York: Morgan, 1975), 209–11. Concerning Cross's background, see the following chapter. On his background, Freedman comments (letter dated 11 November 1999): ". . . parts of the novel by Herman Wouk called *Inside Outside* . . . is autobiographical, and deals in some detail with the year or two that Herman spent learning the trade in my father's 'Joke Factory.' In the book, he calls my father-figure Goldhandler. Herman calls my father 'The King of the Gag Writers,' and in fact my father was, writing for most of the leading comedians of the 20's and 30's: radio, stage, and screen." Freedman further notes that the Ziegfield Follies of 1936 starring Fannie Brice, Bert Lahr, and Bobby Clark drew on the talents of Ira Gershwin for lyrics, Vernon Duke for music, and Freedman's father for sketches; it was the same year he died, at age thirty-eight. Following his college graduation—at the age of seventeen—from the University of California, Los Angeles (UCLA), David Noel Freedman attended Princeton Theological Seminary. After serving as a pastor in Washington, Freedman started the Hopkins program in 1945. Most of this information is mentioned by Albright, who also comments that Freedman "has a brilliant mind" (letter of 5 March 1946 to Sidney Painter, APS archives Albright Corresp. 1946).

127. Albright's work in this area is acknowledged by Freedman in Cross and Freedman, *Studies in Ancient Yahwistic Poetry* (2d ed.), ix–xiii; and it is noted as well by Hillers, "William F. Albright as a Philologian," 54–55.

128. See, for example, Albright, "The Oracles of Balaam," *JBL* 63 (1944): 207–33.

129. Held, "Studies in Ugaritic Lexicography and Poetic Style" (Ph.D. diss., Johns Hopkins University, 1957). See the sample of this work in Held's article, "*Mhs/*mhs* in Ugaritic and Other Semitic Languages (A Study of Comparative Lexicography)," *JAOS* 79 (1959): 169–76.

130. S. J. Lieberman, "Moshe Held (1924–1984)," *JQR* 76 (1985): 1–3; and E. L. Greenstein and D. Marcus in *JANES* 19 (1989): 1–2. See also Sperling, *Students of the Covenant*, 101.

131. For a fine listing of Held's publications and discussion of his method, see C. Cohen, "The 'Held Method' for Comparative Semitic Philology," *JANES* 19 (1989): 9–23.

132. Sperling, *Students of the Covenant*, 103. Cf. Held, "*Mhs/*mhš* in Ugaritic and Other Semitic Languages (A Study of Comparative Lexicography)," 169; C. Cohen, "The 'Held Method' for Comparative Semitic Philology," 9–23. This approach to comparative lexicology was evident in the work of other Assyriologists besides Landsberger; see, for example, the comments of E. A. Speiser, "'Ed in the Story of Creation," *BASOR* 140 (1955): 9–11, esp. 11.

133. For a full list of Albright's doctoral students, see D. N. Freedman, *The Published Works of William Foxwell Albright: A Comprehensive Bibliography* (Cambridge, Mass.: American Schools of Oriental Research, 1975). For Albright and his students, see Long, *Planting and Reaping Albright*.

134. Albright to G. Ernest Wright, 10 March 1944 (APS Albright Corresp. Jan.-Aug. 1944).

135. The correspondence is contained in APS Albright Corresp. 1941.

136. The correspondence is contained in APS Albright Corresp. 1943.

137. The correspondence is contained in APS Albright Corresp. Sept.–Dec. 1944. The dissertation was entitled "Ugaritic Parallels in the Old Testament" (Ph.D. diss., Boston University, 1951). Information on readers courtesy of S. B. Parker, e-mail dated 30 April 1999. Richardson later authored an article entitled "A Ugaritic Letter of a King to His Mother," *JBL* 66 (1947): 321–24.

138. So Albright reports to Paul Bloomhardt in a letter dated 11 October 1945 (APS archives Albright Corresp. 1945).

139. Fitzmyer, in a letter to me dated 22 December 1998. For a precis of Fitzmyer's career up to 1986, see *CBQ* 49, Supplement (1987): 62.

140. Letter dated 29 March 1936 written to Stephen Wise (APS archives Albright box Personal Corresp. 1936–1938). In the same year he received an honorary doctorate from the University of Utrecht as well.

141. Undated letter written in response to Böhl's letter of 26 November 1936 (APS archives Albright box Personal Corresp. 1936–1938).

142. For example, letter to David Noel Freedman dated 26 January 1946 (APS archives Albright box Personal Corresp. 1946).

143. These figures are all mentioned below in this chapter.

144. Paul served in this capacity between his studies with H. L. Ginsberg at the Jewish Theological Seminary and his doctoral program with Ephraim Speiser at the University of Pennsylvania. See Running and Freedman, *William Foxwell Albright*, 301.

145. So Running and Freedman, *William Foxwell Albright*, 11.

146. On returning to Baltimore Albright mentions to his parents that he has joined the First Methodist Church (letter dated 24 November 1929, APS archives [Albright box Corresp.-Misc. 1925–1933]). However, he was married in one Anglican church, and his funeral was held in another.

147. So Running and Freedman, *William Foxwell Albright,* 108. In a letter to his parents written on the S. S. *Exochorda* en route to Boston dated 29 January 1936, Albright details the family trip to the Holy Land and Egypt. He mentions that during their trip to Alexandria, his wife met with the Arabist Fr. Jaussen, head of the Dominican House in Cairo and "her old confessor" (APS archives Albright box Personal Corresp. 1936–1938).

148. For biblical studies at the Ecole Biblique, see *L'Ancien Testament: Cent ans d'exégèse de l'Ecole Biblique* (Cahiers de la Revue Biblique 28; Paris: Gabalda, 1990). For an unappreciative student's view of the Ecole Biblique, see A. E. Breen, *A Diary of My Life in the Holy Land* (Rochester, N.Y.: Smith, 1906), 91–96.

149. So Running and Freedman, *William Foxwell Albright,* 108–9, 426.

150. So in response to reviews "from Methodist seminary professors" to his *From the Stone Age to Christianity,* in a letter to his Aunt Ella (Foxwell), dated 2 June 1941 (APS archive Albright Corresp. 1941).

151. Letter to his father dated 14 November 1937 (APS archives, Albright Corresp. 1936–1938). In the same letter Albright also comments that the number of Jewish rabbis was increasing.

152. As quoted in Running and Freedman, *William Foxwell Albright,* 225.

153. Fitzmyer and Glanzman, pillars of biblical scholarship among American Jesuits, were colleagues at Woodstock College and later at Fordham University. Glanzman never finished his doctorate. For a lovely appreciation of him, see G. P. Fogarty, *American Catholic Biblical Scholarship: A History from the Early Republic to Vatican II* (San Francisco: Harper & Row, 1989), 258.

154. Running and Freedman (*William Foxwell Albright,* 281) cite Albright's reaction to O'Callaghan's death (as told to G. Ernest Wright): "One thing I will never get over: the death of Roger O'Callaghan." See Albright's comments on O'Callaghan in *BASOR* 134 (1954): 4; and Fogarty, *American Catholic Biblical Scholarship,* 234.

155. Information courtesy of Joseph Fitzmyer, letter dated 30 December 1998.

156. O'Callaghan, *Aram Naharaim* (AnOr 26; Rome: Pontifical Biblical Institute, 1948). For his erudition in the area of Ugaritic, see his article, "The Word *ktp* in Ugaritic and Egypto-Canaanite Mythology," *Or* 21 (1952): 37–46.

157. Letter of D. N. Freedman to me, 26 September 1988; and e-mail from A. Gianto, 26 October 1998.

158. Letter to Father W. McClellan, S. J., of Woodstock College, 17 January 1943 (APS archives Albright Corresp. 1943).

159. Letter to George Mendenhall, 6 February 1943 (APS archives Albright Corresp. 1943).

160. Letter of D. N. Freedman to me, 26 September 1988.

161. See Fogarty, *American Catholic Biblical Scholarship,* 241–42. This source quotes Albright's prophetic comments on the papers at the CBA meeting compared with "the numerous papers which expose half-baked theories and wild hypotheses of various kinds" at the Society of Biblical Literature meetings.

162. W. F. Albright, "The Old Testament and Canaanite Language and Literature," *CBQ* 7 (1945): 5–31.

163. See Fogarty, *American Catholic Biblical Scholarship,* 243.

164. Fitzmyer, review of B. Long, *Planting and Reaping Albright, CBQ* 60 (1998): 334–35.

165. See Fogarty, *American Catholic Biblical Scholarship,* 279.

166. See the obituary written by D. J. Wiseman, published in *BSOAS* 35 (1972): 346–48.

167. See the following chapter on Charles University in Prague.

168. Letter to Robinson, dated 16 August 1929, APS archives (Albright box Corresp.-Misc. 1925–1933). Albright would reiterate his praise in a letter written to Alt on

25 May 1931, APS archives (Albright box Corresp.-Misc. 1925–1933). Albright is presumably referring to Mowinckel's work in *Psalmenstudien*. Albright would write (in a letter to George Dahl, dated 28 March 1931): "Mowinckel started out brilliantly, but, in my opinion, has not maintained his early promise."

169. Most of the following information, with the exception of the connections to Dropsie, derives from R. H. Hiers, with H. M. Stahmer, "Theodor H. Gaster, 1906–1992," *UF* 27 (1995): 61–82; and Hiers and Stahmer, "Theodor H. Gaster, Biographical Sketch and Bibliography—a Supplemental Note," *UF* 28 (1996): 277–86.

170. As reported in the obituary in the *New York Times*, 7 February 1992, by Ari L. Goldman.

171. Numbers 12, 14, 15, 16, 17, 18, 19, 20, 21, 22, 24 listed in Hiers, "Theodor H. Gaster, 1906–1992," 85.

172. The sketch of Hiers (ibid., 70) gives the date as 1939 or 1940, but a letter from Louis Finkelstein to Cyrus Adler dated 6 December 1939 (Dropsie College Adler papers, Box 41, FF 6) nails down the date.

173. So Gaster to Cyrus Adler in a letter dated 4 December 1939 (Dropsie College, Adler papers, Box 41, FF 6).

174. R. H. Hiers and H. M. Stahmer in *UF* 27 (1995): 59–114 and *UF* 28 (1996): 277–78 provide a comprehensive list of Gaster's bibliography. *UF* 27 (1995): 87, item #61, gives a date of 1943 for Gaster's dissertation, but 1947 is listed as the date by University Microfilms International (citing volume W1/94–7 of American Doctoral Dissertations). I have been unable to secure a copy of the dissertation. However, in a letter to Albright dated 17 October 1943, Gaster refers to having recently received his doctorate (APS Albright Corresp. 1943–1944).

175. Gaster, *Passover: Its History and Tradition* (New York: Henry Schuman, 1949).

176. So "Interview with Cyrus H. Gordon, Center for Judaic Studies at the University of Pennsylvania, February 3, 1998."

177. Ibid. With respect to learning Egyptian on the job, Gordon speaks of "living up to the illusions of others."

178. Held, "The *YQTL-QTL (QTL-YQTL)* Sequence of Identical Verbs in Biblical Hebrew and in Ugaritic," in *Essays Presented to A. A. Neuman* (ed. M. Ben-Horin; Leiden: Brill, 1962), 281–90; and "The Action-Result (Factitive-Passive) Sequence of Identical Verbs in Biblical Hebrew and Ugaritic," *JBL* 84 (1965): 272–82. Examples of the patterns in the former article are adduced also by Ullendorff, "Ugaritic Studies," 239–40.

179. The *Dropsie College Register*, for years after 1966, continues to list many of the courses taught by Held and Gaster, but none of the teachers of those years conducted a strong research program involving Ugaritic studies, with the exceptions of Nahum Waldman and Stephen Geller (1980–1985). In his capacity as assistant professor of Assyriology, J. Falk, a 1966 Dropsie doctorate, also offered a number of these courses. David Owen, one of Gordon's doctorates from Brandeis, is listed as assistant professor of Assyriology in 1972. Stephen Geller is listed as an Assistant Professor in the Dropsie University Bulletin for 1980–1981, 1981–1982 and later as Associate Professor in the 1983–1984, 1984–1985 Bulletins. The latter also lists Stephen J. Lieberman as Associate Professor. Sol Cohen, a student of S. N. Kramer at the University of Pennsylvania, also offered some courses late in Dropsie College's history. (The institution was named The Dropsie University from September 1, 1969 onward.)

180. For a sketch of Gordon's academic career and interests, see *BA* 59/1 (1996), entirely devoted to the subject. D. T. Tsumura's contribution to this volume focuses on Gordon's contributions to Ugaritic studies ("The Father of Ugaritic Studies," *BA* 59/1 [1996]: 44–50). See further Gordon's bibliography in *Boundaries of the Ancient Near Eastern World: A Tribute to Cyrus H. Gordon* (ed. M. Lubetski, C. Gottlieb, and S. Keller; JSOTSup 273; Sheffield: Sheffield Academic Press, 1998), 533–54.

181. Bella Greenfield, e-mail communication, 25 October 1998. The Greenfields departed for UCLA in 1956.

182. For example, see Levine, "Ugaritic Descriptive Rituals," *JCS* 17 (1963): 105–11; "The Descriptive Tabernacle Texts of the Pentateuch," *JAOS* 85 (1965): 307–18; and *In the Presence of the Lord* (Leiden: Brill, 1974). He coauthored with J. M. de Tarragon, "Dead Kings and Rephaim: The Patrons of the Ugaritic Dynasty," *JAOS* 104 (1984): 649–59; and "The King Proclaims the Day: Ugaritic Rites for the Vintage (*KTU* 1.41//1.87)," *RB* 100 (1993): 76–115. For a profile of Levine, see Sperling, *Students of the Covenant,* 97–98.

183. Tsumura, "The Ugaritic Drama of the Good Gods" (Ph.D. diss., Brandeis University, 1973).

184. Rainey, "The Social Stratification of Ugarit" (Ph.D. diss., Brandeis University, 1962); "The Kingdom of Ugarit," *BA* 28 (1965): 102–25; *The Scribe at Ugarit. His Position and Influence* (Proceedings of the Israel Academy of Sciences and Humanities 3/4:126–43; Jerusalem: Israel Academy of Sciences and Humanities, 1968); "Notes on the Syllabic Ugaritic Vocabularies," *IEJ* 19 (1969): 107–9; "Observations on Ugaritic Grammar," *UF* 3 (1971): 151–72; "Gleanings from Ugarit," *IOS* 3 (1973): 34–62; "Dust and Ashes," *TA* 1 (1974): 77–83; "The Ugaritic Texts in Ugaritica V," *JAOS* 94 (1974): 184–95. For a profile of Rainey, see Sperling, *Students of the Covenant,* 98–100.

185. For example, see Stieglitz, "Ugaritic Commodity Prices," *JAOS* 99 (1979): 15–23; "A Physician's Equipment List from Ugarit," *JCS* 33 (1981): 52–55. See in addition his articles "Ugaritic *Mhd*—the Harbor of Yabne Yam?" *JAOS* 94 (1974): 137–38; "Ugaritic *ḥrd* 'Warrior': A Hurrian Loanword," *JAOS* 101 (1981): 371–72; and "Ugaritic Sky-Gods and Biblical Heavens," *NUS* 35 (1986): 13.

186. Rainey, "The Social Stratification of Ugarit"; and "The Kingdom of Ugarit."

187. Notable exceptions include A. van Selms, *Marriage and Family Life in Ugaritic Literature* (Pretoria Oriental Studies 1; London: Luzac, 1954); I. Mendelsohn, "Samuel's Denunciation of Kingship in the Light of the Akkadian Documents from Ugarit," *BASOR* 143 (1956): 17–22; and later M. Dietrich and O. Loretz, "Die soziale Struktur von Alalakh und Ugarit," *WO* 3 (1966): 188–205; 5 (1969): 57–93.

188. Rainey, "A Canaanite at Ugarit," *IEJ* 13 (1963): 43–45.

189. Rainey, "Ugarit and the Canaanites Again," *IEJ* 14 (1964): 101.

190. For example, see J. Friedrich, "Kanaanäisch und Westsemitisch," *Scientia* 84 (1949): 220–23; and J. Cantineau, "La langue de Ras-Shamra," *Semitica* 3 (1950): 21–34.

191. Albright, *Yahweh and the Gods of Canaan* (London, 1968; repr. Winona Lake, Ind.: Eisenbrauns, n.d.), 116 n. 15.

192. Gordon, "Homer and the Bible: The Origin and Character of East Mediterranean Literature," *HUCA* 26 (1955): 43–108; Astour, *Hellenosemitica: An Ethnic and Cultural Study in the West Semitic Impact on Mycenaean Greece* (Leiden: Brill, 1967).

193. See Ullendorff, "Ugaritic Studies," 242–47.

194. Muhly, "Homer and the Phoenicians: The Relations between Greece and the Near East in the Late Bronze and Early Iron Ages," *Berytus* 19 (1970): 19–64; Negbi, "Evidence for Early Phoenician Communities in the East Mediterranean Islands," *Levant* 14 (1982): 179–82; Puech, "Présence phénicienne dans les îles à la fin du IIe. millénaire," *RB* 90 (1983): 365–95.

195. Niemeyer, "Die Phönizier im Mittelmeer im Zeitalter Homers," *Jahrbuch des Römisch-Germanischen Zentralmuseums Mainz* 31 (1984): 1–94; W. Burkert, *The Orientalizing Revolution: Near Eastern Influence on Greek Culture in the Early Archaic Age* (trans. W. Burkert and M. E. Pindar; Revealing Antiquity 5; Cambridge: Harvard University Press, 1992); Morris, *Daidalos and the Origins of Greek Art* (Princeton: Princeton University Press, 1992); see also her article, "Greece and the Levant," *Journal of Mediterranean Archaeology* 3/1 (1990): 57–66. See also R. Drews, "Phoenicians, Carthage, and the Spartan *Eunomia,*" *AJP* 100 (1979): 45–58. See also the wide-ranging studies by J. P. Brown:

"Kothar, Kinyras, and Kytherea," *JSS* 10 (1965): 197–219; "The Mediterranean Vocabulary of the Vine," *VT* 19 (1969): 146–70; "The Sacrificial Critique in Greek and Hebrew (I)," *JSS* 24 (1979): 159–75; and *Israel and Hellas* (BZAW 231; Berlin/New York: de Gruyter, 1995). The relative rarity of second-millennium West Semitic sources in these studies perhaps points to a methodological difficulty.

196. G. Bass, "A Bronze Age Shipwreck at Ulu Burun (Kas): 1984 Campaign," *AJA* 90 (1986): 269–96; and "Oldest Known Shipwreck Reveals Splendors of the Bronze Age," *National Geographic* 172/6 (1987): 693–733; and G. Bass, C. Pulak, D. Collon, and J. Weinstein, "The Bronze Age Shipwreck at Ulu Burun: 1986 Campaign," *AJA* 93 (1989): 1–29.

197. See M. G. Amadasi Guzzo, " 'The Shadow Line': Réflexions sur l'introduction de l'alphabet en Grèce," in *Phoinikeia grammata, lire et écrire en Méditerranée: Actes du colloque de Liège, 15–18 novembre 1989* (ed. C. Baurain, C. Bonnet, and V. Krings; Studia Phoenicia, Collection d'études classiques 6; Namur: Société des Etudes Classiques, 1991), 293–311; J. Naveh, *Early History of the Alphabet: An Introduction to West Semitic Epigraphy and Palaeography* (Jerusalem: Magnes; Leiden: Brill, 1982); and "Some Epigraphical Considerations on the Antiquity of the Greek Alphabet," *AJA* 77 (1973): 1–8; P. K. McCarter, *The Antiquity of the Greek Alphabet and the Early Phoenician Scripts* (HSM 9; Missoula, Mont.: Scholars Press, 1975); and "The Early Diffusion of the Alphabet," *BA* 37 (1974): 54–68; A. R. Millard, "The Canaanite Linear Alphabet and Its Passage to the Greeks," *Kadmos* 15 (1976): 130–44; M. Sznycer, "Quelques remarques à propos de la formation de l'alphabet phénicien," *Semitica* 24 (1974): 5–12. See also the discussion between F. M. Cross and W. Röllig on the date of the Phoenicians in Sardinia: Röllig, "Paläographische Beobachtungen zum ersten Auftreten der Phönizier in Sardinenien," in *Antidoron Jürgen Thimme* (ed. D. Metzler, B. Otto, and C. Müller-Wirth; Karlsruhe: C. F. Müller, 1982), 125–30; F. M. Cross, "The Oldest Phoenician Inscription from Sardinia: The Fragmentary Stele from Nora," in *"Working with No Data": Semitic and Egyptian Studies Presented to Thomas O. Lambdin* (ed. D. M. Golomb; Winona Lake, Ind.: Eisenbrauns, 1987), 65–74. For the broader discussion, see Cross, "The Evolution of the Proto-Canaanite Alphabet," *BASOR* 134 (1954): 15–24; idem, "Alphabets and Pots: Reflections on the Typological Method in the Dating of Human Artifacts," *Maarav* 3/2 (1982): 121–36; idem, "Early Alphabetic Scripts," in *Symposia Celebrating the Seventy-Fifth Anniversary of the Founding of the American Schools of Oriental Research (1900–1975)* (ed. F. M. Cross; Cambridge, Mass.: American Schools of Oriental Research, 1979), 97–113; E. Puech, "Origine de l'alphabet," *RB* 93 (1986): 161–213; B. Sass, *The Genesis of the Alphabet and Its Development in the Second Millennium B.C.* (Ägypten und Altes Testament 13; Wiesbaden: Harrassowitz, 1988). See also Sass, *Studia Alphabetica: On the Origin and Early History of the Northwest Semitic, South Semitic, and Greek Alphabets* (OBO 102; Freiburg, Switzerland : Universitätsverlag, 1991). See also the old article of R. Carpenter, "The Antiquity of the Greek Alphabet," *AJA* 37 (1933): 8–29.

198. J. C. Waldbaum, "Greeks *in* the East or Greeks *and* the East? Problems in the Definition and Recognition of Presence?" *BASOR* 305 (1997): 1–17.

199. Rendsburg, "Semitic PRZL/BRZL/BRDL, 'Iron,' " *Scripta Mediterranea* 3 (1982): 59–60; Noegel, "The Aegean Ogygos of Boeotia and the Biblical Og of Bashan: Reflections of the Same Myth," *ZAW* 110 (1998): 411–26. For a profile of Rendsburg, see Sperling, *Students of the Covenant,* 131–32.

200. See the account in J. Berlinerblau, *Heresy in the University: The Black Athena Controversy and the Responsibilities of American Intellectuals* (New Brunswick, N.J./London: Rutgers, 1999), 41–43, 179. Berlinerblau was a student of Gordon's at New York University.

201. Gordon's publications on this subject include: "Notes on Linear A," *Antiquity* 31 (1957): 124–30; "Minoica," *JNES* 21 (1962): 207–10; "Eteocretan," *JNES* 21 (1962):

211–14; "The Dreros Bilingual," *JNES* 22 (1963): 76–79; *Evidence for the Minoan Language* (Ventnor, N.J.: Ventnor Publishers, 1966); and *Forgotten Scripts: Their Ongoing Discovery and Decipherment* (rev. ed.; New York: Basic Books, 1982), 131–44. Credit to Gordon in this area varies greatly. See G. A. Rendsburg, "Jan Best and Minoan Linear A," *NUS* 30 (October 1983): 120; and " 'Someone Will Succeed in Deciphering Minoan': Cyrus Gordon and Minoan Linear A," *BA* 59/1 (1996): 36–43, esp. 42. In contrast, classicists have evidently ignored Gordon's work; see, for example, J. Chadwick, *Reading the Past: Linear B and Related Scripts* (Berkeley/Los Angeles: University of California/British Museum, 1987). In our conversation on 18 November 1999, Gordon expressed his view that this oversight was deliberate, since classicists do not control the West Semitic languages necessary to interpret this material.

202. Gordon, "Indo-European and Hebrew Epic," *EI* 5 (1958 = B. Mazar volume): *10–*15. See more recently, in a similar vein, Gordon, "The Near Eastern Background of the Rigveda," in *Ancient Egyptian and Mediterranean Studies in Memory of William Ward* (ed. L. H. Lesko; Providence, R.I.: Department of Egyptology, Brown University, 1998), 117–20. This move resembled Pope's comparison of the goddesses Anat and Kali, a view that has retained the scholarly world's respect (Pope, *Probative Pontificating in Ugaritic and Biblical Literature*, 2 n. 4; cf. D. Pardee, "The New Canaanite Myths and Legends," *BiOr* 37 [1980]: 275). Scholars as different as W. G. Lambert and N. Wyatt have defended similar views. See Lambert, "Old Testament Mythology in Its Ancient Near Eastern Context," in *Congress Volume: Jerusalem 1986* (ed. J. A. Emerton; VTSup 40; Leiden: Brill, 1988), 128; Wyatt, "The Source of the Ugaritic Myth of the Conflict between Ba'al and Yam," *UF* 20 (1988): 375–85. For modifications of his earlier view, see Wyatt, *Myths of Power: A Study of Royal Power and Ideology in Ugaritic and Biblical Tradition* (UBL 13; Münster: Ugarit-Verlag, 1996), 127–29, 244. See also M. S. Smith, *The Ugaritic Baal Cycle. Volume I: Introduction with Text, Translation, and Commentary of the First Two Tablets (KTU 1.1–1.2)* (VTSup 55; Leiden: Brill, 1994), 86–87 n. 167, 113 n. 224.

203. On Gordon's ventures into South America, see his articles, "The Authenticity of the Phoenician Text from Parahyba," *Or* 37 (1968): 75–80; "The Canaanite Text from Brazil," *Or* 37 (1968). Cf. the critical report of F. M. Cross, "The Phoenician Inscription from Brazil: A Nineteenth Century Forgery," *Or* 37 (1968): 437–60; and Gordon's response in his "Reply to Professor Cross," *Or* 37 (1968): 461–63, as well as his book, *Before Columbus: Links between the Old World and Ancient America* (New York: Crown, 1971). Cross further comments in his article, "Phoenicians in Brazil?" *BAR* 5 (1979): 36–43.

204. Gordon conducted seminars on the Ebla texts at New York University, as reported in *NUS* 31 (April, 1984): 13. He published essays on Ebla, for example "Echoes of Ebla," in *Essays on the Occasion of Seventieth Anniversary of the Dropsie University (1909–1979)* (ed. A. I. Katsh and L. Nemoy; Philadelphia: Dropsie University, 1979), 133–39; "West Semitic Factors in Eblaite," in *FUCUS: A Semitic/Afrasian Gathering in Remembrance of Albert Ehrman* (ed. Y. L. Arbeitman; Amsterdam Studies in the Theory and History of Linguistic Science, Series IV—Current Issues in Linguistic Theory 58; Amsterdam/Philadelphia: John Benjamins, 1988), 261–66. See also Gordon's description in *Forgotten Scripts*, 153–72. He has also edited three volumes of *Eblaitica* with G. A. Rendsburg.

205. See Gordon, "Philology of the Ancient Near East: My Seventy Years in Semitic Linguistics," in *Built on Solid Rock: Studies in Honor of Ebbe Egede Knudsen on the Occasion of His 65th Birthday April 11, 1997* (ed. E. Wardini; Institute for Comparative Research in Human Culture Oslo; Series B: Skrifter 1908; Oslo: Novus, 1997), 91–101. See the description also in Gordon, *Ugaritic Textbook* (4th ed.; AnOr 38; Rome: Pontifical Biblical Institute, 1998), x.

206. See L. Srinivasan and C. Gordon, "Canaanite Vocabulary in Bengali and in Some Other Dialects of India," *Mother Tongue* (December 1995): 202–6; and Gordon, *Ugaritic Textbook*, xi.

207. Gordon, *Ugaritic Textbook*, x, xii.

208. Gordon, *A Scholar's Odyssey* (Atlanta: Scholars Press, 2000).

209. Gordon, *Forgotten Scripts: Their Ongoing Discovery and Decipherment* (rev. and enlarged ed.; New York: Basic Books, 1982).

210. According to one reckoning, Gordon trained more than eighty Ph.D.s. See Lubetski and Gottlieb, " 'Forever Gordon,' " 9. Some of these figures, notably Sarna and Sasson, are profiled in Sperling, *Students of the Covenant*.

211. As Jack Sasson pointed out to me.

212. Hunt, e-mail communication, 20 October 1998. Young had at this time published two articles on this text, "With Snakes and Dates: A Sacred Marriage Drama at Ugarit," *UF* 9 (1977): 291–314; and "The Ugaritic Myth of the God Horon and the Mare," *UF* 11 (1979): 839–48.

213. *Ras Shamra Parallels I–II* (ed. L. Fisher; AnOr 49–50; Rome: Pontifical Biblical Institute, 1972, 1975); and *Ras Shamra Parallels III* (ed. S. Rummel; AnOr 51; Rome: Pontifical Biblical Institute, 1981).

214. For example, see Speiser, "An Analogue to 2 Sam 1 $_{21}$, 'AQHT 1 44–45," *JBL* 69 (1950): 377–78.

215. This paper appeared first in Hebrew in *EI* 3 (1953): 63–66 and later in English as "The Terminative Adverbial in Canaanite, Ugaritic, and Akkadian," in *Oriental and Biblical Studies: Collected Writings of E. A. Speiser* (ed. J. J. Finkelstein and M. Greenberg; Philadelphia: University of Pennsylvania, 1967), 494–505.

216. So the recipient of the position, Franz Rosenthal, in conversation on 12 January 1999, and Cyrus Gordon, in conversation on 11 April 1999. See the end of Chapter One on Gordon's relationship with Albright. Some of the following information pertaining to Dropsie College derives from its *Registers*.

217. The details here come from Rosenthal, e-mail communication (and personal communications). The general point is discussed by Gordon, *Pennsylvania Tradition of Semitics*, 66–67.

218. For praise of Speiser, see J. J. Finkelstein, "E. A. Speiser: An Appreciation," in *Oriental and Biblical Studies: Collected Writings of E. A. Speiser* (ed. J. J. Finkelstein and M. Greenberg; Philadelphia: University of Pennsylvania, 1967), 605–16; M. Greenberg, "In Memory of E. A. Speiser," *JAOS* 88 (1968) (= *Essays in Memory of E. A. Speiser* [ed. W. W. Hallo; AOS 65; New Haven: American Oriental Society, 1968]): 1–2; *EncJud* 15:258–59. See further Sperling, *Students of the Covenant*, 71–73.

219. Greenberg, review of Gordon, *The Pennsylvania Tradition of Semitics*, *JQR* 77/ 2–3 (October 1986–January 1987): 226.

220. Finkelstein and Greenberg, *Oriental and Biblical Studies: Collected Writings of E. A. Speiser.*

221. For example, Rin, "Ugaritic–Old Testament Affinities," *BZ* 7 (1963): 22–33.

222. Rin had an interesting family not well known outside Jewish circles. His father, Yehiel Halperin, moved the family from Russia to Palestine in 1921. One of his brothers is Uzzi Ornan, presently emeritus professor of Hebrew language at the Hebrew University, and he was predeceased by another brother, the famous Israeli poet Yonatan Ratosh (1908–1981). Ratosh founded a group called the "young Hebrews," but labeled the "Canaanites" by its opponents; the latter label stuck, and the movement was very influential in Israel in the 1950s. See J. S. Diamond, *Homeland or Holy Land? The "Canaanite" Critique of Israel* (Bloomington/Indianapolis: Indiana University, 1986). Svi Rin himself died at home on 26 September 1998 at the age of eighty-four. (This information is based on a post on Jack Sasson's e-mail list on 28 September 1998, on an e-mail from Jeffrey Tigay on 29 September 1998, and on "Ratosh, Yonathan," *EncJud* 13:1573–74. For further bibliography of Rin, consult *Ugarit-Bibliographie 1967–71* sub Rin.)

223. Information courtesy of S. B. Parker, e-mail dated 30 April 1999.

224. Published as *Numerical Sayings in the Old Testament: A Form-Critical Study* (VTSup 13; Leiden: Brill, 1965).

225. Published as *Amorite Personal Names in the Mari Texts* (Baltimore/London: Johns Hopkins University Press, 1965).

226. Published as *Patterns in the Early Poetry of Israel* (Studies in Ancient Oriental Civilization 32; Chicago: University of Chicago Press, 1963).

227. Published as *The Conflict between El and Baʿal in Canaanite Religion* (Supplement to Numen 3; Leiden: Brill, 1969).

228. Tsevat, *A Study of the Language of the Biblical Psalms* (JBL Monograph Series 9; Philadelphia: Society of Biblical Literature, 1955).

229. Published as *The Hebrew Conception of the World: A Philological and Literary Study* (AnBib 39; Rome: Pontifical Biblical Institute, 1970).

230. Published as *Yahweh versus Baal: A Conflict of Religious Cultures* (New York: Bookman, 1964).

231. For a partial listing of these figures' contributions to Ugaritic, see *CTA*, pp. 293–339.

232. In addition to the works of these authors mentioned above, see Caquot, "Le dieu ʿAthtar et les textes de Ras Shamra," *Syria* 35 (1958): 45–60, and "La divinité solaire ougaritique," *Syria* 36 (1959): 90–101; Fohrer, *History of Israelite Religion* (trans. D. E. Green; Nashville: Abingdon, 1972); Gese's entries in H. Gese, M. Höfner, and K. Rudolph, *Religionen Altsyriens, Altarabiens, und der Mandäer* (Religionen der Menschheit 10, 2; Stuttgart: Kohlhammer, 1970); Jeremias, *Theophanie: Die Geschichte einer alttestamentlichen Gattung* (WMANT 10; Neukirchen-Vluyn: Neukirchener Verlag, 1965); Kaiser, *Die mythische Bedeutung des Meers in Ägypten, Ugarit, und Israel* (BZAW 78; Berlin: Töpelmann, 1958; 2d ed., 1967); Kapelrud, *Baal in the Ras Shamra Texts* (Copenhagen: Gad, 1952) and *The Violent Goddess: Anat in the Ras Shamra Texts* (Oslo: Universitetsforlaget, 1969); Schmidt, *Königtum Gottes in Ugarit und Israel* (BZAW 80; Berlin: de Gruyter, 1961); Albright, *Yahweh and the Gods of Canaan* (New York: Doubleday, 1968); Pope, *El in the Ugaritic Texts* (VTSup 2; Leiden: Brill, 1955); and his contributions in "Syrien: Die Mythologie der Ugariter und Phönizier," in *Wörterbuch der Mythologie* I:1 (ed. H. W. Haussig; Stuttgart; Ernest Klett, 1965), 235–312. See also N. Tromp, *Primitive Conceptions of Death and the Nether World in the Old Testament* (BibOr 21; Rome: Pontifical Biblical Institute, 1969).

233. On "patternism," see the discussion of I. Engnell, "Methodological Aspects of Old Testament Study," in *Congress Volume: Oxford 1959* (VTSup 7; Leiden: Brill, 1960), 18–19.

234. S. H. Hooke, ed., *Essays on the Myth and Ritual of the Hebrews in Relation to the Culture Pattern of the Ancient Near East* (London: Oxford University Press, 1933); Hooke, *The Labyrinth* (London: Oxford University Press, 1935); and *Myth, Ritual, and Kingship* (Oxford: Clarendon, 1958). I. Engnell mentions Hooke's influence on his dissertation published as *Studies in Divine Kingship in the Ancient Near East* (Uppsala: Almqvist & Wiksell, 1943; rev. ed., Oxford: Basil Blackwell, 1967); so Engnell, "Methodological Aspects of Old Testament Study," 17–18.

235. I hasten to add that by Hooke's account myth-and-ritual work emerged independently in England and Scandinavia. See Hooke. "Myth and Ritual: Past and Present," in *Myth, Ritual, and Kingship* (ed. S. H. Hooke), 1–2. Hooke cites Mowinckel's early work as independent of developments in England; see further below. However, a Scandinavian figure such as G. Widengren would characterize the myth-and-ritual approach specifically as British, but with significant connections to work in Scandinavia; see Widengren, "Early Hebrew Myths and Their Interpretation," in *Myth, Ritual, and Kingship* (ed. S. H. Hooke), 152–56.

236. In this discussion, I am largely following D. A. Knight, *Rediscovering the Traditions of Israel: The Development of the Traditio-historical Research of the Old Testament, with Special Consideration of Scandinavian Contributions* (rev. ed.; SBLDS 9; Missoula, Mont.: Scholars Press, 1975), esp. 292–95, 303; and H. Ringgren, "Mowinckel and the Uppsala School," *SJOT* 2 (1988): 36–41. When speaking of the Uppsala figures, Knight prefers the term "circle" to "school" in order to avoid the implication of uniformity. As his fine book demonstrates, there were many areas of disagreement among the various figures involved. Ringgren's viewpoint that one should include all of these figures as members of a wider "Scandinavian school" may ring true at an even a greater distance in time and geography (for example, today in the United States), but it still may be proper to speak of a "Scandinavian approach." However, as the discussion of Gray and Gaster suggests, such an approach was hardly confined to Scandinavia.

237. See the considered remarks of Ringgren, "Mowinckel and the Uppsala School," 36. The discussion here is restricted to figures who used Ugaritic. For the wider range of this work, see Knight, *Rediscovering the Traditions of Israel.*

238. See below for Gray's background.

239. Gaster offered a course entitled "Patterns of Ritual" at Dropsie (*The Dropsie College Register 1959–60*, 28).

240. See Widengren, *Psalm 110 och det Sakrale kungadömet i Israel* (Uppsala: Lundeqvist, 1941); *The King and the Tree of Life in Ancient Near Eastern Religion* (Uppsala: Lundeqvist, 1951); *Sakrales Königtum im AT und im Judentum* (Stuttgart: Kohlhammer, 1955); and "King and Covenant," *JSS* 2 (1957): 1–32; Engnell, *Studies in Divine Kingship in the Ancient Near East*; Ahlström, *Eine Liturgie aus dem Ritual des leidenden Königs* (Lund: Gleerup, 1959). See also Ringgren, "König und Messias," *ZAW* 64 (1952): 120–47; A. Bentzen, *King and Messiah* (London: Lutterworth Press, 1955); A. R. Johnson, *Sacral Kingship in Ancient Israel* (Cardiff: University of Wales, 1955); Kapelrud, "King and Fertility: A Discussion of II Sam. 21:1–14," *NTT* 56 (1955): 113–22.

241. For a succinct discussion of these topics in the works of these scholars, see Knight, *Rediscovering the Traditions of Israel*, 392–95.

242. As noted by H. Frankfort, *Problem of Similarity in Ancient Near Eastern Religions*, 6–8. See Hooke, "Myth and Ritual: Past and Present," 4.

243. See the important studies of R. Ackerman, *J. G. Frazer: His Life and Work* (Cambridge: Cambridge University Press, 1987); and J. Z. Smith, "The Glory, Jest and Riddle: James George Frazer and *The Golden Bough*" (Ph.D. diss., Yale University, 1969). See also M. S. Smith, "The Death of 'Dying and Rising Gods' in the Biblical World: An Update, with Special Reference to Baal in the Baal Cycle," *SJOT* 12/2 (1998): 257–313.

244. In his letter to Millar Burrows dated 14 October 1946, Albright writes: "I am having a time pacifying Mowinckel, who is much too able a scholar and too valuable a stimulator to be treated cavalierly, even if I do not believe a word of his *po^cale ʾawen* and enthronement of Yahweh." (APS archives Albright Personal Corresp. October 1946). Albright was also highly critical of Gaster. For example, in a letter written on 2 March 1937 to the Egyptologist Alan Gardiner, Albright wrote: "He is superlatively bad; I find myself unable to accept a single suggestion, or even to consider a single idea of Gaster's seriously" (APS archives Albright Personal Corresp. 1936–1938). The comments here disclose a general predisposition against Gaster's overall approach. Albright's view of Gaster improved slightly in later correspondence. Note Ernest Wright's comment on Albright's view: ". . . he just goes back on all the myth-and-ritual stuff" (quoted in Running and Freedman, *William Foxwell Albright*, 317). For another negative comment on myth-and-ritual work in American Ugaritic circles, see H. L. Ginsberg, "Interpreting Ugaritic Texts," *JAOS* 70 (1950): 157.

245. Note the emphasis in Albright's thought on the scientific approach to the texts, specifically to what Peter Machinist ("William Foxwell Albright," 395) has called the "di-

agnostic details of the biblical text . . . those that posed questions of language and *realia* and could be said to characterize the text as a whole." Yet no such diagnostic details undergird Albright's claims about Moses' "practical monotheism," a clear example of where Albright's own religiosity at work mutes his scientific or "evolutionist" sensibilities. For some discussion of these questions in Albright's work, see J. M. Sasson, "Albright as an Orientalist," *BA* 56 (1993): 6; W. G. Dever, "What Remains of the House That Albright Built?" *BA* 56 (1993): 25, 33, 39. For a "strong reading" of Albright's theological conservatism, see B. O. Long, "Mythic Trope in the Autobiography of William Foxwell Albright," *BA* 56 (1993): 36–45.

246. Wright to Albright in a letter dated 23 October 1946 (APS archives Albright Corresp. December 1946).

247. See also the classic discussion and critique of the biblical theology movement in B. S. Childs, *Biblical Theology in Crisis* (Philadelphia: Westminster, 1970). For a more recent critique, see Wyatt, *Myths of Power*, 379–98. For another "magnalia dei" scholar in this period with criticisms of myth and ritual, see N. Habel, *Yahweh versus Baal: A Conflict of Religious Cultures* (New York: Bookman, 1964), 31, 63, 79–80, 88, 101.

248. See Wyatt, *Myths of Power*, 417–18; see also the end of this chapter for further discussion.

249. Mowinckel, *Psalmenstudien II. Das Thronbesteigungsfest Jahwäs und der Ursprung der Eschatologie* (Videnskapsselshapets Skrifter. II. Hist.-Filos. Klasse 1921. N. 6; Kristiana: Dybwad, 1922).

250. See also P. Volz, *Neujahrsfest Jahwes* (Tübingen: Mohr, 1912). For the relation between the two feasts, Mowinckel, *The Psalms in Israel's Worship* (2 vols.; trans. D. R. Ap-Thomas; 1962; repr. Sheffield: JSOT, 1992), 1:120–21.

251. Mowinckel, *The Psalms in Israel's Worship*, 1:106–92.

252. Ibid., 1:125, 132, 134, 136, 148, 152, 162, and 174.

253. K. Van der Toorn, "The Babylonian New Year Festival: New Insights from the Cuneiform Texts and Their Bearing on Old Testament Study," in *Congress Volume: Leuven 1989* (ed. J. A. Emerton; VTSup 43; Leiden: Brill, 1991), 343–44; O. Loretz, *Ugarit und der Bibel: Kanaanäische Götter und Religion im Alten Testament* (Darmstadt: Wissenschaftliche Buchgesellschaft, 1990), 96–109; and "Die Rückkehr des Wettesgottes und der königlichen Ahnen beim Neujahrfest in Ugarit und Jerusalem: 'Thronbesteigung' im Blick altorientalisticher Argumentationsforschung," in *'Schnittpunkt' Ugarit* (ed. M. Kropp and A. Wagner; Frankfurt: Lang, 1999), 163–244. See also O. Kaiser, "Kult und Kultkritik im Alten Testament," in *"Und Mose schrieb dieses Lied auf": Studien zum Alten Testament und zum Alten Orient. Festschrift für Oswald Loretz zur Vollendung seines 70. Lebenjahres mit Beiträgen von Freunden, Schülern, und Kollegen* (ed. M. Dietrich and I. Kottsieper; AOAT 250; Münster: Ugarit-Verlag, 1998), 406–8; J. L. Rubenstein, *The History of Sukkot in the Second Temple and Rabbinic Periods* (Brown Judaic Studies 302; Atlanta: Scholars Press, 1995) (my thanks to Dr. Herb Levine for bringing this study to my attention); and H. Ulfgard, *The Story of Sukkot: The Setting, Shaping, and Sequel of the Biblical Feast of Tabernacles* (Beiträge zur Geschichte der Biblischen Exegese 34; Tübingen: Mohr/Siebeck, 1998), 9–11.

254. See A. Jepsen, "Beiträge zur Auslegung und Geschichte des Dekalogs," *ZAW* 79 (1967): 303; M. Weinfeld, "The Uniqueness of the Decalogue and Its Place in Jewish Tradition," in *The Ten Commandments in History and Tradition* (ed. Ben-Zion Segal; trans. G. Levi; Jerusalem: Hebrew University, 1987), 21–27. W. Zimmerli likewise views the statement of divine self-revelation in the Exodus Decalogue and these psalms in terms broader than the Deuteronomic tradition (Zimmerli, *I am Yahweh* [ed. W. Brueggemann; trans. D. W. Stott; Atlanta: John Knox, 1982], 23–28, 104). For further discussion, see J. Jeremias, *Kultprophetie und Gerichtsverkündigung in der späten Königszeit Israel* (WMANT 35; Neukirchen-Vluyn: Neukirchener Verlag, 1970), 125–27; H. J. Kraus, *Psalms 1–59* (trans.

H. C. Oswald; Minneapolis: Augsburg, 1988), 490–91. Van der Toorn, "Babylonian New Year Festival," 339) cites Ps 81:4 as a reference to the fall festival.

255. See M. Z. Brettler, *God Is King: Understanding an Israelite Metaphor* (JSOTSup 76; Sheffield: Sheffield Academic Press, 1989), 145–58. Mowinckel argued (*Psalms in Israel's Worship*, 1:109): "In this poet's imagination this enthronement of Yahweh is an event which has taken place" (i.e., ritually in the annual fall festival). For the standard critique of Mowinckel on this point, see D. Michel, "Studien zu den sogenannten Thronbesteigungspsalmen," *VT* 6 (1956): 40–68; for further references, see D. M. Howard, Jr., *The Structure of Psalms 93–100* (Biblical and Judaic Studies Volume from the University of California, San Diego 5; Winona Lake, Ind.: Eisenbrauns, 1997), 36 n. 2. I am inclined to read *yhwh malak* in these instances simply as "Yahweh reigns" or statively as "Yahweh is king" and to understand the formulation as an affirmation of divine kingship (cf. *yimlōk* in Exod 15:18). What would be ritually true each year is not that Yahweh is king, but that the speakers so affirm it. In support of a present meaning for *mālak* in this context, cf. *bᶜlm yml[k]*, "Baal reig[ns]," in 1.2 IV 32, 34.

256. Van der Toorn, "Babylonian New Year Festival," 343–44. See also I. Nakata, "Problems of the Babylonian Akītu Festival," *JANES* 1/1 (1968): 41–49.

257. See R. de Vaux, *Ancient Israel: Its Life and Its Institutions* (trans. J. McHugh; 2 vols.; London: Darton, Longman and Todd, 1961), 2:502–6; Kraus, *Psalms 1–59*, 60–61; E. Kutsch, "Shavuot," *EncJud* 15:497–98; D. J. A. Clines, *On the Way to the Postmodern: Old Testament Essays, 1967–1998* (2 vols.; JSOTSup 292; Sheffield: Sheffield Academic Press, 1998), 1:371–94. See also B. A. Levine, *In the Presence of the Lord: A Study of Cult and Some Cultic Terms in Ancient Israel* (Leiden: Brill, 1974), 39–41.

258. For a description of the feast, see de Vaux, *Ancient Israel*, 2:495–502. For Sukkot in later sources, see Rubenstein, *The History of Sukkot in the Second Temple and Rabbinic Periods;* and Ulfgard, *Story of Sukkot.*

259. De Vaux, *Ancient Israel*, 2:496.

260. R. Coote, *Amos among the Prophets: Composition and Theology* (Philadelphia: Fortress, 1981), 57. Cf. 2 Macc 10:6–8; Josephus, *Ant.* 13.14.5.

261. *OTPs* 2:321.

262. Danby, *Mishnah*, 194–99.

263. See Rubenstein, *History of Sukkot*, 117–31.

264. Mowinckel, *Psalms in Israel's Worship*, 1:125, 132, 134; M. Delcor, "Rites pour l'obtention de la pluie," *RHR* 178 (1970): 117–32; H. Barstad, *The Religious Polemics of Amos: Studies in the Preaching of Am 2, 7B-8, 4, 1–13, 5, 1–27, 6, 4–7, 8, 14* (VTSup 34; Leiden: Brill, 1984), 72. Barstad would include 2 Sam 23:16, Jer 14–15, and possibly Lam 2:19.

265. See de Moor, *Seasonal Pattern*, 108. Generally for the Mishnaic evidence on the water-libation ritual, see J. Tabori, *Jewish Festivals in the Time of the Mishna and Talmud* (Jerusalem: Magnes, 1995), 198–200.

266. In 1 Sam 7:6, the ritual is to induce God to come in the thunderstorm in order to fight on Israel's behalf, as v. 10 indicates.

267. Mowinckel, *Psalms in Israel's Worship*, 1:125.

268. Bloch-Smith, " 'Who Is the King of Glory?' Solomon's Temple and Its Symbolism," in *Scripture and Other Artifacts: Essays on the Bible and Archaeology in Honor of Philip J. King* (ed. M. D. Coogan, J. C. Exum, and L. E. Stager; Louisville: Westminster John Knox, 1994), 18–31; reprinted and modified in her contribution to M. S. Smith, *The Pilgrimage Pattern in Exodus* (with contributions by E. M. Bloch-Smith; JSOTSup 239; Sheffield: Sheffield Academic Press, 1997), 81–100.

269. Mowinckel, *Psalms in Israel's Worship*, 1:115.

270. For example, C. Patton, "Psalm 132: A Methodological Inquiry," *CBQ* 57 (1995): 643–54, esp. 644–48.

271. On this point, see van der Toorn, "Babylonian New Year Festival," 340–41.

272. Mowinckel, *Psalms in Israel's Worship*, 1:126.

273. For these two references, see van der Toorn, "Babylonian New Year Festival," 341.

274. I thank Victor Hurowitz for help on this formulation.

275. Van der Toorn, "Babylonian New Year Festival," 344.

276. Ibid., 331–44. For further Mesopotamian evidence, see M. E. Cohen, *The Cultic Calendars of the Ancient Near East* (Bethesda, Md.: CDL Press, 1993), 400–453.

277. Mowinckel, *Psalms in Israel's Worship*, 1:121 n. 51.

278. Ibid., 1:184–85.

279. Cross, *Canaanite Myth and Hebrew Epic*, 83.

280. Cohen, *Cultic Calendars of the Ancient Near East*, 400–453.

281. So cited by Mowinckel, *Psalms in Israel's Worship*, 1:131–32; cf. 140.

282. Eaton, *Kingship and the Psalms* (2d ed.; Biblical Seminar; Sheffield: Sheffield Academic Press, 1986), 102–11, 227–28; Gray, *The Biblical Doctrine of the Reign of God* (Edinburgh: T&T Clark, 1979).

283. De Moor, *The Seasonal Pattern in the Ugaritic Myth of Ba'lu: According to the Version of Ilimilku* (AOAT 16; Kevelaer: Butzon & Bercker; Neukirchen-Vluyn: Neukirchener Verlag, 1971).

284. Loretz, *Ugarit-Texte und Thronbesteigungspsalmen: Die Metamorphose des Regenspenders Baal-Jahwe (Ps. 24,7–10; 29; 47; 93; 95–100 sowie Ps. 77,17–20; 114* (UBL 2; Münster: Ugarit-Verlag, 1984).

285. Most of the following information about Gray comes from the summary found on the page facing the title page of his book, *The Canaanites* (Ancient Peoples and Places 38; New York: Praeger, 1964).

286. Gray, *Legacy of Canaan*, vii.

287. The following story comes from James Barr, in a letter dated 11 January 1999, who advises that the tale may be apocryphal: Gray was famous in Palestine for his love of playing the bagpipes, and it was said that the one thing that Jews and the Arabs could agree on was to request jointly that the mayor of a certain town forbid his doing so!

288. Johnstone describes his work on Ugaritic in his 30 November 1998 e-mail to me: "My involvement with Ugaritic stems from my appointment as lecturer in Hebrew and Semitic Languages in Aberdeen in 1962. John Gray was then my head of department and sole colleague. Gray was interested in rapid access to the new Ugaritic texts as they were discovered and suggested to Schaeffer that I be allowed to participate in his excavations at Ugarit. Schaeffer was most cordial in his response and invited me to take part in his work at Enkomi, Cyprus, as well. In all, I did three seasons both at Ugarit and Enkomi. (I published in the Alashia volume as well as Ugaritica.) In my first season at Ugarit, Segert was also present as linguist; also H.-G. Buchholz as archaeologist and Honor Frost (with whom I had later fruitful epigraphical collaboration on the Punic ship at Marsala, Sicily) on the anchors. . . . Schaeffer very kindly gave Gray and me access to Virolleaud's *editio princeps* of the RS 24 season—hence our contributions to *Ugaritica V*. . . ."

289. For an abstract of Watson's thesis, see *NUS* 13 (May 1977): 8.

290. Gray, "Feudalism in Ugarit and Early Israel," *ZAW* 64 (1952): 49–55.

291. In addition to the works of his cited below, see Gray, "Canaanite Kingship in Theory and Practice," *VT* 2 (1952): 193–220; *Social Aspects of Canaanite Religion* (VTSup 15; Leiden: Brill, 1966); "Sacral Kingship in Ugarit," in *Ugaritica VI* (ed. C. F. A. Schaeffer; MRS 17; Paris: Geuthner, 1969), 289–302.

292. William Johnstone provided much of the following information about Gray in a 30 November 1998 e-mail to me.

293. Gray, *Canaanites*, 127. See also Gray, *Legacy of Canaan*, 10–14.

294. Gray, *Canaanites*, 127.

295. Gray, *The KRT Text in the Literature of Ras Shamra: A Social Myth of Ancient Canaan* (Leiden: Brill, 1955), 5–6.

296. Ibid., 5–6.

297. Ibid., 5.

298. Gray, *Biblical Doctrine of the Reign of God* (Edinburgh: T&T Clark, 1979).

299. Gaster, *Thespis: Ritual, Myth, and Drama in the Ancient Near East* (Garden City: Doubleday, 1950; rev. ed., 1961; repr. New York: Norton, 1977). The 1977 edition is cited below.

300. Uptown at Yeshiva University, Ugaritic was occasionally offered by Joshua Finkel (1904–1983). Finkel grew up in Warsaw, immigrated to New York in 1913, was ordained at JTS, and further trained at New York University as well as Dropsie (Ph.D., 1927). He worked primarily in medieval Jewish-Arabic texts (including during a period in Egypt from 1924 to 1926) and taught at Yeshiva University from 1937 to 1971; see *EncJud* 6:1292, and cf. M. Sokolow, "Joshua Finkel (1897[?!]–1983)," *Proceedings of the American Academy for Jewish Research* (1984–1985): 1–3 (references courtesy of R. Stein). In the mid-1950s, Finkel authored a series of articles on Ugaritic texts, especially Keret: "An Interpretation of an Ugaritic Viticultural Poem," in *The Joshua Starr Memorial Volume: Studies in History and Philology* (New York: Conference on Jewish Relations, 1953), 29–58; "The Expedition of King Keret in the Light of Jewish and Kindred Traditions," *Proceedings of the American Academy of Jewish Research* 23 (1954): 1–28; and "A Mathematical Conundrum in the Ugaritic Keret Poem," *HUCA* 25 (1955): 109–49. Finkel's students included Sol Cohen, later a doctorate in Assyriology under S. N. Kramer and E. A. Speiser at the University of Pennsylvania and professor at Dropsie College, who took Ugaritic as a college sophomore from Finkel in a summer session in 1949 (personal communication, 26 January 1999).

301. For the influence of Frazer on Gaster and others in Ugaritic studies, see Smith, "The Death of 'Dying and Rising Gods,'" 263–64. Sperling (*Students of the Covenant*, 81) defends Gaster against some of the heavier abuses of the myth-and-ritual approach of his European colleagues.

302. See R. Ackerman, *J. G. Frazer: His Life and Work* (Cambridge: Cambridge University Press, 1987), 99, 315 n. 5. Incidentally, a trenchant critic of Frazer's second edition of *The Golden Bough* (1899) was Gaster's father (Ackerman, *J. G. Frazer*, 170). In contrast, Gaster was very much influenced by Frazer; see Gaster's use of Frazer's materials in *Thespis*, 41, 49, 84, 217, 359, 367, 423, 424. I have wondered how much the son's interest in Frazer was fueled by the father's dislike for Frazer's work and the son's lifelong animosity toward his father.

303. See Smith, "The Death of 'Dying and Rising Gods,'" 263–64.

304. For a listing of the relevant works by these scholars, see de Moor, *The Seasonal Pattern*, 9–24.

305. *Thespis*, 17, 19, 24–25; cf. Gordon, *Ugaritic Literature*, 185–86.

306. *Thespis*, 128–29.

307. Ibid., 129; Gaster's italics.

308. Ibid., 18.

309. For further discussion and evaluation of Gaster's approach, see R. de Langhe, "Myth, Ritual, and Kingship in the Ras Shamra Tablets," in *Myth, Ritual, and Kingship* (ed. S. H. Hooke; Oxford: Clarendon, 1958), 132–48; Smith, *Ugaritic Baal Cycle*, 60–63.

310. De Moor, *New Year with Canaanites and Israelites* (2 vols.; Kampen: Kok, 1972), 1:6, 2:13. For de Moor's treatment of this text, see de Moor, *Anthology of Religious Texts from Ugarit*, 158.

311. For a detailed study of this text, see Levine and Tarragon, "King Proclaims the Day," 76–115. The problems avoided in the discussion here are addressed in this article. See also Wyatt, *Religious Texts from Ugarit*, 348–56; G. del Olmo Lete, *Canaanite Religion according to the Liturgical Texts of Ugarit* (trans. W. G. E. Watson; Bethesda, Md.: CDL Press, 1999), 25, 26 n. 52, 39, 107–26. It is possible *šmtr* is a verb as many commentators take it; if so, it might be expected that its form would be prefix indicative as with the forms

in lines 3, etc.; however, it is not. Therefore, one might entertain the possibility of a passive participle understood prescriptively.

312. For the larger West Semitic context of the calendar, especially the basic structure of seven-day spring and fall festivals, see D. E. Fleming, "The Israelite Festival Calendar and Emar's Ritual Archive," *RB* 106 (1999): 8–34, esp. 29–32.

313. For discussions of the biblical evidence pertaining to the calendar, see the important study of I. Knohl, *The Sanctuary of Silence: The Priestly Torah and the Holiness School* (Minneapolis: Fortress, 1995), 8–45; and D. E. Fleming, "The Israelite Festival Calendar and Emar's Ritual Archive," 8–34.

314. See the communal atonement ritual of 1.40, translated and annotated in Wyatt, *Religious Texts from Ugarit,* 342–47. For the background of the "Azazel ritual" in Lev 16, see B. Janowski and G. Wilhelm, "Der Bock, der die Sünden hinausträgt: Zur Religionsgeschichte des Azazel-Ritus Lev 16,10.21f," in *Religionsgeschichtliche Beziehungen zwischen Kleinasien, Nordsyrien, und dem Alten Testament: Internationales Symposion Hamburg 17.–21. März 1990* (ed. B. Janowski, K. Koch, and G. Wilhelm; OBO 129; Freiburg, Switzerland: Universitätsverlag; Göttingen: Vandenhoeck & Ruprecht, 1993), 109–69.

315. For example, Yom Kippur attests to the divine determination of life in the "book of life" for the coming year. It is tempting to trace this motif to the Mesopotamian "tablets of fate" that came into play on the seventh day of the seventh month (Tashrit). Indeed, a Mesopotamian text recently published witnesses to this motif associated with this month, which in turn raises the issue of Mesopotamian influence on Yom Kippur. A. Cavigneaux and F. Al-Rawi, "New Sumerian Literary Texts from Tell Hadad (Ancient Meturan): A First Survey," *Iraq* 55 (1993): 91–105, esp. 96–97. I thank Victor Hurowitz for bringing this article to my attention. On the notion of the tablets, see S. M. Paul, "Heavenly Tablets and the Books of Life," *JANES* 5 (1973 = T. H. Gaster Festschrift): 345–53.

316. See D. Marcus, review of de Moor, *New Year with Canaanites and Israelites,* *JAOS* 93 (1973): 589–91.

317. Cross, *From Epic to Canon: History and Literature in Ancient Israel* (Baltimore/London: Johns Hopkins University Press, 1998), 39.

318. For a full discussion, see Smith, "Death of 'Dying and Rising Gods,'" 257–313, esp. 260–69.

319. Ibid., 289–311.

320. Levine and Tarragon, "Dead Kings and Rephaim," 649–59, esp. 656–58; Lewis, *Cults of the Dead in Ancient Israel and Ugarit* (HSM 39; Atlanta: Scholars Press, 1989), 41–43; Anderson, *A Time to Mourn, a Time to Dance: The Expression of Grief and Joy in Israelite Religion* (University Park, Pa.: Pennsylvania State University Press, 1991), 60–67. See in addition to his editions of the text (see below), Pardee's comments in his article, "*Marziḥu, Kispu,* and the Ugaritic Funerary Cult: A Minimalist View," in *Ugarit, Religion and Culture,* 273–87, esp. 274–76; see also Loretz, *Ugarit und der Bibel,* 128–33. I would favor Lewis's view that it is Ammurapi who is told to descend, aided by the illumination of Shapshu.

321. Levine and Tarragon, "Dead Kings and Rephaim," 657. The authors' italics.

322. So Bordreuil and Pardee, "Les textes," 158.

323. So Lewis, *Cults of the Dead,* 43. A third possibility, namely the royal furniture, is contextually plausible, but, again, the parallel wording noted here would militate against this view. For a thorough, critical review, see D. T. Tsumura, "The Interpretation of the Ugaritic Funerary Text *KTU* 1.161," in *Official Cult and Popular Religion in the Ancient Near East: Papers of the First Colloquium on the Ancient Near East—the City and Its Life Held at the Middle Eastern Culture Center in Japan (Mitaka, Tokyo). March 20–22, 1992* (ed. E. Matsushima; Heidelberg: Universitätsverlag C. Winter, 1993), 40–55, esp. 45–52. As Tsumura's discussion indicates, no view is without its difficulty.

324. Levine and Tarragon, "Dead Kings and Rephaim," 657.

325. The prepositional phrase ʿmh could be translated "with her" or "to him." The preposition ʿm commonly means "with" in the sense of accompaniment (e.g., CTA 1.1 IV 14; 1.3 III 24, 25, IV 11–12; 1.5 I 22–23, 24–25, V 8, 10–11, 20) and so it might be thought that ʿmh is to be rendered "with her," namely Anat. Accordingly, *yrd ʿm might seem to mean "to descend with" (as opposed to "to descend to"); so D. Pardee, "The Preposition in Ugaritic," UF 7 (1975): 350, UF 8 (1976): 279 (see also 317–18). Yet ʿm is not uncommon with verbs in the sense of "to, toward": *ytn pnm ʿm in 1.1 IV 21–22; 1.2 I 4, 14, 19; 1.3 III 37, IV 21; 1.4 V 23, VIII 1–4; 1.5 I 9–10, II 14–15, in some cases parallel with tk (e.g., 1.2 I 19; 1.5 II 14–15), and *lsm ʿm in 1.3 III 19 (cf. 1.1 IV 11 and commonly reconstructed elsewhere in the same formulas). Finally, it is to be noted that *yrd l- means "to descend from" (UF 7 [1975]: 350), and no other preposition with *yrd means "to descend to." Therefore, *yrd ʿm may mean "to descend to." Note Pardee's comments on the overlap between l-, "to," and ʿm, "with," in UF 8 (1976): 317–18. Accordingly, Baal might seem to be the object of the preposition in order to indicate Shapshu's role in accompanying Anat to the underworld to locate his corpse.

326. This clause is narrative and not direct discourse, although on purely grammatical grounds it would be possible to render it so ("To him you will descend, O Divine Light, Shapshu"). The larger indicator of narrative derives from the following clause beginning with ʿd (1.6 I 9). This is a subordinating conjunction that begins clauses governed by a preceding independent verb, in this case trd. Anderson (A Time to Mourn, 63–64) divides the lines differently, rendering: "We [Anat and Shapshu] are descending into the netherworld, to the place of Baal/The torch of the gods, Shapshu, descended." This division is unlikely, as "into the netherworld" would be parallel to "to Baal." (His translation omits the prepositional phrase ʿmh.) Furthermore, parallels in 1.161.20–21 and Gen 37:35 makes it unlikely that ʾatr bʿl is to be understood literally as "to the place of Baal."

327. It is this language of the dead king that may lie behind the allusion to bʿl in 1.17 VI 30 and not the storm-god, Baal, as generally thought.

328. Levine and Tarragon, "Dead Kings and Rephaim," 657.

329. Based on ʾard in the parallel in 1.5 VI 25, some scholars emend to ʾard, but the emendation is not necessary. It could be argued that the context with both Anat and Shapshu would comport with the plural form.

330. The description of Anat descending and fetching the corpse of Baal may also help to locate the *Sitz im Leben* of KTU 1.161; the comparison of the two texts would point to KTU 1.161 as a funerary text on behalf of the most recently deceased king, Niqmaddu, as argued by P. Bordreuil and D. Pardee ("Les textes en cunéiformes alphabétiques," in *Une bibliothèque au sud de la ville: Les textes de la 34e campagne (1973)* [RSO 7; Paris: Editions Recherche sur les Civilisations, 1991], 151–63) and Lewis (*Cult of the Dead*, 32), and perhaps not a text commemorating his death, as suggested by Levine and Tarragon ("Dead Kings and Rephaim," 654). In the narrative (1.6 I 11–15), the sun-goddess Shapshu loads the body onto Anat so that she can provide Baal with an appropriate burial and funerary offerings. This narrative detail presumes the sun-goddess's capacity to aid in locating the deceased, and it may also presuppose a role for her in bringing up the deceased in rituals of necromancy. This role is known for Shamash in Mesopotamian ritual of necromancy (see I. Finkel, "Necromancy in Ancient Mesopotamia," AfO 29–30 [1983–1984]: 1–17; Lewis, *Cults of the Dead*, 38) and the same may lie behind the narrative account of Shapshu's setting Baal's corpse on Anat's shoulders in 1.6 I 14–15.

331. The ritual text, KTU 1.161, dates to the late thirteenth century B.C.E. while the Baal Cycle has long been thought to date a century earlier. It has been generally thought that this scribe, responsible for copying the major mythological texts (including the Baal Cycle), worked in the early fourteenth century, during the reign of Niqmaddu II. However, lower dates for Ilimalku the scribe (usually called Ilimilku) named by two of the tab-

lets of the Baal Cycle have been entertained. In 1992, a fragment of a mythological text with Ilimalku's name was reportedly discovered in the house of Urtennu, an official who served Niqmaddu III during the latter part of the thirteenth century. See F. Malbran-Labat, "Les archives de la Maison d'Ourtenu," *CRAIBL* (1995): 447–48; A. S. Dalix, "Exemples de bilinguisme à Ougarit. ʾIloumilku: la double identité d'un scribe," in *Mosaïque de langues mosaïques culturelle: Le bilinguisme dans le Proche-Orient ancien. Actes de la Table-Ronde du novembre 1995 organisée par l'URA 1062 "Etudes sémitiques"* (ed. F. Briquel-Chatonnet; Antiquités Sémitiques 1; Paris: Maisonneuve, 1996), 81–90; and W. Pitard, "The Alphabetic Ugaritic Texts," in *Handbook of Ugaritic Studies* (ed. W. G. E. Watson and N. Wyatt; HdO 1/39; Leiden: Brill, 1999), 54–55. Accordingly, the date of this scribe's literary activity as well as the literary texts attributed to him may be lowered by over a century. According to D. Pardee (personal communication), the hand seems to involve the same scribe, suggesting that the evidence does not involve two scribes by the same name. In either case, direct literary influence need not be posited.

332. *KTU* 1.113 may also bear on the royal cult of the dead (see D. Pardee, *Les textes paramythologiques de la 24ᵉ campagne (1961)* [RSO 4; Paris: Editions Recherche sur les Civilisations, 1988], 170–78), as attested in 1.3 I and 1.17 VI. The front of the text describes musical instrumentation, either described as *nᶜm*, "goodly," or perhaps played by a figure called *nᶜm*. The back of the text consists of a king list originally containing at least thirty-two names and perhaps as many as fifty-two (Pardee, *Les textes paramythologiques,* 173). Despite the differences in details among the texts in question (ibid., 170–78), it would appear that the royal cult of Ugarit invoked the dead ancestors (*KTU* 1.161) and perhaps this cult is reflected in the musical instrumentation in *KTU* 1.113. *KTU* 1.3 I and 1.17 V 28–33 apparently drew on this imagery. A further connection among these texts might involve 1.108, if the figure of *rp'u* who plays music in this text is to be identified with *nᶜm* or is to be viewed as the eponymous tribal figure corresponding or related to the royal figure of *nᶜm*. This figure of *rp'u* leads the musical entertainment of the *ḫbr kṯr ṯbm* (either "the goodly companions of Kothar" or "the goodly ones divined by Kothar"), who may be the Rephaim as suggested by M. S. Smith (in Pardee, *Les textes paramythologiques,* 100 n. 111).

333. This crucial insight about this text was made by J. C. Greenfield, "Une rite religieux araméen et ses parallèles," *RB* 80 (1973): 46–52. Accordingly, this is another reason to entertain the possibility that the *bᶜl* mentioned in 1.17 VI 28–33 is not the god Baal, but the figure of the deceased human "lord."

334. For this problem in Egypt and Mesopotamia, see W. W. Hallo, *Origins: The Ancient Near Eastern Background of Some Modern Western Institutions* (Studies in the History and Culture of the Ancient Near East 6; Leiden: Brill, 1996), 152, 196–210 (esp. 203), 229.

335. Ideally speaking, Kirta cannot die since he is a "son of El," the cliché used in the Baal Cycle for divinities. After all, as indicated in the last of the remarks made by Kirta's son, deities do not die and Kirta belongs to their rank. Yet Kirta is indisputably mortal. So, too, in the Baal Cycle's theological and literary vision of the universe: Baal, the patron of Ugaritic kings, undergoes death. And his death was congruent with the conceptual tension between the divine character of kings and the dynasty and their well-known mortal nature. Yet Baal is a major god, and no major deity with a current cult remains dead in mythological narratives. On many of these texts and their royal background, see esp. J. F. Healey, "The Immortality of the King: Ugarit and the Psalms," *Or* 53 (1984): 245–54.

336. For sleep and death as expressions for one another in the ancient Middle East, see T. H. McAlpine, *Sleep, Divine & Human, in the Old Testament* (JSOTSup 38; Sheffield: Sheffield Academic Press, 1987), 135–49. McAlpine also notes some differences in the u of these two sorts of language. For divine sleep in general, see McAlpine, *Sleep,* 181–99. McAlpine shows, sleep is hardly exclusive to the figures in Frazer's category. Rather, sleep is described as the daily activity of many main deities in Mesopotamian literature

(McAlpine, *Sleep*, 183–86) and of Yahweh (*m. Maʿaśer Sheni* 5.15; McAlpine, *Sleep*, 194–95, 233 n. 15). As McAlpine observes, most of these examples of divine sleep run not on an annual cycle, but on a daily cycle. The biblical language regarding Yahweh's sleep (e.g., Pss 44:24–25; 78:65; 121:3–4) does not involve annual sleep/death à la Dumuzi, but divine sleep during an occasion of human need. McAlpine strongly criticizes attempts to amalgamate these different sorts of divine sleep, which he lays out nicely (*Sleep*, 194–95).

337. For documentation of this point, see Smith, *Ugaritic Baal Cycle*, 104–5.

338. Fitzgerald, review of J. Gray, *The Biblical Doctrine of the Reign of God*, *Interpretation* 35/4 (1981): 415.

339. Futato, "A Meteorological Analysis of Psalms 104, 65, and 29" (Ph.D. diss., Catholic University of America, 1984).

340. Nash, "The Palestinian Agricultural Year and the Book of Joel" (Ph.D. diss., Catholic University of America, 1989).

341. Ginsberg, "A Phoenician Hymn in the Psalter," in *Atti del XIX Congresso Internazionale degli Orientalisti. Roma, 23–29 Settembre 1935–XIII* (Rome: Tipografia del Senato, 1938), 472–76. A number of scholars have gone so far as to suggest that Ps 29 was originally a Canaanite text; see J. L. Cunchillos, *Estudio des Salmo 29: Canto as Dos de la fertilidad-fecundidad. Aportación al conocimiento de la fe de Israel a su entrada en Canaan* (Valencia: La Institución San Jerónimo, 1976). Note also the argument of A. Fitzgerald ("A Note on Psalm 29," *BASOR* 215 [1974]: 61–63) that restoring the divine name Baal wherever Yahweh occurs in Ps 29 significantly improves the psalm's alliteration and assonance.

342. For the weather and Ps 29, see Futato, "A Meteorological Analysis of Psalms 104, 65, and 29." For this reading of Ps 29:9, see pp. 160–61 in the next chapter.

343. For the background of Ps 68, see more recently J. Gray, "A Cantata of the Autumn Festival: Ps. LXVIII," *JSS* 22 (1977): 2–26; J. C. de Moor, *The Rise of Yahwism: The Roots of Israelite Monotheism* (2d ed.; BETL 91; Leuven: Peeters, 1997), 171–88.

344. As observed in detail by Ginsberg, "A Strand in the Cord of Hebrew Psalmody," *EI* 9 (1969 = W. F. Albright volume): 45–50.

345. So also Brettler, *God Is King*, 150, 153, 158. According to Brettler, the idea of foreigners worshiping at Jerusalem is a matter of wishful thinking and the psalms with this theme and therefore the entire complex of Pss 93–100 contain ideal expressions not based on real liturgy. Yet it is possible that such ideal expressions could be incorporated into liturgy, possibly as the reflection of the practice of captives bringing gifts (Ps 68:18, 29) or perhaps vassals submitting tribute to their overlord, the Judean king (see J. J. M. Roberts, "The Religio-political Setting of Psalm 47," *BASOR* 220 [1975]: 129–32). In any case, even in Brettler's literary model, setting remains a desideratum. The study of Howard (*The Structure of Psalms 93–100*) would also point in the direction of a literary model, although he does not address this issue.

346. Mowinckel, *Psalms in Israel's Worship*, 1:117–18 and his comment on 1:106: "granted there *is* such a cultic situation" (Mowinckel's italics).

347. Smith, *Ugaritic Baal Cycle*, 98 n. 189.

348. For further discussion of this position, see ibid., 68–69, 98–99.

349. M. Yon,"Réalités agraires et mythologie d'Ougarit," in *Rites et rythmes agraires* (ed. M. C. Cauvin; Travaux de la Maison de l'Orient 20; Lyon: GIS–Maison de l'Orient, 1991), 53–68.

350. So too A. R. Petersen, *The Royal God: Enthronement Festivals in Ancient Israel and Ugarit?* (JSOTSup 259; Copenhagen International Seminar 5; Sheffield: Sheffield Academic Press, 1998). Unfortunately, the author presents no argumentation for his views. There is no study of primary texts, Ugaritic or biblical. Judgments should be based on evidence, and here Ugaritic texts known since Mowinckel's work, especially *KTU* 1.161, have much to offer, but one would not know this from examining Petersen's discussion. Similarly, the lack of basic secondary sources hardly inspires confidence (e.g., van der Toorn

on the Mesopotamian and biblical evidence for the enthronement festival, Courtois and North on the archaeology of Ugarit, the extensive literature on the *marzeaḥ*). It is odd to be informed on p. 7 that the author was unable to incorporate points from my book, *The Ugaritic Baal Cycle*, even though this volume was published in 1994 and Petersen's study appeared in 1998! More seriously, Petersen's presentation of Mowinckel's theory as it pertains to the Ugaritic texts omits some crucial elements (e.g., Baal as a dying and rising god). Petersen's own view of the Baal Cycle presented in almost exclusively meteorological terms is reductionist.

351. See Wyatt, *Myths of Power*, 131–34.

352. Roberts, "Religio-political Setting of Psalm 47," 129–32. Discussed above is also the defense of van der Toorn, "Babylonian New Year Festival," 331–44. See also Cohen, *Cultic Calendars of the Ancient Near East*, 400–453.

353. For an example, B. Uffenheimer, "Myth and Reality in Ancient Israel," in *The Origins and Diversity of Axial Civilizations* (ed. S. N. Eisenstadt; Albany: State University of New York, 1986), 135, with references on p. 505.

354. In an otherwise fine treatment, F. M. Cross (*Canaanite Myth and Hebrew Epic*, 241–65) describes Judean royal ideology, but without drawing out the *mythos* of this ideology sufficiently. The exception is a fine observation unfortunately buried in a footnote (258 n. 177; see Smith, *Ugaritic Baal Cycle*, 109; addressed below). In contrast, the brunt of Judean royal ideology *mythos* comes out well in P. Mosca, "Ugaritic and Daniel 7: A Missing Link," *Bib* 67 (1986): 496–517. Without engaging the entire debate over this issue, I subscribe to the view that in Judean royal ideology the human and divine king hold parallel realms—terrestrial and cosmic—reinforcing one another and centered on the cosmic mountain against cosmic and terrestrial enemies (Pss 2, 72, 89), that the king partakes of (or participates in, to echo older Thomistic metaphysical language) the power of the divine king (Ps 89:26; see below), that the king is conceived as a royal son on the day of coronation (Ps 2:7), and that the Judean royal ideology possibly included the application of the term *ʾēl/ʾĕlōhîm* to the monarch (Ps 45:7). For discussion, see Smith, "Myth and Myth-Making in Ugaritic and Israelite Literatures," in *Ugarit and the Bible*, 309–21. To this degree we may speak of divine kingship or sacral kingship in Judean royal circles. It is to misframe the question to claim that Israel in general rejected such a view of the king or could not abide such a view of the king. For lack of sources, we should be less confident about what can be said of such a monarchic *mythos* in northern royal ideology. See also Chapter Four below.

355. See J. Jeremias, *Das Königtum Gottes in den Psalmen: Israels Begegnung mit dem kanaanäischen Mythos in den Jahwe-König-Psalmen* (FRLANT 141; Göttingen: Vandenhoeck & Ruprecht, 1987); B. Janowski, "Das Königtum Gottes in den Psalmen: Bemerkungen zu einem neuen Gesamtentwurf," *ZTK* 86 (1989): 389–454.

356. Ahlström, *Aspects of Syncretism in Israelite Religion* (Horae Soederblomianae 5; Lund: Gleerup, 1963).

357. Albright, "The Role of the Canaanites in the History of Civilization," in *The Bible and the Ancient Near East: Essays in Honor of W. F. Albright* (ed. G. E. Wright; New York: Doubleday, 1961), 338 (cited in Petersen, *Royal God*, 92). See already in 1949 a similar statement in Albright, "The Biblical Period," in *The Jews: Their History, Culture, and Religion* (ed. L. Finkelstein; 2d ed.; 2 vols.; Philadelphia: Jewish Publication Society of America, 1949), 1:10: "Among the Canaanites extremely depraved practices were inextricably bound up with religion."

358. See D. R. Hillers, "Criticizing the Abominable: Our Understanding of Canaanite Religion," *JQR* 75 (1985): 253–69; also Hillers, "William F. Albright as a Philologian," 53.

359. Gray, *Canaanites*, 127.

360. Gray, *Legacy of Canaan*, 257.

361. Oldenburg, *The Conflict between El and Ba'al in Canaanite Religion* (Supplement to Numen 3; Leiden: Brill, 1969), xi. Cited in Smith, *Ugaritic Baal Cycle*, xxvii; and Petersen, *Royal God*, 92–93. A similar personal view undermines the later work of G. E. Mendenhall, *The Tenth Generation: The Origins of the Biblical Tradition* (Baltimore/London: Johns Hopkins University Press, 1973), 226; discussed in Smith, *Ugaritic Baal Cycle*, xxviii.

362. Wright, *The Old Testament against its Environment* (Studies in Biblical Theology 2; London: SCM, 1950), 22. On the problematic modern use of myth, see R. A. Oden, Jr., *The Bible without Theology: The Theological Tradition and Alternatives to It* (San Francisco: Harper & Row, 1987), 40–91. For West Semitic myth in the Bible and its political and religious uses, see the discussions of Cross, Emerton, and Greenfield above; and the collections of material in Smith, "Myth and Myth-Making," 293–334; and Wyatt, *Myths of Power*, esp. 417–18.

363. Mendenhall's *The Tenth Generation* is suffused with this perspective. See further his article, "The Worship of Baal and Asherah: A Study in the Social Bonding Functions of Religious Systems," in *Biblical and Related Studies Presented to Samuel Iwry* (ed. A. Kort and S. Morschauser; Winona Lake, Ind.: Eisenbrauns, 1985), 147–58.

364. Mendenhall, *The Tenth Generation*, 223; Habel, *Yahweh versus Baal*, 63.

365. See D. R. Hillers, "Analyzing the Abominable: Our Understanding of Canaanite Religion," *JQR* 75 (1985): 253–69; del Olmo Lete, *Canaanite Religion*, 156–58. For the classic critique of the category of history in biblical scholarship (beginning with Wright), see B. Albrektson, *History and the Gods: An Essay on the Idea of Historical Events as Divine Manifestations in the Ancient Near East and in Israel* (ConBOT 1; Lund: Gleerup, 1967); and more recently I. Cornelius, "The Iconography of Divine War in the Pre-Islamic Near East: A Survey," *JNWSL* 21 (1995): 15–16.

366. For a survey, see Smith, "Myth and Myth-Making," 293–341.

367. For a caution against identifying "fertility" primarily with goddesses or a particular goddess (as opposed to gods), see J. A. Hackett, "Can a Sexist Model Liberate Us? Ancient Near Eastern 'Fertility' Goddesses," *Journal of Feminist Studies in Religion* 5 (1989): 65–76. See the well-placed caution of P. D. Miller against reducing Ugaritic religion to simply a "fertility religion" (Miller, "Aspects of the Religion of Israel," in *Ancient Israelite Religion: Essays in Honor of Frank Moore Cross* [ed. P. D. Miller, Jr., P. D. Hanson, and S. D. McBride; Philadelphia: Fortress, 1987], 59). For a well-placed critique on the issue of nature, see Wyatt, *Myths of Power*, 377 n. 8. For a revisiting of the problem of *hieros gamos* in Mesopotamia (with implications for biblical studies), see J. S. Cooper, "Sacred Marriage and Popular Cult in Early Mesopotamia," in *Official Cult and Popular Religion in the Ancient Near East: Papers of the First Colloquium on the Ancient Near East—the City and Its Life Held at the Middle Eastern Culture Center in Japan (Mitaka, Tokyo). March 20–22, 1992* (ed. E. Matsushima; Heidelberg: Universitätsverlag C. Winter, 1993), 81–96.

368. Here the intellectual trajectory from Mendenhall to N. Gottwald is evident. See Gottwald, *The Tribes of Israel: A Sociology of the Religion of the Liberated Israel 1250–1050 BCE* (Maryknoll: Orbis, 1979).

369. Cross, *Canaanite Myth and Hebrew Epic: Essays in the History of the Religion of Israel* (Cambridge, Mass.: Harvard University Press, 1973).

370. Mettinger, *King and Messiah: The Civil and Sacral Legitimation of the Israelite Kings* (ConBOT 8; Lund: Gleerup, 1976), 254–75. See also J. Day, "The Canaanite Inheritance of the Israelite Monarchy," *King and Messiah in the Ancient Near East: Proceedings of the Oxford Old Testament Seminar* (ed. J. Day; JSOTSup 270; Sheffield: Sheffield Academic Press, 1998), 72–90.

371. Sandmel, "Parallelomania," *JBL* 81 (1962): 1–13. See the further reflections on the Assyriological side by W. W. Hallo, "Albright and the Gods of Mesopotamia," *BA* 56/1 (1993): 18–24.

372. Gordon, "Indo-European and Hebrew Epic," *11.

chapter three

New Texts and Crisis in Comparative Method: 1970 to 1985

The postwar era represented a period of massive synthesis in many areas of language, literature, religion, and history. The period after 1970 was distinguished by the appearance of new texts and journals. The first major new corpus of Ugaritic texts appeared in *Ugaritica V* in 1968.[1] Excavations at Ras ibn Hani, a small port near Ugarit, also produced new texts during this era.[2] This period also witnessed the publication of several tablets stolen from Ras Shamra in 1957.[3] All these texts spurred new activity in the field, reflected especially in the new periodicals, *Ugarit-Forschungen, Aula Orientalis, Studi epigrafici e linguistici, The Newsletter for Ugaritic Studies,* and *Maarav.*

⋈ TEXTS AND TOOLS

Archaeology: French mission's report in *Ras Shamra 1929–1979* (Lyon: Maison de l'Orient, 1979). O. Callot, *Une maison à Ougarit* (RSO 1; Paris: Editions Recherche sur les Civilisations, 1983).

New Texts: Texts from seasons of RIH 77 and 78: P. Bordreuil and A. Caquot, "Les textes en cunéiformes alphabétiques découverts en 1978 à Ibn Hani," *Syria* 57 (1980): 343–73; P. Bordreuil and D. Pardee, "L'epigraphie ougaritique: 1973–1993," in *Le pays d'Ougarit au tour de 1200 av. J.C. Historie et archéologie. Actes du Colloque International, Paris, 28 juin–1ᵉʳ juillet 1993* (ed. M. Yon, M. Sznycer, and P. Bordreuil; RSO 11; Paris: Editions Recherche sur les Civilisations, 1995), 27–32. M. Dietrich, O. Loretz, and J. Sanmartín, *Die keilalphabetischen Texte aus Ugarit: Einschliesslich der keilalphabetischen Texte ausserhalb Ugarits. Teil 1: Transkription* (AOAT 24/1; Kevelaer: Butzon & Bercker; Neukirchen-Vluyn: Neukirchener Verlag, 1976). Hippiatric text editions:

C. Cohen and D. Sivan, *The Ugaritic Hippiatric Texts: A Critical Edition* (New Haven: American Oriental Society, 1983); D. Pardee, *Les textes hippiatriques* (RSO 2; Paris: Editions Recherche sur les Civilisations, 1985).[4] R. E. Whitaker, *Concordance of the Ugaritic Literature* (Cambridge: Harvard University Press, 1972). S. Segert, *A Basic Grammar of the Ugaritic Language* (Berkeley/Los Angeles/London: University of California, 1984). Survey and synthesis: *DBSup* 9 (1979): 1124–1442.

Translations: A. Caquot, M. Sznycer, and A. Herdner, *Textes ougaritiques: Tome I. Mythes et Légends* (LAPO 7; Paris: Cerf, 1974). J. Clear, *Ugaritic Texts in Translation* (2d ed.; Seattle: University of Washington, 1976). M. D. Coogan, *Stories from Ancient Canaan* (Philadelphia: Westminster, 1978). J. C. L. Gibson, *Canaanite Myths and Legends* (2d ed.; Edinburgh: T&T Clark, 1978). G. del Olmo Lete, *Mitos y leyendas segun la tradicion de Ugarit* (Madrid: Ediciones Cristiandad, 1981).

Studies and Commentaries: H. H. P. Dressler, "The AQHT Text: A New Transcription, Translation, Commentary, and Introduction" (Ph.D. diss., Cambridge University, 1976). P. Xella, *Il mito di ŠḤR e ŠLM: Saggio sulla mitologia ugaritica* (Studi Semitici 44; Rome: Istituto di Studi del Vicino Oriente, 1981).

Synthetic Studies on Religion: F. M. Cross, *Canaanite Myth and Hebrew Epic: Essays in the History of the Religion of Israel* (Cambridge: Harvard University Press, 1973). G. Fohrer, *History of Israelite Religion* (trans. D. E. Green; Nashville, Tenn.: Abingdon, 1972). J. Eaton, *Kingship and the Psalms* (London: SCM, 1976; 2d ed., Sheffield: Sheffield Academic Press, 1986). H. Gese, M. Höfner, and K. Rudolph, *Religionen Altsyriens, Altarabiens, und der Mandäer* (Religionen der Menschheit 10.2; Stuttgart: Kohlhammer, 1970). J. Gray, *The Biblical Doctrine of the Reign of God* (Edinburgh: T&T Clark, 1979). K. Koch's essays collected in *Studien zur alttestamentlichen und altorientalischen Religionsgeschichte* (Göttingen: Vandenhoeck & Ruprecht, 1988). B. A. Levine, *In the Presence of the Lord: A Study of Cult and Some Cultic Terms in Ancient Israel* (Leiden: Brill, 1974). T. N. D. Mettinger, *King and Messiah: The Civil and Sacral Legitimation of the Israelite Kings* (ConBOT 8; Lund: Gleerup, 1976); *The Dethronement of Sabaoth: Studies in Shem and Kabod Theologies* (ConBOT 18; Lund: Gleerup, 1982). J. C. de Moor, *The Seasonal Pattern in the Ugaritic Myth of Baʿlu: According to the Version of Ilimilku* (AOAT 16; Kevelaer: Butzon & Bercker; Neukirchen-Vluyn: Neukirchener Verlag, 1971); *New Year with Canaanites and Israelites* (Kampen: Kok, 1972); "The Semitic Pantheon of Ugarit," *UF* 2 (1970): 187–228. *Ras Shamra Parallels I* (ed. L. Fisher; AnOr 49–50; Rome: Pontifical Biblical Institute, 1972). *Ras Shamra Parallels II* (ed. L. Fisher; AnOr 49–50; Rome: Pontifical Biblical Institute, 1975). *Ras Shamra Parallels III* (ed. S. Rummel; AnOr 51; Rome: Pontifical Biblical Institute, 1981).

⊠ TEXTS AND TOOLS, LANGUAGE AND GRAMMAR

The publication of *Ugaritica V* first of all advanced the understanding of Ugaritic grammar, thanks to the polyglot vocabularies with their columns of words giving lexical correspondences in Sumerian, Akkadian, Hurrian, and Ugaritic in syllabic transcription. These lists of Ugaritic words provided the first substantial source of Ugaritic words with vowels. Up to this time, scholars had largely relied on the three *ʾaleph*s in Ugaritic to discern the vowels following the *ʾaleph*s (except in the cases of syllable-closing *ʾi-ʾaleph*), and each of the three *ʾaleph*s could represent either a long vowel or a short vowel, and in some cases a collapsed diphthong.[5] Scholars had also looked to Ugaritic loanwords in the

Akkadian texts from Ugarit in order to determine the vowels in Ugaritic words. The vocalic structures of many West Semitic words from roughly this period were known from the El-Amarna letters. However, the publication of the polyglot vocabulary texts marked a new stage in the field's knowledge of the vowels in Ugaritic words. A series of articles and book-length studies appeared on the Ugaritic words in the polyglots and in Akkadian texts, beginning especially with J. L. Boyd's 1975 University of Chicago dissertation,[6] and culminating in D. Sivan's fine 1984 study,[7] and J. Huehnergard's masterful 1987 book.[8] This period witnessed other important grammatical studies, including H. R. Cohen's monograph on *hapax legomena*,[9] K. Aartun's study of Ugaritic particles,[10] and D. Pardee's important 1974 University of Chicago dissertation on "The Preposition in Ugaritic."[11] Canaanite continued to be a major category in the Ugaritic-biblical discussion,[12] but while the discussion on the linguistic level increased in the number of isoglosses cited, no consensus on major issues emerged.

Also prominent at the outset of the 1970s was research on fourteen other texts published in *Ugaritica V.* The new texts elicited a flurry of scholarly activity, especially in the major venue of *Ugarit-Forschungen.*

This period also witnessed the important concordance of Ugaritic texts by R. E. Whitaker, which stood as a standard reference work for over two decades. S. Pfann supplemented Whitaker's work with his concordance for the *Ugaritica VII* texts in 1980.[13] Yet Whitaker's work was superseded only in 1995, when three works appeared: the three-volume concordance of J.-L. Cunchillos and J. P. Vita, *Concordancia de Palabras Ugaríticas;* M. Dietrich and O. Loretz, *Word-List of the Cuneiform Alphabetic Texts from Ugarit, Ras Ibn Hani, and Other Places;* and Petr Zemánek, *Ugaritischer Wortformenindex.*[14]

This period also witnessed the appearance of several new journals devoted largely to Ugaritic: *Ugarit-Forschungen (UF),* edited by Manfried Dietrich and Oswald Loretz; *Aula Orientalis (AO),* edited by Gregorio del Olmo Lete; *Studi epigraphici e linguistici (SEL),* edited by Paolo Xella; *Maarav,* a journal cofounded by Bruce Zuckerman and Gary Tuttle, two of Marvin Pope's doctoral students in the mid-1970s; and the *Newsletter for Ugaritic Studies (NUS),* edited from 1972 to 1985 by Peter Craigie (Calgary), with Christopher Foley (Saskatoon), Shlomo Izre'el (Tel Aviv), and Wilfred Watson (Dublin and Newcastle) serving as associate editors, and from 1985 to 1990 edited by Foley, with Watson (Newcastle), J. Glen Taylor (Toronto), and J. Sanmartín (Barcelona) serving as associate editors. The newsletter kept the field apprised of all the latest developments in the field and provided a wealth of information about Ugaritic. In particular, Watson offered a series of lexical notes in issues of the newsletter. Finally, in the area of basic resources, this period also marked the appearance of the new and enhanced photographic work of Bruce Zuckerman aided by his brother, Kenneth Zuckerman. Some of their earliest photographs appeared in issues of *Maarav*.[15] These new texts, tools, and journals demonstrate the ongoing vitality of the discipline in this period.

⊠ POETRY

Building on the brilliant studies of H. L. Ginsberg, U. Cassuto, M. Held, M. Tsevat, and S. Gevirtz, the study of poetry entered a new stage at this point. W. G. E. Watson's *Classical Hebrew Poetry* brought to bear a myriad of examples of West Semitic poetic phenomena shared by the Ugaritic texts and Hebrew Bible.[16] Watson's book set a new benchmark with its systematic collection of poetic features in both corpora. It also showed the larger West Semitic literary tradition that encompasses biblical poetry. In his book on West Semitic poetry, D. Pardee attempted a complex analysis of one Ugartic text and one biblical text to demonstrate the complexities of poetic features on multiple levels in both literatures.[17]

The major contribution of the discussion of poetry in this period was the appreciation of the types of parallelism that came to be distinguished from one another. A. Berlin's fine book on poetic parallelism devotes separate chapters to grammatical parallelism (under the rubrics of morphological and syntactical parallelism), lexical and semantic parallelism, and sonant parallelism.[18] While the relationships among these sorts of parallelism continued to be debated,[19] it was clear from this discussion that poetic analysis had moved well beyond the older notational approach, which did not differentiate these sorts of parallelism adequately.

A related issue is identifying the basic unit of West Semitic poetry, which most scholars have assumed to be the couplet or bicolon (as indicated by parallelism between lines). However, research in this period focused on the individual line in its various types (including monocolons).[20] Monocolons with refined poetic features would point to the individual line as a basic block of poetry. For example, Ps 136 with its monocolons followed by the same refrain supports this possibility. Similarly, in Num 12:13 Moses pleads to God on Miriam's behalf in a beautiful monocolon: *ʾēl nāʾ rĕpâ ʾ nāʾ lāh* (rendered literally: "God, please, heal, please, her"). The line provides a fine balance in its chiasm: (A) *ʾēl*, (B) *nāʾ*, (C) *rĕpâ ʾ*, (B') *nāʾ*, (A') *lāh*. The element, *rĕpâ ʾ*, stands in the middle, the elements in B and B' are identical, and in A and A' the letter *l* (lamed), perhaps aided by the gutteral letters, ʾ (*ʾaleph*) and *h* (*he*), signals the connection.

The important poetic phenomenon of alliteration functions more thoroughly on the level of the line than on the level of the couplet.[21] A classic example may be found in the bicolon of *KTU* 1.2 IV 10:

tqḥ mlk ʿlmk	So assume your eternal kingship,
drkt dt drdrk	Your everlasting dominion.

Clearly the alliteration functions effectively within each line, with the consonants *m, l,* and *k* repeated in the first line, and *d, r, k,* and *t* in the second. However, A. Fitzgerald has pointed to alphabetic acrostics for evidence of colonic units (monocolons, bicolons, and sometimes tricolons) and not individual lines as the basic units of West Semitic poetry.[22] O'Connor has made incisive observations regarding the constitutive differences between the unit of the line and the unit of the colon (in particular the bicolon and tricolon). Although further research on the basic units of West Semitic poetry is needed, the traditional fare of colonic analysis, word-pairs and alliteration, represented by the standard works of Avishur,[23] Watson, and *Ras Shamra Parallels I–III,*[24] would now be joined by more linguistically informed treatments, especially in the work of Pardee, Berlin, and O'Connor as well as E. L. Greenstein.[25]

⚍ ADMINISTRATION AND RELIGION

Other trends from the previous period continued. The analysis of ritual texts picked up additional steam under the impetus of J. M. de Tarragon and P. Xella.[26] Tarragon studied terms in sacrificial texts, including words for offerings (the animals, their parts, and other offered materials), types of rituals, cultic personnel, and the deities involved in the offerings. Xella produced the first edition devoted entirely to the ritual texts. The study of letters likewise received a boost from O. Kaiser, S. Ahl, A. L. Kristensen, D. Pardee, and later J. L. Cunchillos.[27] Particularly helpful were the clear correspondences that scholars demonstrated between epistolary formulas in Ugaritic and in Akkadian texts from Levantine sites. In the late 1960s and early 1970s, Rainey observed numerous instances of such parallels. For example, he noted the correspondence for the prostration formula found in letters:

> *l p ͨn ʾadty*   *ana šēpē bēltiya*
> "At the feet of my lady,

> *šb ͨd wšb ͨd*   VII-*šu u* VII TA.ÀM
> seven times (backwards) and seven times (forward)

> *mrḥqtm qlt*   *ištu rūqiš amqut*
> from afar I fall."[28]

As a second case, the use of *ʾaṯr* in the sense of "wherever" in 2.39.34–35 is paralleled in Akkadian *ašar: ʾaṯr ʾiṯ bqt//ašar ibašši,* "wherever it (he) is . . ." (cf. BH *ba ʾăšer* and BH *ʾăšer,* which became a generalized relative pronoun).[29] A final example: Rainey noted that Ugaritic *nǧr ḥwtk,* "guard your life" (2.47.2), is a reflex of the Akkadian expression, *uṣurmi ramanka,* "protect yourself" (EA 119:9,

125:9).[30] Comparison with Akkadian epistolary formulas was a generally reliable, but not foolproof, guide to interpreting words in Ugaritic letters. For example, the use of *mrḥqtm* (*KTU* 2.64.15) cited in the quote above (cf. *mrqḥm* in *KTU* 1.127.31) in the apparent sense, "from a distance" (= *mn + *rḥq[t]m), would seem to be suggested by the comparable Akkadian epistolary formula, *ištu rūqiš,* "from afar" (cf. BH *mērāḥōq*), but many commentators would nonetheless see the Ugaritic form as an adverbial accusative from a noun of the *maqtal* pattern, better translated "at a distance."[31]

Still largely neglected at this stage were administrative texts, apart from the works of A. Rainey, M. Liverani,[32] and M. Heltzer.[33] Heltzer and Liverani applied a two-sector model (namely, the bureaucratic state sector and a kin-based "free sector" based on Marx's concept of the "Asiatic mode of production") to the Ugaritic economy, thereby challenging the older "feudal" economic model applied to Ugarit during the postwar era by A. Alt, J. Gray, and A. Rainey.[34] The two-sector model would remain prominent in discussions of the Ugaritic economy into the 1990s.[35] Finally, numerous Assyriologists turned their attention to either Ugaritic or the Akkadian texts from Ras Shamra; here articles appeared from the hands of A. Archi, D. Arnaud, D. O. Edzard, W. G. Lambert, A. Malamat, A. R. Millard, W. L. Moran, D. Owen, J. Sasson, and D. J. Wiseman.[36] As with the vast archaeological research conducted in this period, the effect of this Assyriological work was to integrate the Ugaritic texts into the wider cultural context of the Late Bronze Age and thereby to provide a healthy counterweight to interest in Ugaritic generated by biblical studies.

Finally, in the wake of *Ugaritica V,* research on deities and other aspects of religion flourished. This period witnessed the completion of one phase of the study of religion initiated in the 1950s by the studies of O. Eissfeldt and M. H. Pope concerning El. By 1985, book-length studies on almost every major deity at Ugarit had appeared, casting light, by the way, on divinities other than Yahweh in Israelite religion. Indeed, it became clear that Israel's understanding of divinity was forged in the same larger West Semitic cultural milieu as that of the authors of Ugaritic texts. This avenue had been pursued for decades by W. F. Albright and many other scholars, but more recent important works by Morton Smith and Gösta Ahlström have signaled a change of direction.[37] Moreover, F. M. Cross's 1973 book of essays, *Canaanite Myth and Hebrew Epic,*[38] masterfully showed many shared fundamental points of religious identity between ancient Israel and its alleged polar opposite, the Canaanites.[39]

Religious topics gaining new attention in 1970–1985 contributed to this major change of perspective. Cults of the dead, for example, assumed new prominence, in part owing to new studies of the topic and in part to the publication of a royal funerary text, RS 34.126 = *KTU* 1.161 (discussed at length in the prior chapter). This text provided a new grounding to the discussion of religious practices associated with the dead and spurred many scholars to pay further attention to the subject. In the mid- and late-1970s, figures including J. F. Healey, O. Loretz, J. C. de Moor, M. H. Pope, and Pope's student, W. J. Horwitz,[40] pursued investigation of funerary and mortuary practices (sometimes referred to as "the cult of the dead"). It became clear that one should understand the Bible's references to such practices to describe Israelite, not Canaanite, behaviors.

In this period, the field remained highly oriented toward religion. Looking back to the learned articles of the late nineteenth and early twentieth century,[41] one can see that the Ugaritic texts, though often themselves fraught with difficulties and questions of interpretation, helped revolutionize the biblical field's understanding of religion. It was particularly in this phase when this revolution was beginning to transpire. In earlier scholarship, "Canaanite" religion and Israelite religion were often set in oppositional terms, a paradigm evidently inspired largely by the anti-Canaanite polemics in the Bible. In contrast, this phase of study showed a realization of how deeply indebted Israel was to its environs in all areas of human activity and thought, including religion. Even as the interest and number of students reached a new apex in this period, underlying problems in the areas of language and literature also emerged, as we will see below with the work of Mitchell Dahood. In order to provide a better idea of the field in this period, let us begin with the figures and centers in the field during the period of 1970–1985 and discuss their research in this context.

⋈ CENTERS OF STUDY

Provided here is only a listing of scholars according to where they studied or taught at the time. For the sake of continuity of academic lineages, this listing includes some figures preceding and following the period covered in this chapter as well as others who took Ugaritic and have conducted their research largely in biblical or archaeological studies. The order is roughly chronological and geographical (with some latitude in groupings). I have written in the word "later" in order to indicate some difference in time frame at a given institution. For the sake of completeness and at the risk of some inaccuracy, I have included some listings of figures at their later faculty posts although technically they were students in this period.

Scandinavia

Norway
   Oslo: A. Kapelrud, later H. Barstad.
   Others: K. Aartun (Stavanger/Oslo).[42]

Sweden
   Uppsala: H. Ringgren[43] and M. Ottoson.[44]
   Lund: B. Johnson, T. N. D. Mettinger, C. Grave, S. Norin.[45]

Denmark
   Aarhus: E. Hammershaimb, K. Jeppesen, F. O. Hvidberg-Hansen.[46]
   Copenhagen: F. Løkkegaard, E. Nielsen, later N. P. Lemche.[47]

Central and Eastern Europe

Germany
   Münster: W. Dietrich, O. Loretz, J. Sanmartín; and students, J. Aboud,
      I. Kottsieper, B. Lang, M. Nissinen, and J. Tropper; also later
      R. Albertz, H. P. Müller.
   Berlin: R. Voigt, later J. Tropper.
   Bochum: J. Ebach, U. Rüterswörden.
   Hamburg: K. Koch and H. P. Müller.
   Heidelberg: R. Rendtorff and students, H. J. Hermisson, D. Michel,
      and C. Macholz.
   Leipzig: W. Herrmann.
   Marburg: O. Kaiser and students, E. Becker, H. Bobzin, A. Fischer,
      I. Kottsieper, C. Levin, J. van Oorschot.
   Munich: W. Richter and M. Krebernik (formerly of Jena).
   Tübingen: W. Röllig and H. P. Rüger, and student B. Janowski (Ham-
      burg, Heidelberg, and now Tübingen).
   Others: D. Kinet (Augsburg); K. Bergerhof; M. Görg; R. Heyer;
      B. Kienast; H. Niehr (now of Tübingen); T. Podella; H. P. Stähli.

Switzerland
   Basel: E. Jenni and student, P. Kustár.
   Bern: J. J. Stamm (now E. A. Knauf).
   Zurich: B. Hartmann, F. Stolz.

Austria
   Vienna: S. Kreuzer.

Hungary
   Budapest: P. Vargyas.

Czech Republic
   Prague: J. Heller, P. Zemánek (Charles University).[48]

Poland: W. Tyloch, J. Wózniak.[49]

Russia: V. V. Ivanov.[50]

Coastal Europe

Netherlands
   Kampen: J. C. de Moor and students, M. Dijkstra, J. Renkema, K. Spronk, W. van der Meer, M. C. A. Korpel, W. T. Koopmans, J. Brinkman, J. Kim, P. Sanders, R. de Hoop.
   Leiden: J. Hoftijzer; later T. Muraoka, K. van der Toorn.
   Amsterdam: M. J. Mulder, later J. W. Wesselius.
   Groningen: C. J. Labuschagne; later H. L. J. Vanstiphout.

Belgium
   Louvain: E. Lipiński; A. Schoors and student, E. Verreet; H. Sauren and student, G. Kestemont.[51]
   Others: P. Swiggers (Belgian National Science Foundation; Leuven).

Mediterranean Europe

France
   Collège de France: A. Caquot and students, P. Bordreuil (CNRS),[52] F. Bron (CNRS),[53] J. L. Cunchillos,[54] A. Lemaire (CNRS), J. Sapin (CNRS).
   Ecole Pratique des Hautes Etudes: A. Caquot, M. Sznycer, and later H. Cazelles (also Institut Catholique) and students, P. Bordreuil, F. Bron, J. L. Cunchillos, A. Lemaire, J. M. de Tarragon, and B. Lang.
   Strasbourg: E. Jacob[55] and student, P. Bordreuil.
   Ecole Biblique (East Jerusalem): R. de Vaux and students, P. Amiet, P. Bordreuil, H. Cazelles, E. Puech (CNRS), J. Sapin, J. M. de Tarragon.
   French archaeological mission to Ras Shamra: H. de Contenson, J. Margueron, and M. Yon (CNRS at Lyon), with P. Bordreuil, O. Callot, A. Caubet, J. C. Courtois, E. and J. Lagarce, R. Stucky, assisted by G. Saadé and joined later by D. Pardee.[56]
   Others: P. Amiet; M. Delcor; M. Sznycer.

Spain
   Barcelona: G. del Olmo Lete, J. Sanmartín, and later J. M. Gálan.
   Madrid: J. L. Cunchillos(-Ilarri) and later students, I. Márquez Rowe, J. P. Vita, J. A. Zamora.

Italy
   Bologna: S. M. Cecchini.
   Florence: P. Fronzaroli.
   Messina: F. Pomponio.

Naples: C. Zaccagnini.

Pontifical Biblical Institute: M. J. Dahood and students, R. Althann, J. Blenkinsopp, A. Blommerde, L. Boadt, K. Cathcart, A. Ceresko, C. Conroy, J. L. Cunchillos, A. Fitzgerald, W. H. Irwin, P. J. Kearney, C. Krahmalkov, J. Krašovec, W. Kuhnigk, W. Michel, G. del Olmo Lete, O. Loretz, T. Penar, L. Sabottka, J. Sanmartín, A. Schoors, N. J. Tromp, W. G. E. Watson, W. A. van der Weiden, H. J.van Dijk, L. Viganò, E. Zurro.

Università "La Sapienza," Rome: G. Garbini, M. Liverani, M. Amadasi Guzzo.

Institute for Phoenician and Punic Civilizations of the Consiglio Nazionale delle Ricerche (C.N. R.): P. Xella, S. Ribichini.

Others: F. Saracino, M. Baldacci.

Studium Biblicum Franciscanum (Jerusalem): A. Niccacci.

United Kingdom

Scotland

Aberdeen: J. Gray and students, W. Johnstone, G. Cowling, P. C. Craigie, K. T. Aitken, W. G. E. Watson, D. J. Weston, J. Elwolde.

Edinburgh: N. Porteous, J. C. L. Gibson, and student, K. T. Aitken; later N. Wyatt, students, D. R. West, S. A. Wiggins, J. B. Lloyd.

Glasgow: B. Cutler, J. Macdonald, later N. Wyatt.

Others: J. R. Porter.[57]

England

Oxford: J. Day and students B. B. Schmidt and S. Weeks.

Cambridge: D. W. Thomas, J. Emerton, and his students, H. G. M. Williamson, G. I. Davies, J. F. Healey, J. M. Hadley.

Durham: T. W. Thacker and his student, M. E. J. Richardson; J. F. Healey (also Dublin and later Manchester).

Hull: L. L. Grabbe.

Liverpool: A. Millard, K. A. Kitchen.

London: E. Ullendorff, D. J. Wiseman, and student, J. F. Healey; J. Wansbrough and student, C. E. G. Tennant.

Manchester: E. Ullendorff, T. L. Fenton, M. E. J. Richardson, G. J. Brooke, A. H. W. Curtis, later J. F. Healey.

Newcastle: W. G. E. Watson.

Wales

Bangor: C. F. Whitley.

Cardiff: J. F. Healey.

Ireland

Dublin: Dermot Ryan, later K. J. Cathcart (also W. G. E. Watson).

Commonwealth Countries

Australia
Sydney: E. C. B. MacLaurin (a student of D. Winton Thomas at Cambridge) and student, W. J. Jobling;[58] F. I. Andersen.

Canada: P. C. Craigie (Calgary), R. Culley (Montreal), H. H. P. Dressler (Vancouver), P. E. Dion (Toronto), W. H. Irwin (Toronto), C. Foley (Saskatoon; student at McMaster).

India: T. W. Swanson (Bangalore).

South Africa
Stellenbosch: A. van Selms' students L. Bronner, F. C. Fensham, C. J. Labuschagne, L. M. Muntingh; later M. B. Brink, W. T. Claasen, F. E. Deist, J. P. J. Olivier, P. J. van Zijl; later P. A. Kruger, D. N. Pienaar, H. F. van Rooy, N. J. G. van der Westhuizen, I. Cornelius.
Pretoria (University of South Africa): H. Dreyer, and students later T. J. D. Bothma, A. Scheurkogel, P. Flint, A. da Silva, J. P. van der Westhuizen; V. Sasson.

Middle East and Asia

Tunisia: M. Fantar.

Syria: A. Abou-Assaf, L. Ajjan, A. Bounni, C. Chaath, F. Jaha, W. Khayata, G. Saadé, H. Safadi, N. Saliby, R. Vitali, B. Zoudhi; later J. Aboud.

Lebanon: R. Saidah, W. Ward.

Israel
Jerusalem—Hebrew University: J. Blau; S. E. Loewenstamm (and students, Y. Avishur and E. Qimron); J. C. Greenfield (1971–1995); also Z. Ben-Ḥayyim (and student, E. Qimron), M. Goshen-Gottstein (and students, A. Bloch, now of Berkeley, and T. Muraoka), S. Morag, C. Rabin, M. Weinfeld, Y. Yadin; A. Hurvitz, and later S. E. Fassberg.
Tel Aviv: A. Rainey, I. Singer, and students, D. Sivan, S. Izre'el.
Beer-sheva: C. Cohen, M. Gruber, D. Sivan.
Haifa: Y. Avishur, T. L. Fenton, M. Heltzer, B. Margalit.
Others: Y. Ben-David; M. Granot; H. Priebatsch.

Japan: D. T. Tsumura; M. Koitabishi; S. Mutoh; M. Sekine; S. Shibayama; A. Tsukimoto.

United States[59]

Northeast
> Harvard: F. M. Cross, T. O. Lambdin, and W. Moran dissertations: P. D. Miller, R. J. Clifford, C. Krahmalkov, D. L. Christensen, R. B. Coote, H. Forshey, L. Clapham, R. E. Whitaker, D. Stuart, J. Levenson, C. E. L'Heureux, R. Rosenberg, J. W. Betylon, E. T. Mullen, H. Wallace, P. L. Day, W. Propp, S. E. Meier, C. L. Seow, G. A. Anderson, R. Hendel, S. M. Olyan, T. J. Lewis, S. Ackerman, H. Page. Also J. J. M. Roberts, P. K. McCarter, J. G. Janzen, J. S. Kselman, W. Bodine, R. Saley, M. D. Coogan, L. Herr, P. Mosca, R. A. Oden, J. Huehnergard, J. A. Hackett, W. Pitard, B. Halpern, R. E. Friedman, T. Hiebert, S. E. Fassberg, D. Gropp, A. Gianto, D. Fleming.
>
> Yale: Pope-Rosenthal dissertations: P. L. Watson, W. J. Fulco, W. J. Horwitz, A. Cooper, R. M. Good, B. Bandstra, R. Heider, M. S. Smith, J. G. Taylor, F. Renfroe. Also J. H. Tigay, G. A. Tuttle, B. Zuckerman, D. Wortman, W. R. Garr. Other students: R. Schultz, T. Longman III, D. Olsen, C. Seitz; G. Brubacher.
>
> Columbia-Jewish Theological Seminary: H. L. Ginsberg, T. H. Gaster, I. Mendelsohn, students, M. Held, J. Milgrom, S. Paul; J. H. Tigay, Y. Muffs, M. Lichtenstein, D. Marcus, H. Tawil, D. Sperling; E. L. Greenstein, C. Cohen, and M. Gruber; later D. Dobrusin.
>
> Brandeis: Cyrus Gordon (1956–1973), D. W. Young, M. Morrison and students, E. Linder, W. C. Kaiser, J. T. Lee, D. T. Tsumura, S. Ahl, S. G. Brown, J. Hunt, R. B. Widbin, E. Wright.
>
> New York University: Cyrus Gordon (1973–1989) and his students, G. A. Rendsburg and K. Spanier; also E. H. Ashley; B. A. Levine and students, V. Sasson, L. B. Kutler, A. M. Merlis, M. L. Brown, P. D. Stern, J. Berlinerblau.
>
> Johns Hopkins: D. R. Hillers, S. Iwry (and later P. K. McCarter), and students, S. B. Parker, B. Batto, D. B. Bryan, A. J. Miller, M. B. Dick, M. L. Barré, J. I. Trujillo, G. I. Miller, F. Dobbs-Alsopp, N. Walls.
>
> Boston University: S. B. Parker and student, E. R. Follis.
>
> Catholic University: A. Fitzgerald and students, E. Mallon, later M. D. Futato, J. Ferrie, K. Nash.

South
> Vanderbilt: D. Knight and student, R. K. Gnuse.[60]

Midwest
> Michigan: G. Mendenhall, students K. Vine, H. Huffmon; later D. N. Freedman, C. Krahmalkov, and students, O. Borowski, M. P. O'Connor, P. Raabe, K. Jackson, D. Howard, A. Hill, A. Bartelt, J. Huddlestun, P. Schmitz, C. G. Libolt.

Chicago: S. Gevirtz,[61] G. W. Ahlström, later D. Pardee and their students, U. Oldenburg, L. M. Kuriakos, D. W. Nasgowitz, W. B. Barrick, J. L. Boyd III, R. Haak, E. M. Bloch-Smith, S. C. Layton, L. K. Handy, C. Miller, D. Clemens, S. W. Holloway, G. A. Long, E. Reymond, and S. L. Gogel.

Hebrew Union College (Cincinnati): M. Tsevat[62] and students, M. Fox and later R. Ratner; later R. F. Dupont.

Southern Illinois University (Edwardsville): M. C. Astour.

West Coast

University of California, Berkeley: J. C. Greenfield (1965–1971) and students, W. J. Fulco, A. Kaye, Z. Zevit (University of Judaism); later, J. Milgrom and student, D. Wright.

Graduate Theological Union of Berkeley: W. J. Fulco and students, A. L. Perlman and C. H. Bowman.

Claremont: S. Rummel, L. (Mack-)Fisher, F. B. Knutson, L. L. Grabbe, J. Khanjian, F. Dickey, M. Floyd.

University of California, Los Angeles: S. Segert (1969–1991).

University of Southern California: B. Zuckerman (and his West Semitic Research project).

The 1983 issue of the *Newsletter For Ugaritic Studies*[63] may serve as a general indicator of Ugaritic studies in this period, even if its survey was not comprehensive. Many countries have one school listed as offering courses on Ugaritic (Australia, Belgium, India, Japan, South Africa, Spain, and Switzerland). Only a handful of countries have more (Canada, France, the United Kingdom, Germany, Israel, the Netherlands, and the United States). The following profiles of some of these centers are meant to be representative, not complete.

Paris: A. Caquot, H. Cazelles, and the French Team

After Syria, France has long been the second home of Ugaritic studies. The original archaeologist of Ras Shamra, C. F. A. Schaeffer, was still productive until his death on 25 August 1982.[64] Despite Schaeffer's many publications, no final archaeological report came from his hands. In 1973–1974 J. C. Courtois and R. North published two learned studies on the archaeology of the site,[65] but much remains unclear.

The study of texts enjoyed major breakthroughs in this period. As already noted, in 1968 C. Nougayrol, J. Laroche, C. Virolleaud, and C. F. A. Schaeffer produced the immensely important volume *Ugaritica V*, with its many newly published texts; *Ugaritica VII* followed a decade later in 1978. This period also witnessed the important 1974 French translation of Ugaritic "myths and legends," by A. Caquot, M. Sznycer, and A. Herdner.[66] (Caquot would also produce a second volume in 1989 with his two students, J. M. de Tarragon, and J. L. Cunchillos.)[67]

Prior to this period[68] Caquot succeeded Virolleaud at L'Ecole Pratique des Hautes Etudes, Section des Sciences Religieuses; from 1973 to 1994 he was professor at the Collège de France. Another important figure at this time was H. Cazelles, at the Ecole des Langues Orientales de l'Institut Catholique in Paris. These two figures have provided the bulk of training in textual studies since the 1960s; their students have included P. Bordreuil, F. Bron, J. L. Cunchillos, J. M. de Tarragon, A. Lemaire, and J. Sapin. Cazelles also taught for several semesters at the Catholic University of America in the late 1970s.[69]

The French team responsible for the publication of the texts and artifacts grew substantially over these decades.[70] From 1971 to 1973, Henri de Contenson succeeded C. F. A. Schaeffer as the director of the excavations of Ras Shamra. J. Margueron directed excavations in 1975 and 1976. Margeurite Yon, herself trained in the archaeology of Cyprus, Iran, and Corsica, became director of the archaeological team in 1979. New talent joined the team, including P. Bordreuil, A. Caubet, O. Callot, and A. Calvet. Bordreuil took up the task of managing epigraphic discoveries of the archaeological mission and began to restudy tablets in the Syrian collections. With Dennis Pardee, who joined the team following a year at Aleppo University as a Fulbright Senior Lecturer in 1980–1981, Bordreuil produced both detailed drawings and higher-quality photographs of new tablets as well as new collations of the older tablets. One of their goals was a comprehensive listing of texts with their archaeological contexts indicated, realized in their joint study, *La Trouvaille épigraphique de l'Ougarit: 1. Concordance.*[71] Together with W. Van Soldt's 1991 *Studies in the Akkadian of Ugaritic,*[72] this work "has signalled a new approach to the archives of Ras Shamra."[73] In addition to the epigraphic work, Yon initiated a broader agenda of archaeological research. In instituting the series Ras Shamra–Ougarit (and editing the volumes), and by adding a range of new talent to the team, Yon has added fresh perspectives to the study of the site. Besides the

Claude Schaeffer, with Odile Schaeffer on his right and Marguerite Yon on his left (Mission de Ras Shamra, 1979). Courtesy of Yves Calvet and the Mission de Ras Shamra.

discovery of new texts, the archaeological team broadened the research into specialized areas of culture (for example, iconography and arts, stone and metal work, and architecture).

The major new discovery of this period was at Ras ibn Hani, in 1977. Led by the joint Syrian-French team under Adnan Bounni and Jacques Lagarce, the excavations would yield a rich harvest of alphabetic texts, especially in 1978, as well as in following years.[74] As the joint archaeological project attests, the French team long enjoyed a very productive relationship with the Syrian directorate of museums and antiquities and the growing group of Syrian scholars in Ugaritic studies. A fine representation of Syrian and French scholarly collaboration of Ugaritic took place in the Colloque International d'Etudes Ugaritiques held in Latakia 10–13 October 1979.[75]

Finally, the tradition of Ugaritic at the Ecole Biblique in East Jerusalem had begun already in the postwar era, where the great Père Roland de Vaux included research and teaching of Ugaritic texts among his many pursuits.[76] In the period of 1970–1985 (and afterward), Ugaritic has been taught at the Ecole by Jean-Michel de Tarragon.[77] One of Tarragon's students was John Elwolde, a significant figure in the production of the Sheffield Dictionary of Hebrew.

Münster: M. Dietrich and O. Loretz

In Germany, many of the established figures discussed in the preceding chapter continued their contributions to the field, but the center of production of tools for Ugaritic studies in the period 1970–1985 became the team of M. Dietrich and O. Loretz, aided by J. Sanmartín. Dietrich had studied in the mid-1950s primarily with Paul Kahle at Tübingen,[78] where he also took an introductory course in Ugaritic with Otto Rössler.[79] Loretz studied with Mitchell Dahood in Rome at the Pontifical Biblical Institute and pursued further studies in Innsbruck, the Oriental Institute in Chicago, and in Münster with von Soden.[80] In 1969, K. Bergerhof and J. C. de Moor joined Dietrich and Loretz in launching what quickly became the most important journal in Ugaritic studies, *Ugarit-Forschungen.*

In 1976, Dietrich and Loretz published with J. Sanmartín their edition of the Ugaritic texts, *Die keilalphabetischen Texte aus Ugarit* (abbreviated as *KTU*). This work collected in one volume nearly all the Ugaritic texts known at that time. Dietrich and Loretz also produced six massive volumes of bibliography, as well as innumerable books and articles on Ugaritic and biblical studies. They have also poured their editorial energy into several monograph series, including Abhandlungen zur Literatur Alt-Syrien-Palästinas, Alter Orient und Altes Testament, and Ugaritisch-Biblische Literatur.[81] A dictionary was also planned in the 1970s,[82] but it did not come to pass. In addition, the two have produced many works of their own (for example, Loretz's many studies devoted to biblical sub-jects in light of the Ugaritic texts).[83] Dietrich and Loretz deserve the field's thanks for this enormous production of scholarship.

As is common in academia, the publication of some of this work did not come without controversy. In particular, a rancorous debate over the quality of *KTU*'s readings broke out in the early 1990s.[84] Questions were raised over the haste with which the original *KTU* was putatively produced; this in turn raised is-sues as to the quality of the readings. Resolution would have to await editions of texts produced with high-quality photographs, an initiative begun especially under the leadership of Bruce Zuckerman.[85] Despite such debate, it is clear that the enterprise of Dietrich and Loretz in Münster has made many contributions to the field, not least in the training of some solid researchers, including J. Aboud, I. Kottsieper, B. Lang, M. Nissinen, and J. Tropper. Many scholars from other countries, including G. del Olmo Lete, M. H. Pope, F. Renfroe, E. Verreet, and P. Xella, have benefited from visits to the Ugarit-Forschung Institut.

The Pontifical Biblical Institute (PBI): R. Follet and M. J. Dahood

The study of Ugaritic at the Pontifical Biblical Institute, meanwhile, is usu-ally associated with the name of Mitchell J. Dahood.[86] His predecessor at the PBI had been R. Follet, an Assyriologist and nephew of the great French Assyriologist, F. Thureau-Dangin.[87] Up through the 1950s, Ugaritic at the PBI was part of gen-eral cuneiform studies; no particular effort was made to connect it to research on the Bible. This approach changed with Dahood's era from 1956 to 1982. An American of Lebanese descent born in Montana on 2 February 1922, Dahood entered the Jesuits on 7 September 1941. After his theological studies, he took a doctorate with W. F. Albright in 1951. In 1954 he was ordained a priest, and in 1956 he arrived at the PBI. After more than a quarter of a century of teaching, Dahood died on 8 March 1982 from a heart attack, while praying in the Chapel of Our Lady of the Well in the Church of Santa Maria in Via located in the center of Rome.[88]

Dahood was an enthusiastic teacher of students from all over Europe and the United States. Joseph Blenkinsopp, a student during Dahood's first two years at the PBI and later a professor at the University of Notre Dame, recalled his teacher's kindness and sense of humor.[89] When Dahood first began teaching Ugaritic at the PBI in 1956, he was required to teach the language in Latin (un-doubtedly one of Dahood's distinctions in the history of Ugaritic). A particular insight into Dahood was provided by Charles Krahmalkov (long a professor at the University of Michigan). He described his time with Dahood:

> My best memories associated with Ugaritic have to do with Mitch Dahood, of blessed memory. I finished my [Harvard] dissertation in Rome, where I got to

know him. For him, Ugaritic, like Phoenician, was HIS language, viz., the language spoken by his ancestors, of which he was exceedingly proud. He did have a dickens of a time attempting to claim parts of the Hebrew Bible for the Phoenicians = Lebanese, but the claim on Ugaritic . . . was comfortable, uncontested and very gratifying for him. The huge output in that period and still to a limited extent continuing today in the area of Biblical Hebrew–Ugaritic literary and linguistic comparisons is for me that part of his legacy that I think of when I look back, because it is associated with genuine personal and a bit of nationalistic involvement and fervor for Ugaritic studies.[90]

According to another student, Dahood assigned as homework the task of finding Ugaritic features in biblical texts.[91] Or, as A. Gianto[92] put it:

His classes of Ugaritic were a reading of the Hebrew Bible in the light of Ugaritic. His classroom discussions became the basis for the three-volume Anchor Bible Psalms commentaries. His warm personality and skill at presenting things generated a contagious interest from the part of the students of biblical studies.

Dahood clearly had a major impact on biblical studies, in part thanks to the vast number of his students, most notably in the present discussion J. L. Cunchillos, C. Krahmalkov, G. del Olmo Lete, O. Loretz, J. Sanmartín, and W. G. E. Watson. For some Roman Catholics, the PBI and Dahood represented the main option open to them. For example, several Catholic Dutchmen came to study with Dahood in the late 1960s (H. J. van Dijk, N. J. Tromp, A. C. M. Blommerde, and W. A. van der Weiden). As expected, knowledge of Dahood's work is better known nowadays among Catholic biblical scholars than in other circles.

While cognizant of Dahood's influence and learning, many of his students have assumed a critical stance toward his work, for reasons which will become clear later in this chapter. It should be remembered that at the PBI, balance would be provided by the presence of many other biblical scholars at different times in Dahood's career, such as Luis Alonso-Schökel, Norbert Lohfink, Roderick MacKenzie, Dennis McCarthy, William Moran, and Ernst Vogt. And following their dissertations pursued under Dahood, most of his students returned to more traditional work on the Bible. Today the response to Dahood's approach among

Mitchell Dahood.
Courtesy of Pontifical Biblical Institute.

his students ranges widely from the self-proclaimed "dedicated Dahoodian," Walter Ludwig Michel (professor of Old Testament at the Lutheran School of Theology in Chicago),[93] to more critical voices, cited later.

Leiden (J. Hoftijzer), Kampen (J. C. de Moor), and Groningen (C. J. Labuschagne)

In the postwar era, the Netherlands also emerged as a center for Ugaritic, this time in Leiden. However, since 1970 Hoftijzer and his successor at Leiden, T. Muraoka, have focused their research on Hebrew and Aramaic. Since taking up his appointment as professor at Leiden in fall of 1991, Muraoka has had no students in Ugaritic.[94] A student in Ugaritic with Hoftijzer, K. R. Veenhof became professor in Assyriology at Leiden, where he taught W. H. van Soldt, who produced a 1986 dissertation on the Akkadian of Ugarit, since published in the AOAT series. This work, as noted above, has helped to change the approach to texts by situating them in their archaeological contexts.[95] Around 1960, Johannes C. de Moor took advanced courses at Leiden, in addition to his doctoral work at the Free University in Amsterdam. At Leiden, de Moor took Ugaritic from Hoftijzer, and he wrote his 1971 dissertation on "The Seasonal Pattern in the Ugaritic Baal Cycle" under W. H. Gispen at the Free University.[96]

A well-known Dutch center for Ugaritic studies beginning in the 1970s was the Theologische Universiteit van de Gereformeerde Kerken at Kampen.[97] There Johannes de Moor assumed a professorship after securing his doctorate from the Free University in Amsterdam and completing additional studies at Leiden. (Lettinga rose to the rank of professor in 1970 at the other theological institution in Kampen, the Theologische Hogeschool van de Gereformeerde Kerken.)[98] At Kampen, de Moor established Ugaritic studies in the 1970s, and during the 1980s he trained a number of doctoral students, especially in the areas of religion and poetry. He supervised several dissertations by such students of Ugaritic as Johan Renkema (1983), Klaas Spronk (1986), M. C. A. Korpel (1990), William T. Koopmans (1990), Jichan Kim (1993), Paul Sanders (1996), and Raymond de Hoop (1998). De Moor was also the co-adviser of Meindert Dijkstra (1980) and William van der Meer (1989). De Moor's students have assumed posts in many Dutch schools. De Moor had occasion to provide instruction also to Edward Noort, T. N. D. Mettinger, and Istvan Karasszon. As this record indicates, Kampen under de Moor was an important school for Ugaritic studies.

At Groningen,[99] in the meantime, Ugaritic started in the late 1960s. Casper Jeremiah Labuschagne, after teaching in his native South Africa, moved to Groningen in 1968.[100] He initiated a small group of students and young teachers (primarily in theology and Semitics) into Ugaritic; it included J. H. Hospers (1921–1993)[101] and C. H. J. de Geus, both later appointed at Groningen. A few years later W. H. P. Römer began to lead the group. However, only in 1975 with the appointment of H. L. J. Vanstiphout did Ugaritic become a regular part of the curriculum in Groningen.

Cambridge (J. A. Emerton), Oxford (J. Day), and Manchester (E. Ullendorff, T. L. Fenton, A. H. W. Curtis, and J. F. Healey)

In his long career at Cambridge, John Emerton, one of G. R. Driver's most eminent students at Oxford, set a high standard for philological and textual precision and erudition. Apart from his numerous articles, he served as longtime editor of *Vetus Testamentum* and editor of many of the congress volumes of the International Organization for the Study of the Old Testament. In addition, Emerton has regularly published seminal articles on Israelite religion that draw on the Ugaritic texts. For example, his 1959 article on "The Origin of the Son of Man Imagery" showed the continuity of imagery of El and Baal in the heavenly council from the Late Bronze Age, represented by the Ugaritic texts, through the Hellenistic period, as reflected in Daniel 7 in the form of the "Ancient of days" and "one like a son of man."[102] This article marked an important advance, as it showed that biblical apocalyptic was the great repository of old mythic material known from the Ugaritic texts. Already in 1895 Hermann Gunkel (1862–1932) had argued that representations of the *Urzeit* in Mesopotamian myth corresponded to material for describing the *Endzeit* in biblical apocalyptic,[103] but Emerton's article demonstrated that the old mythic material lay closer to home in the Ugaritic material. Another important piece penned by Emerton was his early article on the Kuntillet 'Ajrud inscriptions, especially concerning its references to "Yahweh . . . and his asherah." This essay continues to be cited because of its learned details and judicious judgments.[104]

Emerton's better-known students included John Day and John Healey. Now at Oxford, Day wrote his thesis under Emerton, and has since authored many works on West Semitic deities.[105] John Healey, a fine Semiticist presently at Manchester, first studied Ugaritic with Emerton before taking a doctorate under D. J. Wiseman at the University of London. Healey's dissertation addressed evidence for the Rephaim in comparison with relevant Mesopotamian material.[106] A third student of Emerton's was the American Judith Hadley, presently professor at Villanova University and known for her work on Asherah.[107] A fourth student of Emerton's, Robert Gordon, works largely in the biblical field, yet in his capacity as professor at Cambridge he has produced one doctorate in Ugaritic-biblical research, that of P. S. Johnston.[108]

Oxford and Cambridge were not the only English centers for Ugaritic in the postwar era. Thanks to Driver's student, Edward Ullendorff, Manchester has enjoyed a venerable tradition of instruction in the field.[109] In addition to his training at Oxford, Ullendorff studied at the Hebrew University in the late 1930s, and there he learned from H. L. Ginsberg and Umberto Cassuto, among others. Ullendorff's costudents at the Hebrew University included J. Blau, E. Kutscher, and Y. Yadin. Ullendorff went on to teach at St. Andrews (1950–1959), Manchester (1959–1964), and the School of Oriental and African Studies, University of London (1964–1982). Blau taught at Tel Aviv University, and he is best known for his many important articles mostly on comparative grammar.[110]

Manchester would enjoy the services of other figures in the field of Ugaritic, including Terence Fenton, now professor at Haifa,[111] and Mervyn Richardson, himself a student of the Semiticist and Egyptologist T. W. Thacker in Durham. One of Fenton's students at Manchester was A. H. W. Curtis, who has taught there for many years and is best known for an introduction to Ugarit.[112] Fenton authored a fine set of studies on Ugaritic and Hebrew grammar and style. In recent years Richardson's lasting contribution has been his monumental revision and translation of the five-volume *The Hebrew and Aramaic Lexicon of the Old Testament: The New Koehler-Baumgartner in English* (Leiden: Brill, 1994–2000). Richardson and Curtis have been joined at Manchester by Healey. Richardson has retired recently.

Aberdeen (J. Gray) and Edinburgh (J. C. L. Gibson)

The four ancient Scottish universities developed Ugaritic at very different rates, with Aberdeen and Edinburgh leading the way. As noted in Chapter Two, Gray enjoyed a long, productive career at Aberdeen, which lasted into this period, and he taught many figures who would become prominent in their own right.

At Edinburgh, Ugaritic continued to be taught in this period by John Gibson (professor 1962–1994). Like Emerton, Gibson studied at Oxford with Driver.[113] A minister of the Church of Scotland, Gibson had studied at Glasgow in 1948–1956, taking a degree first in Classics and then in Hebrew, Arabic, and Aramaic. Gibson spent 1957–1959 at Oxford just after Driver finished his edition of *Canaanite Myths and Legends* (1956). After Gibson assumed his position at New College at the University of Edinburgh (1962–1994), Driver suggested to him that he produce a fresh edition of *Canaanite Myths and Legends,* which appeared in 1978: "We planned the broad outlines of the revision together and agreed upon most of the changes in format."[114] As Gibson writes about his teacher, "I profited greatly from his notebooks, which he kindly allowed me to use."[115] The new edition marked a great improvement over Driver's 1956 edition:

the layout of the texts was vastly improved and the material was updated.[116] The volume became a standard work in the United Kingdom[117] and beyond.

In the early 1990s, Gibson was joined at Edinburgh by N. Wyatt, who came from a position at Glasgow; together they continue to supervise doctoral students. Unlike Aberdeen and Edinburgh, Glasgow had no formal course work in Ugaritic; instead it formed an afternoon reading group consisting of faculty and other interested parties from different areas (including Bernard Cutler, John Macdonald, [the gifted, late lamented] Robert Carroll, R. P. Gordon, and N. Wyatt).[118] Since moving to Edinburgh, Gibson and Wyatt have trained a number of doctoral students, including S. A. Wiggins and J. B. Lloyd.[119]

Stellenbosch (A. van Selms and F. C. Fensham) and Pretoria (H. J. Dreyer)

In South Africa, the study of Ugaritic began with Adrianus van Selms and the Department of Semitic Languages (founded in 1948) in Stellenbosch.[120] In 1931, van Selms received his doctorate at Utrecht from Professor H. Th. Obbink after studies there and at Leiden with F. M. Th. Böhl. After serving as minister in two small cities in Holland, van Selms moved to South Africa in 1938.[121] His most accomplished student in Ugaritic was probably F. C. Fensham (who died in 1989), but other well-known names include L. Bronner, W. T. Claasen, F. E. Deist, C. J. Labuschagne, and the recently deceased J. P. J. Olivier. Fensham himself was the teacher of the current generation of students of Ugaritic in Stellenbosch, including I. Cornelius and P. A. Kruger. Besides supporting the work of these figures, the Department of Semitic Languages in Stellenbosch was also the impetus behind the establishment of the *Journal of Northwest Semitic Languages* in 1971, a standard among international journals in the field.[122] The University of South Africa in Pretoria has also offered Ugaritic studies; students there under H. J. Dreyer have included T. J. D. Bothma, A. Scheurkogel, and A. da Silva. Bothma wrote his thesis on "Aspects of Ugaritic Syntax within the Framework of Core Grammar" in 1983. Although this is one of the first works on Ugaritic grammar using modern linguistic theory, it has received little attention, perhaps owing to the fact that it was written in Afrikaans. Like its counterpart in Stellenbosch, the Department of Semitics in Pretoria would found its own journal, *Tydskrif vir Semitistiek/Journal for Semitics*, in 1989.

Jerusalem: J. C. Greenfield

An immigrant from the United States, the great Jonas Greenfield, whose earlier career we have already discussed, found his final academic home at the

Hebrew University in 1971, the same year that Loewenstamm retired. Greenfield taught the full range of West Semitic languages and texts, including Ugaritic, until his death in April 1995. Best remembered for his many important contributions to Aramaic language and lexicography, he also returned regularly to questions of Ugaritic. Greenfield also came to reflect on the implications that his detailed research held for the study of literature and culture and their close relation to religion:

> the Biblical writer draws from the poetical resources available to him a number of word pairs and standard epithets and uses them to construct a complex poetic structure, or to set the background framework of the material that he is presenting. It is of minor consequence for this discussion if the resources were written or oral; indeed, a case can be made for the use of both types of material by the Biblical writers, but of that elsewhere.[123]

Based on a number of examples, Greenfield drew the following conclusions about the massive circulation of "Canaanite" religious literary tradition in Israel and Judah:

> It is due to the accident of survival and discovery that the Cannaanite heritage that has reached us comes from Ugarit; but there can be no doubt that similar myths, epics and tales, as well as hymns and prayers circulated in both oral and written form throughout Canaan proper not only in the Late Bronze Age but also in the Iron Age, that is from 1400–600 B.C.E., a period of a thousand years. They were a source of the folklore and the folk religion throughout the area, including monotheistic Judah and Israel. We may also assume that the various cities also had variant versions, using different words and phrases and on occasion crediting different gods with the same deeds.[124]

And indeed, not only the same deeds, but even the names of the same enemies (such as Leviathan, Sea, Death, and Tannin) and homes (Ṣapan; cf. Ps 48:3). Greenfield's formulation represents an extension of Cassuto's basic insight (noted above) regarding a common Canaanite-Israelite literary tradition by drawing larger conclusions about a shared culture.

Unlike many of his contemporaries, Greenfield did not produce Israeli students working primarily in Ugaritic, but he taught foreigners who came to learn from him, including H. Barstad, J. Day, B. B. Schmidt, J. A. Thompson, W. G. E. Watson, and myself.[125] The Ugaritic seminar that I took under him in 1983–1984 attracted an immensely learned group of faculty and students (including Shalom Paul,[126] Avigdor Hurowitz,[127] and Israel Knohl). Since Greenfield's death, his teaching responsibilities in Ugaritic have fallen to two superb scholars, Avi Hurvitz and Steven Fassberg; although neither pursues research primarily in the field of Ugaritic, both regularly refer to it in their studies of Hebrew and Aramaic.[128]

Tel Aviv (I. Singer and A. Rainey), Beersheba (C. Cohen, M. Gruber, and D. Sivan), and Haifa (Y. Avishur, T. L. Fenton, M. Heltzer, and B. Margalit)

At Tel Aviv, I. Singer wrote on Ugaritic subjects and concentrated on Late Bronze Age history.[129] A. Rainey has been a major contributor to the study of Ugaritic, as already noted.[130] Rainey had two particularly good and productive students, D. Sivan and S. Izre'el.[131]

A new core of talent in Ugaritic has been emerging also at Ben Gurion University in Beer-sheva, thanks to the merging of two academic traditions there. Daniel Sivan, an Israeli taught by A. Rainey at Tel Aviv, joined Chaim Cohen and Mayer Gruber, two American students of H. L. Ginsberg and Moshe Held at Columbia-JTS.

Haifa has recruited four teachers of Ugaritic: Y. Avishur, Loewenstamm's star pupil from Jerusalem; T. L. Fenton, a doctorate under Driver at Oxford and later a faculty member at Manchester; M. Heltzer from the former USSR; and B. Margalit, a graduate of the Brandeis program. Avishur's work on parallel pairs marked a high point of research,[132] while nevertheless signaling a shift in the study of Ugaritic, especially in Israel. His research largely involved a massive collection and analysis of variations in word-pairs, just at a time when a shift in literary study was taking place which would diminish the interest in this approach.

Fenton's major contributions involve a series of grammatical studies as well as articles on the influence of the West Semitic mythological tradition of the sea.[133] Fenton convincingly demonstrated the lack of a *yaqattal verbal form in Ugaritic. He has also demonstrated some important patterns of verbal usage in a manner that recalls the fine studies of Moshe Held. On yet a third topic, he examines the reinterpretations of the theomachy motif in biblical texts, especially compared to its attestations in the Baal Cycle. In the case of Exod 14–15, Fenton argues that the division of the Reed Sea is a re-mythologization of that myth with various other connecting links. Heltzer, meanwhile, pioneered major studies on Ugaritic society from the 1970s onward.[134] Margalit, though a graduate of Brandeis and student of Cyrus Gordon, was an autodidact in Ugaritic. He has been a prolific author, with extensive volumes on the Baal Cycle and Aqhat, as well as numerous articles, but his idiosyncratic approaches to Ugaritic poetry and lexicography have met strong criticism.[135] On the other hand, the field has benefited from the attention that he drew to alliteration in Ugaritic poetry as well as his identification of the place names in *KTU* 1.108.2–3 connected with biblical traditions concerning the Rephaim.[136]

McMaster and Calgary: P. C. Craigie

Ugaritic studies in Canada were supported by the energetic presence of Peter Craigie (1938–1985). A native of Lancaster, England, Craigie took an M.A. in Semitic Languages and Literatures in Edinburgh in 1965 and a Master of Theology degree at Aberdeen in 1968. He then received his doctorate in 1970 with a dissertation written under Eugene Combs at McMaster University. From his post in Calgary in 1974–1985, Craigie was a great promoter of Ugaritic studies in North America. Tragically, he died at the young age of forty-seven as the result of an automobile accident. Other McMaster doctoral students included B. Angi ("The Ugaritic Cult of the Dead: A Study of Some Beliefs and Practices That Pertain to the Ugaritians' Treatment of the Dead," 1971), J. L. R. Wood ("Kingship at Ras Shamra: A Study of the Literary, Ritual, and Administrative Documentation," 1972), and C. M. Foley ("The Gracious Gods and the Royal Ideology of Ugarit," 1980). Craigie's students include J. Glen Taylor, who pursued a doctorate at Yale. Besides his labors expended on the *Newsletter for Ugaritic Studies,* Craigie focused his own research on Ugaritic and Hebrew poetry, as well as West Semitic religion.[137]

Columbia–Jewish Theological Seminary: H. L. Ginsberg, M. Held, T. H. Gaster, and E. L. Greenstein

Columbia and Jewish Theological Seminary[138] had become a major center for the study of Ugaritic under H. L. Ginsberg and T. H. Gaster, and later with M. Held.[139] Filling the vacancy left by the death of Isaac Mendelsohn, Held served on the faculty of the Department of Middle East Languages and Cultures at Columbia in 1966–1984, and he was an adjunct faculty member at JTS in 1959–1984. Together, Ginsberg and Held set the highest grammatical and philological standards for the field. Ginsberg and Held supervised many important linguistic West Semitic dissertations, largely in the 1970s produced by H. R. (Chaim) Cohen, Mayer I. Gruber, David I. Marcus, and Hayim Tawil.[140] Held's method continues to be highly influential among his students and colleagues, especially Cohen,[141] who is completing a monograph entitled *The Complete Held Method for Comparative Semitic Philology and Its Application in Modern Biblical Philology.*[142] He also continues work on *A Comprehensive Dictionary of the Ugaritic Language* according to the philological method of his mentor.[143] Along with two coeditors, Daniel Sivan and John Kaltner, Cohen is also producing a companion volume to the English edition of *HALAT.* An important third figure for many years on the Columbia-JTS scene was T. H. Gaster, who supervised Murray H. Lichtenstein's dissertation during this period.[144] Undergirded with the philological depth and poetic sensibility of his teachers, H. L. Ginsberg and M. Held, this thesis developed a comparative study of literary topoi and motifs aided by the broad literary knowledge of T. H. Gaster. Unfortunately, the dissertation was never published.

E. L. Greenstein, twenty years a professor at Jewish Theological Seminary (1976–1996) before joining Tel Aviv's faculty in 1996, has served since 1974 as a coeditor with David Marcus of *Journal of the Ancient Near Eastern Society of Columbia University* (abbreviated either as *JANES* or *JANESCU*).[145]

Yale: M. H. Pope and F. Rosenthal

The early story of Ugaritic at Yale University is recounted in the preceding chapters. Professor from 1949 through 1986, Marvin Pope showed students how to pursue scholarship by his own example in class. He would run down etymologies and information in the books and articles there in the office. And his kindliness and North Carolina wit kept students at ease. In the 1970s Pope took a new turn in his work, reflected in his learned commentary on the Song of Songs.[146] This commentary was especially celebrated for its imaginative and tireless pursuit of the divine backgrounds to the book's descriptions of the lovers and for its encyclopedic range of sources cited. Without any hesitation, Pope addressed Ugaritic texts describing sex and death (whether in the human or divine realm), divine cannibalism, and drunkenness. Pope would see his collected essays appear by the end of his lifetime in 1994 under the papal title of *Probative Pontificating in Ugaritic and Biblical Literature*. Pope also enjoyed the scholarly exchange on the most detailed of points. Moshe Held criticized Pope's watery interpretation of the Biblical Hebrew *hapax legomenon mahămōrôt* in Ps 140:11, but while accepting the criticism ("for this all concerned may give praise and thanks"), Pope offered another point in criticism of Held, namely that Ugaritic *npš* does not show the meaning of "tomb," although this sense of the word develops in later Nabatean and Palmyrene inscriptions.[147]

Pope's colleague Rosenthal is a vastly learned Old World scholar who managed by his massive knowledge and understated manner to overwhelm most students. First appointed at Yale to the Rabinowitz chair in Semitic Languages[148] and later Sterling Professor, Rosenthal provided instruction in the entire range of Aramaic dialects, the field of Arabic and Comparative Semitics. Even the other faculty deferred to Rosenthal's great learning. On one occasion Rosenthal meant to ask us students if there was any question that he could answer, but the question came out as, "Is there any question that I cannot answer?" One intimidated student lunged forward and offered a hearty "No." Momentarily delayed by the students' laughter, Rosenthal smiled and moved to the next point.

The dissertations directed by Pope and read by Rosenthal tended to focus on Ugaritic topics with some Bible, mostly in the areas of religion and myth. In this period, Pope recognized the great amount of material available on deities, especially with the publication of *Ugaritica V,* and it was his plan to have a dissertation treat each deity as well as some of the newly published texts. Accordingly, from the 1960s through the mid-1980s Yale dissertations included: T. Yamashita on Asherah, A. Eaton on Anat, P. L. Watson on Mot, W. J. Fulco on Resheph, G. Heider on Molek, M. S. Smith on Kothar, and J. G. Taylor on Iron Age solar imagery.[149] The late 1960s and onward also witnessed many theses on grammatical topics: D. A. Robertson on linguistic evidence for dating early Hebrew poetry, S. A. Ryder on the *D*-stem (piel in Hebrew), W. J. Horwitz on the so-called word-divider, A. Cooper on a linguistic approach to poetry, R. M. Good on the word ʿ*m,* B. Bandstra on the particle *k,* W. R. Garr on a dialect geography of Iron II West Semitic dialects, and F. Renfroe on Arabic and Ugaritic lexicography.[150] With only a handful of students in most classes, Yale's program produced an ideal mentoring situation. Most of the classes with Pope and Rosenthal took place in their dusty offices in the Hall of Graduate Studies. Pope's was large enough to accommodate three or four students surrounded by the dictionaries and the many other books and articles often consulted during class. With these resources at hand, Pope showed students how he pursued research, and as he taught them how he tracked down leads, he also showed the range of his imagination. In this phase, Pope and Rosenthal were aided by the biblicist Robert R. Wilson, himself their student in the early 1970s, and to a lesser extent, by Brevard S. Childs, who, throughout his career at Yale, always insisted on having doctoral students take Ugaritic, Akkadian, and other extrabiblical languages.

Harvard: F. M. Cross, T. O. Lambdin, and W. L. Moran

The story of Ugaritic at Harvard largely begins in 1956 when Frank Moore Cross joined the faculty of Harvard Divinity School.[151] Cross was born in Marin County, California, where his father attended San Francisco Theological Seminary. (Cross's first memory was getting caught stealing raisins from the Seminary commissary; as he comments: "An appropriate memory for a Calvinist.") At the age of eight, Cross moved with his family to Birmingham, Alabama. Three generations of the family were from southern Alabama, and following family tradition, Cross attended Maryville College (A.B., 1942), where his father was a trustee. Afterward Cross went to McCormick Theological Seminary in Chicago (B.D., 1946), where his father had also studied. There Cross studied under G. Ernest Wright, a student of Albright's prior to the war. Cross's distinguished career was heralded already at this time when McCormick awarded him the Nettie F.

McCormick Fellowship for an essay later published under the title "The Taber-nacle: A Study from an Archaeological and Historical Approach."[152] The judge for the contest was Albright himself, who judged Cross's piece (submitted under the pseudonym, "Uncle Remus") superior to the two other entries ("John Doe" and "Conrado Carducci").

Afterward, Cross attended Johns Hopkins, working with D. N. Freedman on two joint dissertations (discussed in the preceding chapter). After his doctoral training, Cross returned to McCormick, joining his former teacher, G. Ernest Wright, on the faculty before leaving for Harvard to serve in the Divinity School Old Testament Chair in 1956. In 1958, Wright followed Cross to Harvard Divinity School from McCormick, replacing him in the Divinity School Old Testament Chair (later Wright would be named the Parkman Professor of Divinity). At that point Cross assumed the oldest chair in the biblical field in the United States, the Hancock Professorship of Hebrew and Other Oriental Languages, as well as the chairmanship of the Department of Semitic Languages and History (later re-named Near Eastern Languages and Civilizations).[153] Wright served at Harvard until he died of a heart attack on August 29, 1974, at the age of sixty-four. Includ-ing their years as co-faculty at McCormick Theological Seminary, Cross and Wright were colleagues for over two decades.[154]

In 1960 Cross was joined at Harvard by the learned Semitist, Thomas O. Lambdin.[155] Lambdin had been a doctoral student of W. F. Albright and Frank Blake at Hopkins; in 1952 he completed his dissertation entitled "Egyptian Loanwords and Transcrip-tions in the Ancient Semitic Languages." Subsequently he joined the Hopkins faculty and then departed for Har-vard. Lambdin's courses on Historical Grammar and Comparative Semitics were the linguistic hub of the Harvard doctoral program. In these courses, the great structures shared by the Se-mitic languages came to life; so did Lambdin's droll hu-mor. He used to tell students that "Ugaritic is an undeci-phered language."[156] In 1966, another Albright doctorate

Frank M. Cross (at Ashkelon). Courtesy of Frank M. Cross.

and author of an important 1950 dissertation on the Byblian dialect in the Amarna letters, the Assyriologist William L. Moran,[157] joined Cross and Lambdin at Harvard after serving on the faculty of the Pontifical Biblical Institute in Rome. An expert in the Amarna letters, Moran provided over two decades of training in Assyriology at Harvard. His many publications showed, as nicely put by the editors of his *Festschrift,* "a humane quality, a concern for broader issues that expresses the intellectual and vital excitement that he brings to a text."[158] Moran's training in Akkadian was rigorous, demanding, at some times hilarious and at others terrifying, as he asked his students to translate English sentences into Akkadian[159] and to reproduce paradigms for weak verbs not yet studied in class. Sadly, Moran died on 20 December 2000.

Cross advanced in new and powerful ways the old comparative agenda fostered by Albright, first in his 1973 book, *Canaanite Myth and Hebrew Epic,* and later in the 1998 sequel, *From Epic to Canon.*[160] *Canaanite Myth and Hebrew Epic* massively extended the discussion of Israel's religion on a number of fronts. A major contribution was to illustrate the close relations of Ugaritic and Israelite conceptions of divinity. In addition, Cross's analysis represented the culmination of the field's research indicating that Israelite religion belonged to the same larger West Semitic culture as the Ugaritic texts. In time, this insight would contribute further to the view that the Israelites were in many respects "Canaanite," a point already broached in other respects by Cross's contemporaries, such as Morton Smith and Gösta Ahlström.[161] Cross's work had already earned the respect of a wide readership because of its detailed documentation and the depth of the synthesis drawing on approaches deriving from his teachers and the research of the best German and Scandinavian scholars.[162] Cross's synthesis ventured to mediate between the history-of-redemption and mythic frameworks by proposing a tension between the two in biblical literature while seeing the dominance of myth in Canaanite literature.[163] Although the work of Ahlström and later Smith had raised the religious and cultural issues in a new way, it was the depth of Cross's work that moved this discussion into the mainstream of American biblical scholarship. As a result, the relationship of Israelite and Canaanite religion could no longer be posed in primarily oppositional terms.

Together, Cross, Moran, and Lambdin, the gifted students of Albright, now at Harvard, would cover the range of biblical and related West Semitic texts. This range is reflected in the 106 doctoral dissertations that Cross directed.[164] He also served as reader for many other theses written under his fellow Albrightians, Wright and Lambdin, as well as theses supervised by John Strugnell, the great scholar of Dead Sea Scrolls and New Testament, and read later by Cross's students, Paul D. Hanson (1939–), appointed at Harvard in 1971, and Michael David Coogan (1942–), a faculty member at Harvard in the years 1976–1985.[165] Many of the dissertations directed by Cross involve comparisons between Ugarit and ancient Israel, especially in the area of religion. The 1970 dissertation of R. J. Clifford, for example, treated the cosmic or sacred mountain in Ugaritic and biblical texts.[166] (Clifford was appointed at the Weston School of Theology near Harvard [1966–], and along with Cross, he taught Ugaritic at Harvard in the period 1970–1980.) Another early student, P. D. Miller, examined the march of the divine warrior in Ugaritic and biblical texts.[167] R. Whitaker (and later R. Hendel) examined the question of oral composition in the two corpora.[168] C. E. L'Heureux explored the question of El's status in the Ugaritic pantheon as well as the identity of the Ugaritic and biblical Rephaim.[169] Finally in this period, E. T. Mullen investigated the divine council or assembly.[170] This approach to history-of-religion topics would continue at Harvard into the next period. In this period there was one major dissertation on a linguistic topic, the 1979 dissertation of John Huehnergard on the grammar of the Akkadian texts from Ras Shamra.[171] (In the following period, Huehnergard would produce his important work on Ugaritic vocabulary in syllabic transcription in polyglot texts.)[172] In retrospect, we may admire how Cross's powerful research ranged from Ugaritic to the Dead Sea Scrolls. And it is perhaps his penetrating analyses in the area of Israelite religion that have brought him the greatest recognition, but of all the fields, his greatest love is epigraphy.[173]

In the 1970s, Cross and Pope enjoyed friendly exchanges over Ugaritic, in particular over vocalizing Ugaritic words and over one text called "The Birth of the Beautiful Gods" (*CTA* 23 = *KTU* 1.23). Cross had been trained by Albright to vocalize Ugaritic.[174] (Cross writes that "we struggled to vocalize, usually deeply wounding Albright's Semitic sensibilities.")[175] When he defended vocalization in *Canaanite Myth and Hebrew Epic* in 1973,[176] Pope took exception to the book's vocalizations of some Ugaritic words and stated his preference to avoid the potential "fudge factor," as he put it.[177] Yet Pope conceded the value of vocalization, agreeing that, unlike translation, vocalization requires writers to express their interpretations very exactly. Yet vocalization is no easy matter. One Harvard student, Richard Whitaker, recalls an incident illustrating this.[178] Like his teacher Albright,[179] Cross would provide an initial class on Ugaritic grammar and then require students to begin working on a text, which would include analysis of specific words and their etymologies, a vocalization of the text, and translation. Understandably concerned about these difficult assignments (and deeply in awe of Cross as well), students used to find their mentor's most recent studies of the assigned Ugaritic passages and then incorporate his vocalizations into their class preparations of the texts. Once in class after one student had written a vocalized text on the board according to one of his articles, Cross looked at the vocalization and commented that it was not quite right. The incident illustrates that even great scholars could change their minds about their analysis of Ugaritic words.[180]

Cross and Pope also sparred over the depiction of the god El.[181] In his 1955 monograph, *El in the Ugaritic Texts,* Pope addresses El's qualities, his abode, his marital situation, and his diminished status in the pantheon. Pope also recognized El's patriarchal profile, as well as many first-millennium reflexes of the god in West Semitic religion, including in ancient Israel. In *Canaanite Myth and Hebrew Epic,* Cross extended this basic point in studying the extensive influence of El on the descriptions of Yahweh in the Bible, especially with respect to the descriptions of the deity in the heavenly council, the divine appearances in dreams to humans, and the identification of Yahweh with El Shadday in Exod 6:2–3. Indeed, these similarities led to Cross's conclusion that Yahweh was originally a title of El, a position that would elicit its own share of critics. Cross also questioned Pope's view of El as an ineffectual figure fallen from power *(deus otiosus)* and doubted Pope's portrait of El in *KTU* 1.23 as temporarily impotent. Instead Cross saw El in this text as a virile patriarch, more than able in sexual matters.[182] In a 1979 *Ugarit-Forschungen* article punningly entitled "The Ups and Downs in El's Amours,"[183] Pope responded in greater detail that the god suffered from an initial bout of impotence before being coaxed by the two females by magical means. The technical issues involved with 1.23 are complex, and all the issues argued by Cross and Pope illustrate the sorts of difficulties posed by Ugaritic. Their exchanges showed the congeniality and mutual respect of two major American scholars of Ugaritic in this period.[184]

⊠ THE INFLUENCE OF UGARITIC ON BIBLICAL STUDIES

In this period, the enormous influence of Ugaritic on biblical studies may be measured in part by the many dissertations that compared Ugaritic and Hebrew grammatical features, poetic aspects, or religious ones.[185] Many dissertations mentioned above analyzed a single biblical book from the perspective of Ugaritic. Led in number by Harvard in this period, the dissertations produced in the United States alone were very numerous. The comparative agenda flourished in this period, though perhaps with a greater critical attitude, as "parallelomania"[186] was beginning to receive increasing qualification.[187] Internationally, Ugaritic's influence might be measured by the basic tools developed in the biblical field. Dictionaries of biblical Hebrew had already begun to assimilate Ugaritic into their etymological considerations. The best-known example in this period was the revision of the 1953 "Koehler-Baumgartner" Hebrew dictionary,[188] known by the names of its two editors, L. Koehler and W. Baumgartner, professors in Zurich and Basel, respectively. This trend would continue in the area of dictionaries. A representative work of the 1970s and afterward, volumes of the *Theologisches Wörterbuch zum Alten Testament* began to appear in 1970. Entries in the dictionary show consistent inclusion of Ugaritic alongside the better-known languages such as Akkadian, Arabic, and Aramaic. Here we may draw special attention to the guidance and labor of the editors, G. Johannes Botterweck and Helmer Ringgren, especially for their selection of an international group of scholars able to include Ugaritic in their entries. It is to be noted that Ringgren himself has long labored in the field of Ugaritic and the Bible. The popularity of this work might be gauged by the ongoing publication of the volumes in both German and English, the latter under the title *Theological Dictionary of the Old Testament.*[189] This work has become a standard reference work in the field of Hebrew Bible.

Another indicator of Ugaritic's influence was biblical commentaries, at least in the United States. In contrast to the best-known German commentary series of the time, the Biblischer Kommentar, or even the Old Testament Library and Hermeneia series (originally involving a goodly number of translations of German commentaries), the Anchor Bible series was clearly the success story for Ugaritic in biblical commentaries. For this story we have to back up to the series' origins in the early 1960s.[190] The hand behind the series belonged to Cross's old scholarly confrère, David Noel Freedman. The selection of contributors was dominated early on by the old Hopkins network of Albright's students, including Cross (who was assigned Exodus, as well as I and II Samuel), Mendenhall (Numbers), Hillers (assigned Lamentations, but originally also Ruth), and Dahood (Psalms). It also included some Jewish scholars whom some in the Albright school[191] considered compatible with its goals, such as E. A. Speiser (Genesis), H. L. Ginsberg (First Isaiah), and Jonas Greenfield (Tobit). (Freedman only later took up the assignments of Amos and Hosea with Francis Andersen, who originally was selected to do Hosea on his own. Amos was assigned originally to Walter Harrelson. Albright himself took up the mismatched assignment of Matthew with C. S. Mann.)[192] Of the original figures assigned commentaries on the Hebrew Bible in the series, only two, Marvin Pope and Mitchell Dahood, completed volumes by the end of the 1960s. Cross and Ginsberg never published their assigned volumes. And commentaries by the other scholars knowledgeable in Ugaritic were not published until the 1970s.

⋈ MITCHELL DAHOOD AND UGARITIC'S DIMINISHED INFLUENCE ON BIBLICAL STUDIES

What was the effect of this record of publication? It might be argued that the history of the Anchor Bible points to a problematic aspect for Ugaritic studies in the 1970s. The place of Ugaritic in biblical studies was largely determined by that one figure who so energetically completed his commentary assignment first, Mitchell Dahood. This point requires some historical perspective. Beginning in the early 1950s, Dahood was a controversial figure in the field of Northwest Semitic philology.[193] His three-volume Anchor Bible Commentary on the Psalms[194] was the culmination of his comparative method, which allowed him to peruse Ugaritic and other West Semitic languages for cognates or grammatical forms that he thought might underlie difficulties in the Hebrew text of the Bible. Dahood showed a certain reverence for the consonants of the Masoretic Text, but the vowels were not equally sacrosanct, as he showed little reluctance in altering them, based on what he regarded as comparative "evidence." He viewed Ugaritic as part of a single linguistic and cultural continuum with Phoenician and Hebrew. In this approach Dahood was taking to its logical conclusion the comparative approach he learned from W. F. Albright, but he flattened out the differences among different West Semitic languages and cultures and built many questionable conclusions upon others. (Cross quips: "Dahood was also at Hopkins, a year or two behind Moran, Freedman and me. But the Roman dialect of Dahoodian was still gestating.")[195] Many old grammatical and lexicographical conundrums were susceptible to explanation by way of Ugaritic, and these were identified successfully and tested by Albright, Caquot, Cross, Driver, Emerton, Ginsberg, Gordon, Held, and many others. Dahood often picked up older suggestions that in some cases were valid, but then he would propose many more instances of the same usage, and he would leave others to test his assertions. A good example was his proposal to extend H. S. Nyberg's hypothesis of a divine title ʿAliy behind ʿl-, often vocalized as a preposition in the Masoretic Text.[196] Dahood cited the Ugaritic evidence[197] for this title in his work, information just coming to light when Nyberg was preparing his 1935 work. In general, Dahood lost sight of the fact that this case, and others to which he attached importance, were features not of classical Hebrew, but of archaic Hebrew. Such features were exceptions in classical Hebrew and not the rule. They were, to use Ginsberg's phrase, "Canaanite Vestiges."[198] Dahood, however, rewrote these old features back into all sorts of biblical texts, yielding hundreds of "new suggestions." The cumulative effect of all of these proposals was an interpretation of the biblical text that no other reader would recognize.

⋈ A POSITIVE EXAMPLE OF DAHOOD'S METHOD

Let me offer an example of Dahood's way of operating. The last line of Ps 29:9 is often rendered: "and all in his temple say 'Glory!'" The line is generally taken to mean that the worshipers in the temple "say glory" (NJPS, NRSV) or "cry glory" (RSV). It is possible that such a liturgical response to the eastward-moving storm theophany could take place, but more in keeping with the notion of biblical theophanies is not the proclamation, but the appearance of glory. The apparent impediment to this interpretation in this context would be the semantics of the root *ʾmr, which generally means "to say." However, as Dahood rightly saw, "to see" is one meaning of Ugaritic *ʾmr (*KTU* 1.3 I 22) and Akkadian *amāru*, and this meaning may apply in Ps 29:9 as well.[199] In sum, two basic facts support Dahood's solution: divine glory is seen and not said; and the semantic range is supported by cognate languages, made all the more defensible by virtue of the poem's archaic date. Dahood also argued—correctly in my view—that *kullô* is a postpositive referring to the temple, and he translates: "While in his temple—all of it." Because *klw* is attested as a postpositive attached to places,[200] Dahood's view can be sustained, and it is certainly preferable to the view that *klw* is a prose addition.[201]

Yet Dahood's disregard for the vocalized Masoretic Text perhaps misled him at this point. He argued further that *ʾōmēr* is to be read as a noun form *ʾōmer*, and accordingly he translates the final two words of Ps 29:9, "a vision of the Glorious One."[202] The first problem is the morphology of *ʾōmēr* as a noun. The difficulty involves the lack of criteria for this morphological option. Why should Dahood select a nominal form over a verbal form? The second problem involves understanding *kābôd* as a divine title; this is mistaken in my view. "Glory," or better "radiance," tends in biblical texts to be the *visible* manifestation of the divine presence and not a phenomenon *proclaimed*. Moreover, the appearance of divine radiance or glory is presented as an experience. Accordingly, it may be more accurate to translate "and in His temple—all of it—radiance appears." This case illustrates both the strengths and weaknesses of Dahood's work. He followed the tradition of learning and method employed by Albright and his other students, but permitted himself latitude in rewriting the vowels of the text, often with little methodological control.

⬚ DAHOOD AND THE RESPONSE TO HIS WORK: C. H. Gordon, D. Pardee, M. H. Pope, D. N. Freedman, and D. A. Robertson

In Dahood's time, his work was hotly debated. Despite the possibilities opened up by his research, the substantive critiques came quickly. Many articles were produced aimed at disproving many of his claims. Of these, I would single out D. A. Robertson's 1966 review of the first volume of the Psalms commentary, fine reviews by S. E. Loewenstamm and J. C. de Moor and P. van der Lugt on

Dahood's contributions to *Ras Shamra Parallels,* many comments on Dahood's work in James Barr's 1968 *Comparative Philology and the Text of the Old Testament,* and the recent test of Dahood's work by Robert Althann.[203] The range of views on Dahood's work was indeed vast. On the one hand, we meet with the generous assessment offered by Cyrus Gordon, who wrote in 1979:

> Now I've been reading about pan-Ugaritism, and my friend Mitchell Dahood has been capable of overshooting his mark. On the other hand, let me tell you that Father Dahood knows this. This wouldn't surprise him. What I like to do—this is my own predilection—is to find 40 or 50 of each . . . I don't have to overkill. Father Dahood likes to get the last drop out of the lemon when he squeezes it. His work is of inestimable value, but something will have to be done. What is the term they used to use in Washington? Sanitized. That is, to clean up a little bit of the mess, and then we're going to have something refined and excellent.[204]

Gordon was right as to Dahood's awareness of the many problems raised by his work. Once commenting on one of his own "discoveries," Dahood remarked:

> This explanation may sound much like "you name it, we have it," but the plain fact is that the Northwest Semitic morphological and lexical treasure-trove offers the biblical philologist choices unthinkable three decades ago.

With this quote Dahood illustrates both the prizes to be won through such work and the pitfalls. In order to make such new discoveries, Dahood could shop around the putatively single Ugaritic-Phoenician-Hebrew (and later Eblaite) continuum. Yet in a moment of rare academic candor he admitted both to "faulty judgment" and to a failure to "adhere consistently to the enunciated canons of Northwest Semitic grammar."[205]

Despite the note sounded by Gordon, many other scholars in the field were less positive.[206] In the same volume where Gordon's assessment appears, Dennis Pardee, presently the greatest American scholar of Ugaritic, opined:

> I agree that 33% of Dahood's suggestions might be right. Prof. Andersen, in a recent interview, suggested that maybe 25% of someone's contributions might turn out to be correct. My question is: who is going to weed out the 67% or the 75%? It seems to me that it is putting an undue burden on the scholarly community to spend a good deal of its time weeding unacceptable material, and perhaps instead of doing that work, we should be training our students to weed out the unacceptable material themselves, so that the dissertations they publish are maybe 50% correct, or 60% correct, or 70% correct, rather than 25% to 33% correct.[207]

After Pardee contributed his revision of Gordon's numbers, Marvin Pope followed with a citation of Jonas Greenfield's assessment that the question is not simply whether 10 percent of Dahood's ideas are right, but which 10 percent.[208] D. N. Freedman would defend such a score. Speaking of this guess as to the percentage of correct proposals in Dahood's oeuvre, Freedman writes: "I would say that 10% on almost anything biblical would be pretty good for most scholars, even the great ones."[209] Some scholars privately placed the percentage even lower, at 5 percent or less.

D. A. Robertson, himself expert in archaic Hebrew poetry, put the point differently:

> Most serious is that it [Dahood's method] tends to obscure the scholar's primary and fundamental task: to produce studies in the probable, not the possible. Most any theory can be conceived to account for a certain set of facts. But the crucial point is whether an explanation, once conceived, is likely. Dahood has recorded all of his brainstorms, and only very rarely qualified them as probable or improbable. Moreover, all of his proposals are incorporated into the translation, rendering it useless for all public and private use.[210]

The problem was essentially methodological. Other scholars who used a comparative method were far more circumspect in their comparisons than Dahood.[211] They recognized differences as well as similarities between languages, and they used methodological criteria and common sense to maintain both. Dahood, in contrast, was open to many possible readings based on what he saw especially in Ugaritic, and he rarely scrutinized their merits consistently and clearly.[212]

When Dahood offered a seminar at Yale in 1981 (during my student days there), our initial reaction to his approach was decidedly mixed. At one point, I asked him how he might adjudicate between two possible readings of a text (this was my attempt to get him to articulate his method). He responded that he simply chose the solution that struck him as superior. His audience was none too impressed with this answer (nor were we impressed when he divided a single cuneiform sign of "Eblaite" in order to get the end of one word and the beginning of a second). An additional difficulty involved his construction of new discoveries based on prior findings, themselves heavily susceptible to criticism: such a house of cards seemed to be waiting to fall at the removal of a single card from the bottom.

⌘ DAHOOD'S IMPACT AND THE DECLINE OF UGARITIC IN BIBLICAL STUDIES: J. Barr's View

Historically, the issue of Dahood's work involves more than a matter of correctness and error; there is the additional question of influence. Just how influential was his Psalms commentary? As Brevard Childs once put the issue to me, the problems of Dahood's work signaled the demise of Ugaritic for biblical studies. I was stunned by this pronouncement, but from the perspective of biblicists who knew or used only a little Ugaritic, the great work of Caquot, Cross, Emerton, Ginsberg, Held, and Pope was less in view. Childs was hardly alone in his view of the decline of Ugaritic. In his response to criticisms that his 1968 book *Comparative Philology and the Text of the Old Testament* had not paid sufficient attention to Ugaritic, James Barr writes with Dahood's work in mind:

> Insufficient attention to Ugaritic? Well, perhaps. I felt, in writing *Comparative Philology and the Text of the Old Testament,* that the waters of Ugarit had been so muddied by the trampling of those seeking solutions for the Old Testament that it could not, for the present and without extensive and intricate argument, be easily used as secure evidence. . . .

> Ugaritic studies still suffer damage from the *Entdeckerfreude* of those who have exploited them for the elucidation of the Old Testament. I would set it forth as a good principle: if you want to know something reliable about Ugaritic, ask an Ugaritologist who is interested in looking at the material for itself, and not at the material as a quarry from which new quick identifications of Hebrew meanings can be dug.[213]

This gap pointed to deeper rifts in biblical studies, a field that at this point was unprepared to heed the warning given by Ginsberg in 1950: "The specialist can not yet dispense with conscientious sifting of all the better writers on Ugaritica since the birth of the discipline."[214] Even as the method and results of his prodigious output were being severely criticized by specialists of Ugaritic studies, Dahood became typecast as one of the major representatives of Ugaritic to the biblical world. Here again James Barr: ". . . but it is here, among the Drivers and Dahoods of scholarship working on the detailed biblical text, that I find not just an empiricism or positivism but an almost entirely *uncritical* and *unanalytical* empiricism and positivism."[215] During the 1970s many biblicists began to place considerably less premium on Ugaritic studies. Even R. Rendtorff and J. Jeremias, who used Ugaritic to great advantage in their earlier biblical research, paid less attention to Ugaritic after 1980.[216]

⌧ DAHOOD'S WORK IN RETROSPECT:
The Recent Critique by R. Althann

Perhaps most notable among the critiques of Dahood is the recent work by Robert Althann.[217] Althann produced a dissertation under Dahood at the Pontifical Biblical Institute. As one of his students, Althann offers a meticulous examination of his mentor's method. Althann's study addresses several areas of comparison made infamous by Dahood: the "interchangeability" of the prepositions *b-*, *min*, *l-*, and *ʿal*; **taqtul* as an alternative third person masculine prefix indicative verbal form; a third person singular pronominal suffix **-y*; the conjunction *p-*; and vocative particles *kî*, *l-*, and *m-*. The book additionally offers an introduction to the entire discussion, a study of Dahood's debate with James

Barr[218] over the interpretation of Job 3 in light of the comparative method, and some general conclusions. Regarding the prepositions, Althann is highly critical of Dahood, rightly preferring the approach of Dennis Pardee and Ernst Jenni that examines prepositions in combination with verbs. Althann does note some parallel biblical passages where *min* replaces the apparently earlier *b*- (e.g., 2 Sam 22:16 = Ps 18:16). Such cases are relatively rare, and probably indicate what is generally true of the few valid comparisons made by Dahood between Ugaritic and Hebrew, namely that many of these features of Ugaritic grammar are expected to be relatively rare in Biblical Hebrew (BH) and largely confined to early and/or poetic contexts.

Althann rejects Dahood's efforts to find **taqtul* verbal forms or the third person **-y* suffix in BH. The posited instances are susceptible to other interpretations; some are a matter of different grammatical views, while others involve an issue of rhetoric. Here Althann shows poise in discerning the missteps of Dahood.[219] With respect to *p*-, the proposed example of Ps 50:10 is regarded as very probable, Song 3:10 and Hos 4:2 and 7:1 are deemed "probable," and Job 9:12, 20 is taken to acquire greater sense if *p*- is posited. To my mind, the Ugaritic basis for *p*- is solid and the case of Ps 50:10 is persuasive. Vocative *l*- is similarly well attested in Ugaritic, and Althann revisits not only Dahood's discussions, but also treatments by Miller and Pope. The possibilities for vocative *l*- in BH appear more numerous, but as with *b*- in the meaning "from" and for *p*-, this grammatical feature should be expected to be relatively rare in classical Hebrew. Dahood did not recognize this point, finding many cases of such usage in the Psalms in general and in many other biblical texts.

In sum, Althann offers a fair and balanced assessment of Dahood's work. The methodological discussions, especially in the introductory and concluding chapters, are indispensable,[220] while the discussion of proposed grammatical features in specific passages constitutes a particular strength of this book. In sum, then, Dahood's method and conclusions were often off target, but he showed a talent for identifying items in the Masoretic Text that require further examination, and at times he spurred other scholars to more judicious assessments. Althann's book for the most part admirably sifts what may endure in Dahood's work from what was merely innovative.

✄ WIDER DEVELOPMENTS WITHIN BIBLICAL STUDIES

The decline of Ugaritic in biblical studies in this period did not happen simply because of the field's discomfort with Dahood's method. We may point to five factors within the Ugaritic field prompting the decline. First and foremost, the postwar era had witnessed an explosion in primary and secondary literature, and this development accelerated through the 1970s. It seemed impossible to keep fully abreast of developments in both biblical studies and extrabiblical literatures. Second, by the end of this period, Ugaritic seemed to be well harvested; it was now over half a century since the discovery of the first texts.[221] "Parallels" were seen to be of decreasing value to biblical studies.[222] Third, Ugaritic also seemed resistant to full clarification. Without the benefit of vowels apart from the three ʾalephs, the language sometimes seemed as if it would remain poorly understood. Even H. L. Ginsberg in 1950 could make the claim (which Marvin Pope later called "Ginsberg's dictum") that "the only people who have never made mistakes in Ugaritic philology are those who have never engaged in it."[223] It is worth noting as well Ginsberg's lesser-known but pointed 1948 comment about the field: "Each of these texts by itself is a happy hunting-ground for philological sportsmen, abounding as it does in lacunae and obscurities, while the intricate and tantalizing problems of the mutual relations of the texts among themselves can afford even more ambitious nimrods of research scope for weeks and weeks of congenial activity."[224] The point of diminishing returns seemed to pass for many scholars emerging in the field in this period. Fourth, as Ginsberg's comment suggests, the technical knowledge required by the field of Ugaritic seemed daunting to many in the biblical field. Whereas biblicists could easily draw on Ugaritic studies in earlier periods, the growth of Ugaritic studies began to preclude such engagement. Finally, Ugaritic attracted enough problematic proposals that its reputation suffered in the biblical field. Some complained that a journal such as *Ugarit-Forschungen* published a number of far-fetched articles. Even if such pieces were not disproportionate to what is found in other fields, still they did not enhance the reputation of Ugaritic studies.

Beyond the problems of the Ugaritic field itself, at this point it had a new competitor. The appearance of the Ebla texts in the late 1970s (presented to the field in an almost circus-like atmosphere) affected Ugaritic studies in two ways. Either it distracted scholars from Ugaritic, who moved on to Ebla texts (examples include P. Fronzaroli and P. Xella),[225] or it produced an overreaching effort to posit a new West Semitic continuum that reached from Ebla through Ugaritic down to Phoenician and Hebrew; here I would include figures with different levels of background in cuneiform such as Gordon,[226] Dahood,[227] and at least momentarily, D. N. Freedman.[228] This line of approach was only the most recent attempt to subordinate the texts of a Syrian site to the telos of biblical interpretation.

Yet other currents were shifting the course of Ugaritic studies and biblical research by the end of this era. In the United States, the mid-1970s saw a shift away from philological studies to a criticism of the limited ways in which the Bible (especially) had been read. Perhaps the movement of the greatest long-term importance has been feminist study of the Bible.[229] Feminist criticism has helped to unmask long-standing biases and assumptions underlying traditional readings of the text that privileged the viewpoints of ancient authors and ecclesial traditions. Feminist reading has helped further to push readers to read "between the lines," to see the dark side of ancient Israel's history and culture, especially in its horrific treatment of women.

This discussion has allowed scholars to identify biblical texts rendering the deity in female terms and to raise issues as to the female dimension of the deity. None of this agenda in itself would preclude examination of the biblical texts in relation to the Ugaritic texts. Indeed, feminist study applies equally well to the Ugaritic texts. However, since it was the Bible that had long been used to justify subordination of women in the West, it was the Bible that was the battlefield for feminist study, not the Ugaritic texts. Furthermore, the field of Ugaritic demanded close philological attention; such an agenda was not the main focus of many feminist readings. However, when the issue came to religion, interest in goddesses in the Ugaritic texts aided feminist reading, as they helped to show the background of Israelite religion. With the goddesses condemned in the Bible now attested in the Ugaritic texts (Asherah and Astarte), it seems that Israelite religion knew the cult of one goddess (at least) before her eventual exclusion. The discussion here has been healthy: some feminist scholars see the rejection of the goddess as a setback, others as an advance, and yet others do not cast the issue in these terms.[230] In sum, the Ugaritic texts garnered only modest interest from feminist biblical critics.

Feminist criticism would find an ally in another major development in the field, namely, literary readings of the Bible. At the same time as the rise of feminist study of the Bible, the field witnessed the development of "rhetorical criticism," following James Muilenburg's 1968 presidential address before the Society of Biblical Literature.[231] Professor at Union Theological Seminary, Muilenburg in his speech made a "declaration of rhetorical independence" from what he perceived to be the limitations of form criticism. Yet this direction also signaled a shift from philology and poetry of the Ugaritic texts as well. Literary reading could be joined to feminist concerns and perspective, represented, for example, by the influential 1978 study, *God and the Rhetoric of Sexuality*, written by one of Muilenburg's students, Phyllis Trible,[232] or the well-known 1987 study of Mieke Bal entitled *Lethal Love*.[233] Rhetorical criticism and feminist hemeneutics were hardly inimical in principle to the study of Ugaritic poetry; indeed, each is highly compatible to it and very helpful for examining it (as shown by some of its practitioners, such as J. Jackson). However, many rhetorical and feminist critics took little interest in Ugaritic, even in many biblical texts where these approaches might have benefited from a perusal of Ugaritic material.

In the 1970s, another strong wave of literary study swept over the field of Bible.[234] This development involved literary criticism influenced more directly by departments of English and comparative literature. As examples, we may note in order of date works produced by J. P. Fokkelman, M. Fishbane, J. L. Kugel, M. Weiss, R. Alter, and M. Sternberg; works written by U. Simon, Y. Zakovitch and others in Israel; and later the volumes produced by M. Bal and D. Damrosch.[235] Unlike their predecessor S. E. Loewenstamm,[236] most, if not all, of these scholars exhibited little interest in the Ugaritic background of biblical poetry. Falling on deaf ears in biblical studies were the voices of scholars comparing biblical and Ugaritic poetry in the period, such as Y. Avishur, J. C. de Moor, P. C. Craigie, I. Kottsieper, M. C. A. Korpel, O. Loretz, M. P. O'Connor, D. Pardee, and W. G. E. Watson.[237] A few scholars worked both sides, notably E. L. Greenstein,[238] A. Berlin,[239] and, to some extent, D. Pardee.[240] Throughout this entire period the many volumes of L. Alonso Schökel also appeared. These stood in dialogue with scholars on many sides.[241] (In this environment, J. C. Greenfield's contribution to R. Alter and F. Kermode's *The Literary Guide to the Bible* stands out in the volume as something of an oddity,[242] perhaps an indicator of the gulf between literary and philological study at this point.) The role played by Ugaritic in the study of the Bible as literature faded.

Lying behind this literary trend (at least in the United States) was not only a diminished interest in extrabiblical languages and literatures (as well as archaeology, history, textual criticism, and epigraphy). The major shift also involved what it means to read a text. When the meaning of a text is no longer located in historical background or origins and development (diachrony), then reading no longer requires knowledge of such contexts. Reading largely revolves around the conventions and departures from conventions located only in the biblical text (synchrony). In what is commonly grouped today under the rubric of "postmodern" readings,[243] the reader's own time, place, and perspective displace analysis of the ancient texts' conventions. The biblical field also witnessed greater compartmentalization, as successive literary and historical trends swirled around biblical studies through the 1980s: from the older New Criticism, through structuralism, deconstructionism, ideological criticism (feminist and otherwise), the New Historicism, intertextuality, postmodernism, and beyond. These have been complicated further by the emerging interests in social science research (anthropology, sociology, etc.). All told, these various interests have atomized biblical studies. By default, they also reduced any premium paid for philology or comparative literary study. Finally, theology, perhaps reacting against the biblical theology movement, enjoyed at best mixed relations with research in the history of religion. There were important exceptions; fine works were produced on the religion of ancient Israel, for example, T. N. D. Mettinger's series of books;[244] the major two-volume work, *A History of Israelite Religion in the Old Testament Period*,[245] by Claus Westermann's student, Rainer Albertz; and the later studies of many of the students of Cross and Pope students in the United States.

These changes in biblical studies gravely reduced Ugaritic in the eyes of many students of Bible in the late 1980s and afterward. A sea change was at work. In this period, the prestigious traditional practice of Semitic philology and exegesis developed in the nineteenth century ran its full course (and beyond in Dahood's work) in Ugaritic and biblical studies, and calls for intellectual projects influenced by postwar literary and cultural disciplines were growing louder. Even with the publication of new texts, the traditional forms of *Wissenschaft* seemed insufficient in their goals or explanatory capacity. It would require the perspectives afforded by comparative literature and social sciences first to situate both older and newer texts, not to mention material culture, and then to ascertain their broader interrelations and larger cultural significance. Some scholars would view these developments as signs of academic turmoil and a loss in the field's standards, especially in the area of linguistic knowledge. To some extent, this assessment was true; gone were the days when students of the Bible could be expected to study Arabic and Akkadian, Ugaritic and Aramaic. Yet for other scholars, these changes signaled a new intellectual ferment, permitting the entire intellectual project to receive more intensive scrutiny. This reexamination included a renewed look at the basic relationship between Ugarit and ancient Israel. Up to this point in this discussion, it has been the impact of Ugaritic studies on the biblical field that has been emphasized. However, it is equally clear that the biblically driven research on Ugaritic[246] focused on some aspects of the Ugaritic texts and ignored others; and at least in the hands of Dahood and perhaps others, it had also blurred the differences between the languages and cultures attested in the Ugaritic texts and the Hebrew Bible. The many developments during this period opened the door to rethinking the direction and goals of Ugaritic and biblical studies. As a result, the next period would demand the intellectual catholicity both to continue the older, well-grounded practices of philology and exegesis and to engage a broader agenda involving literature and society.

⋈ NOTES

1. J. Nougayrol, E. Laroche, C. Virolleaud, and C. F. A. Schaeffer, eds., *Ugaritica V* (MRS 16; Paris: Imprimerie Nationale/Librairie Orientaliste Paul Geuthner, 1968).
2. See below under Paris.
3. L. R. Fisher, *The Claremont Ras Shamra Tablets* (AnOr 48; Rome: Pontificium Institutum Biblicum, 1972). The background of these tablets is repeated in J. C. Greenfield's review of the volume in *JCS* 29 (1977): 187.
4. Cohen and Pardee have returned to these texts more recently: Cohen, "The Ugaritic Hippiatric Texts: Revised Composite Text, Translation, and Commentary," *UF* 28

(1996): 105–53; Pardee, "Some Brief Remarks on Hippiatric Methodology," *AO* 10 (1992): 154–55; idem, "Quelques remarques relatives à l'étude des textes hippiatriques en langue ougaritique," *Sem* 45 (1996): 19–26.

5. The best article on this topic remains D. Marcus, "The Three Alephs in Ugaritic," *JANES* 1 (1968): 50–60.

6. Boyd, "A Collection and Examination of the Ugaritic Vocabulary Contained in the Akkadian Texts from Ras Shamra" (Ph.D. diss., University of Chicago, 1975).

7. Sivan, *Grammatical Analysis and Glossary of the Northwest Semitic Vocables of the 15th–13th c. B.C. from Canaan and Syria* (AOAT 214; Kevelaer: Bercker & Butzon; Neukirchen-Vluyn: Neukirchener Verlag, 1984).

8. Huehnergard, *Ugaritic Vocabulary in Syllabic Transcription* (HSS 32; Atlanta: Scholars Press, 1987).

9. Cohen, *Biblical Hapax Legomena in the Light of Akkadian and Ugaritic* (SBLDS 37; Missoula, Mont.: Scholars Press, 1978). This work is based on Cohen's 1975 Columbia dissertation.

10. Aartun, *Die Partikeln des Ugaritischen* (2 vols.; AOAT 21/1–2; Kevelaer: Bercker & Butzon; Neukirchen-Vluyn: Neukirchener Verlag, 1974, 1978).

11. Pardee, "The Preposition in Ugaritic," *UF* 7 (1975): 329–78, *UF* 8 (1976): 215–322. See also Pardee, "More on the Preposition in Ugaritic," *UF* 11 (1979 = C. F. A. Schaeffer Festschrift): 685–92.

12. For example, J. Blau, "Hebrew and North West Semitic: Reflections on the Classification of the Semitic Languages," *HAR* 2 (1978): 21–44, republished in Blau, *Topics in Hebrew and Semitic Linguistics* (Jerusalem: Magnes, 1998): 308–32; J. F. Brent, "The Problem of the Placement of Ugaritic among the Semitic Languages," *WTJ* 41 (1978): 84–107; P. van Zijl, *Baal* (AOAT 10; Kevelaer: Verlag Butzon & Bercker; Neukirchen-Vluyn: Neukirchener Verlag, 1972), 2–4 for a brief survey. Sadly, van Zijl died young in the fall of 1976 of a heart attack; see *NUS* 12 (January 1977): 2.

13. *NUS* 22 (September 1980): 8–16.

14. Full references for these works follow in the next section.

15. See the plates at the back of *Maarav* 2/2 (1980) for R. E. Friedman's article, "The MRZḤ Tablet from Ugarit," *Maarav* 2/2 (1980): 187–206. See also *BAR* 9/5 (1983): 70.

16. Watson, *Classical Hebrew Poetry: A Guide to Its Techniques* (JSOTSup 26; Sheffield: Sheffield Academic Press, 1984); see also his later book, *Traditional Techniques in Classical Hebrew Verse* (JSOTSup 170; Sheffield: Sheffield Academic Press, 1994).

17. Pardee, *Ugaritic and Hebrew Poetic Parallelism: A Trial Cut (ʿnt I and Proverbs 2)* (VTSup 39; Leiden: Brill, 1988); idem, "Ugaritic and Hebrew Metrics," in *Ugarit in Retrospect: Fifty Years of Ugarit and Ugaritic* (ed. G. D. Young; Winona Lake, Ind.: Eisenbrauns, 1981), 113–50.

18. Berlin, *The Dynamics of Biblical Parallelism* (Bloomington/Indianapolis: Indiana University Press, 1985). See also her book, *Poetics and Interpretation of Biblical Narrative* (Bible and Literature 9; Sheffield: Almond, 1983; repr. Winona Lake, Ind.: Eisenbrauns, 1994).

19. See the semantic parallelism emphasized in E. L. Greenstein, "How Does Parallelism Mean?" in *A Sense of Text*, *JQR Supplement* (Winona Lake, Ind.: Eisenbrauns, 1982), 41–70; cf. the criticism of R. Alter, *The Art of Biblical Poetry* (New York: Basic Books, 1985), 215 n. 11.

20. See M. P. O'Connor, *Hebrew Verse Structure* (Winona Lake, Ind.: Eisenbrauns, 1981), in particular 4–5, 134–35. For an effort to explain and expand O'Connor's approach, see W. L. Holladay, "*Hebrew Verse Structure* Revisited (I): Which Words 'Count'?" *JBL* 118 (1999): 19–32; and "*Hebrew Verse Structure* Revisited (II): Conjoint Cola, and Further Suggestions," *JBL* 118 (1999): 401–16.

21. I owe this point regarding alliteration within lines to E. L. Greenstein.

22. Fitzgerald, Hebrew Poetry," *NJBC* 1:204. On acrostics more generally, see W. Soll, *Psalm 119: Matrix, Form, and Setting* (CBQMS 23; Washington: Catholic Biblical Association of America, 1991), 5–34; and H. Eshel and J. Strugnell, "Alphabetic Acrostics in Pre-Tannaitic Hebrew," *CBQ* 62 (2000): 441–58.

23. Avishur, *Stylistic Studies of Word-Pairs in Biblical and Ancient Semitic Literature.*

24. *Ras Shamra Parallels I–II* (ed. L. Fisher; AnOr 49–50; Rome: Pontifical Biblical Institute, 1972, 1975); *Ras Shamra Parallels III* (ed. S. Rummel; AnOr 51; Rome: Pontifical Biblical Institute, 1981). See works of other authors cited by Watson, *Traditional Techniques*, 18–22. See also J. C. de Moor and P. van der Lugt, "The Spectre of Pan-Ugaritism," *BiOr* 31 (1974): 3–26. Cf. B. Margalit, *A Matter of "Life" and "Death"* (AOAT 206; Kevelaer: Butzon & Bercker; Neukirchen-Vluyn: Neukirchener Verlag, 1980). For discussion of Margalit's work, see further below the discussion of Haifa in this chapter. For some interesting reflections on Hebrew poetry, see T. Longman, "A Critique of Two Recent Approaches to Hebrew Meter," *Biblica* 63 (1982): 230–54.

25. For further discussion, see below.

26. De Tarragon, *Le culte à Ugarit: D'aprés les textes de la pratique en cunéiformes alphabétiques* (Cahiers de la Revue Biblique 19; Paris: Gabalda, 1980); Xella, *I testi rituali di Ugarit. I: Testi* (Studi Semitici 54; Rome: Consiglio Nazionale delle Ricerche, 1981). See also B. A. Levine, *In the Presence of the Lord* (Leiden: Brill, 1974); R. Rendtorff, *Studien zur Geschichte des Opfers im Alten Testament* (WMANT 24; Neukirchen-Vluyn: Neukirchener Verlag, 1967). For a listing of works by J. Milgrom, see his volume, *Leviticus 1–16* (AB 3; New York: Doubleday, 1991), 103–8. Note also the record album produced by A. D. Kilmer, R. J. Crocker, and R. R. Brown, *Sounds from Silence* (side two: A Hurrian cult song RS 15.30 + 15.49 + 17.387; Berkeley, Calif.: Bīt Enki Records, 1976) with further bibliography; B. Janowski, "Erwägungen zur Vorgeschichte des israelitischen šᵉlamîm-Opfers," *UF* 12 (1980): 231–60; and G. A. Anderson, *Sacrifices and Offerings in Ancient Israel* (HSM 4; Atlanta: Scholars Press, 1987).

27. Kaiser, "Zum Formular der in Ugarit gefundenen Briefe," *ZDPV* 86 (1970): 10–23; Ahl, "Epistolary Texts from Ugarit" (Ph.D. diss., Brandeis University, 1973); Kristensen, "Ugaritic Epistolary Formulas: A Comparative Study of the Ugaritic Epistolary Formulas in the Context of Contemporary Akkadian Formulas in the Letters from Ugarit and Amarna," *UF* 9 (1977): 143–58; D. Pardee, "Ugaritic: Further Studies in Ugaritic Epistolography," *AfO* 31 (1984): 213–30; D. Pardee and R. M. Whiting, "Aspects of Epistolary Usage in Ugaritic and Akkadian," *BSOAS* 50 (1987): 1–31; Cunchillos, "Correspondance," in A. Caquot, J. M. de Tarragon, and J. L. Cunchillos, *Textes ougaritiques: Tome II. Textes religieux, rituels, correspondance* (LAPO 14; Paris: Cerf, 1989), 239–421 (with citation of literature); Cunchillos cites Pardee's other work on letters up to the time of his 1989 book.

28. See *KTU* 2.12.6–11 = 2.24.5–7 = 2.68.4–7; cf. 2.11.5–7, 2.42.4–5. For this example, see Rainey, *The Scribe at Ugarit: His Position and Influence* (Israel Academy of Sciences and Humanities Proceedings 3/4; Jerusalem: Israel Academy of Sciences and Humanities, 1968), 10–11.

29. For this example, see Rainey, "Observations on Ugaritic Grammar," *UF* 3 (1971): 162.

30. For this example, see ibid., 157 (also *CAD* R: 118–19). For another example from epistolary usage, see ibid., 160. For other examples of help for Ugaritic words derived from western peripheral Akkadian texts from Ras Shamra, see Rainey, "Some Prepositional Nuances in Ugaritic Administrative Texts," in *Proceedings of the International Conference on Semitic Studies Held in Jerusalem, 19–23 July 1965* (Jerusalem: Israel Academy of Sciences and Humanities, 1969), 205–11; and "More Gleanings from Ugarit," *IOS* 5 (1975): 25; Pardee and Whiting, "Aspects," 12–14.

31. Sivan, *Grammar of the Ugaritic Language*, 197.

32. For example, Liverani, "La royauté syrienne de l'âge du bronze récent," in *Le palais et la royauté* (ed. P. Garelli; RAI 19; Paris: Geuthner, 1974), 329–56; "Communautés de village et palais royal dans la Syrie du IIème millénaire," *JESHO* 18 (1975): 146–64; "La dotazione dei mercanti di Ugarit," *UF* 11 (1979): 495–504; "Economia delle fattiore palatine ugaritiche," *Dialoghi di archeologia* ns 1/2 (1979): 57–72, translated as "Economy of Ugaritic Royal Farms," in *Production and Consumption in the Ancient Near East* (ed. C. Zaccagnini; Budapest: University of Budapest, 1989), 127–68; "Ville et campagne dans le royaume d'Ugarit: Essai d'analyse economique," in *Societies and Langages of the Ancient Near East: Studies in Honour of I. M. Diakonoff* (ed. M. A. Dandamayev et al.; Warminster, England: Aris & Phillips, 1982), 250–58.

33. Heltzer, *The Rural Community in Ancient Ugarit* (Wiesbaden: Harrassowitz, 1976); idem, *Goods, Prices, and the Organization of Trade in Ugarit* (Wiesbaden: Harrassowitz, 1978). See also his later work, *The Internal Organization of Ugarit* (Wiesbaden: Harrassowitz, 1982).

34. Alt, "Bemerkungen zu den Verwaltungs- und Rechtsurkunden von Ugarit und Alalach," *WO* 2/1 (1954): 7–18, *WO* 2/3 (1956): 234–43, *WO* 2/4 (1957): 338–42. See also Alt, *Kleine Schriften zur Geschichte des Volkes Israel III* (ed. M. Noth; Munich: Beck, 1959), 186–213; Gray, "Feudalism in Ugarit and Early Israel," *ZAW* 64 (1952): 49–55; Rainey, "The Social Stratification of Ugarit" (Ph.D. diss, Brandeis University, 1962); and "The Kingdom of Ugarit," *BA* 28 (1965): 102–25. For a convenient review of this scholarship (on which this summary is largely based), see J. D. Schloen, "The Patrimonial Household in the Kingdom of Ugarit: A Weberian Analysis of Ancient Near Eastern Society" (Ph.D. diss., Harvard University, 1995), 1–149.

35. See Schloen, "Patrimonial Household in the Kingdom of Ugarit," 66–83.

36. For example, Archi, "The Epigraphic Evidence from Ebla and the Old Testament," *Bib* 60 (1979): 556–66; Arnaud, "Mythologie d'Emar et mythologie d'Ougarit," paper presented at the 27th Rencontre Assyriologique Internationale held at the Collège de France, 30 June–5 July 1980; Edzard, "Amarna und die Archive seiner Korrespondenten zwischen Ugarit und Gaza," in *Biblical Archaeology Today: Proceedings of the International Congress on Biblical Archaeology. Jerusalem, April, 1984* (ed. J. Aviram et al.; Jerusalem: Israel Exploration Society, 1985), 248–59; Lambert, "Old Akkadian *Ilaba-* Ugaritic *Ilib,*" *UF* 13 (1981): 299–301; Malamat, *Mari and the Bible* (Studies in the History and Culture of the Ancient Near East 12; Leiden: Brill, 1998); Millard, "Qadesh et Ugarit," *Les annales archéologiques syriennes* 29–30 (1979–1980): 201–5; Moran, "The Sumero-Akkadian Tradition at Ugarit" (paper presented at the annual meeting of the Society of Biblical Literature, 17 November 1979); Owen, "Ugarit, Canaan, and Egypt: New Evidence from Aphek on the 13th Century B.C.E.," in *Ugarit in Retrospect: Fifty Years of Ugarit and Ugaritic* (ed. G. D. Young; Winona Lake, Ind.: Eisenbrauns, 1981), 49–53; Sasson, "Literary Criticism, Folklore Scholarship, and Ugaritic Literature," in *Ugarit in Retrospect*, 81–98; and Wiseman, "Israel's Literary Neighbours in the 13th Century B.C.," *JNWSL* 5 (1977): 77–91. See also J. and A. Westenholz, "Help for Rejected Suitors: The Old Akkadian Love Incantation MAD. V. 8," *Or* 46 (1977): 198–219. Contributions by Egyptologists also deserve mention: for example, K. Kitchen, "Egypt, Ugarit, Qatna, and Covenant," *UF* 11 (1979): 453–64.

37. Ahlström, *Aspects of Syncretism in Israelite Religion* (Horae Soederblomianae 5; Lund: Gleerup, 1963); Morton Smith, *Palestinian Parties and Politics That Shaped the Old Testament* (New York: Columbia University Press, 1971). The topic is important, so I will return to it in more detail below.

38. Cross, *Canaanite Myth and Hebrew Epic: Essays in the History of the Religion of Israel* (Cambridge: Harvard University Press, 1973). Cross and the Harvard program that he built are discussed below.

39. See the critique in C. Conroy, "Hebrew Epic: Historical Notes and Critical Reflections," *Bib* 61 (1980): 1–30. See a partial response on Cross's part in *From Epic to*

Canon: History and Literature in Ancient Israel (Baltimore: Johns Hopkins University Press, 1998), 22–52, esp. 27. See also S. B. Parker, "Some Methodological Principles in Ugaritic Philology," *Maarav* 2/1 (1979): 7–41; and D. R. Hillers, "Palmyrene Aramaic Inscriptions and the Bible," *ZAH* 11/1 (1998): 39.

40. Healey, "Death, Underworld, and Afterlife in the Ugaritic Texts" (Ph.D. dissertation, University of London, 1977); Loretz, "Vom kanaanäischen Totenkult zur jüdischen Patriarchen- und Elternehrung. Historische und tiefenpsychologische Grundprobleme der Entstehung des biblischen Geschichtsbildes und der jüdischen Ethik," *Jahrbuch für Anthropologie und Religionsgeschichte* 3 (1978): 149–204; idem, " 'Ugarit and Biblical Literature': Das Paradigma des Mythos von den rpum–Rephaim," in *Ugarit and the Bible: Proceedings of the International Symposium on Ugarit and the Bible. Manchester, September 1992* (ed. G. J. Brooke, A. H. W. Curtis, and J. F. Healey; UBL 11; Münster: Ugarit-Verlag, 1994), 175–224; see also Dietrich, Loretz, and Sanmartín, "Die ugaritischen Totengeister *RPU(M)* und die biblischen Rephaim," *UF* 8 (1976): 42–52; Dietrich and Loretz, *Mantik in Ugarit: Keilalphabetische Texte der Opferschau, Omensammlungen, Nekromantie* (ALASP 3; Münster: Ugarit-Verlag, 1990); de Moor, "Rapi'uma–Rephaim," *ZAW* 88 (1976): 323–45; Pope, "Notes on the Rephaim Texts from Ugarit," in *Essays on the Ancient Near East in Memory of Jacob Joel Finkelstein* (ed. M. de Jong Ellis; Memoirs of the Connecticut Academy of Arts and Sciences 19; Hamden, Conn.: Archon Books, 1997), 163–82 = *Probative Pontificating in Ugaritic and Biblical Literature*, 185–224. In some respects, a most illuminating study remains W. Horwitz, "The Significance of the Rephaim *rm. aby. btk rpim*," *JNWSL* 7 (1979): 37–43.

41. For example, see G. Hoffman, "Aramäische Inschriften aus Nêrab bei Aleppo. Neue und alte Götter," *ZA* 11 (1896): 207–92.

42. Aartun's work on particles was written while he was studying on a von Humboldt Fellowship with Professor Einar von Schuler at the Freie Universität in Berlin. See Aartun, *Partikeln des Ugaritischen*, 1:vii. Von Schuler had participated in a Ugaritic class at the Kirchliche Hochschule in Berlin with D. Michel in 1965; other participants included V. Haas, F. Gröndahl, and G. Wilhelm (information courtesy of Wilhelm, e-mail dated 30 January 1999). Gröndahl mentions Professors J. Friedrich and E. von Schuler as supervisors for her dissertation published as *Die Personennamen der Texte aus Ugarit* (Studia Pohl 1; Rome: Päpstliches Bibelinstitut, 1967).

43. Ringgren has also taught religious history at Abo Akademi University in Turku, Finland. Finnish scholars have not offered courses in Ugaritic although they have been interested in it. Information courtesy of Antti Laato, e-mail dated 8 February 1999.

44. For some reflections on Uppsala, see the preceding chapter, and H. Ringgren, "Mowinckel and the Uppsala School," *SJOT* 2 (1988): 36–41. Ringgren's predecessors and contemporaries at Uppsala included H. S. Nyberg and I. Engnell. Well-known figures who earlier were students there include G. Ahlström and F. Rundgren, also discussed in the preceding chapter.

45. Despite the long local tradition of biblical studies and the interest in Israelite religion, Lund has offered no formal Ugaritic training apart from the instruction of S. Norin at Lund in the 1980s. So T. N. D. Mettinger, letter dated 7 October 1998. Norin has since moved to Uppsala.

46. Hvidberg-Hansen studied at Copenhagen with Flemming Friis Hvidberg. In Ugaritic, Hvidberg-Hansen was self-taught. His teacher in Arabic was the late Erling Hammershaimb, who was first professor of Old Testament until 1963, when he became professor in Semitic Philology (see further the discussion of Copenhagen in Chapter One). Information courtesy of Hvidberg-Hansen, letter dated 14 January 1999. For Løkkegaard's 1982 review of Hvidberg-Hansen's book on *La déesse Tnt*, see *UF* 14 (1982): 129–40. More recently, Pernille Carstens, a specialist primarily in the Emar texts, has been appointed as assistant professor in the Department of Biblical Studies at Aarhus.

47. Lemche read Ugaritic with Nielsen, himself a student of Baumgartner at Basel (see Chapter Two). Lemche's predecessors at Copenhagen also included Fleming Friis-Hansen (professor in 1930s–1950s) and F. Løkkegaard (see Chapter One). Information courtesy of N. P. Lemche, e-mails on 3, 5, and 7 October 1998. Lemche's own students at Copenhagen more recently include T. Binger and A. R. Petersen.

48. See the discussion of Charles University in Chapter Two.

49. See Tyloch, *Odkrycia w Ugarit a Story Testament* ("Latest Research in Ugaritic and Old Testament Studies") (Warsaw: Polish Academy of Sciences, Committee for Oriental Studies, 1980); Wózniak, "Ugaritic Parallel of Jahwe *melek ʿôlam*," *Folia Orientalia* 20 (1979): 171–73.

50. Ivanov, "The Prehistory of the Ancient Greek, Aegeo-Anatolian, and Italic Alphabets in the Light of the Archives of Ebla and Ugarit," *Balcano-Balto-Slavica* (Moscow, 1979), 1–8 (Russian); and "On the Non-Indo-European Parallels to *ichthus* and *chthon*," *Balcano-Balto-Slavica* 9–10 (Russian). See further articles listed in *NUS* 19 (1979): 4; and 20 (1979): 4, 10.

51. The following information courtesy of A. Schoors, e-mail to me 3 November 1998. For some of Verreet's work, see the following chapter. In this period instruction in Ugaritic largely fell to A. Schoors, professor at Leuven/Louvain. A student of R. de Langhe in the 1960s, Schoors returned to teach at Leuven/Louvain after his studies at the Pontifical Biblical Institute (including classes with Mitchell Dahood). After the split of Leuven/Louvain in 1968, Schoors taught Ugaritic at the Katholieke Universiteit Leuven, and Herbert Sauren sporadically taught the subject at the Université Catholique de Louvain. (Sauren, a Sumerologist, did coauthor one article with his student, G. Kestemont, entitled "Keret, roi du Hubur," *UF* 3 [1971]: 181–221.) Throughout this period Schoors had one doctoral student, Eddy Verreet, whose publications on the verbal system appeared in the late 1980s. Schoors has generally not focussed his research on Ugaritic, with the exception of his contribution to *Ras Shamra Parallels I*. However, he regularly includes Ugaritic in his work on Qoheleth (Ecclesiastes). Schoors's departmental colleague was E. Lipiński, who often made recourse to Ugaritic in his research.

52. The Centre Nationale de la Recherche Scientifique (CNRS) provides funding for many French scholars in this field, as noted by the abbreviation placed after their names.

53. Bron is Swiss. His best-known work is perhaps his dissertation supervised by M. Sznycer and published as *Recherches sur les inscriptions phéniciennes de Karatepe* (Centre de recherches d'histoire et de philologie 2, Hautes études orientales 11; Geneva: Librairie Droz, 1979).

54. *NUS* 30 (October 1983): 14 lists Cunchillos as an instructor at Ecole Pratique des Hautes Etudes at the time.

55. For Jacob's works, see J. G. Heintz, "Bibliographie Edmond Jacob [1979–1998]," *UF* 29 (1997): 199–209.

56. For further information about the archaeological team, see below.

57. For example, Porter, "The Daughters of Lot," *Folklore* 89 (1978): 127–41; "Genesis 19:30–38 and the Ugaritic Text ŠḤR and ŠLM," in *Proceedings of the Seventh World Congress of Jewish Studies: Studies in the Bible and the Ancient Near East* (Jerusalem: World Union of Jewish Studies, 1981), 1–8.

58. See *NUS* 14 (October 1977): 8.

59. Information about dissertations completed in the United States derives from two searches done at University Microfilms International dated 3 October 1985 and 5 November 1998. Names listed after the initial group for a school represent figures who conducted research on Ugaritic primarily apart from their dissertations.

60. Gnuse, "The Dream Theophany of Samuel: Its Structure in Relation to Ancient Near Eastern Dreams and Its Theological Significance" (Ph.D. diss., Vanderbilt University,

1980); published in 1984 by University Press of America (Lanham, Md.). Gnuse has recently produced a work entitled *No Other Gods: Emergent Monotheism in Israel* (JSOTSup 241; Sheffield: Sheffield Academic Press, 1997). He is presently professor at Loyola University of the South in New Orleans.

61. A nice appreciation of Gevirtz appears in Sperling, *Students of the Covenant*, 92.

62. On Tsevat, see ibid., 89–90.

63. *NUS* 30 (October 1983): 12–26. Some schools are missing (e.g., the Ecole Biblique in Jerusalem). The earlier report, published in *NUS* 11 (October 1976): 9–14, is less representative (as noted on p. 14).

64. His last contribution to Ugaritic was his *Corpus des cylindres-sceaux de Ras Shamra-Ugarit et d'Enkomi-Alasia* (with contributions from P. Amiet, G. Chenet, M. Mallowan, K. Bittel, and E. Porada; Paris: Editions Recherche sur les Civilisations, 1983).

65. North's article "Ugarit Grid, Strata, and Find Localizations," *ZDPV* 89 (1973): 113–60; and Courtois' response, "Ugarit Grid, Strata, and Find Localizations: A Reassessment," *ZDPV* 90 (1974): 97–114.

66. Caquot, Sznycer, and Herdner, *Textes ougaritiques: Tome I. Mythes et légends* (LAPO 7; Paris: Cerf, 1974). Bordreuil in a letter dated 28 December 1998: "Chaque semaine, une partie de son [Caquot's] enseignment était consacrée à l'explication des principaux passages des grand textes mythologiques d'Ougarit et je dois beaucoup à la formation que j'ai reçue à ce moment là."

67. Caquot, de Tarragon, and Cunchillos, *Textes ougaritiques: Tome II. Textes religieux, rituels, correspondance* (LAPO 14; Paris: Cerf, 1989).

68. The following information is courtesy of J. M. de Tarragon, e-mail to me, 12 October 1998; and A. Lemaire, e-mail to me, 25 October 1998.

69. Information courtesy of P. J. Kearney, 11 November 1998. While he was on the faculty at Catholic University, Kearney sat in on Cazelles's classes, which he recalled with particular fondness.

70. Much of the following information derives from Pardee's e-mail dated 13 November 1998 and Bordreuil's letter dated 28 December 1998.

71. Bordreuil and Pardee, *La trouvaille épigraphique de l'Ougarit: 1. Concordance* (RSO 5/1; Paris: Editions Recherche sur les Civilisations, 1989).

72. Van Soldt, *Studies in the Akkadian of Ugarit: Dating and Grammar* (AOAT 40; Kevelaer: Butzon & Bercker; Neukirchen-Vluyn: Neukirchener Verlag, 1991).

73. So M. E. J. Richardson, "The Less Inspired Scriptures," in *Ugarit and the Bible*, 281, 291. Richardson's article contributes nicely to this discussion as well.

74. See *NUS* 14 (October 1977): 9; also *UF* 9 (1977): 344. For the texts from seasons of RIH 77 and 78, see P. Bordreuil and A. Caquot, "Les textes en cunéiformes alphabétiques découverts en 1978 à Ibn Hani," *Syria* 57 (1980): 343–73; P. Bordreuil and D. Pardee, "L'epigraphie ougaritique: 1973–1993," in *Le pays d'Ougarit au tour de 1200 av. J.C. Historie et archéologie. Actes du Colloque International, Paris, 28 juin–1er juillet 1993* (ed. M. Yon, M. Sznycer, P. Bordreuil; RSO 11; Paris: Editions Recherche sur les Civilisations, 1995), 27–32.

75. The proceedings were published in *Les annales archéologiques arabes syriennes* 29–30 (1979–1980).

76. J. M. de Tarragon, "Philologie sémitique," in *L'Ancien Testament: Cent ans d'exégèse de l'Ecole Biblique* (Cahiers de la Revue Biblique 28; Paris: Gabalda, 1990), 43. Although few nowadays would associate the name of de Vaux with Ugaritic studies, he did turn to it for his work, offering occasional studies. See, for example, his two articles, "Le cadre historique du poème de *Krt*," *RB* 46 (1937): 362–72; and "Les textes de Ras Shamra et l'Ancien Testament," *RB* 46 (1937): 526–55. H. Cazelles (undated letter, received 12 January 1999) informs me that he studied the Keret (Kirta) text with de Vaux in 1945–1946.

77. See de Tarragon, "Philologie sémitique," 44.

78. So O. Loretz in a letter dated 15 December 1998.

79. So his costudent in the course, Otto Kaiser, in a letter to me dated 15 October 1998.

80. So O. Loretz in a letter dated 15 December 1998.

81. See Loretz's works, including those coauthored with Dietrich and Sanmartín, listed in *SEL* 5 (1988): 1–12, recently supplemented by *"Und Mose schrieb dieses Lied auf"*: *Studien zum Alten Testament und zum Alten Orient. Festschrift für Oswald Loretz zur Vollendung seines 70. Lebenjahres mit Beiträgen von Freunden, Schülern, und Kollegen* (ed. M. Dietrich and I. Kottsieper; AOAT 250; Münster: Ugarit-Verlag, 1998), xiii–xviii. For current information on the Münster team and their work, see http://ugarit.uni-muenster.de/default.htm. This site and its links provide a full bibliography of the series sponsored by Dietrich and Loretz as well as most of their own contributions.

82. See W. G. E. Watson, "The Research Team: 'Ugarit-Forschung,'" *NUS* 13 (May 1977): 10. See more recently also http://ugarit.uni-muenster.de/projekte.htm.

83. See Loretz's works, for example in the UBL series: *Leberschau, Sündenbock, Asasel in Ugarit und Israel: Leberschau und Jahwestatue in Psalm 27, Leberschau in Psalm 74* (UBL 3; Münster: Ugarit-Verlag, 1985); *Regenritual und Jahwetag im Joelbuch: Kanaanäischer Hintergrund, Kolometrie, Aufbau, und Symbolik eines Prophetenbuches* (UBL 4; Münster: Ugarit-Verlag, 1986); *Die Königspsalmen: Die altorientalisch-kanaanäische Königtradition in jüdischer Sicht 1. Psalm 20, 21, 72, 101, 144. Mit einem Beitrag von I. Kottsieper zu Papyrus Amherst* (UBL 6; Münster: Ugarit-Verlag, 1988); and *Ugarit-Texte und Thronbesteigungspsalmen: Die Metamorphose des Regenspenders Baal-Jahwe (Ps. 24,7–10; 29; 47; 93; 95–100; sowie Ps. 77,17–20; 114)* (UBL 7; Münster: Ugarit-Verlag, 1988). See also Loretz's study coauthored with I. Kottsieper, *Colometry in Ugaritic and Biblical Poetry: Introduction, Illustrations, and Topical Bibliography* (UBL 5; Münster: Ugarit-Verlag, 1987).

84. For the bitter exchange over the volume, see in particular Dietrich and Loretz, "A Word from the Editors of *KTU*," *UF* 22 (1990): 1–5, aimed primarily at Dennis Pardee and to a lesser degree at W. G. E. Watson; see also the subsequent "Declaration of Reconciliation" with all the parties involved, mediated by J. C. de Moor in *UF* 23 (1991): 1–7. See further *JAOS* 113 (1993): 614–17 and *JAOS* 115 (1995): 301–3.

85. As reported in *NUS* 31 (April 1984): 2.

86. The information on Follet comes from an e-mail communication, 24 October 1998, from A. Gianto, Dahood's ultimate successor in Northwest Semitic studies. Between 1983 and 1987 Ugaritic was taught at the Pontifical Biblical Institute by P. Proulx and then L. Viganò. Gianto began his teaching duties in 1988. Kevin Cathcart of Dublin provided some supplementary information as well. See further D. J. McCarthy, "P. Mitchell Dahood, S. J. in Memoriam," *Bib* 63 (1982): 298–99; and D. N. Freedman, "Mitchell Dahood, 1922–1982, in Memoriam," *BA* 45/3 (1982): 185–87.

87. For a partial listing of Follet's work on Ugaritic, see Herdner, *Corpus des tablettes*, 305–6 and 320.

88. This information derives from a brochure produced by M. Gilbert, S. J., shortly after Dahood's death. The brochure contains a fine appreciation of Dahood, as well as photographs of him with colleagues and friends.

89. Personal communication, 21 November 1998, cited with permission.

90. C. Krahmalkov, e-mail, 24 October 1998.

91. Michael Dick, personal communication.

92. A. Gianto, e-mail, 24 October 1998.

93. So in his letter to me dated 11 February 1999. Michel completed his 1970 dissertation at the University of Wisconsin at Madison under the title, "The Ugaritic Texts and the Mythological Expressions in the Book of Job." See Michel, *Job in the Light of Northwest Semitic. Volume I: Prologue and First Cycle of Speeches Job 1:1–14:22* (BibetOr 42; Rome:

Pontifical Biblical Institute, 1987); vols. 2 and 3 on the rest of Job are in progress. For a good review of the first volume, see F. C. Fensham, *JNWSL* 14 (1988): 229–30. Michel disposed Marvin Pope favorably to the work of Mitchell Dahood when Michel worked with Pope in 1972, along with B. Zuckerman, on the revision of Pope's Job commentary (so Michel in his 11 February 1999 letter). The other Madison dissertation completed on Ugaritic around this time was produced by Keith Schoville, "The Impact of the Ras Shamra Texts on the Study of the Song of Songs" (1969). Ironically, Walter Michel's student at the Lutheran School of Theology at Chicago, Louis O. Dorn, produced a highly critical study of Dahood's theory that "seeing God" might refer to a post-mortem beatific vision: Dorn, "The Beatific Vision in Certain Psalms: An Investigation of Mitchell Dahood's Hypothesis" (Th.D. diss., Lutheran School of Theology at Chicago, 1980). See also M. S. Smith, " 'Seeing God' in the Psalms: The Background to the Beatific Vision in the Hebrew Scriptures," *CBQ* 50 (1988): 171–83.

94. So T. Muraoka, e-mail communication, 13 October 1998.

95. Van Soldt, *Studies in the Akkadian of Ugarit: Dating and Grammar.*

96. So de Moor, *The Seasonal Pattern in the Ugaritic Myth of Ba'lu: According to the Version of Ilimilku* (AOAT 16; Kevelaer: Butzon & Bercker; Neukirchen-Vluyn: Neukirchener Verlag, 1971), v.

97. Most of the following information comes courtesy of de Moor's two e-mails, 15 and 17 November 1998.

98. Professor de Moor's e-mail of 26 November 1998 informs me that his is the older institution, dating to 1854. The other institution dates to 1945, following a church schism in 1944.

99. The following information about Groningen derives from C. H. J. de Geus, e-mail communication, 6 October 1998.

100. See G. García Martínez, A. Hilhorst, J. T. A. G. M. van Ruiten, and A. S. Woude, "Preface," in *Studies in Deuteronomy in Honour of C. J. Labuschagne on the Occasion of His 65th Birthday* (ed. G. García Martínez, A. Hilhorst, J. T. A. G. M. van Ruiten, and A. S. Woude; VTSup 53; Leiden: Brill, 1994), 3.

101. Hospers did not offer instruction in Ugaritic, but he occasionally wrote on the subject: "Einiges zur ugaritischen Schrift," in *Übersetzung und Deutung: Studien zum dem Alten Testament und seiner Umwelt, Alexander Reinard Hulst gewidmet von Freunden und Kollegen* (Nijkerk: Callenback, 1977), 85–90. For an appreciation, see A. S. van der Woude, "In memoriam J. H. Hospers," *ZAH* 7/1 (1994): 1–2.

102. Emerton, "The Origin of the Son of Man Imagery," *JTS* 9 (1958): 22–42.

103. Gunkel, *Schöpfung und Chaos in Urzeit und Endzeit: Eine religionsgeschichtliche Untersuchung über Gen 1 und Ap Joh 12* (with Heinrich Zimmern; Göttingen: Vandenhoeck und Ruprecht, 1895), esp. 395–98. For a succinct formulation of Gunkel (p. 398): "In der alten Zeit ist ein Mythus der Urzeit, der von Babel nach Israel wandert, in der neuen eine Weissagung über die Endzeit." Other scholars such as Frank Cross would extend Emerton's insight, and it was a student of Cross, Paul Mosca, who demonstrated that royal theology was one conduit of this mythic material through the Iron Age (Cross, *Canaanite Myth and Hebrew Epic*, 17; and P. Mosca, "Ugaritic and Daniel 7: A Missing Link," *Bib* 67 [1986]: 496–517). See further J. J. Collins, *Daniel: A Commentary on the Book of Daniel* (ed. F. M. Cross; Hermeneia; Minneapolis: Fortress, 1993), 286–94. To be sure, the monarchy was but one of several groups transmitting and adapting mythic material in Iron Age Israel. See the discussion of Greenfield's work below; and M. S. Smith, "Myth and Myth-making in Ugaritic and Israelite Literatures," in *Ugarit and the Bible*, 293–341.

104. Emerton, "New Light on Israelite Religion: The Implications of the Inscriptions from Kuntillet 'Ajrud," *ZAW* 94 (1982): 2–20. The article is cited by almost every treatment of the subject, including Keel and Uehlinger, *Gods, Goddesses, and Images of Gods*, 231 n. 94: the "most well-balanced position, now as before, is very likely that of

J. A. Emerton." See Emerton's revisiting of the issues in his essay entitled " 'Yahweh and His Asherah': the Goddess or Her Symbol," *VT* 49 (1999): 315–37.

105. Day's research on this subject is synthesized and extended in his book, *Yahweh and the Gods of Canaan and the Old Testament* (JSOTSup 265; Sheffield: Sheffield Academic Press, 2001). Day in turn has produced one well-known doctorate, the American Brian B. Schmidt, now professor at the University of Michigan, who has produced a controversial book on the Rephaim (Schmidt, *Israel's Beneficent Dead: Ancestor Cult and Necromancy in Ancient Israelite Religion and Tradition* [FAT 11; Tübingen: Mohr/Siebeck, 1994]; cf. the review of M. S. Smith in *CBQ* 58 [1996]: 724–25).

106. Healey produced a series of articles on the subject (published largely in *UF* in the late 1970s and early 1980s) based on his dissertation, "Death, Underworld, and Afterlife in the Ugaritic Texts" (Ph.D. diss., University of London, 1977).

107. For a representative sampling of her work, see Hadley, "Yahweh's Asherah in the Light of Recent Discovery" (Ph.D. diss., Cambridge University, 1989), published as *The Cult of Asherah in Ancient Israel and Judah: Evidence for a Hebrew Goddess* (University of Cambridge Oriental Publications 57; Cambridge: Cambridge University Press, 2000); "Some Drawings and Inscriptions on Two Pithoi from Kuntillet 'Ajrud," *VT* 37 (1987): 180–213; "The Khirbet el-Qom Inscription," *VT* 37 (1987): 50–62; "Chasing Shadows? The Quest for the Historical Goddess," in *Congress Volume: Cambridge 1995* (ed. J. A. Emerton; Leiden: Brill, 1997), 169–84.

108. Johnston, "The Underworld and the Dead in the Old Testament" (Ph.D. diss., University of Cambridge, 1993). Like Schmidt's study (cited above), this work is unduly restrictive in its conclusions and reasoning regarding biblical terminology for the underworld or the so-called cult of the dead in ancient Israel. Indeed, the effort to debunk the notion that BH ʾereṣ can refer to the underworld and ʾĕlōhîm ("divine ones") as a designation for the dead is unconvincing. While Johnston views other scholars as going out of their way to make such points, he clearly goes out of his way to minimize the possibilities. In the former case, he concludes, however, that some texts could have this word with the meaning "underworld" and thereby undercuts his own conclusion. Highly selective use of texts to build a case against devotion to the dead hardly leads to convincing historical conclusions. Finally, generalizations about what ancient Israel thought or "the Yahwistic view" belie the historical diversity in the religious practices and beliefs in ancient Israel. Finally, the backlash of Schmidt and Johnston against positing devotion to the dead in ancient Israel seems driven more by the authors' methods and suppositions than by any lack of data. We should like to have more data, but given the redactors' opposition to such activity, a lack of data is to be expected and therefore what little there is should be taken as more representative historically. I thank T. J. Lewis for his sharing Johnston's work with me as well as his own comments on it.

109. For a precis of his background in Ugaritic, see E. Ullendorff, "Grace in Ugaritic?" in *Ugaritic and the Bible*, 355–56. See also his autobiographical work, *The Two Zions: Reminiscences of Jerusalem and Ethiopia* (Oxford: Oxford University, 1988), 51–52, 54. Ullendorff's Ugaritic research is published in his book, *Is Biblical Hebrew a Language? Studies in Semitic Languages and Civilizations* (Wiesbaden: Harrassowitz, 1977). Some of the information provided here comes from a letter from Ullendorff to me dated 31 December 1998.

110. Blau's papers using Ugaritic are conveniently collected in his collection of essays, *Topics in Hebrew and Semitic Linguistics* (Jerusalem: Magnes, 1998).

111. For Fenton's research, see below in the discussion of Haifa.

112. Curtis, *Ugarit (Ras Shamra)* (Cambridge: Lutterworth, 1985).

113. The information in this paragraph regarding Gibson derives from his undated letter to me, received 18 November 1998. For further information about Driver, see the preceding chapter.

114. Gibson, *Canaanite Myths and Legends* (2d ed.; Edinburgh: T&T Clark, 1978), vii. This passage spells out the differences between the two editions in greater detail.

115. Gibson, letter to me undated (November 1998).

116. This, despite many trenchant criticisms of D. Pardee, *BiOr* 37 (1980): 269–91.

117. So M. E. J. Richardson, "Less Inspired Scriptures," 291.

118. Information courtesy of N. Wyatt, 28 September 1998; cf. *NUS* 30 (October 1983): 18. Cutler and Macdonald are known in the field for their articles in *UF* in the 1970s, for example their coauthored essays, "An Akkadian Cognate to Ugaritic *brlt*," *UF* 5 (1973): 67–70; and "The Unique Ugaritic Text UT 113 and the Question of 'Guilds,'" *UF* 9 (1977): 13–20. Wyatt had one doctoral student in Ugaritic in Glasgow, D. R. West, who has since published two works in the field of "Helleno-semitica": *Some Cults of Greek Goddesses and Female Daemons of Oriental Origin* (AOAT 233: Kevelaer: Butzon & Bercker; Neukirchen-Vluyn: Neukirchener Verlag, 1995); and "Hekate, Lamashtu, and *klbt ʾilm*," *UF* 24 (1992): 383.

119. See S. A. Wiggins, "The Myth of Asherah: Lion Lady and Serpent Goddess," *UF* 23 (1991): 383–94; *A Reassessment of 'Asherah': A Study according to the Textual Sources of the First Two Millennia B.C.E.* (AOAT 235; Kevelaer: Butzon & Bercker; Neukirchen-Vluyn: Neukirchener Verlag, 1993); "Shapsh, Lamp of the Gods," in *Ugaritic, Religion and Culture: Proceedings of the International Colloquium on Ugarit, Religion and Culture. Edinburgh, July 1994. Essays Presented in Honour of John C. L. Gibson* (ed. N. Wyatt, W. G. E. Watson, and J. B. Lloyd; UBL 12; Münster: Ugarit-Verlag, 1996), 327–50; and J. B. Lloyd, "Anat and the 'Double' Massacre of *KTU* 1.3 ii," in *Ugaritic, Religion and Culture*, 151–65. Information courtesy of N. Wyatt, 28 September 1998.

120. The following information derives from I. Cornelius (e-mail communication) and F. C. Fensham, "Ugaritic Studies and South Africa," *JSem* 1/2 (1989): 156–73, esp. 166–67. This article does not comment on Fensham's considerable contributions. On this subject, see H. J. Dreyer, "Frank Charles Fensham—in Memoriam," *JSem* 1/2 (1989): 145–55. For the program in Stellenbosch, readers may consult: http://www.sun.ac.za/localacademic/arts.onos/home.html.

121. See *JNSWL* 12 (1984): 1–3.

122. Readers may consult the home page of the journal: http://www.sun.ac.za/localacademic/arts.onos/jnsl/jnslhome.html.

123. Greenfield, "The 'Cluster' in Biblical Poetry," *Maarav* 5–6 (1990): 160.

124. Greenfield, " 'Cluster' in Biblical Poetry," 167. The case is made also in Greenfield, "The Hebrew Bible and Canaanite Literature," in *The Literary Guide to the Bible* (ed. R. Alter and F. Kermode; Cambridge: Harvard University Press, 1987), 545–60.

125. Watson also took Ugaritic with Gray and Dahood (as noted above) as well as Loewenstamm. Greenfield had taught a number of students in Berkeley (see above). Because of the wealth of Greenfield's research in so many different areas, especially Aramaic, many are unaware that Greenfield was deeply knowledgeable in Ugaritic studies and maintained an interest in it throughout his academic life.

126. For example, Paul's well-known article, "Jerusalem—a City of Gold," *IEJ* 17 (1967): 259–63, produced in a more popular version as "Jerusalem of Gold—a Song and an Ancient Crown," *BAR* 3/4 (1977): 38–40; and "Two Cognate Semitic Terms for Mating and Copulation," *VT* 32 (1982): 492–93.

127. Hurowitz, *I Have Built You an Exalted House: Temple Building in the Bible in Light of Mesopotamian and Northwest Semitic Writings* (JSOTSup 115; JSOT/ASOR Monograph Series 5; Sheffield: Sheffield Academic Press, 1992), 100–105. See also his essay, "The Priestly Account of Building the Tabernacle," *JAOS* 105 (1985): 21–30.

128. For example, Fassberg, *Studies in Biblical Syntax* (Jerusalem: Magnes, 1994), 31, 68, 126 and the listing of words on p. 166 (Heb.).

129. For example, Singer, "Takuhlinu and Haya: Two Governors in the Ugaritic Letter from Tel Aphek," *TA* 10 (1983): 3–25.

130. See above in Chapter Two. For Tel Aviv University's resources in Semitics, see http://spinoza.tau.ac.il/hci/dep/semitic/index.html. For its Bible department, see http://spinoza.tau.ac.il/hci/dep/bible/index.htm.

131. Sivan is best known in Ugaritic studies for his grammar. Izre'el was coauthor with I. Singer, *The General's Letter from Ugarit: A Linguistic and Historical Reevaluation of RS 20.33 (= Ugaritica V No. 20)* (Tel Aviv: Tel Aviv University, Chaim Rosenberg School of Jewish Studies, 1990).

132. Avishur, *Stylistic Studies of Word-Pairs in Biblical and Ancient Semitic Literature.*

133. Most of Fenton's works are mentioned in his article, "Nexus and Significance: Is Greater Precision Possible?" in *Ugarit and the Bible*, 71–91; and "Baal au Foudre: Of Snakes and Mountains, Myth and Message," in *Ugarit, Religion and Culture*, 49–64.

134. For Heltzer's work, see n. 33 above.

135. For highly critical assessments of Margalit's freewheeling procedures for deriving etymologies for Ugaritic words, see D. Pardee, "Ugaritic," *AfO* 28 (1981–1982): 259–72; and F. Renfroe, "Methodological Considerations Regarding the Use of Arabic in Ugaritic Philology," *UF* 18 (1986): 33–74.

136. See Margalit, "Alliteration in Ugaritic Poetry: Its Role in Composition and Analysis," *UF* 11 (1979 = C. F. A. Schaeffer Festschrift): 537–57; "Alliteration in Ugaritic Poetry: Its Role in Composition and Analysis (Part II)," *JNWSL* 8 (1980): 57–80. For Margalit's identification of place names in *KTU* 1.108.2–3, see his article, "A Ugaritic Psalm (RS 24.252)," *JBL* 89 (1970): 292–304.

137. This information derives from C. M. Foley, "In Memoriam [Peter C. Craigie]," *NUS* 34 (October 1985): 2–3; and H. Coward, "Academic Biography of Peter C. Craigie," in *Ascribe to the Lord: Biblical & Other Studies in Memory of Peter C. Craigie* (ed. L. Eslinger and J. G. Taylor; JSOTSup 67; Sheffield: Sheffield Academic Press, 1988), 593–97. Craigie's publications are compiled by Taylor on pp. 603–7; it has since been supplemented by R. G. S. Idestrom and J. G. Taylor, "Addendum to the Bibliography of Peter C. Craigie," *JSOT* 51 (1991): 115–17. For an examination of Craigie's work, see R. G. S. Idestrom, "Some Aspects of Peter C. Craigie's Approach to the Old Testament," *Studies in Religion/Sciences Religieuses* 23/4 (1994): 457–67.

138. The following information comes courtesy of Professor Chaim Cohen, e-mail 6 December 1998.

139. See Chapter One for further information on Ginsberg and Gaster. For Held's background, see Chapter Two.

140. Cohen, *Biblical Hapax Legomena;* Gruber, *Aspects of Nonverbal Communication in the Ancient Near East* (Studia Pohl 12/I–II; Rome: Biblical Institute Press, 1980). Marcus's 1970 thesis, "Aspects of the Ugaritic Verb in the Light of Comparative Semitic Grammar," developed into a series of articles published mostly in *JANES*. For Held's bibliography, see the references listed in Cohen, "The 'Held Method,' " 9 n. 3.

141. The following information comes courtesy of Professor Cohen, e-mail 6 December 1998.

142. Cohen, *The Complete Held Method for Comparative Semitic Philology and Its Application in Modern Biblical Philology* (VTSup; Leiden: Brill, forthcoming).

143. Cohen, *A Comprehensive Dictionary of the Ugaritic Language* (Leiden: Brill, forthcoming).

144. Lichtenstein, "Episodic Structure in the Ugaritic Keret Legend: Comparative Studies in Compositional Technique" (Ph.D. diss., Columbia University, 1979).

145. On Marcus and Greenstein at Columbia-JTS, see Sperling, *Students of the Covenant,* 123–24. For more information on Greenstein, see his Web site at http://spinoza.tau.ac.il/hci/dep/bible/index.htm.

146. Pope, *Job* (AB 15; New York: Doubleday, 1965; rev. ed., 1973); *Song of Songs* (AB 7C; New York: Doubleday, 1977). Pope accepted the offer to produce the latter commentary in a letter dated 22 January 1967 and in a letter dated 13 March 1967, both to D. N. Freedman. Pope proposes a deadline of 31 December 1968 (letters in Yale Divinity School collection). Some of his essays on Ugaritic themes appear in his book *Probative Pontificating in Ugaritic and Biblical Literature.* The introduction to this volume presents a retrospective look on my part at Pope's work, with some recollections of Pope as a person (see esp. pp. 3–4, 12–14).

147. Held, "Pit and Pitfalls in Akkadian and Biblical Hebrew," *JANES* 5 (1973): 173–90; Pope, "A Little Soul-Searching," *Maarav* 1/1 (1978): 25–31. See also Pope's kindly and learned response to Jack Sasson's well-put review (*Maarav* 1/2 [1979]: 177–96) of Pope's commentary, *Song of Songs* (AB 7A; Garden City: Doubleday, 1997) in *Maarav* 2/2 (1980): 207–14.

148. On Rosenthal and the Rabinowitz chair, see W. F. Albright, "Louis Rabinowitz in Memoriam," *BASOR* 146 (1957): 2.

149. See the list in Pope, *Probative Pontificating in Ugaritic and Biblical Literature,* 385–86. The planned dissertations by G. A. Tuttle on the Rephaim texts and by D. Wortman on the snakebite texts were not completed.

150. Listed in ibid., 385–86.

151. A good deal of the following information derives from two letters from Cross, dated 7 December 1998 and 23 January 1999; and from the "Preface" to *Ancient Israelite Religion: Essays in Honor of Frank Moore Cross* (ed. P. D. Miller, Jr., P. D. Hanson, and S. D. McBride; Philadelphia: Fortress, 1987), xi. See *CBQ* 49, Supplement (1987): 52 for further details.

152. Cross, "The Tabernacle: A Study from an Archaeological and Historical Approach," *BA* 10 (1947): 45–68. So letters of Albright to Wright dated 21 and 28 January 1946 and Wright's response dated 15 February 1946, and Albright's official report dated 9 February 1946 (APS archives Albright Corresp. 1946).

153. For a nice appreciation of Cross, see the "Preface" of *Ancient Israelite Religion,* xi–xiii. The same volume contains a bibliography of Cross's publications on pp. 645–56. See also the tributes in the Cross Festschrift in *EI* 26 (1999): ix–xii, with bibliography on pp. xiii–xxiv.

154. See F. M. Cross and G. E. Wright, "The Study of the Old Testament at Harvard," *Harvard Divinity Bulletin* 25 (1961): 14–19. On the doctoral program specifically, see pp. 17–20. For Cross on Wright, see "Preface," in *Magnalia Dei: The Mighty Acts of Gods: Essays on the Bible and Archaeology in Memory of G. Ernest Wright* (ed. F. M. Cross, W. E. Lemke, and P. D. Miller, Jr.; Garden City, N.Y.: Doubleday, 1976). The information about Wright's death derives from the first (unnumbered) page of this volume.

155. For a nice appreciation, see J. Huehnergard, "Lambdin: Probably from the Root *lmd,* 'To Learn,' D 'To Teach,'" in *"Working with No Data": Semitic and Egyptian Studies Presented to Thomas O. Lambdin* (ed. D. M. Golomb; Winona Lake, Ind.: Eisenbrauns, 1987), ix–xii; and R. J. Clifford, "Thomas O. Lambdin," in *"Working with No Data,"* xiii–xiv. The same volume contains a bibliography of Lambdin's publications on pp. 263–64.

156. I was reminded of this well-known quip of Lambdin by P. K. McCarter in a conversation on 22 November 1998.

157. See "William L. Moran: An Appreciation," in *Lingering over Words: Studies in Ancient Near Eastern Literature in Honor of William L. Moran* (ed. T. Abusch, J. Huehnergard, and P. Steinkeller; HSS 37; Atlanta: Scholars Press, 1990), ix–x. The same volume contains a bibliography of Moran's publications on pp. xi–xviii.

158. Ibid., x.

159. According to D. N. Freedman (personal communication, 29 November 1999), this practice goes back to Haupt and the Hopkins program.

160. See n. 39 for critiques of the former.

161. Ahlström, *Aspects of Syncretism in Israelite Religion;* Morton Smith, *Palestinian Parties and Politics That Shaped the Old Testament.* My book, *The Early History of God: Yahweh and the Other Deities in Ancient Israel* (San Francisco: Harper & Row, 1990), xix–xxxiv, 1–40, follows the lead of Smith and Ahlström, but it is especially dependent on Cross as well as Pope in argumentation and sources consulted. My debt to Cross's work will be clear from perusing the references to his works in the book's index of authors.

162. For example, Cross, *Canaanite Myth and Hebrew Epic,* 79–90.

163. Here the influence of his mentor and peers or perhaps his own Presbyterian background might be discerned. See the discussion of Albright and Wright in the section, "Myth-and-Ritual Studies on Both Sides of the Atlantic," on pp. 82–84.

164. By Cross's count, in a letter to me dated 27 November 1998.

165. Cross, letter to me dated 27 November 1998; *CBQ* 49, Supplement (1987): 50, 73.

166. Clifford, *The Cosmic Mountain in Canaan and the Old Testament* (HSM 4; Cambridge, Mass.: Harvard University Press, 1972).

167. Miller, *The Divine Warrior in Early Israel* (HSM 5; Cambridge: Harvard University Press, 1973).

168. Whitaker, "A Formulaic Analysis of Ugaritic Poetry" (Ph.D. diss., Harvard University, 1970); Hendel, *The Epic of the Patriarch: The Jacob Cycle and the Narrative Tradition of Canaan and Israel* (HSM 42; Atlanta: Scholars Press, 1987). For Cross's further thoughts on this subject, see *From Epic to Canon,* 22–52.

169. L'Heureux, *Rank among the Canaanite Gods: El, Ba'al, and the Repha'im* (HSM 21; Missoula, Mont.: Scholars Press, 1979).

170. Mullen, *The Assembly of the Gods: The Divine Council in Canaanite and Early Hebrew Literature* (HSM 24; Chico, Calif.: Scholars Press, 1980).

171. Huehnergard, *The Akkadian of Ugarit* (HSS 34; Atlanta: Scholars Press, 1989).

172. Huehnergard, *Ugaritic Vocabulary in Syllabic Transcription.*

173. So in an interview published in *Bible Review* 8/6 (December 1992): 52. A volume on epigraphy is in the works.

174. See Running and Freedman, *William Foxwell Albright,* 209–11.

175. Cross, letter to me dated 27 November 1998.

176. See especially Cross, *Canaanite Myth and Hebrew Epic,* 21 n. 50.

177. So Pope, "Notes on the Rephaim Texts," n. 90; republished in *Probative Pontificating in Ugaritic and Biblical Literature,* 222 n. 90. For an even more skeptical view of vocalization, see E. Ullendorff, "Grace in Ugaritic?" in *Ugaritic and the Bible,* 359. Note D. Pardee's well-placed criticisms of Ullendorff on this issue; see his review of the volume in *JAOS* 117 (1997): 377–78. For a good example of Pardee's own practice of vocalization, see his book, *Ugaritic and Hebrew Poetic Parallelism,* 1 n. 5. See also his remarks in "Further Studies in Ugaritic Epistolography," *AfO* 31 (1984): 228 n. 45, or mine in *The Ugaritic Baal Cycle,* xxxii–xxxiii.

178. Richard Whitaker, personal communication on 22 November 1998, cited with permission.

179. Cross remarks on Albright's taking one and a half class sessions on Ugaritic grammar before reading the texts in Running and Freedman, *William Foxwell Albright,* 211.

180. John Huddlestun (conversation, 22 November 1998) related a comparable difficulty for doctoral students at the University of Michigan: George Mendenhall would offer one vocalization in his course and then Charles Krahmalkov in his class would suggest another. More recently, Cross has offered a vocalized Ugaritic text with accent marks on words (Cross, *From Epic to Canon,* 101). In a letter dated 7 December 1998, Cross

writes about this particular accented version of vocalized Ugaritic: "My accentuation of Ugaritic is really to show what an accentual meter would look like. The pattern of accent follows a proposal for West Semitic: accent on antepenult if the penult and the ultima are short, on the penult if it is long or in a closed syllable, and on the ultima if it is long. Segholates are treated as monosyllabic nouns. Like all Proto reconstructions, it is tentative, especially in the light of the fact that Proto languages are based on the principle of parsimony, not fact." Cf. the old comment of Albright concerning accent ("The North-Canaanite Epic of 'Al'êyan Ba'al and Môt," *JPOS* 12 [1932]: 206): "Another characteristic of Canaanite at this stage of its development [Ugaritic] is the accent fell on the last long vowel, or in the absence of a long vowel, on the antepenult (counting the case-ending, the penult if we disregard the case-ending)."

181. See F. M. Cross, "El," *TDOT* 1 (1970): 242–61; *Canaanite Myth and Hebrew Epic*, 3–75; Pope, *El in the Ugaritic Texts;* "Up and Downs in El's Amours"; "The Status of El at Ugarit," *UF* 19 (1989): 219–29; reprinted in Pope, *Probative Pontificating in Ugaritic and Biblical Literature*, 47–61. See also Chapter Four below.

182. Cross, *Canaanite Myth and Hebrew Epic*, 24.

183. Pope, "The Ups and Downs in El's Amours," 701–8. See also, Pope, *El in the Ugaritic Texts*, 37–42. The debate turns largely on the word *mmnnm*. For discussion and Cross's more recent view of *mmnnm*, see S. M. Olyan, *Asherah and the Cult of Yahweh in Israel* (HSM 34; Atlanta: Scholars Press, 1988), 42 n. 12. As indicated in his letter of 7 December 1998 to me, Cross may finish an article on this text, so I prescind from citing his current view of *mmnnm*.

184. As a student of both Cross and Pope, it seems to me in retrospect that the positive traits of El presented by Cross and Pope perhaps evoke a bit of their own character and personality. For Cross, El was a vigorous patriarchal ruler. The El represented in Marvin Pope's writings was the kindly and beneficent figure.

185. Note also others by year in the period 1945–1970: W. H. Morton, "The Bearing of the Records of Ras Shamra on the Exegesis of the Old Testament" (Ph.D. diss, Southern Baptist Theological Seminary, 1946); H. N. Richardson, "Ugaritic Parallels to the Old Testament" (Ph.D. diss., Boston University, 1951); C. S. Thoburn, "Old Testament Sacrifice in the Light of the Ugaritic Literature" (Th.D. diss., Boston University, 1954); E. H. Horton, Jr., "The Old Testament Use of 'Molade' in the Light of Ugaritic Parallels" (Ph.D. diss., University of Southern California, 1958); N. C. Habel, "A Conflict of Religious Cultures: A Study in the Relevance of the Ugaritic Materials for the Early Faith of Israel" (Ph.D. diss., Concordia Seminary, 1962).

186. Sandmel, "Parallelomania," *JBL* 81 (1962): 1–13.

187. See S. B. Parker, "Some Methodological Principles in Ugaritic Philology," *Maarav* 2/1 (1979): 7–41, esp. 16.

188. Koehler and Baumgartner, *Lexicon in Veteris Testamenti Libros* (Leiden: Brill, 1953). The dictionary was revised with the help of a third author, J. J. Stamm, *Hebräisches und Aramäisches Lexikon zum Alten Testament* (Leiden: Brill, 1967). See most recently the English translation: *The Hebrew and Aramaic Lexicon of the Old Testament*, by Koehler and Baumgartner, revised by Baumgartner and Stamm, with assistance from B. Hartmann, Z. Ben-Hayyim, E. Y. Kutscher, and P. Reynold (trans. and ed. M. E. J. Richardson, G. J. Jongeling, and L. J. de Regt; Leiden: Brill, 1994–2000).

189. The eleventh volume appeared in 2000; the series in English is published by Eerdmans.

190. For a fascinating read of this history, see Long, *Planting and Reaping Albright*, 60–68.

191. Freedman, but not Wright: so Long, *Planting and Reaping Albright*, 63, 66–67.

192. See the back cover of E. A. Speiser, *Genesis* (AB 1; New York: Doubleday, 1964).

193. For listings of Dahood's works, see E. R. Martinez, S. J., ed., *Hebrew-Ugaritic Index to the Writings of Mitchell Dahood: A Bibliography with Indices of Scriptural Passages, Hebrew and Ugaritic Words, and Grammatical Observations* (Scripta Pontificii Instituti Biblici 116; Rome: Pontifical Biblical Institute, 1967); Martinez, ed., *Hebrew-Ugaritic Index II to the Writings of Mitchell Dahood: A Bibliography with Indices of Scriptural Passages, Hebrew, Ugaritic and Eblaite Words, and Observations, Critical Reviews, Doctoral Dissertations, and Related Writings* (Subsidia Biblica 4; Rome: Pontifical Biblical Institute, 1981).

194. Dahood, *Psalms I.1–50* (AB 16; New York: Doubleday, 1966); *Psalms II. 51–100* (AB 17; New York: Doubleday, 1968); *Psalms III.101–150* (AB 17A; New York: Doubleday, 1970). See also Dahood, *Ugaritic-Hebrew Philology: Marginal Notes on Recent Publications* (BibOr 17; Rome: Pontifical Biblical Institute, 1976). For this work in particular, see the important review of J. C. Greenfield, *JAOS* 89 (1969): 174–78.

195. Cross, letter to me dated 27 November 1998.

196. Nyberg, *Studien zum Hoseabuche: Zugleich ein Beitrag zur Klärung des Problems der alttestamentlichen Textkritik* (Uppsala Universitets Årsskrift 1935.6; Uppsala: Almqvist & Wiksells, 1935), 58–59, 90, 120. Nyberg's work on this point is defended by M. H. Pope in *El in the Ugaritic Texts* (VTSup 2; Leiden: Brill, 1955), 58 n. 20; and in the panel discussion sub C. H. Gordon, "Ugarit in Retrospect and Prospect," in *Ugarit in Retrospect: Fifty Years of Ugarit and Ugaritic* (ed. G. D. Young; Winona Lake, Ind.: Eisenbrauns, 1981), 194. The view is now commonly accepted, for example for 1 Sam 2:10, Pss 18:14 and 68:30, 35. For Dahood on this point, see, for example, Dahood, *Psalms I*, 117; *Psalms II*, 149. Since these volumes lack an index for authors, it is difficult to determine whether Dahood recognized Nyberg's contribution here. For a proper appreciation of Nyberg's work in the biblical field, see J. Barr, *Comparative Philology and the Text of the Old Testament* (Oxford: Oxford University Press, 1968), 72–75.

197. A. Lemaire has pointed out to me that the title apparently appears in the Emar texts in the proper name *al-aḫi* (Emar 144:6; cf. 25:3).

198. In Ginsberg's letter to Albright dated 5 September 1937 (APS archives Albright Corresp. 1936–1938).

199. Cross (*Canaanite Myth and Hebrew Epic,* 154 n. 39) cites the Ugaritic proper name, *a-mur-ᵈbaᶜl,* "I saw Baal"; see also R. de Vito, *Studies in Third Millennium Sumerian and Akkadian Personal Names: The Designation and Conception of the Personal God* (Studia Pohl; Series Maior 16; Rome: Editrice Pontificio Istituto Biblico, 1993), 192, 279; F. Grondähl, *Die Personennamen der Texte aus Ugarit* (Studia Pohl 1; Rome: Pontifical Biblical Institute, 1967), 320. For the verb **ʾmr* in this meaning, see J. Barr, "Etymology and the Old Testament," in *Language and Meaning: Studies in Hebrew Language and Biblical Exegesis* (OTS 19; Leiden: Brill, 1974), 5–6; T. Abusch, "Alaktu and Halakhah Oracular Decision, Divine Revelation," *HTR* 80 (1987): 25. Personal names with the **amur-* element are also attested in Akkadian and Eblaite sources. See de Vito, *Studies in Third Millennium Sumerian and Akkadian Personal Names,* 192, 279; P. Fronzaroli, "Eblaic Lexicon: Problems and Appraisal," in *Studies on the Language of Ebla* (ed. P. Fronzaroli; Quaderni de Semitistica 13; Florence: Istituto di Linguistica e di Lingue Orientali, 1984), 120. The form of the verb in Ps 29:9 is perhaps then a passive-stative **qatul.* In any case, the Masoretes no longer knew the older meaning of **ʾmr.*

200. So Dahood, *Psalms I,* 175, 179. Other BH examples include Ps 8:8; 2 Sam 2:9; Isa 16:7; Jer 18:31; Ezek 29:2; 35:15; Job 34:13; and possibly Num 16:3. See J. C. de Moor and P. van der Lugt, "The Spectre of Pan-Ugaritism," *BibOr* 31 (1974): 9. The postpositive construction is known also in Ugaritic (*KTU* 1.3 VI 14; 1.6 I 65; 1.14 IV 20; often reconstructed in 1.1 III 1* on the basis of 1.3 VI 14) and Aramaic (*KAI* 215:17; 222 A 5; Peshitta Lev 8:21; Peshitta Num 14:21). See I. Avinery, "The Position of the Declined *kl* in Syriac," *Afroasiastic Linguistics* 3/5 (1976): 25. The usage is not restricted to place-names: Ps 8:8 uses the construction after two words for animals; *KTU* 1.6 I 65 uses it after *ʾarṣ,* "land,"

and *KTU* 1.14 IV 20 uses it in a temporal construction. Syriac attests *ldkrʾ klh,* "the whole ram" (Peshitta Lev 8:21) and *bʾrcʾ kwlh,* "in all the earth" (Peshitta Num 14:21). For further discussion, see Avinery, "Position of the Declined *kl* in Syriac," 25.

201. So Cross (*Canaanite Myth and Hebrew Epic,* 154 n. 39), who dismisses the form as "prosaic"; followed by H. Page, "Ethnological Criticism: An Apologia and Application," in *Exploring New Paradigms in Biblical and Cognate Studies* (Macon, Ga.: Mellen, 1996), 100 n. 27.

202. So also Page, "Ethnological Criticism," 100 n. 28. Page gives no reason for his support of Dahood on this point or for the rejection of the verbal reconstruction of his mentor, F. M. Cross (see n. 199 above).

203. Robertson, review of Dahood, *Psalms I, JBL* 85 (1966): 484–86 (cited above); Barr, *Comparative Philology and the Text of the Old Testament* (1968) sub Dahood in the index; Loewenstamm, "Ugarit and the Bible I," *Bib* 56 (1975): 103–18; idem, "Ugarit and the Bible II," *Bib* 59 (1978): 100–122; de Moor and van der Lugt, "The Spectre of Pan-Ugaritism," 6–23; Althann, *Studies in Northwest Semitic* (BibOr 45; Rome: Pontificio Istituto Biblico, 1997). See also O. Loretz, "Die Ugaritistik in der Psalmeninterpretation. Zum Abschluss des Kommentars von M. Dahood," *UF* 4 (1972): 167–69; P. C. Craigie, "Ugarit and the Bible: Progress and Regress in 50 Years of Literary Study," in *Ugarit in Retrospect: Fifty Years of Ugarit and Ugaritic* (ed. G. D. Young; Winona Lake, Ind.: Eisenbrauns, 1981), 99–111; M. S. Moore, "A Short Note on Mitchell Dahood's Exegetical Methodology," *HS* 22 (1981): 35–38; A. Gibson, *Biblical Semantic Logic: A Preliminary Analysis* (New York: St. Martin's Press, 1981), 6, 20, 26, 82–86, 211, 223; and Curtis, "The Psalms since Dahood," 1–10. On Althann, see below.

204. Gordon, "Ugarit in Retrospect and Prospect," in *Ugarit in Retrospect,* 188. Note also the positive appreciation penned by D. N. Freedman, "Editor's Preface," in F. I. Andersen and A. D. Forbes, *Spelling in the Hebrew Bible* (BibOr 41; Rome: Biblical Institute Press, 1986), v–xi.

205. Dahood, *Psalms III.101–150,* xvii.

206. Particularly balanced and highly qualified on both the positive and negative side of the ledger is Curtis, "The Psalms since Dahood."

207. Pardee in the panel discussion sub Gordon, "Ugarit in Retrospect and Prospect," 190.

208. Pope in the panel discussion sub Gordon, ibid., 194.

209. Freedman's letter of 24 October 1998 to me.

210. Robertson, review of Dahood, *Psalms I, JBL* 85 (1966): 484.

211. This point is recognized in J. Barr, *Comparative Philology and the Text of the Old Testament: With Corrections and Additions* (Winona Lake, Ind.: Eisenbrauns, 1987), 365.

212. As a contrast, I would offer the methodology in the work of M. Held, nicely laid out in C. Cohen, "The 'Held Method' for Comparative Semitic Philology," *JANES* 19 (1989): 9–23.

213. Barr, *Comparative Philology and the Text of the Old Testament: With Corrections and Additions,* 359, 369.

214. Ginsberg, "Interpreting Ugaritic Texts," *JAOS* 70 (1950): 160.

215. Barr, *Comparative Philology and the Text of the Old Testament: With Corrections and Additions,* 383.

216. R. Rendtorff and J. Stolz, "Die Bedeutung der Gestaltungstruktur für Verständnis ugaritischer Texte. Ein Versuch zu *CTA* 24 [= *KTU* 1.24] [NK] 5–15," *UF* 11 (1979 = C. F. A. Schaeffer Festschrift): 709–18.

217. Althann, *Studies in Northwest Semitic* (BibOr 45; Rome: Pontifical Biblical Institute, 1997).

218. See Barr's own further reflections in his postscript in *Comparative Philology and the Text of the Old Testament: With Corrections and Additions,* 358–61.

219. With due respect to Althann, I would register some caveats with his study. Occasionally the Ugaritic basis for comparison is insufficiently noted. For example, the basis for positing *taqtul* in the first place goes unmentioned. It is similarly curious that Althann omitted any discussion of the famous comparison of *KTU* 1.5 I 16–19 with Ps 42:2 (pp. 45–46), observed by Held and many others. The former uses ʾaylt with respect to appetite, suggesting the possibility of haplography in Ps 42:2 due to the following *t-* (*kĕʾayyelʿeb taʿărōg); see above p. 109 n. 124. The discussion about vocative particles particularly suffers since Althann wrongly accepts vocative *k-* and *m-* in Ugaritic.

220. Compare C. Cohen's methodological retrospective of the work of his mentor, Moshe Held, in his essay, "The 'Held Method' for Comparative Semitic Philology," 9–23.

221. See the assessments in *Ugarit in Retrospect*. Note in particular Craigie's description of a "pan-Ugaritism" in his contribution, "Ugarit and the Bible," 99–111. Note a similar characterization in de Moor and van der Lugt, "The Spectre of Pan-Ugaritism," 3–26.

222. Sandmel, "Parallelomania," 1–13. See also S. B. Parker, "Some Methodological Principles in Ugaritic Philology," *Maarav* 2/1 (1979): 7–41.

223. Ginsberg, "Interpreting Ugaritic Texts," 156. For Pope's characterization, see his *Probative Pontificating in Ugaritic and Biblical Literature*, 12–13.

224. Ginsberg, review of J. Obermann, *Ugaritic Mythology, JCS* 2 (1948): 139.

225. Fronzaroli was editor of and contributor to *Studies on the Language of Ebla* (Quaderni di Semitistica 13; Florence: Istituto di Linguistica e di Lingue Orientali, Universita di Firenze, 1984) and to many other studies of the Eblaite language and texts. Xella was coauthor with F. Pomponio, *Les dieux d'Ebla: Etude analytique des divinités éblaïtes à l'époque des archives royales du IIIe millénaire* (AOAT 245; Münster: Ugarit-Verlag, 1997).

226. As reported in *NUS* 31 (April, 1984): 13. See the discussion of Gordon at Brandeis in the preceding chapter.

227. For example, Dahood, "Eblaite, Ugaritic, and Hebrew Lexical Notes," *UF* 11 (1979 = C. F. A. Schaeffer Festschrift): 141–46.

228. See Freedman, "The Real Story of the Ebla Tablets: Ebla and the Cities of the Plain," *BA* 41 (1978): 143–64.

229. See the interesting account of C. Murphy, *The Word according to Eve: Women and the Bible in Ancient Times and Our Own* (Boston: Houghton Mifflin, 1998). The book focuses on the backgrounds of different feminist scholars rather than on the details of their research.

230. The bibliography at this point is immense. For its discussion of views and bibliography, see E. S. Gerstenberger, *Yahweh the Patriarch: Ancient Images of God and Feminist Theology* (Minneapolis: Fortress, 1996). For monotheism as an advance for a feminist understanding of the divine, see T. Frymer-Kensky, *In the Wake of the Goddesses: Women, Culture, and the Biblical Transformation of Pagan Myth* (New York: Free Press, 1992); for a nice discussion of Frymer-Kensky's background and work, see Murphy, *Word according to Eve*, 86–91, 104–8. For female imagery applied to the deity of Israel, see, in addition to these two books, M. I. Gruber, *The Motherhood of God and Other Studies* (South Florida Studies in the History of Judaism 57; Atlanta: Scholars Press, 1992). All three of these studies show an awareness and/or some use of the Ugaritic texts.

231. Muilenburg, "Form Criticism and Beyond," *JBL* 88 (1969): 1–18. For Muilenburg's work, see T. F. Best, *Hearing and Speaking the Word: Selections from the Works of James Muilenberg* (Chico, Calif.: Scholars Press, 1984).

232. Trible, *God and the Rhetoric of Sexuality* (Overtures to Biblical Theology; Philadelphia: Fortress, 1978). For some autobiographical reflections, see Trible, "The Pilgrim Bible on a Feminist Journey," *The Auburn News* (Spring 1988): 1–5; for a nice discussion of Trible's background and work, see Murphy, *Word according to Eve*, 40–44, 48–61.

In the 1970s Trible was at Andover Newton Theological School. By the early 1980s she had returned to Union.

233. Bal, *Lethal Love: Feminist Literary Readings of Biblical Love Stories* (Bloomington: Indiana University Press, 1987). For an interesting response, see the review of E. L. Greenstein, *Journal of Religion* 69/3 (1989): 395–96. For a discussion of Bal's background and work, see Murphy, *Word according to Eve,* 117–23.

234. For much of this story, see E. L. Greenstein, *Essays on Biblical Method and Translation* (Brown Judaic Studies 92; Atlanta: Scholars Press, 1989), 20–26.

235. Fokkelman, *Narrative Art in Genesis: Specimens of Stylistic and Structural Analysis* (Assen: Van Gorcum, 1975; 2d ed., 1991); Fishbane, *Text and Texture: A Literary Reading of Selected Texts* (New York: Schocken, 1979); J. Kugel, *The Idea of Biblical Poetry* (New Haven/London: Yale University, 1981); Weiss, *The Bible from Within: The Method of Total Interpretation* (Jerusalem: Magnes, 1984); Alter, *The Art of Biblical Poetry* (New York: Basic Books, 1985); Sternberg, *The Poetics of Biblical Narrative* (Bloomington: Indiana University Press, 1985). For Simon, Zakovitch, and others in Israel, see "The Approach of the Bar-Ilan University Bible Department," *De'ot* 49 (1982): 229–36; Bal, *Lethal Love;* Damrosch, *The Narrative Covenant: Transformation of Genre in the Growth of Biblical Literature* (San Francisco: Harper & Row, 1987).

236. See, for example, the collection of his most important contributions in *Comparative Studies in Biblical and Ancient Oriental Literatures* (AOAT 204; Kevelaer: Butzon & Bercker; Neukirchen-Vluyn: Neukirchener Verlag, 1980).

237. In addition to work cited above, see those listed in Watson, *Traditional Techniques,* 18–31. For the work of Loretz, Kottsieper, and de Moor, see also Loretz, "Die Analyse der ugaritischen und hebräischen Poesie mittels Stichometrie und Konsontenzählung," *UF* 7 (1975): 265–69; and works cited in Loretz and Kottsieper, *Colometry in Ugaritic and Biblical Poetry: Introduction, Illustrations, and Topical Bibliography* (UBL 9; Altenberge: CIS-Verlag, 1987); see also W. van der Meer and J. C. de Moor, eds., *The Structural Analysis of Biblical and Canaanite Poetry* (JSOTSup 74; Sheffield: JSOT Press, 1988).

238. See Greenstein, *Essays on Biblical Method and Translation,* as well as his many contributions to the study of Ugaritic.

239. Berlin, "Parallel Word Pairs: A Linguistic Explanation," *UF* 15 (1983): 7–16; *The Dynamics of Biblical Parallelism* (Bloomington: Indiana University Press, 1985). See also her book *Poetics and Interpretation of Biblical Narrative* (Bible and Literature 9; Sheffield: Almond, 1983; repr. Winona Lake, Ind.: Eisenbrauns, 1994).

240. Pardee, *Ugaritic and Hebrew Poetic Parallelism.*

241. Beginning with his 1957 Pontifical Biblical Institute doctoral dissertation, "Estudios de poéticas hebrea," and followed by several other books and articles. See also the series of books of his listed conveniently in L. Alonso Schökel, *A Manual of Hebrew Poetics* (Subsidia Biblica 11; Rome: Editrice Pontificio Istituto Biblica, 1988), 33, 206.

242. Greenfield, "The Hebrew Bible and Canaanite Literature," in *Literary Guide to the Bible,* 545–60.

243. See the essays collected in G. Aichele et al., eds., *The Postmodern Bible: The Bible and Culture Collective* (New Haven: Yale University Press, 1995).

244. Mettinger, *King and Messiah: The Civil and Sacral Legitimation of the Israelite Kings* (ConBOT 8; Lund: Gleerup, 1976); *The Dethronement of Sabaoth: Studies in Shem and Kabod Theologies* (ConBOT 18; Lund: Gleerup, 1982). His most recent work is *No Graven Image? Israelite Aniconism in Its Ancient Near Eastern Context* (ConBOT 42; Stockholm: Almqvist & Wiksell, 1995). A book on the "dying and rising gods" is in progress.

245. Albertz, *A History of Israelite Religion in the Old Testament Period* (2 vols.; OTL; Louisville: Westminster John Knox, 1994).

246. On this point, see D. Pardee, review of *Ugarit and the Bible, JAOS* 117 (1997): 375–78.

Resurgence in Tools and Method: 1985 to 1999

Many new works that appeared since the mid-1980s and works currently in production indicate the overall health of the field.

⊠ TEXTS AND TOOLS

New Text: RS 1992.2014 (an incantation similar to *CAT* 1.169). See translation and notes by D. Pardee in *Canonical Compositions from the Biblical World*, vol. 1 of *The Context of Scripture* (ed. W. W. Hallo; Leiden: Brill, 1997), 327–28.

Revision of *KTU*: M. Dietrich, O. Loretz, and J. Sanmartín, *The Cuneiform Alphabetic Texts from Ugarit, Ras Ibn Hani, and Other Places (KTU: Second, Enlarged Edition)* (ALASP 8; Münster: Ugarit-Verlag, 1995). See also (based on the 1976 *KTU*) J.-L. Cunchillos and J.-P. Vita, eds., *Banco de datos filológicos semíticos noroccidentales I: Textos ugaríticos. Prima parte: Datos ugaríticos* (Madrid: CSIC, 1993).

Photographic Resources: West Semitic Research Project headed by Bruce Zuckerman makes its initial impact (by year): R. Ratner and B. Zuckerman, "On Reading the 'Kid in the Milk' Inscription," *BAR* 1/3 (1985): 56–58; " 'A Kid in Milk'? New Photographs of *KTU* 1.23, Line 14," *HUCA* 57 (1986): 15–60. W. Pitard, "A New Edition of the 'Rapiʾuma' Texts: *KTU* 1.20–22," *BASOR* 285 (1992): 33–77. M. S. Smith, *The Ugaritic Baal Cycle. Volume 1: Introduction with Text, Translation, and Commentary to the First Two Tablets (KTU 1.1–1.2)* (VTSup 55; Leiden: Brill, 1994). T. J. Lewis, "The Disappearance of the Goddess Anat: The 1995 West Semitic Research Project on Ugaritic Epigraphy," *BA* 59 (1996): 115–21. E. L. Greenstein, "New Readings in the Kirta Epic," *IOS* 18 (1998): 105–23. W. T. Pitard, "The Binding of Yamm: A New Edition of the Ugaritic Text *KTU* 1.83," *JNES* 57/4 (1998): 261–80.

Text Editions: D. Pardee, *Les textes para-mythologiques de la 24e Campagne (1961)* (RSO ⸗ Paris: Editions Recherche sur les Civilisations, 1988); *Les textes rituels* (RSO 12; Paris: Editions Recherche sur les Civilisations, 2000).

The Ugaritic Tablets Digital Edition of *KTU* 1.1–1.24 (UTDE), headed by W. Pitard and B. Zuckerman.

Revised Editions of Grammars: C. Gordon, *Ugaritic Textbook* (Rome: Pontifical Biblical Institute, 1998). S. Segert, *A Basic Grammar of the Ugaritic Language* (4th printing with revisions; Berkeley: University of California Press, 1997).

New Grammars: J.-L. Cunchillos and J.-A. Zamora, *Gramática ugarítica elemental* (Madrid: Ediciones Clásicas, 1995). D. Sivan, *A Grammar of the Ugaritic Language* (HdO 1/28; Leiden: Brill, 1997). J. Tropper, *Ugaritische Grammatik* (AOAT 273; Kevelaer: Bercker & Butzon; Neukirchener-Vluyn: Neukirchener Verlag, 2000). See also J. C. de Moor's study of the syntax of literary Ugaritic (in preparation); and D. D. Testen, *Parallels in Semitic Linguistics: The Development of Arabic la- and Related Semitic Particles* (Studies in Semitic Languages and Linguistics 26; Leiden/Boston/Köln: Brill, 1998).

Dictionaries and Lexical Research: G. del Olmo Lete and J. Sanmartín, *Diccionario de la lengua ugarítica. Vol. I: ʾ(a/i/u)–l* (Aula Orientalis Supplementa 7; Barcelona: Editorial AUSA, 1996); *Diccionario de la lengua ugarítica. Vol. II: m–z* (Aula Orientalis Supplementa 8; Editorial AUSA, 2000). Dictionary of C. Cohen based on M. Held's method, contracted with Brill. See also the republication of J. C. Greenfield's articles *ʾAl Kanfei Yonah: Collected Studies of Jonas C. Greenfield on Semitic Philology* (ed. S. M. Paul, M. E. Stone, and A. Pinnick; 2 vols.: Leiden: Brill, 2001).

Concordances: J.-L. Cunchillos and J.-P. Vita, eds., *Banco de datos filológicos semíticos noroccidentales. II. Concordancia de palabras ugaríticas* (3 vols.; Madrid: Institución Fernandoel Católico, 1995).

Resource for Text Information: P. Bordreuil and D. Pardee, *La trouvaille épigraphique de l'Ougarit: 1. Concordance* (RSO 5/1; Paris: Editions Recherche sur les Civilisations, 1989).

Word Lists: M. Dietrich and O. Loretz, *Word-List of the Cuneiform Alphabetic Texts from Ugarit, Ras Ibn Hani, and Other Places (KTU: Second, Enlarged Edition)* (ALASP 1; Münster: Ugarit-Verlag, 1996). I. Kottsieper, "Indizes und Korrecturen zur 'Word-List of the Cuneiform Alphabetic Texts,'" *UF* 29 (1997): 245–83. Petr Zemánek, *Ugaritischer Wortformenindex* (Lexicographie Orientalis 4; Hamburg: Buske, 1995).

Bibliographies: M. Dietrich and O. Loretz, *Analytic Ugaritic Bibliography 1972–1988* (AOAT 20/6; Kevelaer: Butzon & Bercker; Neukirchen-Vluyn: Neukirchener Verlag, 1996). D. Pardee, "Ugaritic Bibliography," *AfO* 34 (1987): 366–471. J.-L. Cunchillos, *La trouvaille épigraphique de l'Ougarit: 2. Bibliographie* (RSO 5/2; Paris: Editions Recherche sur les Civilisations, 1990).

Handbooks: J.-L. Cunchillos, *Manual de estudios ugaríticos* (Madrid: CSIC, 1992). W. G. E. Watson and N. Wyatt, eds., *Handbook of Ugaritic Studies* (HdO 1/39; Leiden: Brill, 1999).

"Ugaritic in Cyberspace" (Internet):

(1) Edinburgh project: See the article of this name by N. Wyatt and J. B. Lloyd in *UF* 27 (1995): 597; "The Edinburgh Ras Shamra Projects: An Introduction," in *Ugarit, Religion, and Culture: Proceedings of the International Colloquium. Edinburgh July 1994* (ed. N. Wyatt; UBL 12; Münster: Ugarit-Verlag, 1996), 423–30. Online: http://www.ed.ac.uk/~ugarit/home.htm.

(2) Bilingual (English/Spanish) CD-ROM produced by the Madrid Ugaritic team (J.-L. Cunchillos, J. M. Galan, J.-P. Zamora, etc.); contact cunchillos@fresno.csic.es. Ugaritic Philological Data Bank located online: http://www.labherm.filol.csic.es. See also Banco de Datos Filológicos Semíticos Noroccidentales y el Sistema Integrado de Análisis Morfológico de Textos Ugaríticos, headed by J.-L. Cunchillos ("Realizaciones informáticas del Sistema Integrado de Análisis Morfológico de Textos Ugaríticos [SIAMTU]," *Bib* 73 [1992]: 547–59).

(3) InscriptiFact: A Networked Database of Ancient Near Eastern Inscriptions, by B. Zucker-man, M. Lundberg, and L. Hunt, located at www.inscriptifact.com/information/.
(4) Ugarit-Forschungstelle, by M. Dietrich and O. Loretz, located at http://ugarit.uni-muenster.de/.
(5) Marking Systems in the Ancient Near East (including Ugaritic texts), located at http:// soho.ios.com/~arobe/. Contact online arobe@soho.ios.com. Further links to be found online: http://faculty.washington.edu/~snoegel/okeanos.html.
(6) See the listing of resources by ABZU online: http://www-oi.uchicago.edu/OI/DEPT/ RA/Research_Arch.html. Also http://www-oi.uchicago.edu/OI/DEPT/RA/ABZU/ABZU_ REGINDX_MESO.HTML#6. See also the list at www.uni-mainz.de/~lehmann/link. html#ugr.
Archaeological and Historical Research: M. Yon, *The City of Ugarit at Tell Ras Shamra* (Winona Lake, Ind.: Eisenbrauns, 2001, in press); *Le centre de la ville, 38ᵉ–44ᵉ campagne (1978–1984)* (RSO 3; Paris: Editions Recherche sur les Civilisations, 1987). M. Yon, P. Bordreuil, and D. Pardee, "Ugarit," *ABD* 6 (1992): 695–721. See work of M. Yon; Callot and Margueron are preparing an architectural study of the palace.
New work on alphabet based on A. G. Lundin (Loundine), "L'origine de l'alphabet," *Cahiers de L'Institut de Linguistique de Louvain* 11/1–2 (1985): 173–202; "L'abécédaire de Beth Shemesh," *Muséon* 100 (1987): 243–50. Also the publication of a new abecedary, RS 88.2215, in P. Bordreuil and D. Pardee, "Un abécédaire du type sud-sémitique découvert en 1988 dans les fouilles archéologiques françaises de Ras Shamra-Ougarit," *CRAIBL* (1995): 855–60.
Study of Iconography: P. Amiet, *Corpus des cylindres de Ras Shamra–Ougarit II: Sceaux–cylindres en hématitie et pierres diverses* (RSO 9; Paris: Editions Recherche sur les Civilisations, 1992). O. Keel and C. Uehlinger, *Göttinen, Götter, und Gottessymbole* (Freiburg: Herder, 1992). I. Cornelius, *The Iconography of the Canaanite Gods Reshef and Baʿal: Late Bronze Age I Periods (c. 1500–1000 BCE)* (OBO 140; Freiburg, Switzerland: Universitätsverlag; Göttingen: Vandenhoeck & Ruprecht, 1994). T. N. D. Mettinger, *No Graven Image? Israelite Aniconism in Its Ancient Near Eastern Context* (ConBOT 42; Stockholm: Almqvist & Wiksell, 1995). K. van der Toorn, ed., *The Image and the Book: Iconic Cults, Aniconism, and the Rise of Book Religion in Israel and the Ancient Near East* (Contributions to Biblical Exegesis and Theology 21; Leuven: Peeters, 1997).
Proper Names: D. Pardee, "An Evaluation of the Proper Names from Ebla from a West Se-mitic Perspective: Pantheon Distribution according to Genre," in *Eblaite Personal Names and Semitic Name-Giving: Papers of a Symposium Held in Rome 15–17, 1985* (ed. A. Archi; ARES 1; Rome, 1988), 119–51; "Ugaritic Proper Names," *AfO* 36–37 (1989–1990): 390–513. W. G. E. Watson, "Ugaritic Onomastics (1)," *AO* 8 (1990): 113–27; "Ugaritic Onomastics (2)," *AO* 8 (1990): 243–50; "Ugaritic Onomastics (3)," *AO* 11 (1993): 213–22. M. Dietrich and O. Loretz, *Analytic Ugaritic Bibliography 1972–1988* (AOAT 20/6; Kevelaer: Butzon & Bercker; Neukirchen-Vluyn: Neukirch-ener Verlag, 1996) under "subjects."
Translations: D. Amir, *Gods and Heroes: Canaanite Stories Which Were Found in Ugarit* (Kibbutz Dan, Golan: Bet Ussishkin, 1987). A. Caquot, J. M. de Tarragon, and J. L. Cunchillos, *Textes ougaritiques: Tome II. Textes religieux, rituels, correspondance* (LAPO 14; Paris: Cerf, 1989). F. O. Hvidberg-Hansen, *Kanaʿanaeiske myter og legender: Tekster fra Ras Shamra-Ugarit. Dansk oversaettelse med kommentar I–II* (2 vols.; Bibel og historie 13; Aarhus: Aarhus University Press, 1990). M. Dietrich and O. Loretz, *Mythen und Epen in ugaritischen Sprache* (Texte aus der Umwelt des Alten Testaments 3/6; ed. O. Kaiser; Gütersloh: Mohn, 1997). J. C. de Moor, *An Anthology of Religious Texts from Ugarit* (Nisaba 16; Leiden: Brill, 1987). See also J. C. de Moor and K. Spronk, *A Cuneiform Anthology of Religious Texts from Ugarit* (Leiden: Brill, 1987). D. Pardee and others in W. W. Hallo, ed., *The Context of Scripture* (Leiden: Brill, 1997). S. B. Parker, ed.,

Ugaritic Narrative Poetry (Writings from the Ancient World; Atlanta: Scholars Press, 1997). Z. and S. Rin, *'Alilot Ha'Elim* (Philadelphia: 'Inbal, 1996). N. Wyatt, *Religious Texts from Ugarit: The Words of Ilimilku and His Colleagues* (Biblical Seminar 53; Sheffield: Sheffield Academic Press, 1998).

Studies and Commentaries: B. Margalit, *The Ugaritic Poem of AQHT* (BZAW 182; Berlin: Walter de Gruyter, 1989). S. B. Parker, *The Pre-biblical Narrative Tradition* (SBL Resources for Biblical Study 24; Atlanta: Scholars Press, 1989); *Stories in Scripture and Inscriptions: Comparative Studies on Narratives in Northwest Semitic Inscriptions and the Hebrew Bible* (New York: Oxford University Press, 1997). M. S. Smith, *The Ugaritic Baal Cycle. Vol. 1: Introduction with Text, Translation, and Commentary to the First Two Tablets (KTU 1.1–1.2)* (VTSup 55; Leiden: Brill, 1994); *The Ugaritic Baal Cycle. Vol. 2* (in preparation). G. Theuer, *Der Mondgott in den Religionen Syrien-Palästinas: Unter besonderer Berücksichtigung von KTU 1.24* (OBO 173; Freiburg, Switzerland: Universitätsverlag; Göttingen: Vandenhoeck & Ruprecht, 2000). D. P. Wright, *Ritual in Narrative: The Dynamics of Feasting, Mourning, and Retaliation Rites in the Ugaritic Tale of Aqhat* (Winona Lake, Ind.: Eisenbrauns, 2001).

Synthetic Studies: M. Baldacci, *La scoperta di Ugarit: La città-stato ai primordi della Bibbia* (Spa: Piemme, 1996); *Il libro dei morti della antica Ugarit: Le più antiche testimonianze sull'Aldilà prima della Bibbia* (Spa: Piemme, 1998). F. M. Cross, *From Epic to Canon: History and Literature in Ancient Israel* (Baltimore: Johns Hopkins University Press, 1998). J. Day, *Yahweh and the Gods and Goddesses of Canaan* (JSOTSup 265; Sheffield: Sheffield Academic Press, 2001). W. Herrmann, *Von Gott und den Göttern: Gesammelte Aufsätze zum Alten Testament* (BZAW 259; Berlin: de Gruyter, 1999). J. Jeremias, *Das Königtum Gottes in den Psalmen: Israels Begegnung mit dem kanaanäischen Mythos in den Jahwe-König-Psalmen* (FRLANT 141; Göttingen: Vandenhoeck & Ruprecht, 1987). J. Day, ed., *King and Messiah in the Ancient Near East: Proceedings of the Oxford Old Testament Seminar* (JSOTSup 270; Sheffield: Sheffield Academic Press, 1998). T. J. Lewis, *Cults of the Dead in Ancient Israel and Ugarit* (HSM 39; Atlanta: Scholars Press, 1989). Also a survey of Israelite religion (Anchor Bible Reference Library; New York: Doubleday, in preparation). O. Loretz, *Ugarit und die Bibel: Kanaanäische Götter und Religion im Alten Testament* (Darmstadt: Wissenschaftliche Buchgesellschaft, 1990). P. D. Miller, *The Religion of Ancient Israel* (Library of Ancient Israel; Louisville, Ky.: Westminster John Knox, 2000). J. C. de Moor, *The Rise of Yahwism: The Roots of Israelite Monotheism* (BETL 91; Leuven: Peeters/University Press, 1990; 2d ed., 1997). P. Mosca, "Ugaritic and Daniel 7: A Missing Link," *Bib* 67 (1986): 496–517. H. Niehr, *Religionen in Israels Umwelt: Einführung in die nordwestsemitischen Religionen Syrien-Palästinas* (Die neue Echter Bibel: Ergänzungsband zum Alten Testament 5; Würzburg: Echter, 1998). G. del Olmo Lete, *La religión cananea según la liturgia de Ugarit: Estudio textual* (Aula Orientalis Supplementa 3; Barcelona: Editorial AUSA, 1992). Translation: *Canaanite Religion according to the Liturgical Texts of Ugarit* (trans. W. G. E. Watson; Bethesda, Md.: CDL, 1999). G. del Olmo Lete, ed., *Semitas occidentales (Emar, Ugarit, Hebreos, Fenicios, Arameos, Arabes preislámicos)* (Mitología y Religión del Oriente Antiguo II/2; Barcelona: Editorial AUSA, 1995). M. S. Smith, *The Early History of God: Yahweh and the Other Deities in Ancient Israel* (San Francisco: Harper & Row, 1990); *The Origins of Biblical Monotheism: Israel's Polytheistic Background and the Ugaritic Texts* (New York: Oxford University Press, 2001). K. van der Toorn et al., eds., *Dictionary of Deities and Demons* (Leiden: Brill, 1996; rev. ed., 1999). G. J. Brooke, A. H. W. Curtis, and J. F. Healey, eds., *Ugarit and the Bible: Proceedings of the International Symposium on Ugarit and the Bible. Manchester, September 1992* (UBL 11; Münster: Ugarit-Verlag, 1994). N. Wyatt, W. G. E. Watson, and J. B. Lloyd, eds., *Ugarit, Religion and Culture: Proceedings of the International Colloquium on Ugarit, Religion and Culture. Edinburgh, July 1994. Essays Presented in Honour of Professor John C. L.*

Gibson (UBL 12; Münster: Ugarit-Verlag, 1996). M. Dietrich and I. Kottsieper, eds., *"Und Mose schrieb dieses Lied auf": Studien zum Alten Testament und zum Alten Orient. Festschrift für Oswald Loretz zur Vollendung seines 70. Lebenjahres mit Beiträgen von Freunden, Schülern, und Kollegen* (AOAT 250; Münster: Ugarit-Verlag, 1998). N. Wyatt, *Myths of Power: A Study of Royal Power and Ideology in Ugaritic and Biblical Tradition* (UBL 13; Münster: Ugarit-Verlag, 1996); *Serving the Gods* (Sheffield: Sheffield Academic Press, 2000). Z. Zevit, *The Religions of Ancient Israel: A Synthesis of Parallactic Approaches* (London and New York: Continuum, 2001).

This most recent period has witnessed huge advances in the production of tools of all kinds. In addition to dictionaries, concordances, translations, bibliographies, commentaries, and other basics are the text editions being created in various quarters, including the revised edition of *KTU*, the collations of D. Pardee, and the photographic editions of B. Zuckerman and his colleagues. In addition, two new concerns have come to the fore. The first is the archaeological evidence for the archival context of Ugaritic texts. This work was advanced by the 1989 survey of P. Bordreuil and D. Pardee, and the 1991 study of W. von Soldt.[1] It has since been pursued by other scholars, such as R. S. Hess and A. Rosengren Petersen.[2] The second is the study of iconography. The major event in the study of West Semitic religious iconography was the 1992 work of O. Keel and C. Uehlinger, *Göttinen, Götter, und Gottessymbole*.[3] The major event on the more specific question of Israelite iconography and aniconism was clearly T. N. D. Mettinger's 1995 book, *No Graven Image? Israelite Aniconism in Its Ancient Near Eastern Context*.[4] Beyond the appearance of new tools and data, several other trends also emerge in this period.

⚔ ALPHABET AND GRAMMAR

Since 1985 new issues have emerged concerning the nature of the Ugaritic alphabet.[5] A re-examination of the Beth Shemesh tablet, usually dated to the thirteenth century B.C.E., led to its identification as an abecedary that reflected not the West Semitic order of letters of the longer alphabet, but the order of letters found in the shorter South Semitic alphabets (such as South Arabic and Ethiopic).[6] In arguing this case, A. G. Loundine,[7] followed by J. Ryckmans and E. Puech,[8] showed the antiquity and geographical range of this alphabet.[9] Another abecedary discovered at Ugarit in 1988 and published in 1995 showed a high affinity with the sequence of letters in the Beth Shemesh tablet and the South Semitic alphabets.[10] Taken together, these discoveries indicate the geographical range of both the shorter and longer cuneiform alphabets, as well as their connections with the South Semitic alphabets. It is possible, to be sure, that the exemplars of the shorter alphabet did not derive from Ugarit. Nor is it clear that a single order of letters underlies all the texts written in the shorter alphabet. Finally, the variations among the abecedaries urge caution against hasty generalizations.

A further issue about the alphabet came to the fore in this discussion, namely, the question of which alphabet reflected the original number of letters. If the South Semitic tradition was as old as the West Semitic tradition, then perhaps the longer Ugaritic alphabet was secondarily created by adding letters. This new view, defended by M. Dietrich and O. Loretz,[11] has been severely criticized by E. A. Knauf and B. Sass.[12] A longtime observer on the Ugaritic alphabet, F. Rosenthal, has recently weighed in on this issue,[13] noting the similarity between the Ugaritic and South Arabian forms for the letter *th.* He comments on this correspondence: "It guarantees the original existence of the two signs in the linear alphabet . . . and might constitute an additional argument in favor of the bold hypothesis . . . that South Arabian as a Semitic language entered the Arabian peninsula from the north near the end of the second millennium B.C. and probably earlier."[14] The debate continues.

Finally, news came in November 1999 that inscriptions with pictographic letters dating between 1900 and 1800 B.C.E. have been discovered at Wadi el-Hol

Oswald Loretz, Cyrus Gordon, and Manfried Dietrich. Courtesy of Cyrus Gordon.

(lying on an ancient trade route on the western side of the Nile, north of Thebes).[15] This discovery pushes back the date of known alphabetic writing by two to three centuries, and it would also locate the development of the alphabet in Egypt's heartland. Previously, the earliest known alphabetic inscriptions in the Egyptian sphere were texts dating to ca. 1500 B.C.E., from the Sinai peninsula (at Serabit el-Khadem). With this discovery, Ugaritic alphabetic writing seems hardly to belong to early alphabetic writing, which must be dated half a millennium earlier.

The research on grammar remains some of the most exciting work being conducted today. In 1995, the Spanish-speaking world received its first major Ugaritic grammar, thanks to J.-L. Cunchillos and J.-A. Zamora.[16] The first grammar of the language in modern Hebrew was produced by D. Sivan.[17] For the English-speaking community, a new edition of Sivan's grammar, revised and translated by A. F. Rainey,[18] is replacing the older grammars of Gordon and Segert, which themselves have appeared recently in revised form.[19] Great acumen has been applied to the study of Ugaritic and Hebrew grammar, as reflected in the work of many good scholars, including W. R. Garr, J. Huehnergard, D. Pardee, D. Sivan, J. Tropper, and E. Verreet. Especially noteworthy are the grammars of Sivan and Tropper. Moreover, studies drawing more broadly on linguistic theory have begun to make inroads into Ugaritic. Examples include the studies of voicing and devoicing in Ugaritic by W. R. Garr and R. Voigt.[20] Part of the recent discussion of language at Ugarit has involved bilingualism at Ugarit and in particular the relationship between Hurrian and Ugaritic in some ritual texts.[21]

⋈ SCRIBAL HISTORY AND LANGUAGES, AND THE QUESTION OF UGARITIC AS "CANAANITE"

This period witnessed two significant advances in the understanding of Ugarit's scribal history. The first involves the dating of the scribal activity of the figure generally known as Ilimilku (although van Soldt has made a cogent case for an alternative spelling, Ilimalku, a proposal largely ignored by the field).[22] It has been generally thought that this scribe, responsible for copying the major mythological texts (including the Baal Cycle), worked in the early fourteenth century, during the reign of Niqmaddu II. However, in 1992 a fragment of a mythological text with Ilimalku's name was reportedly discovered in the house of Urtennu, an official who served Niqmaddu III during the latter part of the thirteenth century. Accordingly, the date of this scribe's literary activity as well as the literary texts attributed to him may have to be lowered by over a century, unless there was more than one scribe by this name.[23]

A second advance involves a more precise treatment of language influences at Ugarit. Van Soldt has attributed the shifting influence of various foreign languages at Ugarit to political developments.[24] Hurrian influence at Ugarit during the reigns of its earliest kings may be attributable to the presence of Mitannian teachers in Syria during the final period of the empire of Mitanni. After the defeat of this empire, Assyria filled the vacuum in Syria. This is why an Assyrian scribe is found to have lived at Ugarit. Concomitant contacts with Babylon were also established, and Middle Babylonian became the scribal norm at Ugarit, albeit with local influence.

Over the last decade the classification of Ugaritic itself has come under scrutiny. The term "Canaanite" continues to be used by the field.[25] It remains defensible as a linguistic term, as B. Isaksson has argued, although it is hardly necessary. It is a shorthand way of referring not only to Late Bronze Age "Canaanite" of Ugarit and that underlying the Akkadian of the El Amarna letters, but also to Iron Age Hebrew and Phoenician on the one hand, as opposed to Aramaic on the other. The term itself is not crucial, as indicated by Ginsberg's older proposal for an alternative designation, "Phoenic."[26] Clearly, what matters more is not the terminology of "Canaanite" but the pattern of isoglosses, especially innovations, that the term designates. In fact, we have witnessed a further major shift in the field concerning the term "Canaanite." For decades, this word has served as code for "not Israelite," and Ugaritic served to provide examples of "Canaanite culture." However, in declaring Israelite to be Canaanite, more recent scholarship such as H. Barstad's book on Amos[27] has taken up the earlier observations of G. Ahlström and Morton Smith[28] (not to mention Isa 19:18).

This work has resulted in understanding "Canaanite practices" as eminently Israelite. This trend was becoming evident from studies of the so-called cult of the dead in the mid- and late-1970s. The shift was complete by the time of the next scholarly generation, including B. A. Levine and J. M. de Tarragon, K. Spronk, T. J. Lewis, M. S. Smith, E. M. Bloch-Smith, B. B. Schmidt, O. Loretz, and H. Niehr.[29] The same shift of perspective applies to the study of deities, for example in S. M. Olyan's treatment of Asherah,[30] as well as the phenomenon of magic, as observed by F. H. Cryer.[31] Research on West Semitic religion, for example by M. S. Smith and H. Niehr, likewise reflect this shift.[32] This change in viewpoint represents what Wim van Binsbergen has called "the reduction of mythical elements" in a scholarly field: "To the extent that disciplines are established and professionalized, they are routinized structures for the reduction of mythical elements in their members' scholarly statements."[33] The period 1970–1985 saw a turn away from the distinction between "Canaanite" and "Israelite" in the biblical guild and from the use of Ugaritic to support it. Now even as a new perspective has been gaining ground in the field, the term "Canaanite" has been denounced as a historical term (though it may not be as much of a historical ghost as N. P. Lemche, for example, thinks).[34]

The term "Canaanite" thus continues to serve in two very different discussions about ancient evidence, one about language classification, the other about cultures. For example, in the proceedings of the 1992 Manchester conference on Ugaritic and biblical studies,[35] four essays use "Canaanite" as a term for a culture (J. Day, J. C. L. Gibson, L. L. Grabbe, and G. del Olmo Lete), and one paper deals with "Canaanite" as a term for language (J. Tropper). "Canaanite" as both a cultural and linguistic term is an old term in the field.[36] As long as these two uses cross each other's path, "Canaanite" will remain problematic as a heuristic term for the purposes of modern scholarly analysis. Evidence of a sea change with the Europeans' use of the term may be seen by Grabbe's parsing of the difficulties and the call for an avoidance of the term "Canaanite."[37] In contrast, Pardee's fine delineation of the issues ends by advocating a retention of the term: " 'Old Northwest Semitic' would certainly be more precise than 'Canaanite,' but it is so cumbersome!"[38] I prefer myself "West Semitic," since a cumbersome term, if more accurate, would nonetheless be preferable to scholars. Given the long-established usage of the term, Pardee's view will likely prevail. However, in the United States, awareness of the problem may be gauged by the change in title of one program unit of the Society of Biblical Literature; the unit long called "Israelite and Canaanite Religion" was billed as "Israelite Religion in Its West Asian Setting" in the 1999 program.

⌘ THE RELIGIONS OF UGARIT AND ANCIENT ISRAEL

The period since 1985 has also witnessed fine comparative studies for Ugaritic and the Bible, both for particular deities and for divinity more broadly. Some of these studies continue the Harvard tradition of dissertations investigating a given topic attested in Ugaritic and Israelite texts. These include H. N. Wallace's treatment of the divine garden on the holy mountain;[39] G. A. Anderson's survey of sacrificial terminology;[40] T. J. Lewis's study on religious devotion to the dead;[41] S. A. Meier's work on the messenger angel;[42] and H. R. Page's examination of the motif of cosmic rebellion.[43] This period also witnessed innovations, notably M. C. A. Korpel's extensive examination of anthropomorphisms[44] and the recent explosion of studies of deities, especially Asherah. The culmination of all this "deity-study" is the *Dictionary of Deities and Demons in the Bible*, which has appeared in a revised, second edition.[45]

The recent craze in Asherah studies[46] is due in large measure to the discovery of the Kuntillet 'Ajrud and Khirbet el-Qom inscriptions, and it is now augmented by the newer inscriptions from Tel Miqne. At this point the range of opinion about Asherah as a goddess in Israel is best represented by contrasting S. M. Olyan's acceptance of the goddess in his 1988 monograph, *Asherah and the Cult of Yahweh in Israel,* with C. Frevel's considerably circumscribed and critical 1995 study, *Aschera und der Ausschliesslichkeitanspruch YHWHs.*[47] My own 1990 book, *The Early History of God,*[48] raised questions about whether the symbol lost its original association with the goddess, a view disputed by the majority of the field, but largely compatible with Frevel's. O. Keel and C. Uehlinger's important work on iconography, *Gods, Goddesses and Images of God,*[49] dubiously combines the two views, arguing that the symbol of the asherah lost its associations with the goddess by the eighth century, only to regain them by the second half of the seventh century. The jury seems still to be out on these undeniably complex issues.

These works have been supplemented by Keel's 1998 *Goddesses and Trees, New Moon and Yahweh* (largely a response to Frevel).[50] Additional Mesopotamian material has been supplied by P. Merlo's 1998 study, *La dea Ašratum–Aṯiratu–Ašera.*[51] S. Ackerman has also situated the issues against the larger issue of popular religion in ancient Israel.[52] The field now has the long-awaited book of J. M. Hadley on the subject of Asherah.[53]

Extending the older research on El by Pope and Cross (discussed in Chapter Three), B. A. Levine has demonstrated the ongoing existence of the cult of El in first-millennium West Semitic religion. In particular, his work stresses the regional variation in the survival of cultic devotion to El.[54] C. F. A. Schaeffer (followed by N. Wyatt[55] and tentatively by myself)[56] has argued that El may have been the original god connected with the Exodus from Egypt and that this event was secondarily associated with Yahweh when the two gods were identified in Israelite tradition. Levine has keenly observed that Num 23:22 and 24:8 (cf. 23:8) associate the Exodus not with Yahweh, but with El: "El who freed them from Egypt has horns like a wild ox." (This description also evokes El's attribute animal at Ugarit, the ox, reflected in his title "Bull El.") The poems in Num 23–24 contain the name of Yahweh (23:8, 21; 24:6), but El is attested almost three times as often as Yahweh (23:8, 19, 22, 23; 24:4, 8, 16, 23). Accordingly, Levine seems to be correct in suggesting that these poems preserve an old repertoire of El tradition, now synthesized with references to Yahweh. If this is correct, then these texts witness to El as the god of the Exodus. C. L. Seow has similarly elucidated the complex of El language and imagery surrounding the presentation of the Shiloh cult in 1 Sam 1–3,[57] indicating that El was probably the local god of the site and that Yahweh was secondarily identified with him. This pattern of secondary incorporation of Yahweh, an outsider god from the south, was probably repeated at other sites in the hill country.[58]

N. Walls's study of Anat has used social science perspectives to enhance the study of divinities. Walls locates Anat as "frozen" in time prior to the patriarchal constraints of marriage and childbirth. Anat is a young woman, unattached to any male, and therefore her place in the pantheon stands unresolved.[59] She is not fully under the control of patriarchal authority, for she may defy El, and she is not beholden to a husband. Moreover, her passion and intensity cannot be controlled. In this respect, Anat resembles the Sumerian Inanna (perhaps under the influence of Akkadian Ishtar, with whom she was identified), who is, in the words of T. Frymer-Kensky, "sheer force, rage, and might, with a physical power, that exists in a somewhat uneasy relationship to the orderly world of the hierarchical pantheon."[60] Generally, Ugaritic myth seems more concerned with the status and relations among competing males than among females, so that some relations remain largely unexpressed. (This point may apply to Athtart as well: the relations of these goddesses remain unclear compared to the males of the pantheon's second tier.) My only misgivings with Walls's book regard his arguments against Anat's sexual activity in the admittedly very difficult texts, *KTU* 1.10 and 1.12. R. M. Good[61] has well noted regarding Walls's apparent predisposition on the issue of Anat's sexual activity: "Is it unfair to observe that in sexual matters Walls wants to defend Anat's honor, which, as Groucho Marx might say, is more than she ever did?" Certainty on this point is not yet possible. It may be noted, however, that Egyptian culture imported West Semitic deities, and Egyptian texts attest to Anat as the spouse of Seth, commonly understood to be roughly the Egyptian equivalent of Baal. For example, the Egyptian story, "The Contest of Horus and Seth for the Rule," presents Anat and Astarte together as the daughters of Re and the wives of Seth.[62] Walls (as well as P. L. Day) follows Te Velde in challenging the value of this particular text.[63] As his chief argument, Te Velde notes that no other text calls Anat the consort of Seth. The uniqueness of this rendering of Anat as the wife of Seth might be viewed as militating in favor of the text's authenticity as a witness to the West Semitic tradition. However, Te Velde also retranslates the passage in question, making "the Seed" Seth's spouse and leaving to Anat only the task of interceding on behalf of Seth before her father, Re. Unfortunately, Walls and Day apparently overlook a sixth- or fifth-century Aramaic funerary stele from Egypt that calls Baal "the husband of Anat."[64] The little weight afforded by the Egyptian evidence may be sufficient to tip the balance slightly in favor of the older view that Anat and Baal were indeed consorts, at least in some traditions. I do not think that this conclusion significantly undermines Wall's overall study. Viewing Anat as set at a particular point in life recalls the basic point about Ugaritic mythology that the deities are frozen in time; Anat's moment may indeed be one poised between the constraints of her father's household and those of any would-be husband.

Walls's study illustrates a shift in the comparative approach to mythology and religion. A new comparativism has emerged in broader-based studies informed by social science methodologies. Besides Walls's book, social science material has played a major role in the ongoing discussion between L. K. Handy and J. D. Schloen,[65] both of whom have invoked Max Weber's work in order to understand the structure of divinity in the Ugaritic myths. The question is whether the primary terminology in the Ugaritic texts supports presenting the pantheon as divine family (so Schloen) or divine bureaucracy (so Handy). In either case, both studies point to a newer approach to divinity. Instead of focusing on particular deities, both studies seek to understand the larger concepts of family and council informing the understanding of divinity more generally. Such a combination of traditional philological *Wissenschaft* with perspectives derived from the social sciences marks a healthy advance for Ugaritic and biblical studies.[66]

At this stage of scholarship, regional and temporal variation in religion, set in a wider West Semitic context (without the old battles between "Canaanite" versus "Israelite" religion), seems to have received due recognition. We have also seen a more searching examination of the categories of myth and ritual in ancient Near Eastern studies, for example in A. Livingstone's fine work, *Mystical and Mythological Explanatory Works of Assyrian and Babylonian Scholars.*[67] His observations and questions posed by scholars in other fields have been making an impression on Ugaritic and biblical studies.[68] Here again with the wealth of Assyriology aiding the study of Ugaritic, the result has been a multiplicity of relations entertained for myth and ritual. Finally, we may note Gary A. Anderson's use of ritual theory to study mourning and lamentation.[69] His study is well founded on a long line of scholarship on the anthropology of mourning and celebration, and its application to Ugaritic and biblical texts helps to integrate the understanding of religion into its larger social context.

⋈ UGARITIC LITERATURE AND SOCIETY

We may note in passing that with this increased use of social science has come an enhanced use of literary study.[70] A particularly fine example in this period derived from the hand of Simon Parker in 1989.[71] His book examines the stock type-scenes and motifs in different Ugaritic, Hittite, Mesopotamian, and biblical texts. By paying careful attention to the general features of these types, Parker is able to discern departures from the expected norms and then to highlight the particular thematic thrust of specific texts. Here he is successful in noting the depth of family concerns running through the Aqhat text. Similarly, his analysis of the Kirta (Keret) epic recognizes the threats posed to kingship in the various parts of the text, but focuses particular attention on the benevolence, wisdom, and power of El in his support of Kirta's kingship.

In this period we may also note two books by Y. Avishur. His 1994 study, *Studies in Hebrew and Ugaritic Psalms,* turns to current issues in comparing biblical and Ugaritic poetry.[72] His 1999 volume, *Studies in Biblical Narrative,* locates Ugaritic narrative poetry within the larger context of biblical and ancient Near Eastern narrative.[73] Finally, one of the approaches made in biblical studies which has come into Ugaritic studies recently is intertextuality.[74]

The study of literature in Ugaritic and biblical studies has occasionally inspired strong claims about ancient Israel religion. For example, in his book *The Art of Biblical Narrative,* R. Alter makes the following claim about biblical narrative as distinguished from myth:

> What is crucial for the literary understanding of the Bible is that reflex away from the polytheistic genre had powerfully constructive consequences in the new medium which the ancient Hebrew writers had fashioned for their monotheistic purposes.[75]

This claim has an enormous appeal on a first reading, and indeed the suggestion that genres engender modes of discourse about divinity has had considerable influence on writers in wider fields. For example, in a volume of essays entitled *Figuring the Divine,* P. Ricoeur borrows Alter's notion here in order to argue that theology is closely tied to genre.[76] Speaking of the theology of biblical narrative, Ricoeur writes: "it is a theology that calls for the narrative mode as its major hermeneutical mode."[77] Alter's influence on Ricoeur perhaps runs deeper, for both men view genres as generating modes of discourse about divinity. Because this approach has been gaining ground in Ricoeur's work, which assumes its validity for biblical genres, the recent critique of S. B. Parker deserves notice. In an in-depth study of different genres in West Semitic inscriptions and the Bible, he notes:

> Despite his explicit commitment to a synchronic criticism of the Bible, Alter's comparative statement is diachronic—and quite misleading. First, Alter confuses literary categories (genre) and theological categories (monotheism, polytheism). Certainly, many ancient Near Eastern narratives are polytheistic in their depiction of the world, most famously the great poems in the mythic-epic tradition, but in many others, especially prose narratives, only one god or no gods appear. This suggests that the Hebrew writers did not shape a new medium but exploited and developed a well-established one. Second, although the Bible has been generally received since its compilation and closure as a monotheistic book, "the ancient Hebrew writers" were by no means all monotheists. Our literary understanding of the Bible as a whole may depend on our appreciation of its monotheism and "the monotheistic purposes" of those who determined its final shape, but our literary

understanding of the work of the "ancient Hebrew writers," writing long before that later momentous transformation of their material into a religious canon, requires that we recognize sometimes a complete disregard of the divine realm and other times the nuances of the relations among and the kind of reality accorded a variety of divine beings. In other words, ancient Near Eastern narrative cannot be lumped together under the term "polytheistic genre," and ancient Hebrew writers did not fashion "a new medium" for "monotheistic purposes."[78]

Clearly, Alter's claims are problematic, and Ricoeur's wide-ranging explorations into the relations between biblical genre and theology, which depend upon Alter's work, will require further discussion.

Finally, this period has benefited from a renewed examination of Ugaritic economy and society. The 1995 dissertation by J. D. Schloen offers an important challenge to the older economic models proposed for ancient Ugarit.[79] Schloen criticizes both the "feudal" model proposed in the postwar era by A. Alt, J. Gray, and A. Rainey, as well as the two-sector model developed by M. Heltzer and M. Liverani in the 1970s. Instead, in keeping with the attested importance of clan and families, Schloen proposes a "patrimonial household model" at all levels of Ugaritic society, including the monarchy and its mechanisms of rule.

⊠ THE SOCIAL CONTEXTS OF TEXTS

Recent shifts in thinking have resulted in another development well-known now in biblical studies, namely, the relating of texts to the different segments of societies that produce them. Texts may not represent cultures as wholes. Instead, texts are representations of the perspectives of various factions in the ongoing religious histories of Ugarit or Israel: so-called official versus popular; domestic versus public; elite versus peasant; or male versus female. The work of K. van der Toorn on the domestic and gender issues in religion deserves special note here, especially his impressive 1996 book, *Family Religion in Babylonia, Syria, and Israel*[80] and his simpler yet still useful 1994 monograph, *From Her Cradle to Her Grave*.[81] We need more historical and sociological refinements of these categories, as promised by the 1996 work on popular religion by J. Berlinerblau and revisited by him in a 1999 article.[82]

Still, "popular" and "official" religions continue to be useful categories. For example, Pardee's 1996 article reaffirms evidence for a royal funerary cult in *KTU* 1.161 and a popular mortuary (i.e., post-funerary) cult in 1.17.[83] How research will qualify these categories and their dynamic interrelationships remains to be seen. Moreover, scholars in the Ugaritic and biblical studies should compare and contrast the construction of these categories in other fields.[84]

All these changes in perspective afford some freedom to the discipline in seeing phenomena in both comparison and contrast simultaneously. Let me return to the example of the Rephaim for a moment. For about half a century, scholars contrasted the biblical attitude toward death with what was seen in the Ugaritic material as a Canaanite "embrace of death." Then the field viewed the biblical material as a reflection of an inner-Israel conflict between a popular devotion to the dead and priestly and Deuteronomic restrictions on such activity.[85] The Israelite situation has recently been viewed in more complex terms, especially with the integration of important archaeological studies, for example, in E. M. Bloch-Smith's groundbreaking 1992 study, *Judahite Burials and Beliefs about the Dead*.[86] Accordingly, how are scholars to view the Rephaim, found in Ugaritic *(rp'um)* and biblical texts *(rĕpā'îm)?* Recent studies understand the Rephaim in both corpora as heroic deceased ancestors. Both the Ugaritic and the biblical views of the Rephaim are the products of the societies that produced the texts. For Ugarit, *KTU* 1.161 makes it clear that the Rephaim represent the ancient cultural tradition with which the monarchy (and perhaps other sectors of the society) identified itself. Given the Israelite devotion to the dead, a similar view may have obtained throughout much of Iron Age Israel. A reaction to widespread practices appears in Deuteronomic texts, where the Rephaim represent the ancient cultural tradition of Israel's putative predecessors in the land, the Canaanites. In short, "Rephaim" signal cultural distance or "disidentification." The Rephaim then are cultural markers of identity, insiders for the Ugaritic monarchy and society as well as for Israelite popular religion, but outsiders for Deuteronomic authors. The putatively ancient cultural tradition of the Rephaim allows various groups to lay claim to political identity and authority. The comparative lesson is this: within greater similarities lie important differences that provide additional insight into those who produced the texts.

⊠ UGARIT AND UGARITIC *IN SITU*

The preceding chapter alludes to the disjunction between Ugaritic and biblical studies, even as the comparative agenda continues with increasing sophistication. The "pan-Ugariticism" in biblical studies of earlier decades is long past. Simplistic drawing of Ugaritic and biblical parallels has passed from fashion, allowing more attention to be paid to locating Ugarit within its larger societal and ecological context. In a healthy development, the field is coming to understand Ugarit on its own terms, apart from biblical studies.

A related development involves situating Ugaritic and Ugarit within their larger ancient Syrian context, revealed from other sites, some known for decades (Mari), others discovered more recently (Emar, Munbaqa/Tel Ekalte, 'Ain Dara, Suḫu).[87] The field appropriately no longer focuses solely on ancient Israel or the

Bible. Here French scholars have been especially active working on the material from Mari and Emar, but the contributions of others working on Emar texts, including G. Beckman, P. Carstens, J. M. Durand, D. Fleming, R. S. Hess, J. Huehnergard, T. J. Lewis, O. Loretz, W. Pitard, K. van der Toorn, and W. van Soldt also deserve mention. The field also continues to be aided by Amorite material, collected by the painstaking efforts of H. Huffmon and I. J. Gelb, and more recently by R. Zadok.[88] All these discoveries have forced scholars interested in situating the Bible in its wider West Semitic context to take a longer (perhaps more scenic) route in traveling the historical and cultural distances between Ugarit and ancient Israel.[89] The effect of such work is to locate the Ugaritic texts in the more proximate setting of late-second-millennium Syrian studies. Categorizing Ugaritic culture as "Canaanite" seems increasingly less helpful. Such an intellectual situation in no way diminishes the deep cultural and linguistic relations between the Ugaritic and biblical texts; instead, such relations will be understood more richly.

⋈ THE CURRENT STATE OF UGARITIC STUDIES

Since 1985, a handful of the older academic centers has carried on the tradition of Ugaritic research, and a few new ones have emerged. The following survey covers institutions that include doctoral-level work. Beyond these schools are many other scholars who also conduct important research on Ugaritic and the Bible. Moreover, many dissertations have been undertaken in recent years; those from 1994 on appear below.

The French Team, and P. Bordreuil and D. Pardee (the University of Chicago)

The members of the French mission to Ras Shamra continue their vast and important textual and archaeological program. After completing two decades as director of the French team (1978–1998), M. Yon has been succeeded by Y. Calvet (1999–). Yon's study of the city of Ugarit is now in English.[90] Pierre Bordreuil, the team's chief epigrapher, and Dennis Pardee, a team epigrapher, are collaborating on the publication of the Ugaritic tablets discovered from 1986 to 1992 (to appear under the direction of Daniel Arnaud), as well as those from 1994 to 2000.[91] A number of previously discovered unpublished tablets (mostly Akkadian) have been assigned to Arnaud and to Sylvie Lackenbacher, Florence Malbran-Labat, Béatrice André-Salvini, and Mirjo Salvini. Some unpublished fragments of alphabetic and syllabic texts have been given to Annie-Sophie Dalix and Carole Roche. In 1987, Dalix completed her dissertation, "Ilumilku, scribe d'Ougarit au XIIIe siècle avant J. C.," under Bordreuil's direction.[92] Bordreuil is directing two

other dissertations, Roche's on "Les per-
sonnages de la cour d'Ugarit à la fin du
XIIIe siècle"; and that of Claude Chanut,
entitled "Les matières premières à Ugarit
à l'âge du bronze récent: Bois, pierres, et
métaux à partir des données des textes et
de l'archéologie." As a long-range project,
Bordreuil and Pardee continue work on
new editions of the alphabetic tablets by
literary genre. Pardee has already published editions for the hippiatric texts and
the "para-mythological" texts.[93] His edition of the ritual texts has just appeared,
while the epistolary texts are in preparation. Other texts will follow.

Dennis Pardee (at Ras Shamra).
Courtesy of Yves Calvet.

Meanwhile, research on the archaeology of the site has been renewed in recent
years, as witnessed by work on prehistoric
archaeology by H. de Contenson,[94] and
on Bronze Age archaeology by M. Yon and the rest of the team.[95] O. Callot and
J. Margueron are preparing an architectural study of the palace. Broader exami-
nations of the culture of Ugarit have been undertaken in recent years, including
studies of architecture by O. Callot[96] and research on objects in various media at
Ugarit by A. Caubet and F. Poplin.[97]

In the United States,[98] the University of Chicago has maintained a steady
presence in the field of Ugaritic, thanks to Pardee and his students. Pardee is currently the only professor in the United States who has devoted the vast bulk of his
research to Ugaritic studies. In 1999, D. Clemens completed his dissertation, "A
Study of the Sacrificial Terminology at Ugarit: A Collection and Analysis of the
Ugaritic and Akkadian Textual Data," under Pardee. Two dissertations are also in
progress under Pardee: J. A. Fine, "The Socio-economic Organization of Metal-
workers during the Late Bronze Age Period at Ugarit"; and R. C. Hakley, "Ugaritic
Epistolography, Containing the Edition of Twenty-One New Letters."[99]

Münster: M. Dietrich and O. Loretz

The team at Münster has also continued its steady program of work even as
its heads, Dietrich and Loretz, have reached retirement age, leaving the future of
Ugaritic studies there unclear. The preceding chapter includes a discussion of the
achievements of this center.

Edinburgh: Gibson and Wyatt

At Edinburgh, doctoral studies continue under J. C. L. Gibson and N. Wyatt. J. B. Lloyd completed a dissertation in 1994 on "The Goddess Anat: An Examination of the Textual and Iconographic Evidence from the Second Millennium B.C."[100] The Edinburgh group is sponsoring further projects on deities, in a series of dissertations that recalls those supervised by Marvin Pope at Yale from the 1960s through the 1980s. In the early 1990s, Steve Wiggins wrote on Asherah,[101] and Wyatt reports Edinburgh students currently at the pre-dissertation stage working on Mot/Mawet (J. A. Armstrong) and El (R. Allan).

W. G. E. Watson at Newcastle

At Newcastle, W. G. E. Watson continues his prodigious research. He has just completed his English translation of G. del Olmo Lete's *La religión cananea según la liturgia de Ugarit: Estudio textuel,* under the title *Canaanite Religion according to the Liturgical Texts of Ugarit.* Watson is presently preparing a collection of articles on lexicography, proper names, and particles.

N. P. Lemche at Copenhagen

At Copenhagen, N. P. Lemche has sponsored research by A. R. Petersen, who published a monograph under the title, *The Royal God: Enthronement Festivals in Ancient Israel and Ugarit?*

J. C. de Moor and Kampen

At Kampen, work on Ugaritic likewise continues. Professor Johannes de Moor is pursuing two major projects: a new edition of his *Anthology of Religious Texts from Ugarit,* with the help of Dijkstra and Korpel; and a volume on the syntax of literary Ugaritic. He is also directing H. Marsman's dissertation on "The Social and Religious Position of Women in Ugarit and Israel."[102] M. Dijkstra has renewed the study of West Semitic worship as attested in the pictographic inscriptions at Serabit el-Khadem.[103]

Barcelona (G. del Olmo Lete and J. Sanmartín) and Madrid (J. L. Cunchillos)

While many other programs have been reconfigured or dropped, research in Barcelona and Madrid has accelerated. G. del Olmo Lete (Barcelona) and J. L. Cunchillos (Madrid) have managed to produce two important new centers with their own full-scale research projects and funding. Olmo Lete and Sanmartín have published their two-volume Ugaritic dictionary. They also directed the 1995 thesis of Ignazio Márquez Rowe on "El ilku en Ugarit. Estudio textual y contextual acerca del sistema tributario territorial" (University of Barcelona, 1995).[104]

Cunchillos's team, including J. P. Vita and J. A. Zamora, has also been very productive. Noted above is the 1995 three-volume concordance of Cunchillos and Vita, *Concordancia de palabras ugaríticas*. Also important is the computerbase of Ugaritic texts in the Banco de Datos Filológicos Semíticos Noroccidentales y el Sistema Integrado de Análisis Morfológico de Textos Ugaríticos headed by Cunchillos.[105]

Rome: P. Xella, A. Gianto, and P. Merlo

Xella works for the Centro Nazionale del Ricerche in Rome and sometimes teaches Ugaritic at Tübingen. In 1988, the Pontifical Biblical Institute appointed A. Gianto, a product of the Harvard program under Cross and Moran. At the Pontifical Lateran University in Rome, P. Merlo occasionally writes on Ugaritic subjects.[106]

Ben Gurion University of the Negev: C. Cohen, D. Sivan, and M. Gruber

In Israel, work on Ugaritic continues.[107] At Ben Gurion, C. Cohen is working on a companion volume to the English edition of HALAT with two coeditors, Daniel Sivan (also of Ben Gurion) and John Kaltner (of Rhodes College in Memphis, Tennessee); the volume is scheduled for completion in 2007. Cohen also pursues research for *A Comprehensive Dictionary of the Ugaritic Language*. In 1999 Aicha Rahmouni completed her dissertation, "The Divine Epithets in the Ugaritic Texts," under Cohen and Sivan. Under Cohen and Avi Hurvitz of the Hebrew University, J. N. Ford is pursuing a doctoral dissertation, "Ugaritic Prophylactic Magic: The Texts and Their Place within the Ancient Near Eastern Magical Tradition."

Tel Aviv University: E. L. Greenstein

At Tel Aviv University, Anson Rainey has recently retired. In the field of Ugaritic, he has a worthy successor in E. L. Greenstein. Few scholars have conducted as much research in the various areas of grammar and lexicography, poetry and literature of Ugaritic and the Bible as Greenstein. At present, he is working on a series of articles and a book on the art of Canaanite narrative.[108] This research includes observations on how different genres portray deities.

New York University: B. A. Levine, D. E. Fleming, and M. S. Smith

The main figure in Ugaritic studies at this university has been Baruch A. Levine, whose extrabiblical work focuses on Ugaritic and Israelite ritual texts. In particular, he has collaborated with Jean-Michel de Tarragon on studies of Ugaritic ritual texts, and they have worked on relationships between the religions of Ugarit and Israel.[109] In recent years, Levine has produced major commentaries on Leviticus for a series published by the Jewish Publication Society[110] and on Numbers for the Anchor Bible.[111] These works use Ugaritic material to illuminate problems in the biblical text. Levine also serves as an academic adviser to Brill for the area of Ugaritic studies. His colleague at New York University, Daniel E. Fleming, uses Ugaritic in his discussions of ritual information from Emar and the Bible.[112] New York University has yielded one recent dissertation that draws on Ugaritic: A. F. Robertson, "Word Dividers, Spot Markers, and Clause Markers in Old Assyrian, Ugaritic, and Egyptian Texts: Sources for Understanding the Use of Red Ink Points in the Two Akkadian Literary Texts, Adapa and Ereshkigal, found in Egypt" (1994). In 2000, Levine retired from the university, and I succeeded to his post.

Harvard: J. Huehnergard, J. A. Hackett, and L. E. Stager

At Harvard, Ugaritic continues to be taught by a pair of leading American West Semiticists, John Huehnergard and Jo Ann Hackett, both Harvard students of Cross, Moran, and Lambdin. The study of Ugaritic society is supported further in the area of iconography by Irene Winter. In addition, the archaeologist Lawrence E. Stager, in conjunction with Huehnergard and Hackett, sponsors research on Ugarit and Ugaritic. Overall the program at Harvard is incomparable in the number and strength of its appointments in the wider biblical field, and Ugaritic continues as part of the program. As noted above, Harvard has produced several dissertations in recent years: A. Brody, "Maritime Religion of the Canaanites and the Phoenicians: Aspects of the Specialized Sacral Beliefs and Practices of Levantine Seafarers" (1996), published under the title, *"Each Man Cried Out to His God": The Specialized Religion of Canaanite and Phoenician Seafarers;* M. H. Feldman, "Luxury Gods from Ras Shamra–Ugarit and Their Role in the International Relations of the Eastern Mediterranean and Near East during the Late Bronze Age (Fourteenth Century B.C., Thirteenth Century B.C., Syria)" (1998); E. C. McAfee, "The Patriarch's Longed-For Son: Biological and Social Reproduction in Ugaritic and Hebrew Epic" (1996); and J. D. Schloen, "The Patrimonial Household in the Kingdom of Ugarit: A Weberian Analysis of Ancient Near Eastern Society" (1995). A fifth is in the works: J. L. Ellison, "A Paleographic Study of the Cuneiform Alphabetic Texts from Ras Shamra/Ugarit." Related dissertations include: J. Fox, "Noun Patterns in the Semitic Languages" (1996); P. Mankowski, "Akkadian Loanwords in Biblical Hebrew" (1997); E. Pentiuc, "Studies in the Emar Lexicon" (1997); A. Emery, "Weapons of the Israelite Monarchy" (1998); J. Monson, "Architecture in Israel" (1999); P. Korchin, "Markedness and Semitic Philology" (in progress).[113]

Other North American Schools: Montreal, Yale, Penn, and Duke

Though not a traditional center of Ugaritic studies, the University of Montreal recently produced a dissertation by L. Karkajian, "La maisonnée patrimoniale divine à Ougarit: Une analyse wébérienne du dieu de la mort, Mot" (1999). Directed by Dr. Robert David, the dissertation is now published on the Internet by Presses Universitaires de Montréal at: www.pum.montreal.ca/theses/pilote/karkajian/these.html.

At Yale, the passing of Marvin Pope has meant a series of temporary appointments: mine lasted from 1987 to 1993, and F. W. Dobbs-Allsopp (a Hopkins doctorate under D. Hillers and P. K. McCarter) stayed from 1995 to 1999. No doctoral work specifically involving Ugaritic has appeared from Yale apart from R. Whitekettle's 1995 dissertation, entitled "Human Reproduction in the Textual Record of Mesopotamia and Syria-Palestine during the 1st and 2nd Millennia B.C.," and D. Green's dissertation in progress, tentatively titled "Narrating Domestic Achievements: A Study in Ancient Near Eastern Royal Propaganda." In West Semitics and biblical studies, the future configuration of Yale's program is unclear.

The University of Pennsylvania's program in Bible, led by Jeffrey Tigay, sometimes offers Ugaritic. Finally, other American institutions continue to make sporadic contributions to Ugaritic studies. For example, Duke produced one doctorate in 1993: W. D. Whitt, "Archives and Administration in the Royal Palace of Ugarit (Syria)."

Finally, compared to a generation ago, research today on Ugaritic involves a wider group of biblical and ancient Near Eastern scholars situated at many different institutions. While the number of centers has diminished, the number of scholars who include Ugaritic in their research agenda has continued at about the same level as in the period 1970–1985. The work of many scholars on Ugaritic continues to provide important data about Late Bronze Age Syria as well as crucial data for understanding ancient Israel. The following discussion provides just one example of the latter.

⚔ THE CONCEPTUAL UNITY OF POLYTHEISM AND MONOTHEISM IN UGARITIC AND BIBLICAL TEXTS

Polytheism and Monotheism from W. F. Albright to J. C. de Moor

To illustrate the continuing importance of Ugaritic to biblical studies, we may look at studies of the issue of Israelite monotheism.[114] Chapter One of this book examines works on monotheism dated to roughly the time of the discovery of the Ugaritic texts. Chapter Two discusses G. E. Mendenhall's view of polytheism as the deification of the production of fertility and power in direct contrast to the covenantal religion of Moses.[115] Utilizing Ugaritic in great detail are current works ranging from Johannes C. de Moor's *Rise of Yahwism* to my study entitled *The Origins of Biblical Monotheism*.[116] According to de Moor, the monotheism of Akhenaten set off a crisis of polytheism in Late Bronze Age Canaan. Polytheism no longer adequately explained reality, leading to a cultural and religious pessimism. De Moor sees this religious pessimism reflected in the Ugaritic mythological texts, especially in the manner in which El is abused and diminished.[117] This religious environment led in the Iron I period to Israelite monolatry.[118] De Moor also posits a pre–Iron I basis for Yahweh, for example identifying *yw* in *KTU* 1.1 IV with the name Yahweh. Few scholars today would follow either this hypothesis or de Moor's proposal that Late Bronze Age polytheism suffered a "crisis of faith," thereby paving the way for the early emergence of monotheism.[119] Ugaritic informs not only de Moor's analysis of Late Bronze Age history and culture, but also his interpretation of Israelite poetic sources, which he regards as usable guides to early Israelite history. I confess to being skeptical on all these points, but, by the same token, de Moor's research deserves attention. It does challenge some underexamined presuppositions of many scholars in the field.

The Emergence of Monotheistic Rhetoric in Late Monarchic Social and Political Dynamics

As noted in Chapter One's discussion of Meek and Albright on Israelite monotheism, the historical intelligibility and literary character of monotheistic declarations and theologies continues to require a more detailed discussion than the field has offered to date. Like de Moor's book, my study, *The Origins of Biblical Monotheism*,[120] relies on Ugaritic to situate both early Israelite polytheism and monotheism. More specifically, Ugaritic texts reveal two basic notions that provided conceptual unity in both Ugaritic and Israelite polytheism, namely the divine council and the divine family. These two constructs of divinity also illuminate the development of Israelite monotheism in the seventh and sixth centuries. In short, Ugaritic texts provide a distant backdrop for Israelite developments. Let me illustrate. Two perspectives on changes in Judean society are required to see the emergence of monotheistic statements in the seventh and sixth centuries. The first involves the theological intelligibility of a single deity to Judeans. While the language of council continues strongly in biblical texts after the Exile, the metaphor of the divine family largely disappears. What generally remained is a system headed by the chief god, his consort, subordinate deities (some as members of his retinue), astral bodies, and servant-messengers, all of which later Israelite tradition reduced further to a single god and various retainers. In contrast, Ugaritic and early Israelite polytheism expressed conceptual unity in other terms, notably in imagery concerning divine family relationships. Accordingly, we may hypothesize that, since the strongest form of social identity at Ugarit was the family, it stands to reason that the polytheistic family first and foremost may have provided the most "natural" expression of the singleness or coherence of divinity. In early Israel, meanwhile, a similar family structure long obtained (see, e.g., Ps 82), but by the seventh century the lineage system had perhaps eroded.[121] Israelite texts dating to roughly the same period as the earliest clear expressions of monotheism in Second Isaiah proclaim both that the righteousness of parents cannot save their children (Ezek 14:12–23) and that children would no longer be punished for the sins of the fathers[122] (Deut 24:16;[123] Jer 31:29–30; Ezek 18, cf. 33:12–20). For Iron IIb Judah, we may therefore posit a corollary working hypothesis: A culture with a diminished lineage system, one perhaps less connected to traditional family patrimonies due to societal changes in the eighth through sixth centuries,[124] might be more predisposed to hold to individual human accountability for behavior and to see an individual deity accountable for the cosmos. (Individual accountability on the human and divine levels may be viewed as a development concomitant with monotheism, not necessarily its cause.) Accordingly, later Israelite monotheism lost the divine family, perhaps reflecting Israel's weakening family lineages and patrimonies. In sum, the Ugaritic material helps us understand the divine family as a means of conceptual unity in polytheism. This material can aid in identifying traces of the same concept in early biblical tradition, and in understanding the diminution of this language in Iron II Israel.

Ugaritic texts also shed light on another social factor in the development of Judean monotheism, that is, on Israel's political and social decline in the face of Assyria and Babylonia.[125] Within this context, Israel elevated the understanding of its deity's mastery of the world, concluding that, while Israel was now no nation, the gods of other nations, including the greatest powers, were not really gods. Yahweh was the sole force over everything. The worldview in LXX and DSS Deut 32:8–9 had earlier posited that all the nations had their own patron gods, and Yahweh was Israel's.[126] This idea was expressed in conflictual terms in the worldview of the so-called royal psalms, a number of which contrast two sets of powers. On one side are Yahweh and his "anointed," the Judean king, who together rule from Jerusalem (Ps 2), viewed ideologically as the center of the world (cf. Pss 46, 48, and 87). On the other are the kings of the nations. Ideally speaking, they are to submit to the authority of Yahweh and his human regent on earth. Yahweh, the divine warrior-king, extends some of his own power over the cosmic enemies to the human king. According to Ps 89:26, the human king's power is to extend to Sea, the sometimes hostile, sometimes compliant cosmic force in the

Bible: "And I [Yahweh] shall set his hand [the Judean's king's] on Yam(m), and on River(s) his right hand."[127] The divine and human kings centered at Zion, the cosmic mountain, together oppose the divine and human enemies in the world. All enemies are to be defeated and submissive to the royal rule imposed by the divine king and carried out by his human counterpart. Clearly the Ugaritic material plays a role in situating this worldview. It is common to relate the language of Baal's conflict with Yamm to "Yahweh's combat with the Sea," to echo the title of C. Kloos's 1986 book.[128] Yet the relationship runs deeper. Arguably, the Baal Cycle also reflects this political "parallel" or "mirroring" worldview, with the divine and human kings arrayed against their cosmic and terrestrial enemies, respectively. In this case, we might say that here the Ugaritic and biblical material illumine each other.

In sum, the Ugaritic texts show some affinity with early Israelite material, and inner-Israelite changes manifest a departure from worldviews attested in both the Ugaritic and early Israelite texts. Technically speaking, Keel and Uehlinger are right in stating that the Ugaritic texts "are not primary sources for the religious history of Canaan and Israel,"[129] but these texts do provide some of the larger background behind the development of Israelite religion. Although the temporal, geographical, and cultural distances between the Ugaritic and biblical texts deserve attention,[130] it is precisely the differences within their larger similarities that sharpen our understanding of Israelite religion, in particular its differentiation from the larger West Semitic culture of which the Ugaritic texts constitute the most extensive extrabiblical textual witness.

⋈ THE FUTURE OF UGARITIC STUDIES

To turn to the future, we may reasonably hope that Ugaritic studies have many more contributions to make, both to biblical studies and to research on Late Bronze Age Syria. The texts and tools promised by the field within the next decade will be impressive. While it is difficult to prognosticate about future developments in a field, some trends are discernible.

Texts and Tools

Approximately sixty-four new Ugaritic texts from a family archive (Urtennu), as well as three hundred Akkadian texts from Ras Shamra, have recently come to light.[131] Texts from the 1986–1992 campaigns are to be published under the general editorship of D. Arnaud. Texts from 1994 and 1996 are still being studied. Just as the field of Ugaritic studies was reinvigorated by the publication of the texts in *Ugaritica V,* so too new texts may provide the basis for significant discoveries.

In the future, the field may expect the appearance of more and better basic tools in many different languages.[132] In the area of grammar, a revision of Sivan's grammar might be considerably more comprehensive in its examples, in its division between prose and poetry, and in its presentation of paradigms and indexes of grammatical features. J. Tropper has recently provided an important reference grammar which may spur further study.[133]

Furthermore, rapid changes in publishing technology will continue to increase. Here the work of J. L. Cunchillos Ilarri and his team offers great promise.[134] They are creating a comprehensive West Semitic data bank, the goal of which is the automatization of the process of interpreting the texts in these languages. All the Ugaritic texts have been loaded into the data base. The next steps involve the creation of concordances of words in their contexts (with ongoing updates) and the development of a morphological analyzer. At present, work continues on the identification of roots and the analysis of syntax. Eventually this work will be applied to Phoenician and Punic, then Aramaic, Palestinian dialects, and finally texts in syllabic scripts (starting with Akkadian texts from El-Amarna and Alalakh). Digital images will accompany all of these materials except Ugaritic. How the work of Cunchillos Ilarri's team will dovetail with the efforts of B. Zuckerman, W. Pitard, T. J. Lewis, et al. also to digitize Ugaritic texts remains to be seen. In any case, it may be hoped that the plans for digitalized editions will extend to all the Ugaritic texts.

Grammatical Studies

Development of basic tools will aid future linguistic research. Moreover, the increased use of linguistic theory will continue to advance the study of all West Semitic languages. The linguistic study of Ugaritic generally lags behind the investigation of Biblical Hebrew. For example, discourse analysis has made an impact on the study of Biblical Hebrew,[135] but little or none on Ugaritic. Similarly, entire volumes are now devoted to the linguistic study of Hebrew,[136] but not to Ugaritic, with the exception of a 2000 master's thesis *(memoria de licenciatura)* by A. Piquer Otero, entitled "Estudios de sintaxis verbal ugarítica en *El Combate de Ba'lu y Yammu*," directed by L. Vegas Montaner of the Universidad Complutense de Madrid. The standard grammars of Ugaritic mostly employ a relatively traditional model of grammar[137] (although there are many advances in the sections on syntax in Sivan's grammar). In contrast, the Hebrew grammar of C. H. J. van der Merwe, J. A. Naudé, and J. H. Kroeze shows a discernible shift toward deploying linguistic theory, especially in its attention to the semantic-pragmatic functions of words and their use as discourse markers.[138] It is necessary to retain the strengths of traditional grammar (especially in its grasp of comparative data) as concepts and categories drawn from linguistics continue to be applied to the study of the West Semitic languages. (Another area receiving attention involves the study of grammatical differences between direct discourse and narrative in biblical Hebrew, although a full-length grammar of the biblical Hebrew presented in direct discourse remains a desideratum of the field.) Furthermore, there are many specific issues in need of greater investigation. Three questions involving verb morphology may serve as examples.

1. Many grammatical treatments in the past have assumed in the literary texts three indicative forms, the suffixed **qatala* and the prefixed **yaqtul* preterite past and the prefixed **yaqtulu* present-future. This schema has appeared most recently in D. Sivan's grammar.[139] In his review of the book, E. L. Greenstein has argued that the two prefixed indicative forms are variants and no longer separate forms in the Ugaritic literary texts.[140] He notes several contexts where the two alleged forms are juxtaposed or parallel passages where they appear to function interchangeably. Accordingly, he suggests that the prefixed indicative form is a "historical present" in the literary texts and that the suffixed form provides backgrounding to the narrative as related by the prefixed form. Whether the prefixed forms are to be translated as "historical present" or "past" is unclear. Moreover, the use of the suffixed forms in 1.96.1–2 followed by the prefixed forms in lines 4–5 (regardless of the genre)[141] militates against Greenstein's position. Watson has noted that **qtl*- forms "can often open a narrative passage." In some passages, these forms are followed by **yqtl* forms.[142] This syntax corresponds to the classical Hebrew syntax of suffixed forms plus "*waw*-consecutive"[143] prefixed forms. To illustrate the morphological-syntactical similarity of the two constructions:

Ugaritic poetry: **qtl* + **yqtl* + **yqtl*

Biblical Hebrew prose: **qtl* + **w-yqtl* + **w-yqtl*

No one would suggest that only backgrounding is involved in the biblical examples (although such a feature might exist in some cases). Instead, both constructions begin a narrative line with the suffixed form and continue with the prefixed forms. The two forms both refer to the same time frame. Nevertheless, the challenge posed by Greenstein's argumentation is substantial, and it will represent a point of departure for future discussions of these issues.

2. An important issue about the verbal system involves the distinction made by A. Rainey between the energic indicative and the energic volitive.[144] Following Rainey, Sivan cites as examples *yrʾaʾun* (*KTU* 1.5 II 6), *tlʾuʾan* (1.14 I 33), and *tmdln* (1.19 II 8–9), all singular energic indicative forms in narrative contexts. Sivan further suggests *tmtn* in a question (1.16 I 3–4). Establishing the energic indicative requires marshalling more examples for Ugaritic and Biblical Hebrew. A parade context for the Ugaritic indicative energic is 1.6 II 31–35:

bḥrb tbqᶜnn	With a sword she splits him,
bḫṭr tdrynn	With a sieve she winnows him.
bʾišt tšrpnn	With a fire she burns him,
brḥm tṭḥnn	With millstones she grinds him,
bšd tdrᶜnn	In a field she sows him.

Cross vocalizes all of these verbs as indicative forms.[145] *KTU* 1.19 III 40–41 provides another case: *ybqr . . . ybqrnn*, "he buries . . . , he buries him." The context is clearly narrative (and therefore not volitive), and the subject is clearly singular. Two further examples may appear in the second line of the two bicolons in 1.2 I 18//34:

tn ʾilm dtqh	Give up, O Gods, the one whom you obey,
dtqyn hmlt	The one whom you obey, O Multitude.
tn ʾilm dtqh	Give up, O Gods, the one whom you obey,
dtqynh hmlt	The one whom you obey, O Multitude.

The second case adds the resumptive suffixed *-h*, but otherwise the two cases are identical. The form is clearly singular, since the vocative, *hmlt*, is singular. Moreover, the context shows that the verb is indicative, not volitive.[146] As these cases all suggest, the best test for an indicative energic involves a singular form in a non-volitive context, especially in narrative. Accordingly, a BH example is perhaps furnished by the poem of Exod 15 (as with many archaic features). Exodus 15:2 reads:

zeh ʾēlî wěʾanwēhû	This is my god, and I will glorify him,
ʾělōhê ʾābî	
waʾărōmĕmenhû	The god of my father, and I will exalt him.

The final verb is clearly indicative and singular; accordingly, one may suspect an old energic indicative form. However, more persuasive examples of the form should be adduced before it is viewed as firmly established.[147]

   3. A difficult morphological question involves an obscure verbal form identified and discussed by R. Williams.[148] According to Williams's well-known article on the *G*-passive stem in Biblical Hebrew, there is a **qutal* passive participle (distinguished from the far more common **qatul* passive participle). For example, Williams identifies the form in Exod 3:2, Judg 13:8, 2 Kgs 2:10, Isa 18:2, 7, 48:12, and Prov 25:19. In the first of these passages, Moses is tending his flock on Mount Horeb when he turns aside to see the burning bush, called *hassěneh*, which is "not consumed" *(ʾênennû ʾukkāl)*. The verbal form is unlikely to be a *D*-stem passive ("pual") perfect as in the MT pointing, since this root has an active *G*-stem but no active *D*-stem and since **ʾên-* usually governs a participle.

Recourse to the *G*-stem passive participle *qatul* is also unlikely given the absence of *waw* in the consonantal writing; only if the form were defective and the Masoretic vocalization incorrect could this form be posited. The form may be an alternative *qutal* form of the *G*-stem passive participle. M. H. Pope noted many of the cases involved and suggested that the same morphological base may lie behind the form *haššûlammît* in Song 7:1–2.[149] These examples raise a number of issues, especially as to the origin of the form. Its closest morphological base is the *G*-passive indicative suffixed form *qutal.* Accordingly, G. Becker suggests that *qatul* is the passive participle of *G*-stem active perfect *qatala* form while *qutal* is the passive participle of a *G*-stem passive perfect *qutala* form.[150] The reasoning is logical; the proposal would benefit from further corroboration.

Whether the form occurs in Ugaritic is difficult to determine, given the language's lack of clearly indicated vowel patterns. Only a first *aleph* root of the pattern **ʾuCC,* attested where a passive participle might be expected, would indicate a possible *qutal* passive participle in Ugaritic. The only example that leaps to mind is the controverted word *ʾuzr,* in *KTU* 1.17 I 2–3, 6–8, 9–11, 11–13. In his translation of 1.17 I 2, S. B. Parker renders *ʾuzr ʾilm ylḥm,* "Girded, [Daniel] gives food to the gods."[151] In the note to his translation, N. Wyatt identifies the form as a *G*-passive participle (without specifying the morphology).[152] This case meets the morphological and syntactical criteria for a *qutal* participial form. Sivan also identifies the form as a *G*-stem passive participle, but offers the phonological interpretation that the form may have involved assimilation of the first vowel to the second (i.e., **ʾuzuru < **ʾazuru).[153] If so, then this form would provide no evidence of an original *qutal* form in Ugaritic, and might hint at a more complex development behind the Hebrew forms. Whether Ugaritic or Biblical Hebrew contains more examples of this form also requires further investigation.

Lexicography and Semantics

Lexicographical research has long benefited from comparison of words in different languages. The second volume of a new Ugaritic dictionary has appeared recently. As the fields of lexicography and semantics continue to make headway in biblical studies,[154] more sophisticated lexicographical research will also be pursued for Ugaritic. One dimension of lexicography, not sufficiently appreciated to date, involves the semantics of roots that have coalesced in a Semitic language.[155] Ugaritic shows coalescence of a few originally different roots, including initial **w-/y-.* Biblical examples should theoretically be more numerous, as this language reflects coalescence of more consonants. As a result, two originally different roots appeared to ancient speakers of these languages as different meanings of a single word. We may briefly consider one instance well-known from Ugaritic, and three other possible examples involving both Ugaritic and Hebrew.

Ugaritic offers a good example of coalescence of first *w-/y-* roots and their subsequent semantic coalescence with the word *yd*. The Ugaritic word is literally "hand," but it is also a term for "love," with the further connotation of "penis." Two originally different roots seem to underlie Ugaritic *yd*, namely the primitive biconsonantal *yd*, "hand" and the triconsonantal *wdd*, "love."[156] In both Ugaritic and Hebrew, these two have coalesced, and the meaning of the former seems to have affected the semantics of the latter. It would appear that the semantic connotation of "love" underlying *wdd* has come to exert a connotation on the meaning of *yd*, "hand," by taking on the nuances of "passion" and "penis." The usage may be illustrated by two passages. Ugaritic *yd* is sometimes a euphemism for penis, as in CTA 1.23.33–35:

tʾirkm yd ʾil kym	El's penis extends like the sea,
wyd ʾil kmdb	Indeed, El's penis, like the flood.
ʾark yd ʾil kym	El's penis extends like the sea,
wyd ʾil kmdb	Indeed, El's penis, like the flood.

Pope argues for wordplay here: as love is involved, the Ugaritic texts present concrete actions, not abstractions.[157] *KTU* 1.4 IV 38–39 likewise uses both *yd* and *ʾahbt* in a sexual manner. After Athirat's journey to El, he offers her food and drink and then more:

Or, does the love *(yd)* of El the King excite you,

The affection *(ʾahbt)* of the Bull arouse you?

It is evident that, to the users of Ugaritic, the original semantics of love and hand had merged. Other examples might be adduced, for example *ypʿ* ("to arise") and *wpʿ* ("to shine forth") in 1.3 III 37–38, or *nʿm* ("attractive")[158] and *nǵm* (term for a singer)[159] in 1.3 I 18–19 (cf. Pss 81:3; 135:3; 147:1), or possibly *ʿlm* ("eternity")[160] and *ǵlm* ("darkness," based on the BH usage of this root,[161] possibly Ugaritic *ǵlmt*, "darkness" [?][162] and supported by the Targum) in Eccl (Qohelet) 3:11.[163] In sum, the semantics of the lexicon require further consideration. These handfuls of examples indicate areas of research needed for Ugaritic grammar and its possible correspondences in Biblical Hebrew.

Poetry

In the area of poetry, the new trends developing since 1970 continue to engage critics. One area in need of further exploration concerns the structural relationships between colons (what I like to call the "microlevel") and whole poems or parts of the longer narrative poems (what I would label the "macrolevel"). As the discussion in Chapter Three notes, work on the microlevel received a tremendous amount of attention beginning in the 1970s, and some authors explored features shared by these two levels, and since then work has progressed, thanks to W. G. E. Watson and others.[164] Especially in biblical poetry, several features exhibited in colons are replicated over larger units of poetry. Various poetic phenomena regularly associated with the poetry within colons can be shown to apply as well to clusters of colons. For example, poetic parallelism, a hallmark of West Semitic poetry, exists in the construction of groups of colons or even entire poems. For example, the colons of *KTU* 1.2 I 24–28 and Ps 27:1 show the structure aba'b', a basic pattern found within colons.[165] Major sections of poems may be parallel in content or theme. Reflecting different sorts of balance, poems of about twenty-five verses or less usually divide into major units of two, three, or four major sections (as indicated by refrains, discussed below).[166] A good example of such balance is Ps 1, which balances two major sections, vv. 1–3 and 4–5, and then closes with a final statement reflecting on the two types of persons described in the two major sections.

Sonant parallelism does not occur only within pairs of words in colons; it also functions across the macrolevel, for example in Ps 8: the particle "how, what" *(mâ)*, occurs in the *inclusio*n of vv. 2 and 10, and the third appears in the middle of the psalm in v. 5;[167] the consonants *shin* and *mem* appear in different sections: in "name" (**šēm*) in both vv. 2 and 10, "heavens" (**šāmayim*) in vv. 2b and 9a, "your heavens" *(šāmĕkā)*, the second word in v. 4, and "you made him rule" *(tamšîlēhû)*, the first word in in v. 7.

Chiasm appears at every level of Hebrew rhetoric, from the colon to the arrangement of the whole Pentateuch![168] It is also common on the level of the overall structures of individual psalms. Many psalms arrange groups of colons in chiastic or concentric structures. For example, Ps 1 exhibits the following chiastic arrangement:

> A: the just defined in contrast to wicked's company (v. 1)
>> B: the just defined in terms of divine teaching (v. 2)
>>> C: comparison of the just with fruitful tree (v. 3a–c)
>>>> D: all the just does prospers (v. 3d)
>>>> D': not so, the wicked (v. 4a)
>>> C': comparison of the wicked with chaff (v. 4b)
>> B': the wicked defined in terms of divine judgment (v. 5a)
> A': the wicked defined in contrast with the upright's company (v. 5b)

The chiastic arrangement here might be viewed as contributing to the psalm's meaning. While the parallelism of sections delineates the two types of people, the chiastic structure here reinforces the contrasts between them. Other psalms, such as Pss 3, 8, 11, 12, and 15, manifest chiasm as a macrostructure.

Repeated words or phrases, a feature found within colons, also function to organize psalms or parts of psalms.[169] In some cases these are the feature on the macrolevel corresponding to word-pairs on the microlevel. The question, "How long?" is posed four times in a row in the first half of Ps 13. (The same question is found in sections of Mesopotamian laments.)[170] Similarly, Ps 29 uses the word *qôl* ("voice") seven times in the body of the poem. Key words or phrases may be combined with other structures such as chiasm, for example, in Ps 8:3–4 and 7–9, where the key phrase, "the works of your fingers/hands," is part of its chiastic structure. Another example of a key phrase used with a larger chiastic structure appears in Ps 12. This poem uses the key-phrase *běnê ʾādām*, "humanity" (literally "sons of a human"), in vv. 2 and 9, in sections A and A':

A v. 2: prayer for help, with invocation of Yahweh, and complaint
  B vv. 3–4 characterization of liars' speech
    C v. 5 direct discourse of liars
    C' v. 6 direct discourse of Yahweh
  B' v. 7 characterization of Yahweh's speech
A' vv. 8–9 prayer for help, with invocation of Yahweh, and complaint

In this example, the key phrase helps to reinforce the frame that vv. 2 and 8–9 form around the rest of the psalm.

While inclusions frame the body of a psalm, refrains occur at the end of stanzas. Or, to put it differently, a refrain "is a verse that is repeated at regular intervals in a poem"[171] (although some minor variations may appear in the refrains). A preeminent example of the refrain occurs in Pss 42–43 (like Pss 9–10, Pss 42–43 form a single poem). According to P. Raabe, other examples of psalms with refrains are Pss 39, 46, 49, 56, 57, 59, 67, and 80.[172] Psalms 46, 49, 56, 57, 59, and 80 all have internal refrains plus a final refrain, while Pss 39, 56, and 67 show internal refrains with no final refrain. Refrains are important for the study of Hebrew poetry more generally. Refrains divide poems into two (Pss 49, 57, 99), three (Pss 42–43, 46), or four parts (Pss 59, 80), indicating a highly developed sense of symmetry.[173] Division into units of two, three, or four parts is not exclusive to poems with refrains. Rather, it seems to constitute the basic division within poems of about twenty-five verses or less. Both inclusion and refrains are analogous to parallelism within a colon.

Ellipsis, a feature common in the second line of bicolons or the third line of tricolons, also appears in the imagery of stanzas. For example, the first part of Ps 1 mentions both the tree that stands for good people as well as its product, "its fruit," but the second section of the psalm omits any mention of the plant that stands for the wicked and discusses only the product of the plant, "the chaff." This ellipsis focuses attention on the bad end to which the wicked come.

In sum, then, the fundamental formal features of Hebrew poems are balance and repetition. These two features occur on both the smallest level, in bicolons and tricolons, and on the largest level, the poem or its stanzas. Parallelism, too, is found both within the small unit of the colon and the large unit of the whole poem. More specific features, such as chiasm, wordplay, and ellipsis, exist on both levels. West Semitic poetry replicates many structures at various levels of complexity. Hebrew poetry achieves a remarkable aesthetic, with small and large units mirroring one another in diverse ways. It deserves further study.

Religion, Iconography, and the Problematic Nature of Modern Categories

In the future, many long-standing areas of inquiry will continue. For example, the study of deities shows no signs of abating. It might be worth pursuing a "deity geography," namely plotting the known cultic sites of West Semitic deities in different periods and noting changes over time. Such a "macro-examination" may show the changing configurations of cults, and thus provide a deeper understanding of the deities themselves.

In addition to works on texts and archaeology, the field will continue to benefit from studies of iconography. As noted at the outset of this chapter, the 1992 study of Othmar Keel and Christoph Uehlinger, *Göttinen, Götter, und Gottessymbole*, is presently the standard work on the iconography of West Semitic religions, and it has been followed by many other works focusing attention on what iconography reveals about the religion of Ugarit, Israel, and their neighbors.[174] This area of research is greatly enhancing scholarly interpretation of the past. In their book, Keel and Uehlinger offer many methodological comments, and they occasionally use the language of grammar for iconography.[175] To follow up their analogy between language and iconography, the field would certainly benefit from a "grammar of iconography," that is, a more systematic explication of the system of visual imagery and its relationships to other sources, applied to the record from the Middle Bronze Age through the Iron Age. Such a work, if truly feasible, would help provide a rigorous way of integrating iconographic information into the larger reconstruction of ancient cultures. Such a study would help those working with texts and other artifacts to understand the theoretical basis for the interpretation of iconography. In sum, such work would engender a healthy methodological dialogue among scholars of antiquity.

Enhanced tools in religion and iconography should also help scholars to assess their own thinking more deeply. Over the last few years, I have been deeply impressed by the ongoing influence of scholarly categories developed in the nineteenth and early twentieth centuries. For example, Sir James George Frazer's *Golden Bough* has had a profound influence on the formation of the religious categories of "dying and rising gods" or sacred kingship.[176] Frazer did identify some important factors, but he flattened out differences within categories and abstracted examples of such categories from their cultural settings.

Standard analytic terminology and categories appropriately continue to be questioned. For example, the category "religion" has come to be regarded as a relatively modern term of discourse developed in post-Enlightenment Western society to justify an ideologically constructed "secular" world.[177] Accordingly, it represents a category alien to the ancient world. As the ongoing discussion of this term illustrates, the analysis of the ancient world faces an increasing theoretical challenge. On the one hand, scholars in ancient studies have found analytical help in social sciences and comparative literature. On the other hand, enlisting the aid of other fields requires an engagement with their problems. The vocabulary used to discuss phenomena in the world, ancient or modern, is becoming increasingly problematized. For example, in his 1999 Charles Homer Haskins Lecture, Clifford Geertz expressed the difficulty with the term "culture":

> Everyone knows what cultural anthropology is about: it's about culture. The trouble is that no one is quite sure what culture is. Not only is it an essentially contested concept, like democracy, religion, simplicity, or social justice, it is a multiply defined one, multiply employed, ineradicably imprecise. It is fugitive, unsteady, and encyclopedic, and normatively charged, and there are those, especially those for whom only the really real is really real, who think it vacuous altogether, or even dangerous, and would ban it from the serious discourse of serious persons. An unlikely idea, it would seem, around which to try to build a science. Almost as bad as matter.[178]

An equally great difficulty involves the limits of knowledge and method. Mark Taylor well warns of the theoretical problems involved:

> Critics of theology often embrace the methods of social sciences ranging from history and psychology to sociology and anthropology with an enthusiasm bordering on the religious. As it assumes ever greater importance, methodology approaches the status of "queen of the sciences" once reserved for theology. The Cartesian promise of a proper method is, in fact, a secularized version of theology's dream of an unconditional principle of principles. For those with eyes to see, theology casts a long—perhaps inescapable—shadow.[179]

While the fields of ancient studies will continue to expunge outdated anthropological paradigms and to turn for guidance to social science literature present,y available, they will meet major theoretical challenges.

Similar questions obtain in the literary study of biblical and Ugaritic tex The past two decades have seen increasing calls for a more rigorous scrutiny ot readers' assumptions and methodologies. For example, the authors of the 1995

Postmodern Bible call for a radical assessment of reading strategies and their ideological agendas.[180] The work largely rejects historical criticism in favor of more recent "postmodern" literary methodologies. It would be easy to level criticisms at this book. Despite his clear sympathy for postmodern reading, R. P. Carroll offers a critique of *The Postmodern Bible* on its own terms.[181] He attacks the lack of the study of the Bible in *The Postmodern Bible,* its effort to make a bid for intellectual hegemony within the biblical guild, its "highly authoritarian and totalizing ideology of its own (made up of so many parts race and gender and so many parts egalitarianism)," its uncritical posture toward the "new gods" of postmodernism, and its lack of any writers who are not privileged whites.

Moreover, the authors of this book ignore or take for granted the gains made by historical criticism, such as philological study. They set up historical criticism and "the biblical guild" as barely unvariegated hypostases, even straw men, to serve their ideological purposes. Indeed, it is regularly claimed that "the notion of a stable text with determinate meanings" is a hallmark of historical criticism, but it is historical criticism in the biblical field that has helped to undermine the notion of a stable text by showing the limits of its own approach. Moreover, the book's call to challenge reigning structures of power and meaning begs for its own self-critical ideological analysis, but such substantive self-scrutiny is absent.[182] This point leads to the ideological paradox of the readings put forward by the authors of *The Postmodern Bible:* they garner prestige for their own methods and viewpoints by means of the Bible, a collection of texts deriving their massive prestige in the West from religious traditions that the authors themselves play down or ignore. That is, the book lacks a coherent discussion of the authors' epistemology: how do they know what they know about their methodologies? The book is further marred by an uncritical use of psychoanalysis and other postmodern modes of reading, an uncritical presentation of radical political commitments, and an unprofessional claim to authority in invading intellectual territory of modern history.[183] In sum, the authors seem to regard historical critics as naive, even as they try to coopt historical criticism (though without providing any epistemological coherence or intelligibility as to how this linkage is to be made).[184] In the end, the very sort of intellectual naivete attributed to historical criticism mars this book.

One might list other problems that the book does not face fairly. However, such criticism would miss the fundamental value that such work holds. All biblical interpreters, whether historical or postmodern, need to be critically aware of their own reading biases and the shifting ground of their own interpretive location; this point is incontrovertible. The circular character of historical-critical arguments is equally evident. Furthermore, any interpreter should applaud "discussions of what you can know and how you can know it . . . how you as a subject of knowledge are shaped . . . and who benefits ultimately from what you claim to know."[185] Even if historical criticism's "foundations shake" at the repeated waves of ahistorical (and perhaps antireligious) methods washing over it, its theoretical basis will ultimately be stronger from the engagement. General theories, whether traditional or modern, will give way to the "postmodern" readings of literature and culture, capable of offering open-ended, tentative possibilities (the description of this intellectual landscape is a contribution of *The Postmodern Bible*).[186] Instead of searching for a grand unified theory of reading, it may be more intellectually productive in the long run to entertain intersections between interpretations and approaches operating out of widely varying frames of reference.

Such a view of matters does not validate the stereotypical critique of the biblical guild found in *The Postmodern Bible* or other works. Critics who condemn the field as hostile to either nonspecialists or scholars who do not subscribe to its "accepted reading strategies and conclusions" are poor readers of biblical scholarship. In the last two decades, historical criticism has hardly been the hegemonic enterprise that its critics have made it out to be. Few fields have been as open to nonspecialists and dissenting scholars as the biblical guild. (The success of a work such as *The Postmodern Bible* is proof of this very point.) The dissenters have not just stormed the gates; they are respectable members of the so-called guild who secure tenure and develop doctoral programs espousing their approaches in reading. Indeed, biblical studies meets one postmodern criterion; it is "unruly" and "decentralized,"[187] insofar as it constitutes a series of atomized subspecialties or intellectual boutiques, rarely coercing so-called dissenters who demonstrate basic knowledge of primary sources.

Scholars of Ugaritic and Bible should continue to insist on a rigorous knowledge of primary sources even as the discipline engages recently developed methods. All who enter biblical studies should have their insights noted, appreciated, and refined, as the Bible is hardly the private domain of scholars. By the same token, the research of specialists or nonspecialists alike legitimately deserves criticism if it does not exhibit knowledge of primary sources. A field lacking basic professional standards is by definition not professional, and failure to invoke such standards surrenders its identity as an arena for rigorous research.

In the end, there will not be any easy combination of historical-critical methods with postmodern approaches. However, as a positive result of such intellectual interaction, future research will contextualize its methods and results with increasing theoretical complexity.

Ugaritic and/or Biblical Studies

Perhaps it would be appropriate to conclude this survey with a word of caution. Ugaritic studies will be successful *despite* a major negative trend. For about three decades, the field has atomized into a host of subspecialties. In contrast, older scholars such as Albright and Mowinckel combined deep learning of many different aspects of the ancient record with the courage to synthesize them. On the one hand, the task requires fundamental textual and archaeological analysis. The field will not flourish without a solid knowledge of the languages and material culture involved. On the other hand, the field of Ugaritic and biblical studies will push ahead as the works of its practitioners cumulatively undertake more complex models of cultural analysis for Ugarit and Israel. Accordingly, researchers will need to be prepared to interact with perspectives and frameworks derived from other disciplines. For example, biblical scholars have pursued a considerable amount of social science research since the 1970s, and the subsequent discussion—perhaps predictably—has included consideration of the difficulties involved in applying models developed from research on contemporary societies.[188] In the 1990s, such issues have been faced with increasing sophistication.[189] In the future, the field as a whole will require knowledge of Ugaritic and the Bible, along with the developing disciplines of social science, as well as the capacity to produce larger syntheses with a mastery of minutiae, all with the awareness of great gaps and differences within the larger continuities between Ugarit and Israel. No one person can accomplish all this. Still, one may hope for works that do manage to combine traditional philological and historical investigations with study of the various sorts of realia brought to light by texts or archaeological evidence, and then relate them in a critical manner to pertinent discussions in other disciplines. The Ras Shamra–Ougarit series has provided some examples of such work for Ugarit proper; the task of the field will require extending this sort of investigation.

This point leads to another emerging development. Although the field of Ugaritic may prosper despite the increasing lack of historical study in the biblical field, the short-term effect may be neglect from the biblical side. However, the long-term effect could well involve the recontextualizing of Ugaritic studies within the larger Syrian setting of the Late Bronze Age. In part this will derive from a new account of the archaeology of Ugarit. In the future, we will have to take the scenic route from Ugaritic to ancient Israel via other Levantine sites of the second and first millennia. There is no longer any direct route, a blessing in disguise. We will learn much more about Ugarit and ancient Israel by taking such a long route. Moreover, we will benefit from the current distance between biblical and Ugaritic studies, as we test some of the new methods and tools available in biblical studies and apply them to Ugaritic studies. In the end, such learning will help us abandon facile comparisons in favor of more complex ones.

In retrospect, the Ugaritic texts have fulfilled their promise for biblical studies. No older corpus from Syria or Mesopotamia, no roughly contemporary corpus such as the Mari texts, the El-Amarna letters, or the Emar texts (though these still hold considerable promise!), or even later texts such as the Dead Sea Scrolls, have made the same impact on the understanding of Israel's languages and culture. When we turn to Iron Age Israel, in particular the origins and early development of ancient Israelite culture or the origins of biblical literature and religion, it is the corpus of Ugaritic texts that has transformed the understanding of these areas. This they have done for over seventy years and, we may hope, will continue to do.

⋈ NOTES

1. Bordreuil and Pardee, *La Trouvaille épigraphique de l'Ougarit: 1. Concordance* (RSO 5/1; Paris: Editions Recherche sur les Civilisations, 1989); van Soldt, *Studies in the Akkadian of Ugarit: Dating and Grammar* (AOAT 40; Neukirchen-Vluyn: Neukirchener Verlag, 1991).

2. Hess, "A Comparison of the Ugarit, Emar, and Alalakh Archives," in *Ugarit, Religion and Culture*, 75–83; and Rosengren Petersen, "Where Did Schaeffer Find the Clay Tablets of the Ugaritic Baal-Cycle," *SJOT* 8 (1994): 45–60; republished in *The Royal God: Enthronement Festivals in Ancient Israel and Ugarit?* (Copenhagen International Seminar 5; JSOTSup 259; Sheffield: Sheffield Academic Press, 1998), 72–85. Anthony Appa, a doctoral candidate at Harvard, has written an unpublished paper on this topic, and Duncan Burns, a graduate student at Sheffield, is pursuing this topic at present.

3. Keel and Uehlinger, *Göttinen, Götter, und Gottessymbole* (QD 134; Fribourg: Herder, 1992); now in English as *Gods, Goddesses, and Images of God in Ancient Israel* (trans. T. Trapp; Minneapolis: Fortress, 1998). For Ugarit, see also P. Amiet, *Corpus des cylindres de Ras Shamra–Ougarit II: Sceaux–cylindres en hématitie et pierres diverses* (RSO 9; Paris: Editions Recherche sur les Civilisations, 1992); I. Cornelius, *The Iconography of the Canaanite Gods Reshef and Ba'al: Late Bronze Age I Periods (c. 1500–1000 BCE)* (OBO 140; Freiburg, Switzerland: Universitätsverlag; Göttingen: Vandenhoeck & Ruprecht, 1994); and his follow-up article, "The Iconography of the Canaanite Gods Reshef and Baal: A Rejoinder," *JNWSL* 24 (1998): 167–77; and M. Klingbeil, *Yahweh Fighting from Heaven: God as Warrior and as God of Heaven in the Hebrew Psalter and Ancient Near Eastern Iconography* (OBO 169; Freiburg, Switzerland: Universitätsverlag; Göttingen: Vandenhoeck & Ruprecht, 1999). See also Cornelius's articles: "Anat and Qudshu as the 'Mistress of Animals': Aspects of the Iconography of the Canaanite Goddesses," *SEL* 10 (1993): 21–43; "The Visual Representation of the World in the Ancient Near East and the Hebrew Bible," *JNWSL* 20 (1994): 193–218; "The Iconography of Divine War in the Pre-Islamic Near East: A Survey," *JNWSL* 21 (1995): 15–36.

4. Mettinger, *No Graven Image? Israelite Aniconism in Its Ancient Near Eastern Context* (ConBOT 42; Stockholm: Almqvist & Wiksell, 1995). See the essays largely in response to Mettinger in *The Image and the Book: Iconic Cults, Aniconism, and the Rise of Book Religion in Israel and the Ancient Near East* (ed. K. van der Toorn; Contributions to Biblical Exegesis and Theology 21; Leuven: Peeters, 1997); and T. J. Lewis's important review article entitled "Divine Images: Aniconism in Ancient Israel," *JAOS* 118 (1998): 36–53 (with extensive bibliography).

5. For the issues raised in this paragraph, see the survey in W. W. Hallo, *Origins: The Ancient Near Eastern Background of Some Modern Western Institutions* (Leiden: Brill, 1997), 35–38.

6. See also A. K. Irvine and A. F. L. Beeston, "New Evidence on the Qatabanian Letter Order," *Proceedings of the Seminar for Arabian Studies* 21 (1988): 35–38.

7. Loundine (= Lundin), "L'origine de l'alphabet," *Cahiers de l'Institut de Linguistique de Louvain* 11/1–2 (1985): 173–202; and "L'abécédaire de Beth Shemesh," *Muséon* 100 (1987): 243–50. For a rejection of Loundine's interpretation, see E. A. Knauf, "The Migration of the Script, and the Formation of the State in South Arabia," *Proceedings of the Seminar for Arabian Studies* 19 (1989): 1–8.

8. Ryckmans, "A. G. Lundin's Interpretation of the Beth Shemesh Abecedary: A Presentation and Commentary," *Proceedings of the Seminar for Arabian Studies* 18 (1988): 123–29, and "Aux origines de l'alphabet," *Bulletin Séance. Académie royale des Sciences d'Outre Mer* 32 (1986/3): 311–33; E. Puech, "La tablette cunéiforme de Beth Shemesh, premier témoin de la séquence des lettres du sud-sémitique," in *Phoinikeia grammata, lire et écrire en Méditerranée: Actes du colloque de Liège, 15–18 novembre 1989* (ed. C. Baurain, C. Bonnet, and V. Krings; Studia Phoenicia, Collection d'études classiques 6; Namur: Société des Etudes Classiques, 1991), 33–47.

9. Cf. Sass (*The Genesis of the Alphabet*, 167) dates the South Arabian borrowing to the eleventh–tenth centuries based on the similarity of some South Arabian letter forms with those attested in Phoenician. Another abecedary, this time written in a North Arabian script with a twenty-eight-letter alphabet, was discovered at Khirbet es-Samra (halfway between Amman and Bosra) in 1989. See W. J. Jobling, "The Ugaritic Alphabet and the Khirbet es-Samra Ostracon," in *Ugarit and the Bible*, 151–58.

10. See P. Bordreuil and D. Pardee, "Un abécédaire du type sud-sémitique découvert en 1988 dans les fouilles archéologiques françaises de Ras Shamra-Ougarit," *CRAIBL* (1995): 855–60.

11. Dietrich and Loretz, *Die Keilalphabete: Der phönizisch-kanaanäischen und altarabischen Alphabete in Ugarit* (ALASP 1; Münster: Ugarit-Verlag, 1988); "The Cuneiform Alphabets of Ugarit," *UF* 21 (1989): 101–12; and "Die Keilalphabete aus Ugarit," in *Phoinikeia grammata, lire et écrire en Méditerranée: Actes du colloque de Liège, 15–18 novembre 1989* (ed. C. Baurain, C. Bonnet, and V. Krings; Studia Phoenicia, Collection d'études classiques 6; Namur: Société des Etudes Classiques, 1991), 49–67; and Loretz, "The Ugaritic Script," in *Handbook of Ugaritic Studies*, 81–89. For a qualified acceptance of some of Dietrich and Loretz's positions, see P. Swiggers, "Linguistic Considerations on Phoenician Orthography," in *Phoinikeia grammata* (ed. Baurain, Bonnet, and Krings), 116–17. See in another vein, B. E. Colless, "Recent Discoveries Illuminating the Origin of the Alphabet," *Abr-Nahrain* 26 (1988): 30–67.

12. Knauf, "The Migration of the Script, and the Formation of the State in South Arabia"; Sass, "The Beth Shemesh Tablet and the Early History of the Proto-Canaanite, Cuneiform, and South Semitic Alphabets," *UF* 23 (1991): 315–25. See also idem, *The Genesis of the Alphabet and Its Development in the Second Millennium B.C.* (Ägypten und Altes Testament 13; Wiesbaden: Harrassowitz, 1988), 161–68. See also H. Hayajneh and J. Tropper, "Die Genese des altsüdarabichen Alphabets," *UF* 29 (1997): 183–98.

13. Rosenthal, review of Gordon, *Ugaritic Handbook, Or* 18 (1949): 254–56; see Chapter Two.

14. Rosenthal, review of Garbini and Durant, *Introduzione alla lingue semitiche*, *JAOS* 166 (1996): 280.

15. Reported by John Noble Wilford, "Egyptian Carvings Set Earlier Date for Alphabet," *New York Sunday Times* (14 November 1999): 1, 16 (Section A); and J. Darnell, F. W. Dobbs-Alsopp, P. K. McCarter, Jr., and B. Zuckerman, "The Wadi el-Hol Inscriptions: Paleo-Canaanite Writing of Extreme Antiquity Discovered in Upper Egypt" (paper presented at the Annual Meeting of the Society of Biblical Literature, Boston, 22 November 1999).

16. Cunchillos and Zamora, *Gramática ugarítica elemental* (Madrid: Ediciones Clásicas, 1995).

17. Sivan, *Ugaritic Grammar* (Biblical Encyclopaedia Library; Jerusalem: Mosad Bialik, 1993) (Heb.).

18. Sivan, *A Grammar of the Ugaritic Language* (HdO 1/28; Leiden: Brill, 1997).

19. Gordon, *Ugaritic Textbook* (AnOr 38; revised reprint; Rome: Pontifical Biblical Institute, 1998); Segert, *A Basic Grammar of the Ugaritic Language* (4th printing; Berkeley: University of California Press, 1997).

20. Garr, "On Voicing and Devoicing in Ugaritic," *JNES* 45 (1986): 45–52; Voigt, "On Voicing and Devoicing in Ugaritic," in *Semitic Studies in Honour of Wolf Leslau on the Occasion of His Eighty-Fifth Birthday* (ed. A. S. Kaye; 2 vols.; Wiesbaden: Harrassowitz, 1991), 2:1619–31.

21. See W. Mayer, "The Hurrian Cult at Ugarit," in *Ugarit, Religion and Culture,* 205–12; D. Pardee, "L'ougaritique et le hourrite dans les textes rituels de Ras Shamra– Ougarit," in *Mosaïque de langues mosaïques culturelle: Le bilinguisme dans le Proche-Orient ancien. Actes de la Table-Ronde du novembre 1995 organisée par l'URA 1062 'Etudes Sémitiques'* (ed. F. Briquel-Chatonnet; Antiquités Sémitiques 1; Paris: Maisonneuve, 1996), 63–80.

22. Van Soldt, *Studies in the Akkadian of Ugarit: Dating and Grammar,* 21 n. 182; and "The Written Sources: 1. The Syllabic Akkadian Texts," in *Handbook of Ugaritic Studies,* 35 n. 52.

23. See F. Malbran-Labat, "Les archives de la Maison d'Ourtenu," *CRAIBL* (1995): 447–48. See also Dalix, "Exemples de bilinguisme à Ougarit. 'Iloumilku: La double identité d'un scribe," in *Mosaïque de langues mosaïques culturelle,* 81–90; and W. Pitard, "The Alphabetic Ugaritic Texts," in *Handbook of Ugaritic Studies,* 54–55.

24. Van Soldt, *Studies in the Akkadian of Ugarit: Dating and Grammar,* 522–23; see also his summary in "The Written Sources: 1. The Syllabic Akkadian Texts," 45. For Hurrian influence at Ugarit, see the works cited in the preceding note.

25. See the remarks of O. Loretz, "Ugariter, 'Kanaanaeer,' und 'Israeliten,'" *UF* 24 (1992): 249–58; Pardee, review of Loretz, *Ugarit and the Bible, JAOS* 117 (1997): 375–78.

26. H. L. Ginsberg, "The Northwest Semitic Languages," in *The World History of the Jewish People. Vol. II. Patriarchs* (ed. B. Mazar; Tel Aviv: Jewish History Publications, 1967), 102–24.

27. For example, Barstad, *The Religious Polemics of Amos: Studies in the Preaching of Am 2, 7B-8, 4, 1–13, 5, 1–27, 6, 4–7, 8, 14* (VTSup 34; Leiden: Brill, 1984).

28. Ahlström, *Aspects of Israelite Syncretism in Israelite Religion* (Lund: Gleerup, 1963); and *Royal Administration and National Religion in Ancient Palestine* (Studies in the History of the Ancient Near East 1; Leiden: Brill, 1982); Smith, *Palestinian Parties and Politics That Shaped the Old Testament* (New York: Columbia University Press, 1971).

29. Levine and de Tarragon, "Dead Kings and Rephaim: The Patrons of the Ugaritic Dynasty," *JAOS* 104 (1984): 649–59; Spronk, *Beatific Afterlife in Ancient Israel and in the Ancient Near East* (AOAT 219; Kevelaer: Butzon & Bercker; Neukirchen-Vluyn: Neukirchener Verlag, 1986), and the review of Smith and Bloch-Smith, "Death and After-life in Ugarit and Israel," *JAOS* 108 (1988): 277–84; Lewis, *Cults of the Dead in Ancient Israel and Ugarit* (HSM 39; Atlanta: Scholars Press, 1989), and "Toward a Literary Translation of the Rapiuma Texts," in *Ugarit, Religion and Culture,* 115–49; Loretz, *Ugarit und die Bibel: Kanaanäische Götter und Religion im Alten Testament* (Darmstadt: Wissenschaft-liche Buchgesellschaft, 1990), 128–39; and "Nekromantie und Totenevokation im Meso-potamien, Ugarit, und Israel," in *Religionsgeschichtliche Beziehungen zwischen Kleinasien, Nordsyrien, und dem Alten Testament* (ed. B. Janowski; OBO 129; Freiburg, Switzerland: Universitätsverlag; Göttingen: Vandenhoeck & Ruprecht, 1993), 285–318; Schmidt, *Is-rael's Beneficent Dead: Ancestor Cult and Necromancy in Ancient Israelite Religion and*

Tradition (FAT 11; Tübingen: Mohr/Siebeck, 1994), 100–120; and my review in *CBQ* 58 (1996): 724–25; Bloch-Smith, *Judahite Burials and Beliefs about the Dead* (JSOTSup 123; Sheffield: Sheffield Academic Press, 1992). See also the articles devoted to this topic by H. Niehr, R. Wenning, J. F. Healey, K. van der Toorn, and T. Podella in *Theologische Quartalschrift* 177/2 (1997). A book-length work by Niehr is in progress.

30. Olyan, *Asherah and the Cult of Yahweh in Israel* (SBLMS 34; Atlanta: Scholars Press, 1988). For further discussion of this topic, see below.

31. Cryer, *Divination in Ancient Israel and Its Near Eastern Environment: A Socio-historical Investigation* (JSOTSup 142; Sheffield: Sheffield Academic Press, 1994). See the review by V. Hurowitz in *JQR* 87 (1997): 416–20.

32. Smith, *The Early History of God: Yahweh and the Other Deities in Ancient Israel* (San Francisco: Harper & Row, 1990); and Niehr, *Religionen in Israels Umwelt: Einführung in die nordwestsemitischen Religionen Syrien-Palästinas* (Die neue Echter Bibel: Ergänzungsband zum Alten Testament 5; Würzburg: Echter, 1998).

33. W. van Binsbergen, "Black Athena Ten Years After: Towards a Constructive Reassessment," *TALANTA: Proceedings of the Dutch Archaeological and Historical Society* 28–29 (1996–1997): 59. See further pp. 11–64, esp. 56–61.

34. Lemche, *The Canaanites and Their Land: The Tradition of the Canaanites* (JSOTSup 110; Sheffield: JSOT, 1991). See the critiques of A. Rainey, "Who Is a Canaanite? A Review of the Textual Evidence," *BASOR* 304 (1996): 1–15; N. Na'aman, "The Canaanites and Their Land: A Rejoinder," *UF* 26 (1994): 397–418. Lemche responds to the first in an article, "Greater Canaan: The Implications of a Correct Reading of EA 151:49–67," *BASOR* 310 (1998): 19–24; and he answers the latter in his essay, "Where Should We Look for Canaan? A Reply to Nadav Na'aman," *UF* 28 (1996): 767–72. See also the remarks of D. Fleming, " 'The Storm God of Canaan' at Emar," *UF* 26 (1994): 127–30. Fleming adds the datum of ^{d}IM *ša ki-na-i*, which he renders "the Storm-God of Canaan" (Emar 446:107–8). See further R. S. Hess, "Occurrences of 'Canaan' in Late Bronze Age Archives of the West Semitic World," *IOS* 18 (1998): 365–72; and N. Na'aman, "Four Notes on the Size of Late Bronze Age Canaan," *BASOR* 313 (1999): 31–38.

35. Brooke, Curtis, and Healey, *Ugarit and the Bible: Proceedings of the International Symposium on Ugarit and the Bible. Manchester, September 1992.* Grabbe wisely places the term in quotation marks.

36. See B. Isaksson, "The Position of Ugaritic among the Semitic Languages," *Orientalia Suecana* 28–29 (1989–1990): 54–70. See also the three treatments by J. Huehnergard: "Remarks on the Classification of the Northwest Semitic Languages," in *The Balaam Text from Deir 'Alla Re-evaluated: Proceedings of the International Symposium Held at Leiden 21–24 1989* (ed. J. Hoftijzer and G. van der Kooij; Leiden: Brill, 1991), 282–93; "Languages (Introductory)," *ABD* 4 (1992): 155–70; and "Semitic Languages," in *Civilizations of the Ancient Near East* (ed. J. M. Sasson; 4 vols.; New York: Charles Scribner's Sons/Macmillan, 1995), 4:2117–34. Cf. J. F. Healey and P. C. Craigie, "Languages (Ugaritic)," *ABD* 4 (1992): 227: "it is wiser to regard Ugaritic simply as a pre-Canaanite Northwest Semitic language." The problem with this formulation is the attestation of the term "Canaanite" prior to Ugaritic; see Pardee, review of Loretz, *Ugarit and the Bible, JAOS* 117 (1997): 375–78.

37. Grabbe, " 'Canaanite': Some Methodological Observations in Relation to Biblical Study," in *Ugarit and the Bible,* 113–22.

38. Pardee, review of *Ugarit and the Bible,* 375–77.

39. Wallace, *The Eden Narrative* (HSM 32; Atlanta: Scholars Press, 1985).

40. Anderson, *Sacrifices and Offerings in Ancient Israel: Studies in their Social and Political Importance* (HSM 41; Atlanta: Scholars Press, 1987).

41. Lewis, *Cults of the Dead in Ancient Israel and Ugarit* (HSM 39; Atlanta: Scholars Press, 1989).

42. Meier, *The Messenger in the Ancient Semitic World* (HSM 45; Atlanta: Scholars Press, 1988).

43. Page, *The Myth of Cosmic Rebellion: A Study of Its Reflexes in Ugaritic and Biblical Literature* (VTSup 65; Leiden: Brill, 1996).

44. Korpel, *A Rift in the Clouds: Ugaritic and Hebrew Descriptions of the Divine* (UBL 8; Münster: Ugarit-Verlag, 1990).

45. K. van der Toorn, B. Becking, and P. W. van der Horst, eds., *Dictionary of Deities and Demons in the Bible* (Leiden: Brill, 1995; 2d ed., 1999).

46. For recent surveys, see J. A. Emerton, " 'Yahweh and his Asherah': The Goddess or Her Symbol," *VT* 49 (1999): 315–37; and S. A. Wiggins, "Asherah Again: Binger's Asherah and the State of Asherah Studies," *JNWSL* 24 (1998): 231–40.

47. Olyan, *Asherah and the Cult of Yahweh in Israel* (SBLMS 34; Atlanta: Scholars Press, 1988); Frevel, *Aschera und der Ausschliesslichkeitanspruch YHWHs* (BBB 94; 2 vols.; Weinheim: Beltz Athenäum, 1995). Olyan's monograph originated as a chapter of his dissertation. Interestingly, his doctoral adviser, Frank Cross, does not share Olyan's view of the asherah as a symbol of the goddess: "In any case I must reject any attempt to make it a proper name." He prefers a position closer to the view of another former student of his, P. K. McCarter, that the asherah was "a conventionalized tree of life, a cult object, or a hypostasis of an aspect of ʾEl." Finally, he comments: "If you want syncretism in the Hebrew Bible, there is plenty of material to be found without manufacturing it." (All three quotes are taken from a letter to me dated 7 December 1998.) For McCarter's view, see his article, "Aspects of the Religion of the Israelite Monarchy: Biblical and Epigraphic Data," in *Ancient Israelite Religion: Essays in Honor of Frank Moore Cross* (ed. P. D. Miller, Jr., P. D. Hanson, and S. D. McBride; Philadelphia: Fortress, 1987), 137–55.

48. Smith, *Early History of God,* 80–97.

49. Keel and Uehlinger, *Gods, Goddesses, and Images of God in Ancient Israel,* 228–48, 332, 369–70.

50. Keel, *Goddesses and Trees, New Moon and Yahweh: Ancient Near Eastern Art and the Hebrew Bible* (JSOTSup 262; Sheffield: Sheffield Academic Press, 1998).

51. Merlo, *La dea Ašratum–Aṯiratu–Ašera: Un contributo alla storia della religione semitica del nord* (Mursia: Pontificia Università Lateranese, 1998). This work contains other relevant bibliography, including work by S. A. Wiggins cited below.

52. Ackerman, *Under Every Green Tree: Popular Religion in Sixth-Century Judah* (HSM 46; Atlanta: Scholars Press, 1992).

53. Hadley, *The Cult of Asherah in Ancient Israel and Judah: The Evidence for a Hebrew Goddess* (University of Cambridge Oriental Publications 57; Cambridge: Cambridge University Press, 2000).

54. Levine, "The Balaam Inscription from Deir 'Alla: Historical Aspects," 337–38; "The Plaster Inscriptions from Deir 'Alla: General Interpretation," in *The Balaam Text from Deir 'Alla Re-evaluated* (ed. J. Hoftijzer and G. van der Kooij; Leiden: Brill, 1991), 58–72. See especially his forthcoming commentary, *Numbers 21–36* (AB 4B; New York: Doubleday). On El iconography in the first millennium, see Keel and Uehlinger, *Gods, Goddesses, and Images of God in Ancient Israel,* 154, 311–12.

55. Wyatt, "Of Calves and Kings: The Canaanite Dimension in the Religion of Israel," *SJOT* 6 (1992): 78–83; *Myths of Power: A Study of Royal Power and Ideology in Ugaritic and Biblical Tradition* (UBL 13; Münster: Ugarit-Verlag, 1996), 33. I do not accept a number of the arguments forwarded by Wyatt.

56. Smith, "Yahweh and the Other Deities of Ancient Israel: Observations on Old Problems and Recent Trends," in *Ein Gott allein? JHWH-Verehrung und biblischer Monotheismus im Kontext der israelitischen und altorientalischen Religionsgeschichte* (ed. W. Dietrich and M. A. Klopfenstein; OBO 139; Freiburg, Switzerland: Universitätsverlag; Göttingen: Vandenhoeck & Ruprecht, 1994), 207–8.

57. Seow, *Myth, Drama, and Politics of David's Dance* (HSM 46; Atlanta: Scholars Press, 1989), esp. 9–54.

58. On these issues involving El and Yahweh, see further Smith, "Yahweh and the Other Deities of Ancient Israel," 197–234.

59. See N. Walls, *The Goddess Anat in Ugaritic Myth* (SBLDS 135; Atlanta: Scholars Press, 1992). See also P. L. Day, "Why Is Anat a Warrior and Hunter?" in *The Bible and the Politics of Exegesis: Essays in Honor of Norman K. Gottwald on His Sixty-Fifth Birthday* (ed. D. Jobling, P. L. Day, and G. T. Sheppard; Cleveland, Ohio: Pilgrim, 1991), 141–46, 329–32; and "Anat: Ugarit's 'Mistress of Animals,' " *JNES* 51 (1992): 181–90.

60. Frymer-Kensky, *In the Wake of the Goddess: Women, Culture, and the Biblical Transformation of Pagan Myth* (New York: Free Press, 1992), 65.

61. Good, "The Sportsman Baal," *UF* 26 (1994): 147–63, esp. 149 n. 8.

62. *ANET*, 200–201. For further examples of the identification of Seth with Baal in New Kingdom Egypt, see R. Stadelmann, *Syrisch-palästinensische Gottheiten in Ägypten* (Probleme der Ägyptologie 5; Leiden: Brill, 1967), 27–47; *ANET*, 249; Cornelius, *Iconography of the Canaanite Gods Reshef and Ba'al*. The identification of Baal and Seth may be reflected in the divine name Bolchoseth, found on amulets, *defixiones*, and in formularies dating to the Hellenistic-Roman period. For discussion, see J. G. Gager, ed., *Curse Tablets and Binding Spells from the Ancient World* (Oxford: Oxford University Press, 1992), 266.

63. *ANET*, 15. See Te Velde, *Seth, God of Confusion: A Study of His Role in Egyptian Mythology and Religion* (Problem der Ägyptologie 6; Leiden: Brill, 1967), 29–30; seconded by Walls (*Goddess Anat in Ugaritic Myth*, 144–52) and P. L. Day ("Anat: Ugarit's 'Mistress of Animals,' " 186, and "Why Is Anat a Warrior and Hunter?" 141–46, 329–32).

64. A. Dupont-Sommer, "Une stèle araméenne d'un prêtre de Ba'al trouvée en Egypte," *Syria* 33 (1956): 79–80.

65. L. K. Handy, *Among the Host of Heaven: The Syro-Palestinian Pantheon as Bureaucracy* (Winona Lake, Ind.: Eisenbrauns, 1994); J. D. Schloen, "The Patrimonial Household in the Kingdom of Ugarit: A Weberian Analysis of Ancient Near Eastern Society" (Ph.D. diss., Harvard University, 1995), now published as *The House of the Father as Fact and Symbol: Patrimonialism in Ugarit and the Ancient Near East* (Studies in the Archaeology and History of the Levant 2; Harvard Semitic Museum; Winona Lake, Ind.: Eisenbrauns, 2001). For a critique of Handy's work, see Wyatt, *Myths of Power*, 329–30.

66. For a fine study combining biblical and Syro-Mesopotamian texts as well as anthropological material, see S. M. Olyan, "What Do Shaving Rites Accomplish and What Do They Signal in Biblical Ritual Contexts?" *JBL* 117 (1998): 611–32. See also Olyan, *Rites and Rank: Hierarchy in Biblical Representations of Cult* (Princeton, N.J.: Princeton University Press, 2000).

67. Livingstone, *Mystical and Mythological Explanatory Works of Assyrian and Babylonian Scholars* (Oxford: Clarendon, 1986).

68. For example, M. S. Smith, "The Death of 'Dying and Rising Gods' in the Biblical World: An Update, with Special Reference to Baal in the Baal Cycle," *SJOT* 12/2 (1998): 257–313.

69. G. A. Anderson, *A Time to Mourn, a Time to Dance: The Expression of Grief and Joy in Israelite Religion* (University Park, Pa.: Pennsylvania State University, 1991).

70. K. T. Aitken, *The Aqhat Narrative* (JSSSup; Manchester: 1990), based largely on his 1978 Edinburgh doctoral dissertation; T. L. Hettema, " 'That It Be Repeated': A Narrative Analysis of *KTU* 1.23," *JEOL* 31 (1989–1990): 77–94; J. M. Husser, "The Birth of a Hero: Form and Meaning of *KTU* 1.17 i-ii," in *Ugarit, Religion and Culture*, 85–98.

71. Parker, *The Pre-biblical Narrative Tradition* (SBL Resources for Biblical Study 24; Atlanta: Scholars Press, 1989).

72. Avishur, *Studies in Hebrew and Ugaritic Psalms* (Jerusalem: Magnes, 1994).

73. Avishur, *Studies in Biblical Narrative: Style, Structure, and the Ancient Near Eastern Literary Background* (Tel Aviv: Archaeological Center, Tel-Aviv University, 1999).

74. See the essays in J. C. de Moor, ed., *Intertextuality in Ugarit and Israel: Papers Read at the Tenth Joint Meeting of the Society for Old Testament Study and Het Oudtestamentisch Werkgezelschap in Nederland en Belgie* (OTS 40; Leiden: Brill, 1998).

75. Alter, *The Art of Biblical Narrative* (New York: Basic Books, 1981), 29; quoted in Parker, *Stories in Scripture and Inscriptions*, 137.

76. Ricoeur, *Figuring the Sacred: Religion, Narrative, and Imagination* (ed. M. Wallace; trans. D. Pellauer; Minneapolis: Fortress, 1995), 181–91, 317.

77. Ibid., 182.

78. Parker, *Stories in Scripture and Inscriptions*, 137–38.

79. See n. 65 above.

80. Van der Toorn, *Family Religion in Babylonia, Syria, and Israel: Continuity and Change in the Forms of Religious Life* (Studies in the History and Culture of the Ancient Near East 7; Leiden: Brill, 1995).

81. Van der Toorn, *From Her Cradle to Her Grave: The Role of Religion in the Life of the Israelite and the Babylonian Woman* (Bible Seminar 23; Sheffield: JSOT Press, 1994). See also M. I. Gruber, *The Motherhood of God and Other Studies* (South Florida Studies in the History of Judaism 57; Atlanta: Scholars Press, 1992).

82. Berlinerblau, *The Vow and the 'Popular Religious Groups' of Ancient Israel: A Philological and Sociological Inquiry* (JSOTSup 210; Sheffield Academic Press, 1996); and "Preliminary Remarks for the Sociological Study of Israelite 'Official Religion,'" in *Ki Baruch Hu: Ancient Near Eastern, Biblical, and Judaic Studies in Honor of Baruch A. Levine* (ed. R. Chazan, W. W. Hallo, and L. H. Schiffman; Winona Lake, Ind.: Eisenbrauns, 1999), 153–70. For some of the potential and issues in Berlinerblau's book, see my review in *JSS* 43 (1998): 148–51.

83. See Pardee, "*Marziḥu, Kispu,* and the Ugaritic Funerary Cult: A Minimalist View," in *Ugarit, Religion and Culture*, 273–87.

84. For some studies of popular religion in European studies (by year), see N. Z. Davis, "Some Tasks and Themes in the Study of Popular Religion," in *In the Pursuit of Holiness in Late Medieval and Renaissance Religion* (ed. C. Trinkaus and H. A. Oberman; Leiden: Brill, 1974), 307–36; P. M. Vovelle, "La religion populaire: Problèmes et méthodes," *Le monde alpin et rhodanien* 5 (1977): 7–32; H. Vrijhof and J. Waardenburg, eds., *Official and Popular Religion: Analysis of a Theme for Religious Studies* (Religion and Society 19; The Hague: Mouton, 1979); and K. L. Jolly, *Popular Religion in Late Saxon England: Elf Charms in Context* (Chapel Hill, N.C./London: University of North Carolina Press, 1996).

85. See the works cited in n. 23 above.

86. Bloch-Smith, *Judahite Burials and Beliefs about the Dead* (JSOTSup 123; JSOT/ASOR Monograph Series 7; Sheffield: Sheffield Academic Press, 1992); see also her article, "The Cult of the Dead in Judah," *JBL* 111 (1992): 213–24. See the responses in A. Cooper and B. R. Goldstein, "The Cult of the Dead and the Theme of Entry into the Land," *Biblical Interpretation* 1/3 (1993): 285–303, esp. 301 n. 37; and R. Tappy, "Did the Dead Ever Die in Biblical Judah?" *BASOR* 298 (1995): 59–68.

87. See R. S. Hess, "A Comparison of the Ugarit, Emar, and Alalakh Archives," in *Ugarit, Religion and Culture*, 75–84. See also in the same volume M. Dietrich, "Aspects of the Babylonian Impact on Ugaritic Literature and Religion," 33–48.

88. Huffmon, *Amorite Personal Names in the Mari Texts* (Baltimore: Johns Hopkins University Press, 1965); Gelb, *A Computer-Aided Analysis of Amorite* (AS 21; Chicago/London: University of Chicago, 1980); Zadok, "On the Amorite Material from Mesopotamia," in *The Tablet and the Scroll: Near Eastern Studies in Honor of William H. Hallo* (ed. M. E. Cohen, D. C. Snell, and D. B. Weisberg; Bethesda, Md.: CDL Press, 1993), 315–33.

89. The issues are put nicely by D. Pardee, "Background to the Bible: Ugarit," in *Ebla to Damascus: Art and Archaeology of Ancient Syria* (Washington, D.C.: Smithsonian Institution, 1985), 253–58. The issue of Ugarit's larger context surfaces in several essays in *Ugarit: Ein ostmediterranes Kulturzentrum im Alten Orient: Ergebnisse und Perspektiven der Forschung. Band I: Ugarit und seine Umwelt* (ed. M. Dietrich and O. Loretz; ALASP 7; Münster: Ugarit-Verlag, 1995).

90. Yon, *La cité d'Ougarit sur le tell de Ras Shamra* (Paris: Editions Recherche sur les Civilisations, 1997); now *The City of Ugarit at Tell Ras Shamra* (Winona Lake, Ind.: Eisenbrauns, 2001).

91. This information and the following come from several conversations with Pardee as well as a detailed letter from Bordreuil, dated 28 December 1998.

92. For now, Dalix, "Exemples de bilinguisme à Ougarit. 'Iloumilku: La double identité d'un scribe," in *Mosaïque de langues mosaïques culturelle*, 81–90.

93. Pardee, *Les textes hippiatriques* (RSO 2; Paris: Editions Recherche sur les Civilisations, 1985); *Les textes paramythologiques de la 24e campagne (1961)* (RSO 4; Paris: Editions Recherche sur les Civilisations, 1988). On the hippiatric texts, see further Pardee, "Quelques remarques relatives à l'étude des textes hippiatriques en langue ougaritique," *Sem* 45 (1996): 19–26. For C. Cohen's work on this subject, see the listing at the beginning of the preceding chapter.

94. De Contenson, *Préhistoire de Ras Shamra* (RSO 8; 2 vols.; Paris: Editions Recherche sur les Civilisations, 1992).

95. For her contributions, see the listing in *Handbook of Ugaritic Studies*, 821–22, under Yon.

96. Callot, *Une maison à Ougarit: Etudes d'architecture domestique* (RSO 1; Paris: Editions Recherche sur les Civilisations, 1983); and *La tranchée "Ville Sud": Etudes d'architecture domestique* (RSO 10; Paris: Editions Recherche sur les Civilisations, 1994).

97. For articles by these authors, see the listing in *Handbook of Ugaritic Studies*, 770, under Caubet.

98. Information about dissertations completed recently in the United States derives from a search done at University Microfilms International dated 5 November 1998.

99. For Fine's thesis topic, see http://www-oi.uchicago.edu/OI/DEPT/RA/DISPROP/Fine_diss.html. Information on the other two dissertations derives from D. Pardee, e-mail communication on 21 October 1998.

100. To be published as *The Goddess Anat: An Examination of the Textual and Iconographic Evidence from the Second Millennium B.C.* (Münster: Ugarit-Verlag, 2000). See also Lloyd, "Anat and the 'Double' Massacre of *KTU* 1.3 ii," in *Ugarit, Religion and Culture*, 151–65. See in the same volume Lloyd, and Wyatt, "The Edinburgh Ras Shamra Project: An Introduction," 423–30.

101. See Wiggins, "The Myth of Asherah: Lion Lady and Serpent Goddess," *UF* 23 (1991): 383–94; *A Reassessment of 'Asherah': A Study according to the Textual Sources of the First Two Millennia B.C.E.* (AOAT 235; Kevelaer: Butzon & Bercker; Neukirchen-Vluyn: Neukirchener Verlag, 1993); "Shapsh, Lamp of the Gods," in *Ugarit, Religion and Culture*, 327–50. Wiggins's work largely offers a critique of what he regards as the excess of past claims made about Asherah and Shapshu.

102. Information courtesy of Professor de Moor, e-mail, 26 November 1998.

103. Dijkstra, "Semitic Worship at Serabit el-Khadem (Sinai)," *ZAH* 10 (1997): 89–97, which announces I. D. G. Biggs and M. Dijkstra, *Corpus of Proto-Sinaitic Inscriptions (CPSI)* (AOAT 41; Neukirchen-Vluyn: Neukirchener Verlag, forthcoming).

104. This information comes courtesy of W. van Soldt, e-mail on 11 November 1998. Márquez Rowe studied with van Soldt at Leiden for one semester.

105. Announced in his article, "Realizaciones informáticas del Sistema Integrado de Análisis Morfológico de Textos Ugaríticos (SIAMTU)," *Bib* 73 (1992): 547–59.

106. Merlo, "Über die Ergänzung '*št*' in *KTU* 1.23:59," *UF* 28 (1996): 491–94.

107. This information comes courtesy of Professor Cohen, e-mail 6 December 1998.

108. This information comes courtesy of Professor Greenstein, e-mail 10 February 1999.

109. See J. M. de Tarragon, "Philologie sémitique," in *L'Ancien Testament: Cent ans d'exégèse de l'Ecole Biblique* (Cahiers de la Revue Biblique 28; Paris: Gabalda, 1990), 44.

110. Levine, *The JPS Torah Commentary: Leviticus* ויקרא (Philadelphia/New York/Jerusalem: Jewish Publication Society, 1989).

111. Levine, *Numbers 1–20* (AB 4; Garden City, N.Y.: Doubleday, 1993); *Numbers 21–36* (AB 4B; New York: Doubleday, 2000).

112. For a recent example, see Fleming, "The Israelite Festival Calendar and Emar's Ritual Archive," *RB* 106 (1999): 8–34; also *Time at Emar: The Cultic Calendar and Rituals from the Diviner's House* (Mesopotamian Civilizations 11; Winona Lake, Ind.: Eisenbrauns, 2000).

113. Information courtesy of John Huehnergard, e-mail 18 November 1998.

114. For important basic works on monotheism in ancient Israel, see O. Keel, ed., *Monotheismus im alten Israel und seiner Umwelt* (BB 14; Freiburg, Switzerland: Katholisches Bibelwerk, 1980); *Gott, der Einzige: Zur Entstehung des Monotheismus in Israel* (QD 104; Freiburg, Germany: Herder, 1985) (reference courtesy of W. H. Propp); B. Uffenheimer, "Myth and Reality in Ancient Israel," in *The Origins and Diversity of Axial Civilizations* (ed. S. N. Eisenstadt; Albany: State University of New York, 1986), 164–66; Dietrich and Klopfenstein, *Ein Gott allein?*; A. Schenker, "Le monothéisme israélite: Un dieu qui transcende le monde et les dieux," *Bib* 78 (1997): 436–38; R. Gnuse, *No Other Gods: Emergent Monotheism in Israel* (JSOTSup 241; Sheffield: Sheffield Academic Press, 1997); and W. H. Propp, "Monotheism and 'Moses': The Problem of Early Israelite Religion," *UF* 31 (1999): 537–75.

115. Mendenhall, *The Tenth Generation: The Origins of the Biblical Tradition* (Baltimore: Johns Hopkins University Press, 1973), esp. 223; and "The Worship of Baal and Asherah: A Study in the Social Bonding Functions of Religious Systems," in *Biblical and Related Studies Presented to Samuel Iwry* (ed. A. Kort and S. Morschauser; Winona Lake, Ind.: Eisenbrauns, 1985), 147–58.

116. M. S. Smith, *The Origins of Biblical Monotheism: Israel's Polytheistic Background and the Ugaritic Texts* (New York/Oxford: Oxford University Press, 2001).

117. De Moor, *Rise of Yahwism*, 71–102. See also de Moor, "The Crisis of Polytheism in Late Bronze Age Ugarit," *OTS* 24 (1986): 1–20.

118. De Moor, *Rise of Yahwism*, 298. De Moor sees monolatry as tantamount to monotheism, but does not explain why actual monotheistic expressions arise so much later in Israel's history, namely in the seventh and sixth centuries. Instead of viewing monolatry as a virtual monotheism, I would see monotheistic claims as particular expressions of Judean monolatry in the seventh and sixth centuries. See below.

119. See Wyatt, *Myths of Power*, 326–27.

120. Smith, *Origins of Biblical Monotheism*, especially Part Three.

121. This development is discussed by J. Blenkinsopp, "The Family in First Temple Israel," 88, and J. J. Collins, "Marriage, Divorce, and Family in Second Temple Judaism," 105, both in *Families in Ancient Israel* (ed. L. Perdue et al.; Louisville, Ky.: Westminster John Knox, 1997).

122. See B. Halpern, "Jerusalem and the Lineages in the Seventh Century BCE: Kinship and the Rise of Individual Liability," in *Law and Ideology in Monarchic Israel* (ed. B. Halpern and D. W. Hobson; JSOTSup 124; Sheffield: Sheffield Academic Press, 1991), 11–15. See further Halpern, "Sybil, or the Two Nations? Archaism, Kinship, Alienation, and the Elite Redefinition of Traditional Culture in Judah in the 8th–7th Centuries B.C.E.," in *The Study of the Ancient Near East in the Twenty-First Century: The William*

Foxwell Albright Centennial Conference (ed. J. S. Cooper and G. M. Schwartz; Winona Lake, Ind.: Eisenbrauns, 1996), 295, 317–18, 323, 326.

123. Reference courtesy of Saul Olyan.

124. See Halpern, "Jerusalem and the Lineages in the Seventh Century BCE," 11–107. See further Halpern, "Sybil, or the Two Nations?" 291–338.

125. Different commentators have recently discussed the role of Mesopotamian empires in Israel's religious development in the Iron II period: W. Dietrich, "Der eine Gott als Symbol politischen Widerstands. Religion und Politik im Juda des 7. Jahrhunderts," in *Ein Gott allein?* 463–90; J. H. Tigay, *The JPS Torah Commentary: Deuteronomy* דברים (Philadelphia/Jerusalem: Jewish Publication Society, 1996), 433; P. Machinist, "The Fall of Assyria in Comparative Ancient Perspective," in *Assyria 1995: Proceedings of the 10th Anniversary Symposium of the Neo-Assyrian Text Corpus Project. Helsinki, September 7–11, 1995* (ed. S. Parpola and R. M. Whiting; Helsinki: Neo-Assyrian Text Corpus Project, 1997), 179–95, esp. 184.

126. Based on the readings 4QDeutq: *bny ᵓl[*; 4QDeutj: *bny ᵓlwhym[*; LXX *huion theou* (cf. LXX variants with *angelon* interpolated). For the evidence, see E. Tov, *Textual Criticism of the Hebrew Bible* (Minneapolis: Fortress; Assen/Maastricht: Van Gorcum, 1992), 269; J. A. Duncan, *Qumran Cave 4. IX: Deuteronomy, Joshua, Judges, Kings* (ed. E. Ulrich and F. M. Cross; DJD 14; Oxford: Clarendon Press, 1995), 90; noted also in BHS to Deut 32:8 note d. For older bibliography, Smith, *Early History of God*, 30 n. 37; and A. Schenker, "Le monothéisme israélite," 438.

127. Cross, *Canaanite Myth and Hebrew Epic*, 258 n. 177; Smith, *Ugaritic Baal Cycle*, 109.

128. Kloos, *Yhwh's Combat with the Sea: A Canaanite Tradition in the Religion of Ancient Israel* (Amsterdam: G. A. van Oorschot; Leiden: Brill, 1986). On this topic, see also J. L. Cunchillos, *Estudio des Salmo 29: Canto al Dos de la fertilidad-fecundidad. Aportación al conocimiento de la fe de Israel a su entrada en Canaan* (Valencia: La Institución San Jerónimo, 1976); and J. Day, *God's Conflict with the Dragon and the Sea: Echoes of a Canaanite Myth in the Old Testament* (University of Cambridge Oriental Publications 35; Cambridge: Cambridge University Press, 1985).

129. Keel and Uehlinger, *Gods, Goddesses, and Images of God*, 396.

130. Ibid., 395–96.

131. See M. Dietrich and O. Loretz, "Neue Tafelfunde der Grabungskampagne 1994 in Ugaritic," *UF* 26 (1994): 21.

132. For example, in a letter dated 5 December 1998, Professor Segert informs me of his ongoing work on Czech translations of the Ugaritic texts, a project that he has been working on since the 1950s.

133. Tropper, *Ugaritische Grammatik*. See also Tropper, "Ugaritic Grammar," in *Handbook of Ugaritic Studies*, 92.

134. The following summary derives from Cunchillos Ilarri's contribution, "Storage and Analysis of the Texts," in *Handbook of Ugaritic Studies*, 747–54; and his e-mail to me dated 8 February 1999.

135. For example, see R. E. Longacre, *Joseph, a Story of Divine Providence: A Text Theoretical and Textlinguistic Analysis of Genesis 37 and 39–48* (Winona Lake, Ind.: Eisenbrauns, 1989); the essays in R. D. Bergen, ed., *Biblical Hebrew and Discourse Analysis* (Dallas: Summer Institute of Linguistics; Winona Lake, Ind.: Eisenbrauns, 1994); D. A. Dawson, *Text-Linguistics and Biblical Hebrew* (JSOTSup 177; Sheffield: Sheffield Academic Press, 1994); M. Eskhult, "The Old Testament and Text Linguistics," *OrSu* 43–44 (1994–1995): 93–103; and N. Winther-Nielsen, *A Functional Discourse Grammar of Joshua: A Computer-Assisted Rhetorical Structure Analysis* (CBOT 40; Stockholm: Almqvist & Wiksell, 1995). See also G. Payne, "Functional Sentence Perspective: Theme in Biblical Hebrew," *SJOT* 5 (1991): 62–82.

136. See, for example, the essays in W. R. Bodine, ed., *Linguistics and Biblical Hebrew* (Winona Lake, Ind.: Eisenbrauns, 1992).

137. However, note the works of A. T. Bothma, "Aspects of Ugaritic Syntax within the Framework of Core Grammar" (D.Litt. diss., University of South Africa, 1983 [Afrikaans]); and R. W. B. Webb, "A Structuralist Approach to the Ugaritic Language" (M.A. thesis, University of Melbourne, 1973).

138. Van der Merwe, Naudé, and Kroeze, *A Biblical Hebrew Reference Grammar* (Biblical Languages: Hebrew 3; Sheffield: Sheffield Academic Press, 1999).

139. Sivan, *Grammar of the Ugaritic Language*, 96–108.

140. Greenstein, review of Sivan, *A Grammar of the Ugaritic Language*, *IOS* 18 (1998): 409–13.

141. For further notes and discussion, see Smith in Parker, ed., *Ugaritic Narrative Poetry*, 224–28.

142. Watson, *Traditional Techniques in Classical Hebrew Verse* (JSOTSup 170; Sheffield: Sheffield Academic Press, 1994), 249. See further Smith, *Ugaritic Baal Cycle*, 53–55; following Fenton, "The Hebrew 'Tenses' in the Light of Ugaritic," in *Proceedings of the Fifth World Congress of Jewish Studies* (Jerusalem: World Union of Jewish Studies, 1973), 4:35.

143. For objections to the term, "converted *waw*," see Fenton, "Nexus and Significance: Is Greater Precision Possible?" in *Ugarit and the Bible*, 81–85. Fenton seems also to disparage "*waw*-consecutive." Like all scholars who see the old **yaqtul* preterite behind the *waw*-consecutive, he rightly suggests that the form represents a "fixed syntagm," but there is little new in this point. He further deduces incorrectly that " 'consecution' is an irrelevance." I understand "consecutive" to mean serial; and the *waw* does mark the serial character of the syntax of verbal forms.

144. Rainey, "The Ancient Hebrew Prefix Conjugation in Light of Amarnah Canaanite," *HS* 27 (1986): 4–19; Sivan, *A Grammar of the Ugaritic Language*, 96–108, esp. 102–3.

145. Cross, *Canaanite Myth and Hebrew Epic*, 117–18. Of course, in the fourth verb, *tṯhnn*, the first *n-* is part of the root. I proposed these verbs as examples of the indicative energic in Ugaritic class at the University of Pennsylvania on 10 February 1999.

146. I first proposed this Ugaritic example and the following biblical instance in my Ugaritic class at the University of Pennsylvania on 3 February 1999.

147. Cf. T. Zewi, *A Syntactical Study of Verbal Forms Affixed by -n(n) Endings in Classical Arabic, Biblical Hebrew, El-Amarna Akkadian, and Ugaritic* (AOAT 260; Münster: Ugarit-Verlag, 1999).

148. Williams, "The Passive *qal* Theme in Hebrew," in *Essays on the Ancient Semitic World* (ed. J. W. Wevers and D. B. Redford; Toronto/Buffalo: University of Toronto, 1970), 43–50.

149. Pope, *Song of Songs* (AB 7; Garden City, N.Y.: Doubleday, 1977), 599–600.

150. Becker, " 'The Pa'ul, the Po'el of Which Has Not Been Specified' according to R. Yonah Ben Janah," *Leš* 56 (1992): 213–21 (Heb.).

151. Smith in Parker, ed., *Ugaritic Narrative Poetry*, 51.

152. Wyatt, *Religious Texts from Ugarit: The Words of Ilimilku and His Colleagues* (Biblical Seminar 53; Sheffield: Sheffield Academic Press, 1998), 251 n. 6.

153. Sivan, *A Grammar of the Ugaritic Language*, 122.

154. See, for example, J. F. A. Sawyer, *Semantics in Biblical Research: New Methods of Defining Hebrew Words for Salvation* (SBT, 2d series 24; London: SCM, 1972); A. Gibson, *Biblical Semantic Logic: A Preliminary Analysis* (New York: St. Martin's Press, 1981), 126–64; J. Lübbe, "Hebrew Lexicography: A New Approach," *Journal for Semitics* 2 (1990): 1–15; S. Morag, "The Structure of Semantic and Associate Fields in Biblical Hebrew and Classical Arabic," in *"Sha'arei Talmon": Studies in the Bible, Qumran, and the*

Ancient Near East Presented to Shemaryahu Talmon (Winona Lake, Ind.: Eisenbrauns, 1992), 137*–143* (Heb.); *ESF Workshop on the Semantics of Classical Hebrew = ZAH* 6/1 (1993): 1–127.

155. For example, J. Blau, " 'Weak' Phonetic Change and Hebrew *śin,*" *HAR* 1 (1977): 67–119; republished in Blau, *Topics in Hebrew and Semitic Linguistics* (Jerusalem: Magnes, 1998), 50–103.

156. See M. Delcor, "Two Special Meanings of the יד," *JSS* 12 (1967): 234–40; A. Fitzgerald, "Hebrew *yd* = 'Love' and 'Beloved,'" *CBQ* 29 (1967): 368–74; Caquot, Sznycer, and Herdner, *Textes ougaritiques,* 205 n. i; Seow, *Myth, Drama, and the Politics of David's Dance,* 110 n. 88.

157. Pope, "The Ups and Downs of El's Amours," *UF* 11 (1979): 706.

158. For *n^cm* predicated of deities in West Semitic proper names, see F. L. Benz, *Personal Names in Phoenician and Punic Inscriptions* (Studia Pohl 8; Rome: Pontifical Biblical Institute, 1972), 362; N. Avigad, *Corpus of West Semitic Stamp Seals* (revised and completed by B. Sass; Jerusalem: Israel Academy of Sciences and Humanities/Israel Exploration Society/Institute of Archaeology, Hebrew University of Jerusalem, 1997), 515.

159. See the secondary literature and further discussion in T. J. Lewis, *Cults of the Dead in Ancient Israel and Ugarit* (HSM 39; Atlanta: Scholars Press, 1989), 52; Smith, *The Ugaritic Baal Cycle,* 65 n. 126.

160. So C. L. Seow, *Ecclesiastes* (AB 18C; Garden City, N.Y.: Doubleday, 1997), 163.

161. *BDB* 761.

162. See de Moor, *Anthology of Religious Texts from Ugarit,* 65 n. 297.

163. The word *^côlām* has been taken generally in four ways:

1. "eternity," based on the common BH usage, including Eccl 1:4, 10; 2:16; 3:14; 9:6; and 12:5 (so LXX; ibn Ezra);
2. "that which is hidden, concealed";
3. "knowledge," based on Arabic **^clm;* and
4. "world," based on the later Hebrew meaning of this word.

For these alternatives, see G. A. Barton, *A Critical and Exegetical Commentary on the Book of Ecclesiastes* (ICC; Edinburgh: T&T Clark, 1912), 105; R. Gordis, *Koheleth—the Man and His World: A Study of Ecclesiastes* (3d ed.; New York: Schocken, 1968), 231. The last of the four is favored by Gordis. For a discussion of these suggestions, see W. Leslau, *Comparative Dictionary of Ge'ez (Classical Ethiopic)* (Wiesbaden: Otto Harrassowitz, 1987), 61. The fourth meaning has also been claimed for Ugaritic, in the expression *mlk ^clm,* "king of the universe," attested in *KTU* 1.108.1. See *UT* 19:1858; cf. A. Cooper, " *MLK 'LM:* 'Eternal King' or 'King of Eternity'?" in *Love & Death in the Ancient Near East: Essays in Honor of Marvin H. Pope* (ed. J. H. Marks and R. M. Good; Guilford, Conn.: Four Quarters, 1987), 1–7. However, the imputed meaning is apparently anachronistic. In an unpublished short piece entitled "Darkness and Eternity," Marvin Pope favored this etymology and meaning for *^clm* in this passage. The essay is part of Pope's unpublished papers held in the Yale Divinity School Library.

164. To cite two very different authors: R. Alter, *The Art of Biblical Poetry* (New York: Basic Books, 1985); and D. Pardee, *Ugaritic and Hebrew Poetic Parallelism: A Trial Cut ('nt I and Proverbs 2)* (VTSup 39; Leiden: Brill, 1988); idem, "Ugaritic and Hebrew Metrics," in *Ugarit in Retrospect: Fifty Years of Ugarit and Ugaritic* (ed. G. D. Young; Winona Lake, Ind.: Eisenbrauns, 1981), 113–50. For Watson's work, see his book *Traditional Techniques.*

165. Smith, *Ugaritic Baal Cycle,* 300.

166. Exceptional in this regard is Ps 136, with a refrain at the end of every line.

167. L. Alonso Schökel, *A Manual of Hebrew Poetics* (Subsidia biblica 11; Rome: Editrice Pontificio Istituto Biblico, 1988), 198.

168. For a brief discussion of the chiastic arrangement of the Pentateuch, see M. S. Smith, *The Pilgrimage Pattern in Exodus* (JSOTSup 239; Sheffield: Sheffield Academic Press, 1997), 285–308.

169. See Alonso Schökel, *A Manual of Hebrew Poetics*, 192–93.

170. See *ANET*, 390; B. R. Foster, *Before the Muses: An Anthology of Akkadian Literature* (2 vols.; Bethesda, Md.: CDL Press, 1993), 2:566, 686.

171. So the definition adopted in P. Raabe, *Psalm Structures: A Study of Psalms with Refrains* (JSOTSup 104; Sheffield: Sheffield Academic Press, 1990), 164.

172. Ibid., 29–153.

173. Ibid., 165.

174. See the works cited in n. 3 above.

175. Keel and Uehlinger, *Gods, Goddesses, and Images of God in Ancient Israel*, 120 ("vocable" and "sentences"), and 126 ("paratactic").

176. For discussion of Frazer as well as his influence and methodological problems, see Smith, "The Glory, Jest and Riddle," 366–75; "Dying and Rising Gods," in *The Encyclopedia of Religion* (ed. M. Eliade; New York: Macmillan; London: Collier Macmillan), 4:521–27; W. Burkert, *Structure and History in Greek Mythology and Ritual* (Berkeley: University of California, 1979), 100; J. P. Södergard, "The Ritualized Bodies of Cybele's Galli and the Methodological Problem of the Plurality of Explanations," in *The Problem of Ritual: Based on Papers Read at the Symposium on Religious Studies Held at Åbo, Finland on the 13th–16th of August, 1991* (ed. T. Ahlbäck; Scripta Instituti Doneriani Aboensis; Stockholm: Almqvist and Wiksell, 1993), 175–76. For the biblical and ancient Middle Eastern fields, see the citations of Smith, "The Glory, Jest and Riddle," 40 n. 43; and more recently, H. Barstad, *The Religious Polemics of Amos: Studies in the Preaching of Am 2, 7B-8, 4, 1–13, 5, 1–27, 6, 4–7, 8, 14* (VTSup 34; Leiden: Brill, 1984), 84 n. 45, 148–51; and Walls, *The Goddess Anat in the Ugaritic Texts*, 5–6, 68. H. Frankfort's points made in his *Kingship and the Gods: A Study of Ancient Near Eastern Religion as the Integration of Society & Nature* (Chicago/London: University of Chicago Press, 1948, 286–94) still stand. For further discussion, see Smith, "Death of 'Dying and Rising Gods,'" 257–313.

177. See J. Z. Smith, "Religion, Religions, Religious," in *Critical Terms for Religious Studies* (ed. M. C. Taylor; Chicago/London: University of Chicago, 1998), 269–84; see also in the same volume M. C. Taylor, "Introduction," 6–13. Note also T. Fitzgerald, "The Ideology of Religious Studies," *Bulletin of the Council of Societies for the Study of Religion* 28/2 (April 1999): 39–41, and his book, *The Ideology of Religious Studies* (New York/Oxford: Oxford University Press, 1999).

178. Geertz, "A Life of Learning," Charles Homer Haskins Lecture for 1999 (American Council of Learning Societies Occasional Paper, No. 45; New York: American Council of Learning Societies, 1999), 9.

179. Taylor, "Introduction," 13.

180. G. Aichele et al., eds., *The Postmodern Bible* (New Haven/London: Yale University Press, 1995).

181. Carroll, "Poststructuralist Approaches: New Historicism and Postmodernism," in *Biblical Interpretation* (ed. J. Barton; Cambridge: Cambridge University Press, 1998), 58–60.

182. The brief note on the issue in *Postmodern Bible* ("Introduction," 5) hardly qualifies.

183. To cite some specifics: (1) the call for "a *transforming* biblical criticism, one that undertakes to understand the ongoing impact of the Bible on culture . . ." (ibid., 2; author's italics) would require a serious, professional training in modern history and culture, but no recognition of this point is made; and (2) the author's use of psychoanalytic language (even when read critically as on pp. 218–19), despite the often totalizing character of psychoanalytic discourse and the scientific problems attendant in psychoanalysis.

For a critique of the latter from a scientific perspective, see J. S. Hobson, *Dreaming as Delirium: How the Brain Goes Out of Its Mind* (Cambridge: MIT Press, 1994), esp. 57, 212, 214, 218, and note in particular the intriguing tirade against a hermeneutics of psychoanalysis by "religious scholars" on 209–10. Hobson, in turn, tends to reduce the importance that the content of dreams may hold for individuals and their self-understanding.

184. See the weak attempt in *Postmodern Bible*, 64.

185. "Introduction," ibid., 4.

186. See specifically 8–15. See also G. Benavides, "Modernity," in *Critical Terms for Religious Studies* (ed. M. C. Taylor; Chicago: University of Chicago Press, 1998), 186–204.

187. "Introduction," *Postmodern Bible*, 9.

188. For examples, see B. O. Long, "Recent Field Studies in Oral Literature and Their Bearing on Old Testament Criticism," *VT* 26 (1976): 187–98; and R. R. Wilson, *Prophecy and Society in Ancient Israel* (Philadelphia: Fortress, 1980). See the review of the latter by G. W. Ahlström in *JNES* 44 (1985): 217–20.

189. For examples, see S. Niditch, *Oral World and Written Word: Ancient Israelite Literature* (Library of Ancient Israel; Louisville, Ky.: Westminster John Knox, 1996); and S. M. Olyan, "What Do Shaving Rites Accomplish?" 611–32. Note also M. S. Smith, "The Heart and Innards in Israelite Emotional Expressions: Notes from Anthropology and Psychobiology," *JBL* 117 (1998): 427–36.

Index of Modern Authors